New Horizons in Journalism
Howard Rusk Long, *General Editor*

DEFAMATION
and Public Officials

The Evolving Law of Libel

Clifton O. Lawhorne

Foreword by Howard Rusk Long

Southern Illinois University Press   Carbondale and Edwardsville
Feffer & Simons, Inc.   London and Amsterdam

COPYRIGHT © 1971, by Southern Illinois University Press
All rights reserved
Printed in the United States of America
Designed by Andor Braun
ISBN 0-8093-0454-6
Library of Congress Catalog Card Number 76-93884

TO CLAUDETTA, KELLY, AND JEFFRY

Contents

Development and Divergency

Order and Cohesion

The Law Yesterday, Today, and Tomorrow

Foreword

Perhaps it is only an accident of history that the English culture and institutions that prevailed in the thirteen colonies along the Atlantic were destined to provide the foundations of our North American republic. The men and women who crossed the Atlantic or the Pacific, regardless of national origins, shared a common need to reestablish themselves or to perish. They were the dropouts of their times from a variety of closed systems that destroyed more people than were permitted to escape. Many romantic interpretations are employed to explain the migrations to the New World, but hidden by these fictions are the hard facts of economic pressures, political defeat, and the consequences of apostasy.

In Britain, Church and State had never really consolidated the monolithic structure designed by medieval Europe to keep the people in their place. The uneasy relationship of Crown with Church, of king with nobles, plus the brawling of the English with the Irish, the Scots, and the Welsh, offered more occasions for disagreement and conflict than central authority could always control.

When dissident groups were permitted to leave England to establish beachheads in the western Atlantic, they carried with them their institutions, and while maintaining contact with the homeland, proceeded after the manner suggested by Frederick Jackson Turner to make the adjustments necessary for survival in the New World.

Professor Lawhorne's treatment of the evolving law of libel, by limiting application to questions involving public officials, demonstrates the natural history of a change from extreme repression to something very close to immunity. In the American beginning, those in authority invoked the entire weight of English law to retain for themselves the same overbearing controls previously challenged by them when exercised by others.

Later, although the colonists seldom hesitated to employ the law against dissident neighbors, they learned to bend court decisions to their own needs in the conflict, first with Parliament and later with the Crown. With the collaboration of bench and bar mighty blows for liberty were struck in the years preceding the American Revolution. Professor Lawhorne points out that newspaper editors of the emerging nation, in fact, enjoyed unbridled license in their political controversies until the lawmakers of the new republic, including the legislatures of the various states, began to produce the statutes intended to grant relief in the courts to persons attacked in the press.

There must be some merit in any attempt to impose upon an irresponsible press the rules of truth and fair play. But even as the states increased in number, laws multiplied and jurisdictions proliferated. Far into the twentieth century the law of libel remained a hodgepodge of statute and decision so incomprehensible that most newspapermen accepted as an occupational hazard the prospect of a libel suit, properly ignored until the arrival of the process server.

Personal journalism is a phrase descriptive of the relationship of the American newspaper editor with men in public life during much of the nineteenth century. Mark Twain's burlesque account of "Journalism in Tennessee" first published in the *Buffalo Express* on September 4, 1869, carries the measure of truth so often found in overblown creations of this nature. That the courts were no factor in this relationship is well demonstrated in the instructions of the fictional chief editor to his new assistant:

> Jones will be here at three—cowhide him. Gillespie will call earlier, perhaps—throw him out the window. Ferguson will be along about four—kill him. That is all for today, I believe. If you have any odd time, you might write a blistering article on the police—give the chief inspector rats. The cowhides are under the table; weapons in the drawer—ammunition there in the corner— lint and bandages in the pigeonholes. In case of accident, go to Lancet the surgeon, down-stairs. He advertises—we take it out in trade.

Not even to a new assistant was it necessary to spell out how to handle the wedding of the county clerk's daughter or the personal news of any other official generous to the newspaper in the placing of legal notices.

Of course public officials did take editors to court, as Professor Lawhorne's cases show. Even so, the adversary system developed by the political parties caused the man in office to become fair game for the editorial spokesman of the party out of office. The muckrakers with their documented exposure of corruption in public life gave respectability to the practice of subjecting the officials to hatred, ridicule, and contempt. No longer was the public official sacrosanct under the rule that "the greater the truth the greater the libel," a doctrine intended to extend the infallibility of the king to all who served him. Public opinion in the popular expression, "turn the rascals out," supported the principle of accountability of public officials and the watchdog role of the press. And, as Professor Lawhorne suggests in his demonstration of the responsiveness of the judiciary to public opinion and the social environment, could the courts be far behind with supporting decisions?

Although there remain problems of definition, it seems to be the law of the land that the public official can defend himself from published attacks upon his acts and his character only if he is able to prove malice and outright disregard for the truth. This leads to such questions as to the ability of the entrenched politicians to change the law by amendment to the Constitution, by challenging the Supreme Court for decisions impinging upon the legislative process, or by changing the composition of the Court. Will the Court itself, under pressure from within or from without, find it expedient to dress the balance tilted so far against the public official?

Any thought of the future must take it into consideration that today's journalism is the product of vast corporations with great financial responsibility. This is in contrast with a nineteenth-century journalism in the hands of impecunious editors, who, for practical purposes, were responsible only in physical encounter.

Howard Rusk Long

Carbondale, Illinois
November 7, 1970

Preface

Through the years, journalists in the United States have been plagued with uncertainty as to what they could, or should, write about public officials and candidates for public office. In considering what to write, they have been forced, since the dawn of this nation, to balance their ideas as to what the public should know against their ideas as to what the libel laws would allow them to report. Such balancing has not always been easy because of the difficulty in knowing what constitutes libel, especially in commenting about public officials and public figures. Though every state has its libel laws—either statutory or common—these laws have been largely what the judges have said they were. And the judges from state to state and from year to year have greatly varied their rulings. In short, a patchwork of libel laws grew up from jurisdiction to jurisdiction, with some overall standardization but without national uniformity.

Differences prevailed until 1964, when the United States Supreme Court in the case of *New York Times* v. *Sullivan* issued a broad mandate that established a uniform standard for libel as it pertains to public officials. The Supreme Court in this case held, in effect, that journalists have a constitutional right, in the absence of actual malice, to publish even defamatory falsehoods about the public conduct of public officials. And actual malice was defined as knowledge of falsity or reckless disregard of falsity. The decision, binding on all state courts through the United States Constitution's First and Fourteenth Amendment guarantees for free speech and press, brought order and cohesion to an otherwise disturbed area of libel jurisprudence.

The stabilization of the law resulted from a slow evolution that has taken place through the history of the United States. Today's liberal rule evolves from the harsh English common law in the colonial period that prohibited, under threat of punishment for sedition, any critical statement whatsoever about government or government officials. In the intervening three centuries, changes in the laws of libel reflect an ever-increasing liberty to discuss public officials. Yet, as far as can be determined, no comprehensive treatment has been given to these changes.

The purpose of this volume, then, is 1) to trace the evolution of the law as it applies to libeling public officials, in an attempt to provide a better understanding of present day legal principles and, possibly, of what to expect in the future; 2) to examine not only modifications in public policy, but also how, when, where, and, in as far as possible, why they occurred; 3) to identify the trends that have developed; and 4) to provide a comprehensive treatment of the changing libel laws as they affect newspaper discussion of public officials, in an effort to familiarize journalists with an area of jurisprudence closely associated with their everyday activity.

This work is designed not for attorneys, but for journalists and others who discuss public officials. The information that forms the foundation for the study is available to members of the bar, at least to those with the time, inclination, and library facilities to conduct the research. But the information is isolated; it is scattered throughout thousands of law books, some of which detail court decisions older than the nation. Normally the content of these law books remains a mystery to the general public. Yet the general public and those who communicate to the public are the ones who should know about the development and current status of their right to discuss their government and their government officials. Hence, a major contribution of this work perhaps will be in the compilation itself, the combining of bits and pieces of information heretofore secluded in many legal volumes.

The hypothesis is that the law of defamation as it pertains to public officials is not a product of any one period in United States history, but rather a composite built upon what has gone before, shifting only to meet the needs of particular periods or the needs of specific geographic areas within a particular period. This hypothesis has been born out by research, which has shown that the law has been, and is, fluid, expanding and contracting in accordance with prevailing views. Because of this, there is ample reason to believe that prevailing views, combined with experiences of the past, will control the future direction of the law of libel as it pertains to public officials.

In chronicling the experiences of the past and the present, this volume is divided into six parts. Part one focuses on the colonial period. It examines the roots of the English common law of seditious libel, the enforcement of criminal laws in the American colonies, and the emergence of truth as a defense in colonial prosecutions for statements critical of the governors. Part two examines the formation of libel laws in the United States from the nation's inception until the Civil War. Discussions are centered on Sedition Law prosecutions and state trials, at first for any criticism of public officials, then for true criticism made with bad motives, and finally for false criticism only. The shift from criminal libel prosecutions to civil libel actions is traced, along with the varying decisions of judges in different states.

Part three examines the initial development of privileged discussion, with some courts allowing a libel-free privilege for falsehoods if publishers had probable cause for believing them true and other courts limiting privilege only to fair comment and criticism. Part four details the development and divergency in the law of libel as it pertains to public officials. The lack of state court uniformity through the first half of the twentieth century in underscored. Additionally, the privilege to publish fair and accurate reports of public proceedings is examined, and a trend toward greater privilege of discussing officials following World War II is identified.

Part five centers on the decisions of the United States Supreme Court that initiated a constitutional privilege to discuss public officials. The effect these decisions had on state court rulings is detailed. Part six contains a summary of the law through the years and ends with a discussion of alternatives and consequences that may apply in the future.

The range of discussion in this volume is, in some respects, rather narrow. Only those segments of the libel laws which concern public officials and candidates for office are considered. Similarly, no attempt is made to deal with any media of communication other than newspapers, except for the purpose of clarity. Further, the study is based entirely on court decisions about libel; it touches on statutory law only when necessary.

I am particularly indebted to the editors, newspapermen, attorneys, and public officials who, during my twelve-year newspaper career, offered me guidance and information concerning libel. They helped lay the foundation for this volume. Additionally, I readily and gratefully acknowledge the advice and cooperation of Dr. Bryce W. Rucker, Dr. Jim Allee Hart, and Dr. Howard R. Long, all journalism educators; Dr. Randall H. Nelson, professor of government and constitutional law; and Dr. E. Earle Stibitz, professor of English and American literature. They spent long hours reading the manuscript, and their suggestions for polishing the weak spots contributed to whatever value the volume might have. They cannot, however, be held responsible for my shortcomings. The errors are mine alone.

A private note of gratitude is due my wife, Claudetta, and two children, Kelly and Jeffry, who gave me encouragement and understanding while I poured my life into the pages that follow. To them, I dedicate this book.

Clifton O. Lawhorne

Texas Christian University
March 1970

Defamation
and Public Officials

THE
HERITAGE

1. Colonial Heritage from England

Religious, Seditious Libel

A body of law concerning seditious and schismatical libel was built up in England long before the settlement of America. Under this law, it was a crime to publish scandalous matter about the governors and government or to express religious views not in conformity with those sanctioned by the English monarch. The law became quite prominent in prosecutions designed to suppress publications of the Brownists, who were church separatists, and the Puritans, who wished to purify the church from within. Consequently, when members of these two dissident religious groups established permanent English settlements in the Massachusetts Bay Colony of America, they brought at least a passing knowledge of libel with them. In the colonies, furthermore, the Brownish Pilgrims and the Puritans who followed them were as intolerant of those who dissented from their religious views as English officials had been. And

1

it was only six years after the Puritans arrived on the shores of New England that a religious difference caused the first colonial prosecution for what amounts to libeling public officials.

The victim of the prosecution was Roger Williams, who today is remembered as a founder of religious freedom in this country. At the time of the prosecution, in 1635, he was an elder and teacher in the church at Salem, Massachusetts. He was charged with writing circular "letters of defamation, both of the magistrates & churches" and with spreading "newe and dangerous opinions, against the authoritye of magistrates." [1] The letters asked Puritan churches in Massachusetts to rebuke the General Court, governing authority of the colony, for oppression. They were the end result of a rather vigorous attack that Williams had waged against the theocratic government of the Puritans.[2] He was, incidentally, judged by the same men he criticized; and upon his refusal to retract the defamatory statements, the General Court ordered him banished. To escape being sent back to England, Williams fled to the wilderness of today's Rhode Island, where he established a government dedicated to religious toleration.

While the case generally is treated as a religious and political controversy, it nevertheless dealt with written statements that censured governmental officials of the colony. The central issue was defamation. Though the press as such was not involved, Williams's case was the precursor of future American libel suits which pitted the press against public officials.

Puritan officials had ample precedent to follow in punishing Williams. In England, the law specifically had protected officials from scandalous statements since 1275. In that year, due to the unrest resulting from the Barons' Wars, a law was enacted providing that "none be so hardy to tell or publish any false News or Tales, whereby Discord, or Occasion of Discord of Slander may grow between the King and his people, or the Great Men of the Realm." [3] This law and two others, passed in 1378 and 1388, which defined the great men as including governmental officials and nobles and which provided that individuals spreading false statements as well as originators could be indefinitely imprisoned, made up what is known as England's Law De Scandalis Magantum.[4]

These declaratory laws, which did not distinguish between written and spoken defamation, limited punishment only to those making false reports. Nevertheless, after the advent of the printing press and during the reign of Queen Elizabeth, when only licensed printing was allowed, the fine distinction between truth and falsity seems to have been overlooked in English libel cases. The common law doctrine advanced in these cases was that statements reflecting on magistrates were libelous, true or false. The Puritans, at the time of Roger Williams's trial, could draw on at least three major court cases in England which advanced the principle that statements involving religion that excited discontent against the government, as Williams's statements did, were punishable as libel.

The earliest of these cases, in 1588, was brought against Sir Richard Knightly and three others. They were tried in the Star Chamber on a charge that they allowed a "seditious and libelous" pamphlet to be printed on their premises.[5] Knightly and his associates, who had helped hide a press that was used to print one of the Martin Marprelate Tracts, were described in the trial as sectaries who wanted individual church congregational government in England. The judges cited Queen Elizabeth's proclamations to the effect that all Brownist literature and "other seditious books" should be suppressed and burned and that no schismatical and seditious libels would be tolerated.[6] Further, they pointed out that only licensed books could be printed, and then only in London, Oxford, and Cambridge. Then they ruled that the unlicensed pamphlet, entitled *The Supplication to the Parliament*, reflected on Parliament, that it slandered Queen Elizabeth by accusing her of not maintaining religion, and that it caused confusion by tending "to take away her Majesty's prerogative royal," or licensing right.[7] All four defendants were fined and imprisoned, though their sentences were commuted by Queen Elizabeth on intercession of Archbishop Whitgift.

Such leniency was not shown two years later in 1590, when John Udall, a Puritan minister, was tried in England for printing antiepiscopal tracts. It was charged that he "maliciously published a slanderous and infamous libel against the queen's majesty, crown and dignity." [8] The pamphlet, entitled *A Demonstration of Discipline*, contained a passage calling for governments over individual churches "whereby they may take the government out of her majesty's hand, so sobering her majesty to be one of their sheep." [9] At the trial, held at Croydon Assizes, Udall's attorney tried to tell the jury that a malicious intent in writing had to be found before Udall could be determined guilty. However, the judge said this was not so.

The only job of the jurors, he said, was to determine if Udall had written the book, because some six months before all the judges in the land had pronounced the writer, whoever he might be, guilty of a felony.[10] The jury then found Udall guilty, and he was sentenced to death. However, he died in prison before he could be executed.

In all likelihood, jurors in the Udall case were limited in their determination only because England's twelve highest judges, meeting in judicial assembly, already had issued a decree in the matter. Nevertheless, the decision appears to have set a precedent whereby English juries were restricted in libel cases to determining only if accused individuals wrote or published statements alleged to be libelous. From this point on, trial judges assumed the right to determine when statements were actually libelous and hence criminal.

Though the duties of the judge and jury appeared to have been determined, early English prosecutions still had not defined libel; furthermore, as opinions had been the subject of these prosecutions, truth or falsity had not been brought into issue. It was not until 1606, in a third major case prior to the settlement of the American colonies, that declarative statements were made as to what constituted a libel and as to the place of truth as a defense justification. The trial commonly is referred to as the *Case de Libellis Famosis*, which authorities cite as the formal beginning of English libel law.[11]

This case, too, was before the Star Chamber, and, as reported by Lord Coke, involved an "infamous libel in verse" by Lewis Pickering against the dead John, Archbishop of Canterbury and the then living Richard, Bishop of Canterbury.[12] Not only did the case differentiate between libeling private citizens and officials, but it also gave the theory behind libel prosecutions. The Star Chamber opinion was reported as follows:

> Every libel . . . is made either against a private man, or against a magistrate or public person. *If it be against a private man it deserves a severe punishment,* for although the libel be made against one, yet it incites all those of the same family, kindred, or society to revenge, and so tends . . . to quarrels and breach of the peace, and may be the cause of shedding of blood, and of great inconvenience: *if it be against a magistrate, or other public person, it is a greater offence;* for it concerns not only the breach of the peace, but also the scandal of Government; for what greater scandal of Government can there be than to have corrupt or wicked magis-

trates to be appointed and constituted by the King to govern his subjects under him? And greater imputation to the State cannot be, than to suffer such corrupt men to sit in the sacred seat of justice, or to have any meddling in or concerning the administration of justice.[13]

Furthermore, it was declared immaterial whether the libel was true or false or whether the person libeled had a good or bad reputation.[14] An attempt was made to define a libel when the Star Chamber justices stated it "robs a man of his good name, which ought to be more precious to him than his life." [15] Libels against private individuals or officials, alive or dead, were punishable either by indictment or information, the court ruled, and libels could consist of writing, verse, pictures, or signs.

With such heritage concerning libel prosecutions, Puritan magistrates in Massachusetts were on firm ground in finding Williams guilty of defamation for spreading, by circular letter, opinions which were disruptive of their form of government. Still, the Massachusetts General Court showed more leniency than English courts by giving Williams an opportunity to retract his written statements. Furthermore, the sentence of banishment was much less harsh than the prison and death sentences in England. This is not to say that the colonial Puritans did not take strict measures.[16] For instance, shortly after Williams was banned from Massachusetts, John Wheelright and Mrs. Ann Hutchinson were banished for seditious statements, and some sixty persons in various Massachusetts towns were disarmed for fear that the opinions of Mrs. Hutchinson and Wheelright might excite them to revolt.[17] Massachusetts' citizens were warned at the time, in 1637, not to defame any magistrates under threat of imprisonment or banishment.[18]

The danger of defaming the government or the official religion also was stressed in England in 1637. John Bastwick, Henry Burton, and William Prynn, strong Puritans whose views did not coincide with those of the English government then in power, were found guilty in that year of publishing "seditious, schismatical and libellous books" which allegedly accused the bishops of changing services and prayer books to advance Popery.[19] Prynn was a lawyer, and in pleading his case before the Star Chamber, he mapped, to some extent, the history of libel punishments in England. He stated that in Queen Mary's time, the worst punishment for libeling either the king or queen was one hundred pounds and a month's imprisonment, while in Queen Elizabeth's reign the fine was raised to a maximum of two hundred pounds and three months' imprisonment. Then he made this statement:

> Formerly the greatest fine was 200 pounds, though against king or queen: now 5,000 pounds, but against the prelates and that but supposedly, which cannot be proved. Formerly, but three months imprisonment; now perpetual imprisonment. Then, upon payment the fine, no corporal punishment was to be inflicted: but now, infamous punishment with the loss of blood.[20]

He had predicted his punishment well. All three defendants had their cheeks burned and ears cut off; furthermore, they were fined five thousand pounds each and banished to prisons on islands at sea.[21] Later, in 1641 when the Long Parliament met and the Star Chamber was abolished, all three were pardoned, and they returned to England in triumph. One authority asserted that the trial of Prynn and his associates illustrated the causes leading to the abolishment of the Star Chamber,[22] and a Boston newspaper in the period of unrest before the American Revolution claimed that "had not Prynn lost his ears, King Charles would have never lost his head." [23]

English prosecutions for libel, however, did not stop with the rise of the Puritans and the execution of the King. They continued just as forcefully under the Protectorate. For example, Sir Henry Vane, who fought with Oliver Cromwell, was tried, convicted, and imprisoned for a seditious libel "tending to disturbance of the present government and the peace of the Commonwealth." [24] His crime was writing a book proposing "love and union" of all political and religious factions to heal the wounds of the civil war in England. He claimed he simply asserted the principles, spirit, and justice of the cause for which he fought.

Assertion of still other principles in a book written during this period of the Protectorate brought trouble to John Eliot, famous colonial missionary to the Indians. Unfortunately, the book, entitled The Christian Commonwealth, was not printed in England until after the Restoration, and Eliot's assertion that the choice of rulers should be by elections was offensive to the restored monarchy. The General Court of Massachusetts, in May 1661, ordered the book suppressed and printed Eliot's apology for writing "such expression as doe too manifestly scandalize the government of England, by Kings, Lords & Commons, anti-Christian, & justify the late innovators." [25] Eliot apparently had, unlike Roger Williams some twenty-five years before, agreed to a retraction to escape punishment.

Eliot's ideas concerning elections seem only slightly less severe than the idea, advanced in an English book printed by John Twyn in 1663, that the king was accountable to the people. However, Twyn, tried at Old Bailey, received the worst sentence ever meted out for printing a book in England. He was hanged and cut down alive, at which point his body was divided into four quarters. His head and quarters were placed over gates to London.[26] Actually, Twyn was charged with treason, it being alleged that he plotted and imagined the King's death, but the overt act as outlined in the indictment was printing a "seditious, poisonous and scandalous book." [27] In effect, Twyn was accused of committing treason through seditious libel.

Shortly after this, several cases were tried in England in which juries balked at punishing defendants for written and spoken statements. The first was the libel trial of Benjamin Keach in 1665 for writing a religious book, *The Child's Instructor, or, A New and Easy Primmer,* which Chief Justice Hyde claimed "disaffected his majesty's government, and the government of the Church of England." [28] In the trial, jurors could not agree on guilt until threatened with imprisonment by the judge. Though the jury had been instructed to determine only if Keach wrote the book, not if it was libelous, the original judgment was "guilty in part." [29] The judge's threat changed the finding to an unqualified verdict of guilty.

Later, in 1670, jurors freed William Penn and William Mead on a charge of tumultuous assembly and riot, a charge levied after Penn preached in a street. The jury again determined the law by its decision that the incident did not constitute a riot.[30] However, this time the jurors stuck to their verdict. And they were imprisoned for infringing upon what was considered the judge's prerogative of determining law, rather than confining themselves to determining only if Penn and Mead were involved. Shortly after, however, when juryman Edward Bushell was tried for alleged misconduct in the Penn and Mead verdict, all the jurors were exonerated and released.[31] Considerable importance was attached to this trial some sixty-five years later in the colonial libel trial of John Peter Zenger when Zenger's attorney, Andrew Hamilton, cited it as proof that jurymen could not legally be punished for exercising the power of determining the law as well as the facts in a case.[32]

Jurors further showed discontent with libel convictions in the first English libel trial which actually discussed writers of news. The trial, in 1680, was that of Benjamin Harris, then a London bookseller. He was charged with libel for peddling a pamphlet entitled *An Appeal From the Country to the City, for the Preservation of his Majesty's Person, Liberty, Property and the Protestant Religion.*[33] There were fears in England at the time concerning the publicized Popish Plot; and the pamphlet stated, in effect, that neither the people, who elected representatives to Parliament, nor those elected to Parliament, which was dissolved whenever it met, could be blamed if the plot to kill the king and turn the country over to France succeeded. Since the only one left to blame was the king, the presiding judge, Chief Justice Sir William Scroggs, said the pamphlet was "a sly way of casting it upon the king himself." [34] In the trial, Chief Justice Scroggs disclosed that England's judges, following the expiration of the English licensing act,[35] had reached a consensus on court treatment of writers and publishers. He said:

> It is not long since, that all the judges met, by the king's command; as they did some time before too: and they both times declared unanimously, that all persons that do write, or print, or sell any pamphlet, that is either scandalous to public, or private persons; such books may be seized, and the person punished by law; that all books which are scandalous to the government may be seized; and all persons so exposing them, may be punished. And further, that all writers of news, though not scandalous, seditious, nor reflective upon the government or the state: yet if they are writers (as they are free others) of false news, they are indictable and punishable upon that account.[36]

The statement, in effect, served notice that the growing number of news publications in England were subject to libel indictments for false reports.[37] In addition, by this judge-made law, the seller was as guilty as the writer or publisher. Despite Chief Justice Scroggs's declaration, however, jurors at first found Harris guilty only of selling the book, not of libel. Scroggs said such a verdict "was not their business" and threatened to poll individual jury members. Before he did, jurors, apparently fearful of punishment themselves, changed their verdict to guilty. Still, Chief Justice Scroggs told them that their work "was not so prudently done as might have been done." [38] Nevertheless, as a result of this judgment forced from the jurors,

Harris was fined five hundred pounds and placed on good behavior for three years.

Later in the same year, 1680, what appears to be the first libel case involving a newspaper and public officials was tried in England. The same judge presided, and the same Popish Plot fears prevailed; it was also evident that the judges still were bypassing Parliament by declaring their own laws. The trial was at the Guildhall of London and involved Henry Carr, editor of *The Weekly Packet of Advice from Rome*, described in the trial both as "a paper" and as a "single sheet coming out every Friday." [39]

Carr was charged with printing an article implying that officials, because of their inclination toward Catholicism, were blind to justice. The indictment included an allegation that the article was false as well as illegal and malicious, though no evidence was introduced in the trial to prove these allegations.[40] Carr's attorney claimed a guilty verdict could not be rendered since no evidence had been presented to show malice or scandal to the government. However, Chief Justice Scroggs stated that the only question was whether Carr was the author. He said that when all the judges previously had assembled at the King's command, they had decided that the printing of any news publication was illegal unless done with authority.[41] Even if the publication was not scandalous, it was illegal, he said, and as a result the author should be convicted. As Chief Justice Scroggs interpreted it, then, there was no necessity to prove the points in the indictment charging falsity or maliciousness; the printing itself was illegal and thus a libel.

Members of Parliament disagreed with his interpretation. They disagreed so much that impeachment proceedings against Scroggs and three other justices were begun, with Scroggs's decisions in the Harris and Carr cases cited specifically. In the proceedings, it was declared that Harris's fine was excessive and that Carr's newspaper was suppressed illegally and arbitrarily.[42] It also was declared that warrants issued by the courts against publishing "news-books" were illegal. In the articles of impeachment, the House of Commons declared that the judges "were encroaching and assuming to themselves a legislative power and authority" in declaring news publications illegal.[43] It was plain that much of the decision was based on religious views, however, as the articles also claimed Scroggs's decision discouraged Protestantism and countenanced Popery. The

House of Commons impeached Scroggs and the other judges, but the Lords refused to determine the issue.[44] Nevertheless, Scroggs was dropped as a justice. The import seemed to be that unauthorized publication of news in England was not in itself illegal and libelous at this time.[45]

However, it still was quite easy to libel or slander someone during the reign of the Stuarts. For instance, cases against twenty-two men were listed between November 1682 and February 11, 1685.[46] Many of these cases were brought by James, then Duke of York and later James II. In one case, he obtained a judgment of one hundred thousand pounds from Titus Oates, the principal instigator of the Popish Plot stories, in which James's close connection to the Catholic faith was emphasized. After James was unseated in the Glorious Revolution of 1688, Oates was pardoned.

The utter confusion in the libel law by this time, the last year of James II's reign, was shown in the trial of the Seven Bishops. James issued a declaration suspending laws that called for imprisonment of religious nonconformists, and he ordered the bishops to publish the declaration of indulgence in each diocese. The bishops, however, led by the Archbishop of Canterbury, petitioned the king, stating that declarations founded on dispensing power often were found illegal in Parliament and that they could not "in prudence, honour or conscience" publish the declaration.[47] The king brought them to trial, accusing them of publishing a libel in the petition.[48] The four judges split openly in their views as to whether the act was libelous; they also disagreed on their reasons.

For instance, both Lord Chief Justice Sir Robert Wright and Justice Allybone were of opinion that the petition was libelous and that it was immaterial whether the contents were true or false. The chief justice declared that determination as to libel was a point of law for the judges, not the jury, to decide. Further he said that anything which detracted from government or made mischief among the people, as did the bishops' petition, fell within the confines of libel, as set down by the rules of the *Libellis Famosis*.[49] Allybone's opinion was that "no man can write against exercise of government without leave." [50] However, both Justices Holloway and Powell were of the opinion that the petition was not libelous and that determination was for the jury, not the court. Holloway indicated that without malice, there could be no libel, and he said he personally could find no evil intent or sedition. "I cannot think it is a libel," he said in addressing the jury; " 'tis left to you, gentle-men, but that is my opinion." [51] Justice Powell was more forceful in his statement to the jury:

> To make it a libel it must be false, it must be malicious, and it must tend to sedition. As to the falsehood, I see nothing that is offered by the king's counsel, nor anything as to the malice: it was presented with all the humility and decency that became the king's subjects to approach their prince with.[52]

Powell thus rejected the former Chief Justice Scroggs's contention that proof of one segment of the indictment was enough for convic-tion. He, in effect, stated that all three elements in the indictment—falsity, malice, and sedition—had to be proved but had not been.

Following the summations by judges, the jury returned a ver-dict of not guilty, and the seven Bishops were freed. One can only speculate as to the reasons for the verdict, as to whether the over-riding motive was religious or practical. Nevertheless, it is clear that the function of determining the law, as to whether the offence constituted a libel, was taken out of the judges' hands by the jury. The views of Powell and Holloway prevailed on this point; and it was these views, along with those of the other two judges, that are important. They are important because they point to the fact that as the seventeenth century was ending, England did not have a clear-cut common law concerning libel.

SUMMARY

The confusion concerning the common law of libel as shown in the Seven Bishops Case appears to have prevailed from the first days of the printing press, when licensing provisions got in the way of the Statute de Scandalus Magnatum provisions that falsehood made the defamation. The impact of the licensing provisions was apparent in the early 1588 seditious libel trial of Sir Richard Knightly, in which licensing was cited by the Star Chamber justices. Another Star

Chamber case, that of the Libellis Famosis in 1666, declared it to be immaterial whether libelous statements were true or false. Libel indictments of this period did not allege publications to be false. The inclusion of the allegation of falsity in indictments, judging from the pronouncement of Chief Justice Scroggs in the trial of Benjamin Harris, was for the specific purpose of controlling news publications. Further indication of this was the allegation in the first known indictment against a newspaper for libeling public officials, in 1680, that the report was false as well as illegal and malicious.

However, the chief justice in this case, the trial of Henry Carr, refused to let jurors consider the allegations in the indictment. There was precedent for such a move, dating back to 1590 and the trial of John Udall, in which the judge refused to let the jury consider the indictment charge that a book was written maliciously. In both trials, judges said that the works had been prejudged as illegal and that the juries were to determine only if those accused actually wrote the works involved. Despite this special aspect of prior judgment, the cases emerged as legal justification for limiting jurors to the determination only of publication in libel suits. Juries, however, did on occasion attempt to determine questions of law, as to whether a libel actually was involved, and their right to do so was upheld in Bushell's case.

The disagreements among the judges in the Seven Bishops Case, then, simply reflected the uncertainty in the common law of libel as it concerned public officials. One of the major points of uncertainty was the power of the jury. Another evolved around the question as to whether it was necessary or nonessential to prove the allegations in the indictments, such as malice, sedition or falsity. The place of truth as a justification for libel was left muddled by the Seven Bishops Case.

Furthermore, the fact that religion was an element in so many early cases involving libel against officials only served to heighten the confusion. It seemed that judges interpreted any statement as libelous that reflected on an accepted official or prelate, the government in power or the established church. In this period, with the interrelation between government and religion, it was almost predetermined that a libel prosecution would be for seditious libel. And it was not unusual to find the allegation that the publication being prosecuted was schismatical as well.

Among prosecutions for religious views were those of Roger

Williams in the colonies under the Puritans, William Prynn in England under the Stuarts, and Sir Henry Vane in England under the Protectorate. Nevertheless, it appears that in the colonies, where Williams was given a chance to retract his statements and where John Eliot escaped punishment following an apology, the law as enforced was more lenient than in England, where John Twyn was hanged and quartered for stating the king was accountable to the people. Still, the difference between the colonies and England in court justice as it pertained to libeling public officials was only a difference of degree. The Massachusetts General Court had done no more than bend the English common law of seditious and religious libel to meet the conditions of a separate, yet subservient, government in a new country.

2. Clash in the Law of Libel

Colonial Liberalism v. *English Totalitarianism*

Pronounced evidence that colonial courts were bending the English common law of libel to suit conditions of the frontier came in 1692 with the trial of William Bradford of Philadelphia. Bradford, from all evidence obtainable, was the first printer tried in the American colonies for libeling public officials. Furthermore, as far as can be determined, his was the first colonial libel trial heard by a jury. It therefore provided the foundation for American common law as it pertains to libeling public officials. As in most other libel trials up to this time, conflicting religious principles were involved. Still, the harsh, totalitarian procedures of English libel trials, procedures which allowed judges arbitrary power to protect rulers from criticism, were not in evidence during the trial of Bradford. Instead, more libertarian principles were advanced, principles by which fellow citizens determined the fate of those critical of rulers.

Bradford, who in 1692 was the only printer in Philadelphia, upset Quaker magistrates there by printing a pamphlet entitled *An Appeal From the Twenty-Eight Judges To the Spirit of Truth.* The pamphlet was written by George Keith and Thomas Budd as an appeal from a condemnation of their religious views by twenty-eight Quaker ministers. It called Deputy Governor Thomas Lloyd, with whom Keith and Budd had argued in a Quaker monthly meeting, an "impudent man." [1] It also contended that ministers should not serve as magistrates. Keith, Budd, and a Quaker named Peter Boss, who had written a scandalous letter to one of the judges over the incident, were all tried for defamation. Then Bradford, who had

14

been arrested on a warrant charging him with publishing a "malicious and seditious paper" was tried on a grand jury's indictment alleging that his publication had a "tendency to weaken the hands of the magistrates." [2]

The Bradford trial is important because the Quaker judges, instead of arbitrarily determining as a point of law that a libel had been committed, left the decision to the jury. One authority put it this way:

> For the first time, it is believed, in the history of English jurisprudence, a court of competent jurisdiction left to the jury the question of the determination of the seditious character of an alleged libelous paper.[3]

The unanimous decision of the ten judges came after the prosecutor had insisted that jurors were to determine only if Bradford printed the pamphlet. The determination as to sedition, or whether magistrates' "hands" had been weakened, the prosecutor said, was a "matter of Law, which the Jury is not to meddle with." [4] Bradford replied that the prosecutor's contention was wrong, "for the jury are Judges in Law, as well as in matters of Fact." [5] Bradford's position was accepted by Chief Justice Samuel Jennings, who for the court instructed the jury to determine not only whether Bradford printed the pamphlet, but whether sedition was involved.

The judge's action here was described, in one recent study, as surprising.[6] However, Keith's account of the trial, from which all subsequent reports are based, indicates no surprise. It shows, rather, that the judges were yielding to pressure. Jurors demanded either to be dismissed or to be allowed to consider whether the publication was seditious as well as whether Bradford printed it.[7] Further, the judges had been accused by Bradford and two non-Quaker judges of basing the case exclusively on a difference in religious views.[8] Apparently, under this pressure, the judges were determined to be fair.

This attitude of fairness also could be inferred from the judges' earlier action in the trial of Peter Boss, one of Bradford's codefendants. Here, too, the judges deviated from all precedent in English trial procedures to allow Boss to produce evidence toward the truth of his alleged defamatory statements in the letter he wrote Judge Jennings. As a result, jurors did not find him guilty of defamation, but "only guilty of . . . speaking slightingly of a magistrate." [9] The

Quaker judges in Pennsylvania, then, gave jurors considerably more latitude than had been offered any libel trial jury in England prior to this time.

Nevertheless, when jurors finally got Bradford's case, they could not agree on his guilt or innocence. Consequently, he was discharged. It was reported that nine Quakers on the jury thought that Bradford was guilty of both printing and sedition, but the three non-Quakers maintained there had not been evidence presented to show that he even printed the pamphlet.[10] The irreconcilable views of jurors prevented this case from setting a precedent that jurors determined the law. Still, it did set a precedent, in that the judges, unanimously, turned the question of law over to jurors and allowed truth to be pleaded in evidence.[11]

The Bradford case does not stand alone among the early colonial libel trials in which jurors were asked to determine the law. Only four years after Bradford's trial, jurors in the 1696 Massachusetts trial of Quaker Thomas Maule brought in a general verdict to decide the law along with the facts. The jury freed Maule. The importance of Maule's trial, however, does not rest entirely on the fact that jurors made the determination as to libel. It also was important as the first trial before a Massachusetts jury for the crime of printing a libel.[12] Even more important, however, was the fact that jurors in this first case questioned the competency of a civil court to try spiritual issues through an indictment alleging that public officials had been libeled.

Maule was accused of publishing a book, entitled *Truth Held Forth and Maintained*, that contained "divers slanders against the Churches and Government of this Province." [13] Involved were theological opinions critical of Massachusetts civil and religious rulers. These opinions, Maule declared in his address to the jury, were in accordance with sound doctrine and spiritual truth.[14] He in effect argued, just as had Peter Boss, Bradford's codefendant in the earlier trial, that his work was justified because it was true. He further argued that only spiritual issues were involved and that he had broken none of the king's laws. The jury, he said, was not competent to sit in judgment of spiritual issues.[15]

The presiding judge, Thomas Danford, turned the entire case, along with the book, over to the jury for consideration. He asked a conviction on the grounds that Maule was opening a path through which others would follow to destroy the Commonwealth and churches.[16] Jurors nevertheless declared Maule not guilty on the basis that there was insufficient evidence of libel. They explained their belief that religious rather than civil matters were involved and that the matter should be decided by a "jury of devines." [17] They apparently did not feel they could judge whether Maule had written spiritual truths as he had claimed.

Two Maryland residents accused of libeling Governor Francis Nicholson also were tried in colonial courts before the end of the seventeenth century.[18] One, Philip Clarke, was a member of the Maryland House of Delegates. He was found guilty specifically of "divulging false news" about the governor and was sentenced by the Provincial Court to six months in jail.[19] The other man, Gerald Slye, was convicted of writing letters critical of the governor to officials in England. Nicholson claimed the letters were "part false, part scandalous and all malicious." [20] On arraignment, Slye was given a chance to prove the truth of his accusations but could not do so.[21] The Provincial Court sentenced him to five months in jail, but his sentence was remitted after he confessed his wrongs in open court.[22]

The assemblymen, upset over Clarke's imprisonment, also tried to secure his release on the basis that House privilege prevented imprisonment except for treason or for denying surety for breach of the peace. However, Nicholson refused the assembly, claiming that "all rebellions were begun by scandalizing and rendering odious the persons in authority.[23] It is interesting to note that the Maryland Council, which took the governor's side, asserted the assembly could not claim the privileges Parliament claimed because the colonies were subject to the king's laws; furthermore, Nicholson had told the assembly that there was "no custom in this country which amounts to common law." [24]

Such a broad statement by a colonial governor makes one pause to consider its import. If no custom amounting to common law existed for the legislatures to follow, as Nicholson claimed, the same likely was true for the courts. This might account for the more liberal set of standards that were evolving in colonial courts in trials for libeling public officials. Colonial juries, by determining whether publications were libelous, were not following the English common law.

That judges in England still were retaining the right to determine libel was shown in the 1702 trial of William Fuller, who was accused of "falsely, wickedly, maliciously and scandalously" writing and printing libelous statements.[25] His publications stated that persons of public trust were receiving bribes from the Pretender James and the French king. Not only did the indictment specify that the publications were false, but Lord Chief Justice Holt gave Fuller a chance to prove the truth of his statements.[26] However, when he did not produce any witnesses to prove his claim that the charges were true, Lord Holt declared the publications libelous, "for you produced no proof of what you charge them with." [27] He left the jury the duty of determining only if Fuller wrote or published the accusations. The year after the trial, in 1703, Queen Anne issued a proclamation setting up strict punishment for the publication of "any false news or tales." [28]

Although there was no doubt that Lord Holt preserved the judges' prerogative of determining the law, there was a question among United States jurists some one hundred years later as to whether he actually solicited truth as a justification for libel. Because the case was reported in Howell's *State Trials* as a prosecution for a fraud and a cheat, one view was that the case accepted truth only as a defense for fraud.[29] The other view was that the indictment was for libel, despite the case heading, and truth was solicited as a justification for the charge in the indictment.[30]

Judges of a later date also were confused as to the jury's role in the 1704 trial of John Tutchin, again conducted by Lord Chief Justice Holt. Tutchin, publisher of a semiweekly newspaper, was prosecuted for "falsely, seditiously and scandalously" writing and publishing a report that the navy was being mismanaged and that English officials were being bribed with French gold.[31] It was in this case that Lord Holt laid down this famous dictum:

> To say that corrupt officers were appointed to administer affairs, is certainly a reflection on the government. If people should not be called to account for possessing the people with an ill opinion of the government, no government can subsist. For it is very necessary for all governments that people should have a good opinion of it.[32]

After making the statement, he told the jury that it was to consider if the six issues of Tutchin's newspaper, the *Observator*, did not cause an ill opinion of the government's administration.[33] Later, however, he appeared to contradict himself by telling jurors that if they believed Tutchin wrote and published the papers, they were to find him guilty.[34] As if the instructions were not chaotic enough,[35] jurors added to the disorder by finding Tutchin guilty of all charges in the information except writing, which Lord Holt specified they must find for a guilty verdict. The ambiguity was never clarified, as the case was appealed on a technicality and never retried.[36] Still, the case pointed to a difficulty in obtaining convictions for discussing public affairs in England at this time.

Colonial courts also began to find it difficult to prosecute people for public affairs libels, as was evident in the 1723 case of James Franklin, publisher of the *New England Courant*. Here, a grand jury resisted an attempt by the Massachusetts Council and House to force an indictment against Franklin.[37] The officials were incensed because Franklin had taken a satirical slap at ministers' hypocritical prayers concerning public officials.

At the time, Franklin already was in trouble with the hierarchy. Previously he had been publicly censured and imprisoned by the House and Council for what were called scandalous libels,[38] and Dr. Increase Mather, one of the last of the old-line Puritans, had called the *Courant* a "cursed libel" in an address to the public.[39] Nevertheless, the attempt for an actual court indictment did not come until Franklin questioned whether the prayers of ministers for Governor Shute, who some thought was on his way to England to make representations against the province, would not actually be prayers for the ruin of Massachusetts.[40]

It was at this point that members of the House and Council prohibited Franklin from continuing to print his newspaper without a license. They claimed it mocked religion, abused the scriptures, insulted the government, and disturbed the peace.[41] The committee failed at getting an indictment from the grand jury, however, and Franklin continued to publish his newspaper under the name of his brother, Benjamin. Though the Franklin article expressed an ill opinion of government as well as religion, publicity concerning the matter centered on religion. The *Philadelphia Mercury*, which reported the details, stated that "the assembly of the province of Massachusetts-Bay are made up of oppressors and bigots, who make religion the only engine of destruction to the people." [42]

Religion certainly had a part in the prosecution of John Checkley in the same year, 1723. He was indicted at Boston for writing a pamphlet entitled *A Short and Easie Method with the Deists*, which the indictment called a "false and scandalous libel, tending to draw into dispute his present majesty's title to the crown." [43] It also was alleged that the pamphlet scandalized ministers, promoted Catholicism, and caused divisions among people in the province. The jury at Checkley's trial was asked to determine whether the publication was libelous as well as whether he was guilty. However, they refused to do it. The verdict was as follows:

> If the book is false and scandalous libel, we find him guilty. . . .
> But if the said Book, containing a discourse concerning Episcopacy,
> be not a false and scandalous libel; then we find him not guilty.[44]

The question of law, as to whether the religious views were libelous, was returned to the bench. After receiving the verdict, the court ruled that Checkley was guilty of publishing a false and scandalous libel.[45]

The import of this case is that jurors refused to declare a publication containing religious views a libel against the government. Despite the fact that they refused to determine the law, for which there was ample precedent in colonial courts, it is worthy of note that the jurors felt the case turned on the issue of truth or falsity. Perhaps this decision and that in the Maule case account for the fact that Checkley's trial marked the last time a legal prosecution was attempted in Massachusetts for publications defending episcopacy.[46] It would appear that the people of the colonies in this period, during the rise of Deists, religious nonconformists, and apostles of reason, were not prone to declaring statements concerning religion as libel against the governing powers.

Though the threat of prosecution for libel against the government for making religious statements appeared to be a thing of the past, two major questions of earlier libel suits remained. Despite the reliance in colonial trials and in some English trials on truth as a justification for libelous statements, did it in fact constitute a defense under English common law? Further, even though juries both in the colonies and England had made determinations as to whether statements constituted libel, did jurors under English common law really have this right? Both of these questions were answered negatively in 1731 by Lord Chief Justice Raymond in the English trial of Richard Francklin.

Francklin was the publisher of a London newspaper known as the *Craftsman* or the *Country Journal*. On January 2, 1730, he carried in the columns of his publication an article entitled "A Letter

From the Hague," which stated that English ministers were contemplating a treaty with the French emperor in violation of an agreement with the allies of Seville.[47] He was prosecuted for libel on the basis that the letter was malicious and seditious, reflecting on the King and his administrators.

Peculiarly, there was no allegation in the charge that the statement was false. Further, Lord Raymond would allow no evidence to prove the statements true. "It is my opinion," he said, "that it is not material whether the facts charged in a libel be true or false, if the prosecution is by indictment or information." [48] He added that libels were prosecuted because they flowed from malice and disturbed the peace. Malice, he said, was implied from the publication itself, as there was no other way of proving malice except by the publication.[49]

In instructing the jury, Chief Justice Raymond said that he knew some people thought jurors could determine whether statements were libelous, but this was not so. He stated:

> There are two matters of which you are proper judges. But there is a third thing, to wit, whether these defamatory expressions amount to a libel or not? This does not belong to the office of the jury, but to the office of the Court; because it is a matter of law, and not of fact; and of which the Court are the only proper judges . . . for we are not to invade one another's province, as is now of late a notion among some people who ought to know better; for matters of law and matters of fact are never to be confused.[50]

The two matters Raymond referred to as being within the province of the jury were whether Francklin published the newspaper and whether the expressions were about the king and his administrators. The latter decision was necessary because the letter had discussed all the allies of Seville and had talked only of "certain ministers." Chief Justice Raymond stated that when individual's names were not mentioned, it was necessary to file an information by innuendo, which was done in this case. He said the law allowed jurors "to give their verdict whether they think these speechings have the same meaning as mentioned in the information." [51] Jurors brought in a verdict that Francklin published the libel, and he was ordered imprisoned for a year, with an alternative of giving surety for good behavior over a seven-year period.[52]

The elimination of truth as a factor of consideration in

Francklin's case reiterated the declaratory ruling of the 1666 *Case de Libellis Famosis*. However, the fact that the indictment itself dropped the allegation that the letter was false, an allegation that had been in indictments and informations since newspapers first became involved in libel suits, beginning with the trial of Henry Carr in 1680, was in itself noteworthy.[53] The indictment alone, even without Lord Raymond's rulings, was sufficient to underscore the opinion of jurists that truth was immaterial.

SUMMARY

The trial of Francklin, though slipping back to Star Chamber doctrines and striking a blow at libertarian thought, served at this time to stabilize the common law of libel as it pertained to public officials in England. Before this, the common law of libel had been left teetering by the decisions of Lord Holt in the Fuller and Tutchin cases. In Fuller's case, Lord Holt had made the judgment as to libel while leaving only the question of publication to the jury; still, he had solicited proof of truth as a defense. In Tutchin's case, he appeared to reverse himself by giving the jury wide discretion in determining the libelous nature of the newspapers, but in reality, he left his charge unclear; further, he set the standard for determining a libel as being the tendency to promote an ill opinion of government, regardless of truth or falsity. When Lord Raymond tried Francklin, then, he could have made several rulings on the basis of Holt's contradictory dicta. By declaring an undefined malice as the determining factor in libel, with truth immaterial, Lord Raymond actually gave official sanction to Holt's standard that ill opinions of government constituted libel.

As in the Star Chamber Case de Libellis Famosis, there was little doubt as to the law declared from the bench in Francklin's case. When citing the Francklin ruling in the New York libel trial of Harry Croswell some one hundred years later, Justice James Kent had this to say about it:

It is a little remarkable, that the prohibition to the jury to judge the criminality of the libel, and the prohibition to the defendant to give truth in evidence, received together their first authoritative sanction in a court of common law, but this *nisi-prius* decision of Lord Raymond. It seems, however, to have been, from that time, generally taken as the law, without further inquiry or examination.[54]

There is no doubt that Kent's statement was correct so far as the common law of libel in England was concerned, but the colonial law was another thing. There had been no such broad guideline promulgated in the colonies to prevent juries from considering truth and determining libel.

Up to this point the colonial trials of people charged with libeling public officials, unlike those in England, had shown a remarkable consistency in principle. Starting with the first trial of a printer, William Bradford, in 1692, the Philadelphia jury was allowed to determine if the publication was libelous; furthermore his codefendant, Peter Boss, was allowed to introduce evidence of the truth as justification of the libel charged against him. Four years later in Massachusetts, Thomas Maule, in his plea to the jury, claimed he wrote only spiritual truths, and the jury refused to declare his claimed truths a libel. In 1698 in Virginia, Gerald Slye was given an opportunity to prove the truth of his statements against Governor Nicholson, and Philip Clarke was found guilty on the basis that his statements were false. The trial of John Checkley again saw the question of libel turned over to jurors, and their finding was that if it was untrue, his book was libelous. Two threads of consistency hold these trials together. One was justification of libel by truth; the other was jury determination as to whether libel actually was involved.

Furthermore, the cases reflected a definite reluctance of colonists to convict individuals for libel against the government on the basis of religious statements or prosecutions showing an ill opinion of government. The refusal of Maule's jury to determine whether religious statements libeled officials and the sidestepping verdict of Checkley's jury concerning religious views heralded the end of prosecutions in which religion and government were amalgamated in libel suits. As for ill opinions of government, it seems that in at least one case, that of Gerald Slye, a public retraction or confession of wrongs was sufficient to escape punishment. Prosecutions for at least two publications with ill opinions of government floundered before the James Franklin case,[55] in which a grand jury refused an indictment for an article that both mocked religion and expressed an ill opinion of government.

The colonists, then, appeared to be following principles of law somewhat different from the developing common law in England. Indeed, Governor Nicholson even stated there was no custom in the colonies amounting to the common law of England. While this seems somewhat extreme, the totalitarian principles of English libel trials were not reflected in their colonial counterparts. The developing colonial law had a decidedly more libertarian flavor, a flavor which suited the conditions of a new land in which reason was taking the place of theology and tradition. Still, this libertarian flavor as it pertained to trials for libeling public officials had not reached the point of crystallization. It did not evolve into a full concept of colonial justice until the widely publicized trial of John Peter Zenger.

3. Truth as a Defense

The Colonies Stand Alone

Though early libel trials in the American colonies had advanced more democratic principles than similar trials in England, a clear and decisive separation from the English common law of libel did not come until the prosecution of New York newspaperman John Peter Zenger in 1735. Zenger's case was one of landmark proportions for the colonies, as had been the trial of Richard Francklin in England only four years before. However, the two cases promulgated two entirely different principles. Francklin's trial had solidified the English totalitarian view that judges made the determination as to libel by considering if an ill opinion of government had been promoted. The trial of Zenger crystallized the colonial libertarian view that juries determined whether libel was involved on the basis of truth or falsity.

Still, the trial of Zenger differed only in degree from previous colonial trials for libeling public officials. Truth had been previously emphasized in the colonies as justification for publication, and jurors often had determined whether a libel was involved. In the Zenger trial, however, the place of truth in libel trials and the jurisdiction of jurors were joined for the first time as primary points of consideration. Furthermore, Zenger's was the first colonial prosecution in which a newspaperman was accused of publishing articles that libeled a public official. Other newspapermen took up his cause. Because of this and the explosive political situation in New York, the case attracted wide public interest and considerable publicity. As a result, the Zenger trial was given a place of prominence not achieved by previous trials for libel against public officials.[1] And the principles of the case were cited by colonists until the Revolutionary War.[2]

Zenger, publisher of the *New-York Weekly Journal* and an antiadministration propagandist, was charged with libeling Governor William Cosby. The charge was in an information filed by Attorney General Richard Bradley after the General Assembly, which was at odds with the governor, refused action, and after an indictment ordered by the council was refused by a grand jury.[3] Specifically, the information charged Zenger with "printing and publishing a false, scandalous and seditious libel" that placed the king's representative, the governor, in the position of "having no regard for law or justice." [4] Zenger's alleged libelous article, which did not name the governor, was claimed in the information to reflect on Governor Cosby by innuendo. The article quoted a man who moved to Philadelphia as praising the New York Assembly for not being affected by the "smiles or frowns of a governor." [5] The man was further quoted as follows:

> I think the law itself is at an end. We see men's deeds destroyed, judges arbitrarily displaced, new courts erected, without consent of the legislature by which it seems to me, trials of juries are taken away when a governor pleases, men of known estates denied their votes contrary to the received practice, the best expositor of any law; who is then in that province [New York] that call anything his own, or enjoy any liberty longer than those in the administration will condescend to let them do it, for which reason I have left it as I believe more will.[6]

There is no doubt that the portion about displacing justices referred to Governor Cosby's removal of Lewis Morris, leader of the antiadministration group, as chief justice, and his appointment of James DeLancey to the post.

The political differences over the appointment of DeLancey carried over into the courtroom. Zenger's first attorneys, James Alexander and William Smith, were disbarred for claiming Judge DeLancey did not have the approval of the council and hence was not lawfully commissioned to try the case.[7] Andrew Hamilton of Philadelphia was then called upon to take over Zenger's defense.

Despite the opposition to Judge DeLancey, reports of the case make it evident that he was trying to be fair during the trial. He ordered a jury that had been packed by the clerk to be dismissed so another could be selected in the regular manner from freeholders in the presence of both parties.[8] Further, even though he had ruled from the bench during the trial that truth could not be given as evidence to justify a libel, he allowed Hamilton to make an impassioned plea to the jury to the effect that all free citizens had the right to complain about government so long as the complaints were supported by truth.

Hamilton opened his defense by admitting that Zenger published the articles,[9] trying to eliminate the question of publication from the issues involved. However, the attorney general took this as a confession, claiming that under the laws of England, the jury had no other issue to determine but publication and, as a result, must find Zenger guilty. Hamilton disagreed. He said the indictment not only accused Zenger of publishing but also accused him of publishing a false, seditious, and scandalous libel. Then he stated:

> This word false must have some meaning, or else how came it there? I hope Mr. Attorney will not say he put it there by chance, and I am of the opinion this information would not be good without it. . . . The falsehood makes the scandal, and both make the libel.[10]

The attorney general argued, again on the basis of English law, that if the articles were true it would be only an aggravation of the crime. He then quoted the principle laid down in the *Case de Libellis Famosis* and reiterated by Lord Holt that there could be no greater scandal than to claim that corrupt and wicked magistrates had been appointed by the king.[11] His citations were buttressed by similar statements from Judge DeLancey.

In rebuttal, Hamilton claimed that the two were arguing Star Chamber decisions which were "long ago laid aside, as the most dangerous court to the liberties of the people of England that ever was known in that kingdom." [12] The application of the English common law to the colonies also was questioned by Hamilton at this point. He stated:

> What strange doctrine is it, to press everything for law here which is so in England? I believe we should not think it a favour, at present at least, to establish this practice.[13]

Though indicating that the English common law was not established in the colonies, Hamilton himself dipped into English cases to support his argument that truth was justification. Among other cases, he cited those of Tutchin, Fuller, and the Seven Bishops.

Despite his arguments, however, Judge DeLancey ruled he should not be allowed to give truth as evidence. Still, the judge told him if he would treat the court with good manners, "you shall be allowed all the liberty you can reasonably desire." [14]

It was at this point that Hamilton turned to the jury with the statement that "it is to you we must now appeal for witness to the truth of the facts we have offered, and are denied the liberty to prove." [15] Included in his argument to the jury was the following statement:

> The right of complaining or remonstrating is natural: and the restraint upon this natural right is the law only, and that those restraints can only extend to what is false: for as it is truth alone which can excuse or justify any man for complaining of a bad administration, I as frankly agree, that nothing ought to excuse a man who raises a false charge or accusation, even against a private person, and that no manner of allowance ought to be made to him who does so against a public magistrate. . . . Truth ought to govern the whole affair of libels, and yet the party accused runs risk enough even then. For if he fails of proving every tittle of what he has wrote, and to the satisfaction of the court and jury too, he may find to his cost, that when the prosecution is set on foot by men in power, it seldom wants friends to favor it.[16]

In arguing that words should be taken as they are understood, he quoted the Bible to show that it could be made to appear, by attaching the proper innuendos, that the New York governor was being discussed.[17] Hamilton further expressed particular criticism for prosecution by an information filed by the government's lawyer rather than an indictment, which has to come from a grand jury. He stated that informations were arbitrary weapons of men in power.[18] But he particularly emphasized that the jury could not find Zenger guilty unless the article was false.

To this latter contention, the chief justice took exception. He broke into Hamilton's argument with this statement:

> No, Mr. Hamilton: the jury may find that Mr. Zenger printed and published those papers, and leave it to the court to judge whether they are libellous. You know this is very common. It is in the nature of a special verdict, where the jury leave the matter of law to the court.[19]

Hamilton, however, answered the judge with these words:

I know, may it please your honour, the jury may do so; but I likewise know they may do otherwise. I know they have the right,
beyond all dispute, to determine both the law and the fact: and
where they do not doubt of the law, they ought to do so.[20]

Neither the judge's nor Hamilton's words were dogmatic. Each used
the word "may." However, Hamilton later stated that a jury in a
libel case had "at least as good a right to say, whether our newspapers are a libel or not libel, as another jury has to say, whether
killing of a man is murder or manslaughter." [21]

The judge, in his final instruction to jurors, told them the publication had been confessed and the only question was whether the
words were libelous, "and that is a matter of law, no doubt, and
which you may leave to the court." [22] He still used the word "may."
Jurors, in effect, had not been told positively that they had to
let the judge make the determination as to libel. They decided that
they, as well as the judge, might rule on the law. They found
Zenger not guilty of libel.[23]

One modern legal scholar has claimed that Hamilton's argument in the Zenger case was "peppered with grossly distorted precedents." [24] While it is true that Hamilton stressed the portions of
prior English trials that were useful to his arguments, as any good
attorney would do, he was not guilty of grossly distorting them. He
stressed the inconsistencies of English judges in libel cases and said
there was "no greater uncertainty in any part of the law, than about
words of scandal." [25] It is worthy of note that neither Hamilton nor
the attorney general nor Judge DeLancey cited Francklin's case,
which only four years before had been declarative of the law in
England. The reason is simple. Francklin's case apparently had not
been printed in English trial reports that were available in the
colonies.[26] Both the prosecuting attorney and the defense in Zenger's case rested their arguments on English libel suits that had
been tried prior to the Francklin case.

Still, as has been seen, Hamilton had protested the "strange
doctrine" of adopting English common law in colonial courts. In
effect, he argued the common law under protest, and it is plain
from other statements he made that Hamilton felt colonial law
was separate from the English common law. For instance, he argued
at one time that "in these parts of the world, at least" nature and
laws had given people the right to expose arbitrary power by publishing the truth.[27] He further attempted to drive a wedge between

English common law and colonial law by talking about the uncertainty among English judges. He stated:

> How cautious ought we to be in determining by their judgments, especially in the plantations, and in the case of libels? There is heresy in law as well as in religion, and both have changed very much.[28]

While there can hardly be doubt that Hamilton was exploiting the political situation in New York to play on colonists' mistrust of royal administrators, his statements indicate that differences in administering the law in the colonies and in England were usual rather than unusual. In his arguments, Hamilton had alternately cited nature or natural law, the law here, the laws in these parts of the world and, finally, the English common law. He presented a hybrid law to jurors, and it matched their sentiments as well as the temper of the times, the colonial courts and the colonial mind.

That Hamilton's arguments and the jury's verdict received popular support is abundantly clear from the cheers that met Zenger's acquittal in the courtroom and the city's presentation to Hamilton of a gold box with the city's seal.[29] Furthermore, the widespread publicity in both the colonial and British press could not help but sway public opinion toward the ideas that statements critical of government officials were not libelous in the colonies if true, and that it was the province of jurors to determine libel. The case crystallized the colonial concept of justice so far as prosecutions for libeling public officials were concerned.[30]

That truth officially was considered to be a justification for libelous statements in the colonies after the Zenger trial was shown in Boston by a 1741 prosecution initiated against Thomas Fleet, publisher of the *Boston Evening-Post*. Fleet in his issue of March 8, 1741, had carried a story quoting a ship captain to the effect that Parliament had called for all the papers concerning the war between England and Spain, and that shortly Sir Robert Walpole was expected to be arrested. The Massachusetts Council ordered an information against Fleet for libeling the administration of the King. However, Fleet produced five witnesses to prove the truth of the story, and the prosecution ended.[31]

Another example of truth being successfully pleaded in a colonial libel trial came with the prosecution in the 1740s of William Parks, publisher of the *Willamsburg Gazette* in Virginia.

Parks printed a story about a member of the Virginia House of Burgess, stating the representative had been convicted of sheep stealing several years earlier while living in another area. Parks was taken to court for publishing a libel that scandalized the government by reflecting on one entrusted with administering public affairs. However, Parks was allowed to prove the truth of the story by producing records of the court in which the past sheep-stealing trial was held.[32] He was exonerated, and the representative retired in disgrace. Further, the account was carried in newspapers of the time as an example of the free press being a restraint "on wicked men and arbitrary magistrates." [33]

This is not to say, however, that there was no suppression of the press during this period. For instance, the Massachusetts House of Representatives imprisoned Daniel Fowle in 1754 for publication of a pamphlet entitled *Monster of Monsters*, which was an allegorical attack on a current excise bill. House members claimed that the pamphlet was a libel that constituted a "breach of privileges" and that they had authority to commit individuals to jail for such breaches.[34] Fowle was released to see his sick wife, and he published an account of his treatment, claiming the Magna Charta had been violated because he had not been judged in court.[35] The House failed after this to pursue the matter, other than to recompense Fowle some ten years later for his unjust imprisonment.[36] There were several such incidents of legislative harassment of printers during the colonial period.[37] In the only case to reach the English Privy Council on appeal, however, it was ruled in 1758 that "inferior Assemblies in America" had no authority to imprison people for contempt in the form of a libel.[38]

Meanwhile in England, in 1752, the trial of William Owen, a bookseller charged with libeling the House of Commons, appeared suspiciously like a rerun of the Zenger case in America. The information filed against him, despite the holding of Francklin's case, contained the allegation that his pamphlet, which had accused the House of Commons with corruption, partiality, and injustice, was *false* as well as wicked, scandalous, seditious, and malicious. At the trial, the prosecuting attorney, William Murray, who afterwards became Lord Chief Justice Mansfield, proved Owen sold and published the book and said that as a result jurors had to find Owen guilty. However, Owen's attorneys argued, as did Hamilton in Zenger's case, that proving the sale did "not prove all those opprobrious and hard terms laid in the charge against him." They claimed the terms had to be proved if Owen were to be found guilty.[39]

Despite Chief Justice Lee's charge to the jury that Owen had to be found guilty if the fact of publication was fully proved, jurors, as did those in Zenger's case, brought in a verdict of not guilty. Even then the attorney general was allowed to ask them if the evidence had not been sufficient to convince them that Owen sold the book. The report of the trial states that the foreman fluttered but finally answered that the jury would stand by the verdict of not guilty.[40] A note to the case states that jurors would have had to perjure themselves if they said evidence did not prove publication.[41] While the verdict was hailed as England's "third great case in which juryes [sic] have insisted on judging the matter of law as well as of the act," [42] the postverdict questioning and its accompanying threat of perjury prosecution clearly showed jurors did not have this right under the English common law.

It also was quite evident from the widely publicized prosecution of John Wilkes in 1763 that the English common law still did not recognize truth as a defense to libel. Wilkes, a renegade member of Parliament who anonymously published the North Briton, stated in issue No. 45 that the king was making unjustifiable declarations from the throne and that the English crown, through advice from despotic ministers, had "sunk even to prostitution." [43] For this, he was condemned by Parliament and charged by an information with publishing a wicked and seditious libel. The information did not even allege the publication to be false, thus adhering to the principles of Francklin's case that truth or falsity was not a libel issue.

Wilkes, who had fled England, was tried in absentia by Lord Chief Justice Mansfield, who had been the prosecutor in Owen's case. The verdict was guilty, and upon his return to England, Wilkes was imprisoned for twenty-two months.[44] Meanwhile Wilkes, who had been denied his seat in Parliament, to which he was elected six times, was widely acclaimed both in England and in the colonies as a champion of liberty.

Perhaps the publicity attending the Wilkes' prosecution was one factor that caused difficulty in England in making libel prosecutions stand up. This difficulty was nowhere more pronounced than in the 1770 prosecutions of five newspaper publishers and a bookseller for publishing Junius's "Letter to the King." This letter,

Junius No. 35, was termed in the information as a "wicked, scandalous, seditious and malicious" libel. The letter stated that the English government was arbitrarily invading the rights of the people in
England, Ireland, and America. It further vilified the King, stating
the name of Stuart was contemptible, and that the king who imi-
tated the Stuarts should remember that a throne gained by one
revolution could be lost by another.[45] Much was made by defense
attorneys in the separate trials about the allegation of falsity being
left out of the charges. However, in the first of the six trials, that of
bookseller John Almond, Lord Mansfield maintained that the word
"false" had been left out of indictments and informations years
before because it was immaterial to the prosecution.[46] Further,
Mansfield told the jury that it was to determine only if Almond
sold the letter and whether the dashes in the title meant, by innuendo, the King. Jurors obeyed their mandate and found Almond
guilty. But jurors in all the other trials, though they received the
same instructions, acquitted the defendants, those who actually had
printed and published the letter.[47] In one of these trials, that of
Henry Woodfall, printer of the *Public Advertiser*, the jury stipulated that he was guilty of printing and publishing only. In effect,
the jury refused to declare the letter a libel.[48]

While England was having difficulty obtaining libel convictions in the period following the Wilkes case, colonial officials were
finding it almost impossible even to obtain an indictment. The
New York Mercury on November 3, 1766, printed an account of a
grand jury in Williamsburg, Virginia, refusing to indict four men on
charges of libel. The records also show that Chief Justice Thomas
Hutchinson of Massachusetts in 1768 failed at least twice to get
grand juries to indict individuals for libel.[49] Finally, in 1769, Hutchinson made this statement to a grand jury:

> I do not mention the Matter of Libels to you, Gentlemen—I am
> discouraged—My repeated Charges to Grand Juries, on this Head,
> both in this and other Counties, being so entirely neglected. How
> these Juries have got over their Oath, I tremble to think,—but I
> have discharged my own Conscience. In short, I have no Hope
> of the ceasing of this atrocious Crime, but from finding that they
> multiply so fast, are become so common, so scandalous, so entirely
> false and incredible, that no Body will mind them; and that all
> Ranks among us will treat them with Neglect.[50]

It is evident that the mood of the colonists during this period, in the few short years before the Revolution, was not conducive to prosecutions against individuals who libeled officials owing their commissions to England.

Officials, however, did not follow Hutchinson's advice to ignore critical publications. Within two years after his statement, two rather notable attempts were made at prosecutions for libels against government officials in the colonies. One attempt was against Alexander McDougall, who issued a handbill in New York entitled *The Betrayed Inhabitants of the City and Colony of New York*, and the other was against Isaiah Thomas, publisher of the *Massachusetts Spy*. In both cases the old arguments of Andrew Hamilton in the Zenger case were revived and printed in newspapers of the day to show that truth justified a libel.

McDougall was arrested after James Parker, publisher of the *New York Gazette* and *Post Boy*, unwillingly admitted that he had printed two of McDougall's handbills critical of the New York Assembly.[51] Both handbills claimed the assembly was abusing the liberties of the people. McDougall was thrown into jail to await indictment and trial. At this point newspapers and pamphleteers in the city revived the Zenger case, pointing to its principles as being the public policy of the colonies in libel suits. Parker in his newspaper printed Hamilton's arguments in behalf of Zenger, as did John Holt in his *New York Journal*.[52] Holt went even further and reproduced a fifty-three-page pamphlet containing the entire Zenger trial report.[53] However, Hugh Gaine, the publisher of the *New York Gazette* who has been referred to in newspaper histories as a turncoat,[54] issued a sixty-page pamphlet in support of the English common law and against the Zengerian principles.[55] McDougall himself issued at least one broadside from jail critical of the rubber-stamp procedures under which he was being prosecuted. He stated:

> The Assembly might as well invite the council, to save the trouble of formalities, to take their seats in the house of assembly, and place the lieutenant governor in the speaker's chair, and then there would be no waste of time in going from house to house.[56]

Despite the propaganda warfare, McDougall was indicted. Further, he was called before the assembly to account for the handbills, but he refused to discuss them because of the pending trial, pleading he would not be tried twice for the same offense.[57] As a result, he was held in contempt by the assembly and imprisoned.

Meanwhile, Parker died. There then was no witness to prove that McDougall, who had never admitted authorship, wrote the handbills. The prosecution for libel was dropped. However, Mc-Dougall, by this time famous, remained in prison on the contempt sentence until the legislature adjourned.[58]

Unlike McDougall, Thomas was never imprisoned. His offense was printing an article in his newspaper, signed Mucius Scaevale, which stated Hutchinson, who had become governor of Massachusetts, was tyrannical and a "monster in government." Further the article stated:

> I cannot but view him [Hutchinson] as a usurper, and absolutely deny his jurisdiction over the people; and am of the opinion, that any act of assembly consented to by him in his pretended capacity of Governor, is *ipso facto,* null and void and consequently not binding on us.[59]

As a result of the article, the Massachusetts Council ordered him to appear before it, but he refused. The attorney general was ordered to prosecute Thomas for libel, and Thomas replied by printing in his newspaper various letters of support along with the Zenger arguments that truth was a defense to libel.[60] When the case came before the grand jurors, they refused to indict him.[61] The episode did not mark the end of Thomas's opposition to officials, however, as less than a year later he printed an article critical of the King for using bayonets to enforce laws unapproved by the colonies.[62] Though noted lawyer James Otis, who offered to defend Thomas, said the situation was "touch and go, by God," neither an information nor an indictment was attempted.[63]

SUMMARY

So it was that in this last attempt at prosecution in the colonies for libel against government officials, as well as in the near prosecution of McDougall during the same year, the Zenger doctrine was re-

vived. It was America's court heritage, not that of England, that was looked to in the arguments as to the law that were waged in the public press. There can be no doubt that the press, in this period of heightened feeling against governmental control by England, benefited by publicizing the colonial court heritage. But the heritage was nonetheless real; it was one that began with the prosecution of William Bradford and that was consistently sustained in libel trials until crystallized in the arguments of the Zenger prosecution. It was a heritage of law that permeated the entire history of libel prosecutions in eighteenth-century colonial history.

This colonial concept of justice, that juries determined libel by using the standard of truth, was entirely different from that established under the English common law. True, it was becoming more and more difficult to obtain convictions in English libel prosecutions, as was demonstrated in the trials of Owen and those who printed Junius's "Letter to the King." Nevertheless, English judges adhered strictly to the totalitarian view that they alone determined if libel was involved. Furthermore, the public policy in England, as differentiated from the practiced colonial policy, was that publications promoting an ill opinion of government were malicious and consequently libelous, even if true. Jurors, under the English common law, were instructed to determine only if accused individuals published or sold works adjudged libelous.[64] Even Judge DeLancey, who tried to abide by the English common law in the Zenger case, did not expressly forbid jurors to bring in a verdict concerning the libelous nature of the publication. The courts in the American colonies and England, then, had followed divergent paths in formulating their respective laws of libel as they pertained to public officials. The colonies, in this respect, stood apart from England, and alone.

Still, the libertarian principles that had been advanced in colonial trials for libel were not accepted by all in the American colonies. Many of the colonists, especially those who had worked and lived in England, were in complete sympathy with English views. These people, such as New York newspaperman Hugh Gaine, looked to the court heritage of England, to the principles of the English common law, as the controlling factor in justice. That this English common law as it pertained to libel and public officials had not lost its impact in America was particularly evident in this country's court decisions after the United States won its independence. So far as the new nation's courts were concerned, the English common law and the law as practiced in the colonies were entwined into one common heritage. But for this particular period, when a whole people, the colonists, were on the threshold of discarding their English ties and of going their own separate and independent way, the Zengerian principles were paramount and consistent with ideas of liberty.

THE
FORMATIVE
YEARS

---

4. A New Nation

Criticism of Public Officials a Crime

Newspapers in the period immediately following the Revolutionary War enjoyed an almost unrestrained freedom to discuss, criticize, and comment on government and government officials.[1] Many individuals of the time felt that in the new United States there could no longer be a libel against government, that the old English common law of seditious libel had ended with the Declaration of Independence.[2] There was a basis for this belief. While the new states had not abandoned the English common law, it had been stipulated in some state constitutions that only the English common law as it had been interpreted in the colonies was now in force.[3] And the portion of the common law dealing with seditious libel had been modified in the colonies. Colonial juries had rejected, in trial after trial, the English doctrine that publications promoting an ill opinion of government or officials, whether true or false, constituted

39

criminal libel. The colonial concept, as it evolved in these trials, was that truthful statements about public officials were not libelous. This was the heritage that had been passed to a new nation. Further the various states guaranteed press freedom in their new constitutions.[4] Despite this, it soon became abundantly clear that the common law of seditious libel was not dead. Within fifteen years after independence, criticism of public officials in the United States became a crime.

One of the earliest published views concerning criminal libel came from Eleazer Oswald, publisher of the *Independent Gazeteer* in Philadelphia. Upon an indictment for a political libel against the director of a private girls' school in 1788, he commented in his newspaper as follows:

> The doctrine of libels being a doctrine incompatible with law and liberty, and at once destructive of the privileges of a free country, in the communication of our thoughts, has not hitherto gained any footing in Pennsylvania. . . . I may well suppose, the same love of liberty yet pervades my fellow-citizens and that they will not allow the freedom of the press to be violated, upon any refined pretence, which oppressive ingenuity or courtly study can invent.[5]

Although Oswald was never tried on the libel indictment, he was summarily convicted of contempt of court for publications growing out of the case. Pennsylvania Chief Justice McKean, commenting on libels, said at the time that nothing in the Pennsylvania Constitution changed the common law of England regarding the liberty of the press.[6]

This certainty of Judge McKean was not shared by jurists in all states, as was reflected a year later in correspondence between Massachusetts Chief Justice William Cushing and future president John Adams. Cushing in a 1789 letter asking Adams's views on libel, reviewed the English law, pointing out that truth could not be pleaded there in defense to a libel indictment. "The question is," he wrote, "whether it is law now here?" [7] While apparently not sure of the law of criminal libel as it should be applied from the bench, Cushing added that it was his personal belief that "falsity must be a necessary ingredient in a libel." [8] Adams, also a lawyer, replied that he believed truth should be allowed in evidence, but that juries also should consider whether publications were for the public good before acquittals were allowed in libel trials.[9]

A statement in Cushing's letter leaves no doubt that he was

not in sympathy with the English common law of seditious libel.
Pointing to the Massachusetts constitutional provision that the free
press should not be restrained, and discussing the right to freely
scan the conduct of those in government, Cushing wrote:

> I think the liberty tends to the security of freedom in a State,
> even more directly and essentially than the liberty of printing upon
> literary or speculative subjects in general. Without this liberty of
> the press could we have supported our liberties against the British
> administration? or could our revolution have taken place? Pretty
> certainly it could not, at the time it did. . . . This liberty of pub-
> lishing truth can never effectually injure a good government, or
> honest administrators; but it may save a state from the necessity
> of a revolution, as well as bring one about, when it is necessary.[10]

As chief justice of Massachusetts, Cushing never had an opportu-
nity to make his views official. Shortly after his correspondence with
Adams, he became one of the first justices of the United States
Supreme Court.

Despite Cushing's views, it soon became evident that the English common law of seditious libel was very much in force in his
state of Massachusetts. In 1791, Edmund Freeman, young publisher
of the *Herald of Freedom* in Boston, was indicted and prosecuted
for publishing ill opinions of a Massachusetts legislator, John Gardiner.[11] The three judges of the Massachusetts Superior Court differed
in their charges to the jury. Justice Sumner, disagreeing with the
English common law, quoted the Massachusetts Bill of Rights and
said Freeman had a right to express his views as long as he kept
them "within the bounds of truth." [12] However, the majority ruling,
by Chief Justice Sargent and Justice Dana, held that the English
common law of criminal libel had not been altered by the state
constitution.[13] One legal historian has said that the decision attracted attention throughout the United States and was a "great
shock" to laymen and many attorneys.[14]

Interestingly, however, the two judges did appear to voice reservations concerning the English libel doctrine. Dana, who pointed
out to the jury that truth was not allowed in evidence in English
courts, made this statement:

> Yet, perhaps the Charter here may lay down a different principle,
> and admit truth of charges contained in a libel to amount to a com-
> plete justification, as it is otherwise in civil action upon a libel.[15]

Both Sargent and Dana stressed that the truth of the publication was not at issue in the trial. The article concerned a political difference of the time, and Freeman's attorneys had not raised the issue of truth.

The court fight centered around the question of malice, and Freeman's attorneys apparently were successful in contending that there was no malicious intent. In fact, they made quite a point of Gardiner's being a representative of the people and stressed the need to scrutinize the conduct of public men.[16] Jurors, whose foreman was Paul Revere, found Freeman not guilty. They did not appear to be ready to find a newspaper publisher guilty of a crime for publishing matter promoting ill opinions of government officials. In what was believed to be the first trial for libeling a public official in the new nation,[17] then, the old English common law of criminal libel was revived only to be rejected by jurors. Furthermore, there was a strong indication that truth would be accepted as a justification for a libel against a public official in Massachusetts.

Pennsylvania, meanwhile, had gone much further than Massachusetts in protecting the freedom of the press. Constitutional reforms of 1790 in Pennsylvania provided that citizens were free to investigate public officials in their public capacities. Coupled with this was another provision that publications proper for public information could be justified by truth in all prosecutions for criminal libel.[18] Pennsylvania was the first state to include this guarantee in a constitution, though Delaware and Kentucky followed suit two years later, in 1792, and Tennessee made similar provisions in its constitution in 1796.[19]

The new Pennsylvania constitution forced Chief Justice McKean to modify the views he expressed in Oswald's case concerning the application of the English common law to the press. Still, he was not forced to accept truth as a complete defense in prosecutions for libeling officials. The reason was simple. A standard for determining what publications were proper for public information was left unresolved by the new constitution. McKean, then, had considerable leeway, as was shown when he tried to obtain a grand jury indictment against William Cobbett of *Porcupine's Gazette* in 1797.[20] He told grand jurors that publications criticizing the government or officials had to be "decent, candid and true," that they had to be for "reformation and not for defamation," and that they had to have an "eye solely to the public good."[21] He pronounced a standard, as Adams had before him, that good motives as well as truth were necessary to justify a libel.

Cobbett had been accused of libeling the Spanish ambassador to the United States. The article at issue had been printed in Cobbett's Federalist newspaper after the ambassador had objected to the Federalist's Jay Treaty with England. It stated that the ambassador, who was engaged to McKean's daughter, was controlled by the French, was frivolous and degenerate, and was "half Don and half Sans Culotte." [22] Specifically referring to the attack, McKean told the grand jurors:

> Libeling has become a kind of national crime, and distinguishes us not only from all the states around us, but from the whole civilized world. . . . The contest has been, who could call names in the greatest variety of phrases, who could mangle the greatest number of characters; or who could excell in the magnitude and virulence of these lies.[23]

He added that Cobbett had won the contest as the greatest libeler. Despite this and the judge's instructions as to what was proper for public information, grand jurors refused to indict Cobbett. His publication was only typical of the partisan party press of the time, which was free to make scurrilous attacks upon public figures with few restraints.[24]

The press at this period in the United States had broken into two great segments, following the political parties that had evolved after Washington's inauguration. Both segments, whether Whig (Republican) or Federalist, were completely intolerant of political opponents. As one newspaper historian has said:

> Coarse personalities, vulgar ribaldry, malicious slanders were poured forth, until it seemed to sober minded men that unrestrained freedom of discussion was leading to the triumph of anarchy.[25]

The activities of this partisan press were tolerated, however, until the war scare of 1798. At this time, Federalist members of Congress, frantically preparing for an expected war with France, took the position that excessive attacks by elements of the Whig press against the United States government and the Federalist officials then in power was criminal.[26]

It was questionable, however, whether legal action could be taken to stop press comments. Supreme Court Justice Samuel Chase in April 1798, issued an opinion that indicated the federal government could not prosecute newspapermen on common law indictments. Sitting on circuit court in Philadelphia, which also was the seat of Congress at the time, Justice Chase announced in *United States* v. *Worrall* that the United States, unlike the states, had no common law. Since all national law came from the Constitution or Congress, he said, individuals could not be prosecuted in federal courts for common law crimes.[27] He further stated that Congress had to pass a law to define an offense and set punishment for it before there could be a criminal prosecution of any type in federal court. Judge Chase's decision, evidence indicates, was one of the factors leading to the Sedition Act that soon was passed by Congress.[28]

Perhaps a more immediate stimulant for a Sedition Law, however, was Benjamin Franklin Bache's *Philadelphia Aurora*, an Antifederalist organ which was becoming more vehement by the day. Bache objected to war preparations, claiming they started because France had not received American ambassadors but were continuing despite the opening of negotiations by France at that very moment with American envoy Elbridge Gerry, a Whig.[29] Bache was indicted under the common law for seditious libel on the same day that the Sedition Act was introduced in the United States Senate.[30] The timing does not appear to be a coincidence. One authority has indicated that the Sedition Law was considered necessary by Federalists because they did not feel the prosecution of Bache would stand up under common law.[31] It is definite that Bache's articles were cited in Senate debates on the act,[32] and Thomas Jefferson wrote at the time that the purpose of the Sedition Act was to suppress the Whig press.[33]

Debates did not long delay the passage of the act. It went into effect on July 14, 1798, less than three months after Chase's decision questioning common law jurisdiction of federal courts and less than twenty days after Bache was indicted. Terms of the law were as follows:

> If any person shall write, print, utter or publish . . . any false, scandalous and malicious writing or writings against the government of the United States, or . . . Congress . . . or the President . . . with intent to defame the said government or either house of . . . Congress, or the said President, or to bring them . . . into contempt or disrepute, or to excite against them . . . the hatred of

the good people of the United States, or to stir up sedition within
the United States, or to excite any unlawful combinations . . .
for opposing or resisting any law of the United States, or any act
of the President . . . or to resist, oppose or defeat any such law
or act . . . then such person, being thereof convicted . . . shall
be punished by a fine not exceeding two thousand dollars, and by
imprisonment not exceeding two years.[34]

An important feature of the act was that anyone prosecuted was allowed to present the truth of the publication in evidence for his defense. The act also specified that jurors could determine whether
publications were libelous and if publishers were guilty.

The Sedition Law was adopted despite the First Amendment
to the Constitution, which stated that no law could be passed
abridging press freedom.[35] The question as to whether press freedom
actually was abridged brought on a controversy that has waged
through the years. An answer was never given by the Supreme
Court, which was not confronted with a Sedition Law case. However, the United States House Committee on the Judiciary in 1840,
at a time fines levied under the law were being refunded, stated
that the Sedition Law was "unconstitutional, null, and void, passed
under a mistaken exercise of undelegated power." [36]

Considering that the United States government had not previously imposed restrictions on the press, the Sedition Law certainly
was an abridgment of press freedom as then known. Prior to the
law, it had not been a crime to libel the national government or its
officials. With the law, it was. Further, the all-inclusive language of
the law could be interpreted to apply to legitimate criticism of the
federal government, criticism which voiced opinions that could not
be gauged by a yardstick of truth. In this light, the law restricted
what could be published and was in violation of the First Amendment mandate.

Still, the national government through the Sedition Law had
assumed no more power than had many state governments. All the
states exercised the right to bring libel indictments for published
statements critical of their government or public officials. And press
freedom in these cases had never been extended beyond the right
to present truth in evidence at the trial and to have a jury make the
determination as to libel. The Sedition Law protected this phase of
press freedom, in a sense nationalizing and formalizing it.

The Sedition Law, then, as far as the court trial itself was concerned, granted all the freedom that the American and colonial press had ever known. But at the same time the law set standards for libel that muzzled press criticism of the United States government. It made libel a household word, and one scholar has said that in the United States the "law of libel may be considered as commencing with the passing of the Sedition Law." [37] While this is extreme, one must admit that the law gave official sanction to the idea that criticism of public officials was a crime.

Less than three months after the Sedition Law was passed, Republican Congressman Matthew Lyon of Vermont was indicted for allegedly stirring up sedition and bringing into contempt President Adams and the United States government.[38] His crime was sending two letters to the *Vermont Gazette* for publication. He was the author of one letter, which included the following statement:

> Whenever I shall, on the part of the Executive, see every consideration of the public welfare swallowed up in a continual grasp for power, in an unbounded thirst for ridiculous pomp, foolish adulation, and selfish avarice: when I shall behold men of real merit daily turned out of office, for no other cause but independency of sentiment . . . when I shall see the sacred name of religion employed as a state engine to make mankind hate and persecute one another, I shall not be their humble advocate.[39]

The other letter reportedly was from Joel Barlow, an American diplomat and man of letters then in France. The letter stated that after Adams's speeches against the French, "we wondered that the answer of both houses had not been an order to send him to a mad house." [40]

At the trial, Lyon insisted that the Sedition Law was unconstitutional and that his statements showed only legitimate opposition to the party in power. But Supreme Court Justice William Patterson, presiding over the Vermont circuit court, told the jury that constitutionality was not its concern. The only questions before the jury, Patterson said, were: "Did Mr. Lyon publish the writing given in the indictment? Did he do so seditiously?" [41] Lyon, acting as his own attorney, attempted to prove the truth of his published opinions by asking Justice Patterson to attest to Adams's pompishness. This Patterson refused to do, and Lyon called no other witness. He claimed that he was spirited into Vermont's Federalist territory for the trial and that the jury was packed with Federalist sympathizers.[42]

The jury found him guilty, and he was fined one thousand dollars and sentenced to four months in jail. While in jail, he was reelected to Congress. Apparently the common citizens of Vermont supported Lyon's criticism of those in control of government, criminal or not.

The next major trial under the Sedition Law was that of Anthony Haswell, the printer of the *Vermont Gazette*. The trial was a result of the Lyon case. While Lyon was in jail, Haswell's newspaper carried an article addressed "To The Enemies of Political Persecution." The article was critical of the sheriff's holding Lyon and stated that Lyon was "holden by the oppressive hand of usurped power." [43] It further stated that the "administration publicly notified that Tories, men who had fought against our independence, who had shared in the desolation of our homes and the abuse of our wives and daughters, were men who were worthy of the confidence of the government." [44]

At the trial, Justice Patterson, again presiding, refused to admit testimony from the secretary of war that the government had acknowledged appointing Tories to office.[45] He said this would not show that these men shared in desolating homes and abusing wives and daughters. In short, he ruled the offered proof did not fully justify the charge. Justice Patterson also ruled that Haswell did not have to be the author of the article to be liable for it, as the article was in his newspaper. Haswell had claimed it was inserted without his knowledge by James Lyon, clerk of Congressman Lyon.

After dispensing with defense claims, Patterson told the jury: "If the jury believe, beyond a reasonable doubt, that the intent was defamatory, that the publication was made, they must convict." [46] Jurors found Haswell guilty, and he was sentenced to two months in jail and fined two hundred dollars. While Patterson set down two major rules in libel cases, that justification must be as broad as the charge and that publishers were responsible even if they did not write libelous articles, it appears that he did usurp the jury's function by not allowing it to hear and make its own judgment on testimony concerning the government's employment of Tories.

Another trial that generated wide interest was that of Dr. Thomas Cooper, who was indicted for libeling President Adams.[47] Cooper, an Antifederalist or Republican, was accused in print of vacillating, trying unsuccessfully to get a government post from Adams, a Federalist. Cooper replied in a newspaper article that the charge was partially true. He said he had written Adams for a position some two years before, when Adams was first in office and was in "the infancy of political mistake." Listing what he thought were subsequent mistakes, Cooper wrote:

> Nor had he [Adams] yet interfered, as president of the United States, to influence the decisions of a court of justice—a stretch of authority which the monarch of Great Britain would have shrunk from—an interference without precedent, against law and against mercy. This melancholy case of Jonathan Robbins, a native citizen of America, forcibly impressed by the British, and delivered up, with the advice of Mr. Adams, to the mock trial of a British court-martial, had not yet astonished the republican citizens of this free country; a case too little known, but of which the people ought to be fully apprised, before the election, and they shall be.[48]

The indictment claimed the statement was false, scandalous, and malicious, that it brought Adams into contempt and disrepute, and that it turned the "hatred of the good people of this country against him." [49]

Cooper, at his trial, claimed his article was justified by truth, that it was an involuntary publication for self-defense, and that the public and not private character of Adams had been attacked.[50] He later wrote that it was a "notorious and universal belief" of the majority of the population that Adams had instructed Judge Bee of South Carolina to turn Robbins over to the British as a deserter, and that a person should not be required to provide strict proof of facts commonly believed and that "cannot honestly be contradicted." [51] However, Supreme Court Justice Samuel Chase, a Federalist presiding over the Pennsylvania circuit court where the trial was held, said Adams could not refuse to turn Robbins over to the British because of the Jay Treaty. Robbins, he said, was accused of murder on a British ship. Further, Chase said that Adams had contacted the South Carolina judge only to inquire into evidence of Robbin's criminality.[52]

It is evident from the trial record that Judge Chase transcended his position as judge to become an advocate. It also is evident that he succeeded in giving reasons for Adams's action but did not destroy Cooper's story. Still, Chase called Cooper's account "false and scandalous," said it was "actuated by improper motives," and claimed it was made only to injure Adams's character and to influence the next election.[53] "Take this publication in all its parts,"

Judge Chase said, "and it is the boldest attempt I have known to poison the minds of the people." He told the jurors that Dr. Cooper had to prove every charge to be true, and that if he did not, they had to consider if the charges were made maliciously.[54] The jury found him guilty.

The trial is particularly important because of the theories concerning the Sedition Law that were advanced by Justice Chase and Dr. Cooper. Chase made the following statement in support of the law:

> There is no civilized country that I know of, that does not punish such offences; and it is necessary to the peace and welfare of this country, that these offences should meet with their proper punishment, since ours is a government founded on the opinions and confidence of the people. . . . All governments which I ever read or heard of punish libels against themselves. If a man attempts to destroy the confidence of the people in their officers, their supreme magistrate, and their legislature, he effectually saps the foundation of the government. A Republican government can only be destroyed in two ways; the introduction of luxury or the licentiousness of the Press. This latter is the more slow, but more sure and certain, means of bringing about the destruction of government. The legislature of this country, knowing this maxim, has thought proper to pass a law to check this licentiousness of the press.[55]

Chase, then, looked to what other governments did as support for the Sedition Law and, in effect, adopted the English doctrine that promotion of ill opinions of public officers was a crime. His view was countered by that voiced by Cooper:

> In the present state of affairs, the press is open to those who will praise, while the threats of the law hang over those who blame the conduct of the men in power. . . . Nor do I see how the people can exercise on rational grounds their elective franchise, if perfect freedom of discussion of public characters is not allowed. Electors are bound in conscience to reflect and decide who best deserves their suffrage; but how can they do it, if these prosecutions *in terrorem* close all the avenues of information, and throw a veil over the grossest misconduct of our periodical rulers? [56]

Cooper's plea for "perfect" freedom of discussion perhaps was as extreme a view as Chase's. However, his six-month jail sentence and four-hundred-dollar fine does not now appear justified. Many felt it was unjustified at the time. His imprisonment, as was the entire

Sedition Law, was a popular subject for electioneering declamation in the race between Adams and Thomas Jefferson.

Though the Sedition Law issues probably were best stated in the trial of Dr. Cooper, the most famous of the libel trials under the Sedition Law was that of James Callender. Callender, who previously had been adjudged an outlaw in Scotland for fleeing a seditious libel trial there,[57] was accused in 1800 of libeling President Adams also. He was the author of a tract, *The Prospect Before Us*, which was published prior to the Jefferson-Adams presidential race. Again the case of sailor Jonathan Robbins, who was turned over to the British, was cited. Callender wrote:

> You will choose between that man whose life is unspotted by crime, and that man whose hands are reeking with the blood of the poor, friendless Connecticut sailor. . . . Take your choice, then, between Adams, war and beggary, and Jefferson, peace and competency.[58]

Callender also accused Adams of deserting and reversing all his principles, of trying to force the United States into an alliance "with the British tyrant" and into a war with France, of attempting to destroy all men who disagreed with him, and of persecuting Antifederalist office holders.[59]

Callender, like Dr. Cooper, was tried before Judge Chase, in the federal circuit court at Richmond, Virginia. One of the issues in Callender's trial was the constitutionality of the Sedition Law. Three of Callender's attorneys claimed the law was not in force as it was contrary to the Constitution. They attempted to get the jury to declare it unconstitutional, saying jurors had a right to consider both the law and fact, and this included the right to consider the Constitution, as it was the supreme law of the land. One of the attorneys told the jurors:

> If the law of Congress under which we are indicted, be an infraction of the Constitution, it has not the force of a law, and if you were to find the traverser guilty, under such an act, you would violate your oaths.[60]

But Judge Chase stopped the presentation, claiming the jury had no right to consider whether a law was contrary to the Constitution. It is noteworthy that the judge did claim at this time, before Chief Justice John Marshall's decision instituting judicial review, that the judiciary was the "only proper and competent authority" to decide unconstitutionality.[61] "If the jury should exercise that power," Justice Chase said, "they would thereby usurp the authority entrusted by the Constitution of the United States to this court." [62]

Callender's attorneys also argued that his work was mostly opinion and that a line should be drawn between fact and opinion.[63] Again Justice Chase objected, saying:

> This construction admits the publication, but denies its criminality. . . . The traverser charges him [Adams] with being a murderer and a thief, a despot and a tyrant! Will you call a man a murderer and a thief, and excuse yourself by saving it is but a mere opinion —or that you heard so? . . . The question here is, with what intent the traverser published these charges? Are they false, scandalous and malicious, and published with intent to defame? [64]

In effect, Justice Chase stated that a person's expressed opinions were subject to prosecution as well as allegations of fact.

The defense attorneys also were thwarted by Justice Chase in attempts to call separate witnesses to prove different parts of the publication. The judge said partial justifications were inadmissible and that it was only a "popular argument" to claim that separate witnesses could prove separate parts of the charge until all was proved.[65] Chase continually stopped the defense attorneys in their arguments, until they all walked out of the court.[66] The jury found Callender guilty, and he was imprisoned for nine months and fined two hundred dollars.

The trial record, then, shows that Callender was denied the right to present evidence of truth, despite the provisions of the Sedition Law stipulating that it could be introduced. Chase, like Justice Patterson earlier, demanded all-inclusive proof of truth from each witness, or no proof at all. Chase's conduct here was one of the factors leading to his impeachment trial. Five of the articles of impeachment considered by senators resulted from Callender's trial. The necessary two-thirds vote was not forthcoming for impeachment, but Chase actually was voted guilty by a majority for not allowing partial testimony from one witness and for "crude, contemptuous and indecent conduct" during the trial.[67]

People in practically every section of the United States felt the effects of the Sedition Law. One historian states that only in New Hampshire and in Rhode Island were there no prosecutions under its terms.[68] Though there is uncertainty as to how many people were arrested as Sedition Law violators, one count places the total at twenty-five, with fifteen indictments, eleven trials and ten convictions.[69] The brunt of the government's attacks under the law was felt by the Republican or Whig press. Such papers as the *Aurora* of Philadelphia, the *Examiner* of Richmond, Virginia, the *Time Piece* and the *Argus* of New York, the *Bee* of New London, Connecticut, and the *Register* of Mount Pleasant, New York, were affected by indictments. Benjamin Franklin Bache of the *Aurora*, whose articles possibly stimulated the law, died before he could be tried.

As prosecutions mounted under the Sedition Law, agitation against the law also grew, possibly coming to a climax with the Virginia and Kentucky resolutions.[70] Animosity toward the law also was evident in the Adams-Jefferson presidential campaign. While evidence is insufficient to attribute Adams's defeat and Jefferson's election to the presidency to the Sedition Law,[71] there is no doubt that it played a major part in supplying meaningful oratory in the hotly contested campaign. The Sedition Law, which had been passed with a provision that it expire on March 3, 1801, died a natural death with the Adams administration. After Jefferson assumed the presidency, he pardoned all who had been convicted under the law.[72] Congress later reimbursed those who had been fined.[73] The force of the Sedition Law ended with the defeat of the Federalists.

Some of the prosecutions for seditious libel while the Sedition Law was in effect were in state courts rather than in federal courts. There is, however, no systematic body of knowledge concerning these state prosecutions for libeling public officials during this period. Reports in the various states concerning criminal law are sketchy; information must be obtained largely from newspapers of the day.[74] The indictments in these state courts were at common law, not statutory law. And the common law that was in force, as was pronounced by Justice Dana in the 1799 trial of Abijah Adams in Massachusetts, was the common law of England.

Adams, an editorial clerk for his brother, Thomas Adams, publisher of the *Independent Chronicle* in Boston, was tried for publishing an article critical of Massachusetts legislators for not joining Virginia and Kentucky legislators in resolutions calling the Alien and Sedition Laws unconstitutional. The article claimed Massachusetts legislators had violated their oaths to protect the sovereign and independent state of Massachusetts by disclaiming the right to

decide on the constitutionality of a law of Congress.[75] Chief Justice
Dana, who stated in the trial that the English common law was the
"precious birthright of every American," [76] refused to listen to the
defense contentions that English common law principles were inconsistent with the Massachusetts constitution. However, Dana did
allow Adams's attorneys to present evidence of truth as a defense.
And the account of the trial in Adams's newspaper claims the
jurors' verdict indicated that they were impressed by this evidence.[77]
The jury's verdict was peculiar. It found the article in question to be
a libel, but it found Adams guilty only of printing.[78] One could infer
that jurors perhaps felt the libel was justified. But on the strength
of the partial verdict, the court pronounced Adams guilty and sentenced him to thirty days in jail. An account of the trial, questioning
the application of the English common law to American courts,
was carried in the *Independent Chronicle* for several weeks after
the trial.[79]

Another 1799 prosecution, this one in New York, resulted from
the insistence of Alexander Hamilton, who claimed that he was
libeled by an article in the *New York Argus*, a Republican newspaper. The article was a reprint of one from the *Philadelphia Aurora*
claiming that Hamilton was at the bottom of an effort to put the
latter paper out of business by pecuniary means.[80] The article also
questioned where Hamilton would get the money, as he appeared to
be penniless, and it was suggested the money might be coming from
the British secret service.[81] Hamilton, in demanding the prosecution,
claimed the article was false and sought to discredit him and those
in the Federalist administration.[82]

The issue of truth or falsity was not raised in the New York
trial. Truth was not considered a defense to libel in that state.[83]
The printer of the *Argus*, David Frothingham, claimed the article
was not criminal and that it was printed without malice. Hamilton,
who was then inspector-general of United States forces,[84] testified
that the *Aurora*, where the article first appeared, was hostile to the
government and that he personally was accused of working against
the interest of the United States government by being on the British
payroll.[85] The jury found Frothingham guilty but asked for the
mercy of the court. The court, however, sentenced him to four
months in jail and fined him one hundred dollars.

While the Adams and Frothingham trials took place during
the period of the Sedition Law, common law prosecutions survived

after the Sedition Law had expired. This was especially true in
Massachusetts. In 1802, John S. Lillie, the editor of the *Constitutional Telegraph* in Boston, was imprisoned for three months after
being found guilty of libel for referring to Chief Justice Dana as a
tyrant and as the "Lord Chief Justice of England" who was enforcing the "execrable engine of tyrants the Common Law of England
in criminal prosecutions." [86] Another Massachusetts trial followed
in 1803, when editor William Carolton of the *Salem Register* was
found guilty of common law libel and sentenced to two months in
jail and fined one hundred dollars. It is noteworthy that in this case,
with the agreement of the prosecuting attorney, evidence was
allowed as to the truth of Carolton's publication.[87]

Some of these early common law trials, then, allowed truth as
a defense; others did not. Where testimony of truth was presented,
it appears that it was not considered a full justification for a libel.
Issues more prominently turned on malice or lack of malice. Regardless of justifications, however, the application of the common law
of seditious libel by American jurists is credited by one scholar as
being a major factor in causing the entire body of the English
common law to become ever more obnoxious to Americans.[88]

SUMMARY

It was the application of this English common law of seditious libel
in state courts and the enforcement of the Sedition Law by federal
courts that caused the complexion of press freedom in the early
days of the United States to change radically. Newspapers began the
postrevolutionary period as free as newspapers had been anywhere,
anytime in history.[89] But this unrestrained freedom led to what
many considered to be excessive criticism of government and officials. As a result, restrictive measures were taken. Some of the states
took court action through common law indictments. Congress
passed the Sedition Law to restrict comments concerning the na-

tional government. Under both the common law and the Sedition Law, criticism of public officials was considered a crime.

Early attempts at enforcing the English common law, such as in the Freeman case in Massachusetts and the Cobbett case in Pennsylvania, were rejected by juries. These juries, unlike the judges, perhaps were not ready to say that publications promoting an ill opinion of government were criminal. Judges themselves were not in agreement. Chief Justice Cushing of Massachusetts believed truth was a complete defense in a libel case, but a successor, Chief Justice Dana, would assert only that truth might be complete justification. In Pennsylvania, Chief Justice McKean early announced that the state constitution did not change the English common law; later, however, with constitutional reforms, he accepted truth as a defense provided the publication was for the public good, for reformation and not defamation. There was little uniformity in the various states concerning newspaper prosecutions, other than the fact that such prosecutions were sanctioned.[90]

Prosecutions were expanded into the federal courts with the passage of the Sedition Law in 1798. With the reservations that truth was a legal defense to libel and that jurors could determine the law as well as fact, the Sedition Law adopted the old English common law concept completely. Publications that promoted an ill opinion of government were criminal. Even legitimate opposition to those in control of government, which Matthew Lyon's publications appear to have been, were causes for indictment.

Despite the provision that truth could be used as a defense under the Sedition Law, neither Anthony Haswell, Thomas Cooper, nor James Callender were afforded the moral, and perhaps legal, right to do this. Callender and Haswell were prohibited from calling witnesses to prove the truth of portions of their alleged libelous statements. While such prohibitions might have fit the letter of the law, that the justification must be as broad as the charge, they hardly afforded the defendents the protection to which they were entitled under the law. Furthermore, such prohibitions denied juries the right to hear testimony necessary to make judgments concerning the law as well as the facts. In Dr. Cooper's trial, Justice Chase became an active prosecutor who apparently tried the defendant for "improper motives" in electioneering rather than for false statements.

Several points of law evolved from the Sedition Law trials. Both Justices Patterson and Chase held that justification must be as broad as the charge. Each also ruled that juries had no concern with the constitutionality of a law passed by Congress. Patterson in Haswell's case ruled that a publisher of a newspaper is responsible for libelous articles even though he is not personally aware of the articles. And Chase in Callender's case ruled that opinions as well as fact were subject to prosecution.

The Sedition Law was the last libel law ever passed by Congress.[91] After all the evidence is weighed, it appears clear that the law was an abridgment of press freedom guaranteed by the United States Constitution. Nevertheless, the law died a natural death, its constitutionality never being considered by the Supreme Court. One benefit of the law, perhaps, was the promotion of the idea that truth was a defense to a charge of libeling the government or its officials.

This criterion of truth, however, was not in complete accord with standards set in state courts where the old English common law of libel prevailed. Truth was not an ingredient in the New York prosecution of David Frothingham, nor was it recognized as a complete justification in the Massachusetts trials of Abijah Adams and William Carolton. As one authority has said, it appears evidence of truth was allowed simply to disprove malice.[92] The relevancy of truth in these common law suits was left unclear. It was evident, however, that publications promoting an ill opinion of government or public officials were, under the common law, still a crime.

5. Truthful Accounts

Defense to Criminal Libel

Though early state cases firmly established that newspaper attacks upon government officials were subject to criminal prosecutions under the common law, such prosecutions became much harder to sustain in the first quarter of the nineteenth century. The reason was the establishment of criteria by which newspapermen could defend themselves. In the early common law cases, there were no set criteria. Evidence of truth often had been allowed, but its relevancy was questionable, and it by no means was accepted as a complete defense or as a full justification for libel. Further, claims of honest criticism often had fallen short of refuting charges of malice and sedition, which had fluid connotations. But after the turn of the century, a series of court cases, constitutional reforms, and statutory provisions gave prominence to the defenses of truth and honest intent to inform citizens about their officials.[1]

These defense standards made it much more difficult for public officials to prove, especially beyond a reasonable doubt, that newspapermen were guilty of libel. This was especially true during the second quarter of the nineteenth century during the so-called growth of democracy.[2] Some court jurisdictions liberalized defense standards even further. Occasionally the showing that a publication was made with belief in truth was enough to cause a reasonable doubt of guilt. Thus, criminal libel prosecutions in the United States began to move further away from the English doctrine that any publication promoting an ill opinion of government or its officials was criminally libelous.

Perhaps the one trial that did more than any other in the early

57

nineteenth century to crystallize standards for the defense of criminal libel prosecutions was that of editor Harry Croswell in New
York. The case itself was indecisive, as the four New York Supreme
Court judges were evenly divided in their opinion. The impact of
the case, possibly because Alexander Hamilton was one of Croswell's defense attorneys, was significant. It led to a New York
statute providing that truthful articles published with good motives
and for justifiable ends did not constitute libel.

Croswell, editor of the *Wasp* of Hudson, New York, was accused of "wickedly, maliciously and seditiously" printing a libel
against President Thomas Jefferson on September 9, 1802. The
article claimed that Jefferson had paid convicted libeler James Callender for publishing *The Prospect Before Us* and for vilifying
George Washington and John Adams.[3] The original trial judge,
Chief Justice Morgan Lewis, based his decision on the English common law. He refused to let the trial jury consider the truth of the
allegations or to let it determine if a libel was involved. In true
English fashion, he determined the publication libelous and left
only the question of publication to the jury.[4] The case went to the
Supreme Court in 1804 on a motion for a new trial, based on a
claim that the judge misdirected the jury.

Alexander Hamilton, in arguing Croswell's appeal, claimed, as
Andrew Hamilton had in Zenger's case seventy years before, that
jurors had to decide both the law and the fact since the two were so
blended in criminal cases. "The law cannot adjudge a paper to be a
libel," he said, "until a jury have found the circumstances connected
with the publication." [5] He also argued that truth was necessary to
determine the circumstances and intent. In summing up his case,
he made these points:

1] The liberty of the press consists in the right to publish, with
impunity, truth, with good motives, for justifiable ends, though
reflecting on government, magistracy, or individuals.
2] That in determining the charater of a libel, the truth or
falsehood is, in the nature of things, a material ingredient, though
the truth may not always be decisive; but being abused may still
admit of a malicious and mischievous intent, which may constitute
a libel.[6]

These views often have been considered original with Hamilton.

The phraseology, however, is only a variation of that expressed earlier by former President John Adams and Pennsylvania Chief Justice Thomas McKean.[7]

There can be no doubt, however, that Hamilton's forceful presentation had its effect on the court, despite the divided judgment. Justice James Kent, whose opinions were joined by Justice Smith Thompson, adopted Hamilton's argument almost verbatim. Kent specifically stated that "it is the particular intent and tendency that constitutes the libel," and that truth or falsehood was "a very material and pertinent consideration" in determining intent.[8] Jurors, he stated, had a right to consider the fact of publication, the truth of the innuendoes, the intent and tendency of the publication as well as whether libel was involved.[9] Then he made this statement:

> I adopt, in this case, as perfectly correct, the comprehensive and accurate definition of one of the counsel at the bar (Gen. Hamilton) that the liberty of the press consists in the right to publish, with impunity, truth, with good motives, and for justifiable ends, whether it respects government, magistracy, or individuals.[10]

He stressed further that each jury would have to determine how far truth had been used for commendable purposes or abused for malicious purposes.[11]

In a conflicting opinion, Chief Justice Morgan Lewis, joined by Justice Brockholst Livingston,[12] said that under the common law, as it came from England, the judge determined the law and truth was immaterial. He also made this statement: "Truth may be as dangerous to society as falsehood, when exhibited in a way calculated to disturb the public tranquility, or to excite a breach of the peace." [13] However, even Chief Justice Lewis appears to have been affected by Hamilton's argument. He admitted that many disagreed with his views, but said that as a judge he had to pronounce the law as he found it. He invited legislation to change the law, stating that he would "leave the alteration of it, when found convenient, to that body to whom the Constitution has confided the power of legislation." [14]

The legislature did alter the law. W. W. Van Ness, who had been Hamilton's co-attorney in the Croswell case, introduced a bill in 1805. In addition to allowing jurors to determine both the law and the fact, the bill provided:

> That in every prosecution for writing or publishing any libel, it
> shall be lawful for the defendant, upon the trial of the cause, to give
> in evidence, in his defence, the truth of the matter contained in
> the publication charged as libellous: provided always that such evi-
> dence shall not be a justification, unless, on the trial, it shall be
> further made satisfactorily to appear, that the matter charged as
> libellous, was published with good motives and for justifiable ends.[15]

This defense was later written into the New York Constitution,[16]
and it served as a model for similar insertions in other state constitutions. Meanwhile, it had a direct effect on the Croswell case. During
the appeal hearing, a new trial had not been granted because of the
divided court. After the law was passed, the court unanimously
awarded a new trial, though it was never held.[17] The contention
that Jefferson paid Callender was never proved nor disproved in a
court of law.

Both the Croswell case and the resulting New York law made
it clear that truth was not a complete defense to a libel indictment.
Motives as well as truth were at issue. For this reason, it has been
claimed that the Hamiltonian doctrine narrowed the right to publish matters concerning public affairs.[18] To an extent this is true,
especially when it is compared to the colonial doctrine or the Sedition Law, both of which provided that truth constituted a defense
to criminal libel. But the colonial doctrine had been modified in the
postrevolutionary trials at common law, and the relevancy of truth
had not been standardized as a defense in the states. Also judges, in
trying the Sedition Law cases, had made a mockery of the provision
that truth was a defense. Even in Pennsylvania, where the constitution provided that truth was a defense when publications were
proper for public information, the place of truth had been diminished by the question as to what was proper for publication. The
Croswell case and the law that followed at least set a standard and
gave truth an undenied prominence and relevancy as a defense to
criminal libel.

While it was established in New York that truth about officials
was not libelous when published with good motives for justifiable
ends, definitions for good motives or justifiable ends were not established. This was left to other cases, and such cases were not long
in coming. Within seven years after the Croswell case, it had been
established by appellate courts in three states that truthful statements that were published to honestly inform the public about

government officials were neither malicious nor seditious and consequently not libelous. An honest attempt to inform the public, then, apparently was considered both a good motive and a justifiable end.

The first of these cases was tried in Pennsylvania in 1805, as a result of an article by Joseph Dennie in the *Port Folio*. The Philadelphia newspaper article claimed that a democratic form of government was futile, weak, wicked, sinister, and scarcely tolerable. In stating that a democracy leads to despotism and anarchy, Dennie wrote:

> It is on trial here, and its issue will be civil war, desolation and anarchy. No wise man but discerns its imperfections; no good man but shudders at its miseries; no honest man but proclaims its fraud, and no brave man but draws his sword against its force.[19]

Dennie was indicted and tried for libel on the basis that he "seditiously, maliciously and wilfully" intended to cast contempt and hatred on the state and the United States.[20]

At the trial, Judge Jasper Yeates told the jury that individuals were responsible for what they spoke, wrote, or printed. Quoting Alexander Hamilton from the Croswell trial, he also stated that if the truth were used wantonly or to disturb the peace of families, it was libelous.[21] But he countered by saying that "it is no infraction of the law to publish temperate investigations of the nature and forms of government." [22] Then he told jurors that they must decide that Dennie's article either was "seditious, with evil intent" or was "honestly meant to inform the public." [23] The jury found Dennie not guilty.[24] The importance of the case was in Judge Yeates's charge. By placing publications that honestly intended to inform the public outside the realm of sedition, he gave meaning to the press guarantees in the Pennsylvania Constitution.[25]

The Dennie case allowed truth and honest intent to inform the public as a defense only for publications about government, but the doctrine was soon extended to cover comments about public officials as well. The extension came in an 1808 appeal before the Massachusetts Supreme Judicial Court. The case involved, *Commonwealth v. Clapp*,[26] is perhaps as important as any early American libel case. Unlike *People v. Croswell*, which pointed to the faults of English common law and depended on a state law to change it, the Clapp case completely modified common law prosecutions for libel in Massachusetts.[27] As a precedent cited in other states, it had a profound effect throughout the country.[28]

William Clapp had nothing to do with newspapers. His crime was posting notices to the effect that a public auctioneer, appointed by the government, was a "liar, a scoundrel, a cheat and a swindler." [29] He was tried for libel, at which time he offered truth in evidence. The court rejected his proffered evidence, however, and Clapp was found guilty. He appealed for a new trial. In the appeal judgment, Chief Justice Parsons laid down dictum that was to have far-reaching effect on newspaper publications concerning public officials.

Judge Parsons did not reverse the verdict against Clapp, however, because the libeled auctioneer was merely an appointed official, not an elected official. The judge made the following observation:

> And when any man shall consent to be a candidate for a public office conferred by the election of the people, he must be considered as putting his character in issue, so far as it may respect his fitness and qualifications for the office. And publications of the truth on this subject, with the honest intention of informing the people, are not a libel. For it would be unreasonable to conclude that the publication of truths, which it is the interest of the people to know, should be an offence against their laws. And every man holding a public elective office may be considered as within this principle; for as a re-election is the only way his constituents can manifest their approbation of his conduct, it is to be presumed that he is consenting to a re-election if he does not disclaim it. For every good man would wish the approbation of his constituents for meritorious conduct. For the same reason, the publication of falsehood and calumny against public officers or candidates for public offices, is an offence most dangerous to the people, and deserves punishment; because the people may be deceived, and reject the best citizens, to their great injury, and it may be to the loss of their liberties.[30]

Parsons, in effect, swept away completely the old English common law concept that publications promoting an ill opinion of government or its elected officials were libelous. For such publications to be libelous, he said, they had to be both false and injurious. This included candidates as well as office holders. Perhaps the most important point he made was that the public is entitled to truthful information about officials in order to secure good government.

With this premise, it was impossible to escape the conclusion that truthful publications which honestly intended to give the public information about their elected officials were not criminal under the common law of libel.

The doctrine that people were entitled to information about their officials also was adopted in the libel prosecution *Commonwealth v. Morris*, an 1811 case in Virginia.[31] The court, in making its ruling, first cited the state constitution, which stated that magistrates were servants of the people and responsible to them. Continuing, the court said,

> It follows as a necessary consequence that the people have a right to be informed of the conduct and character of their public agents. In the case of an indictment or information for a libel against public officers, or candidates for public office, truth is a justification. . . . And this forms an exception to the general rule established by law.[32]

The decision went on to announce, however, that truth could not justify a libel against a public official unless it tended to show that the individual libeled was unfit for office. The ruling, in effect, limited inquiries to official conduct, closing the door to investigations of a public official's private affairs.

These three key cases—in Pennsylvania, Massachusetts, and Virginia—arrived at approximately the same conclusion. At first glance, it would appear that the three decisions had different foundations. For instance, the Pennsylvania decision sprang from specific constitutional guarantees for press freedom to inform the public. In Massachusetts, the decision was based on common law, but on a modified common law that took democracy and good government into consideration. In Virginia, the holding rested on a constitutional provision that government was derived from the people and that the people had a right to know what their officials were doing. It was the Virginia decision that was the key. A close analysis of all three cases shows that the overriding influence involved was the people's right to know about their government.

The people's right to know, then, was changing the old English common law that made it a crime to publish ill opinions of government or its officials. Starting with the *Croswell* case, prominence was given to truth as a defense, provided it was published with good motives for justifiable ends. Other appellate cases strongly indicated that the requirement of good motives and justifiable ends was met by an honest intent to inform citizens about public officials. Further, these cases did not stand alone. Similar opinions were voiced by other judges, and state after state began to adopt constitutional guarantees protecting the press in criminal prosecutions.

The various state constitutional guarantees took two major forms. Some state constitutions provided that truth was a defense to libel if publications were made with good motives and for justifiable ends, as in New York.[33] Others provided that truth was a defense in all instances where publications were proper for public information.[34] These constitutions, by and large, premised their libel protection provisions with the statement that people were free to investigate the affairs of their government. The press' protections, then, stemmed from the people's rights, and recognition of these rights was causing a shift in the common law of libel.

Though the criminal law of libel was shifting in state courts, the question of federal prosecution was unresolved until 1812. In that year the United States Supreme Court received an appeal from two newspapermen who were convicted in the federal circuit court of Connecticut in 1806 for publishing an article promoting an ill opinion of President Jefferson and the Congress. The two men, editors Hudson and Goodwin of the *Connecticut Currant*, had published an article on May 7, 1806, charging Jefferson and the Congress with secretly voting two million dollars as a present to Napoleon Bonaparte for permission to make a treaty with Spain for Florida.[35] Despite the earlier ruling of Judge Chase that the United States had no common law jurisdiction in criminal cases, the two editors were indicted, tried and convicted under the common law for the crime of seditious libel. The appeal did not reach the Supreme Court until six years later.

The Supreme Court decision was announced by Mr. Justice Johnson, who said the only question was whether United States courts had common law jurisdiction in criminal cases. He said the answer had long since been settled in public opinion and that such jurisdiction had not been asserted for many years.[36] Then he held that the United States courts "possess no jurisdiction but what is given them by the power that creates them."[37] The only other possible source of jurisdiction would be from implied powers, he said. "But jurisdiction of crimes against the state is not among those powers," he said. "All exercise of criminal jurisdiction in common law cases, we are of the opinion, is not within their implied powers." [38]

. While the decision only reaffirmed the opinion voiced by Judge Chase some thirteen years before, it was a decision of the highest judicial body in the nation. And it effectively removed the United States courts from common law prosecutions, including those in criminal libel cases. So far as the federal courts were concerned, there no longer was a crime of libeling public officials. The only avenue left for common law prosecutions was that of the state courts, and this avenue had been significantly narrowed by the various state court decisions, constitutional reforms, and laws that promoted an unfettered press.[39]

Coincidental with state court acceptance of truth and good motives as a defense, the number of criminal prosecutions for libeling officials dropped drastically.[40] Between the War of 1812 and the Civil War, research yields only three of these criminal libel cases reaching the appellate courts of the various states.[41] During the same period, however, the state appellate courts determined at least ten times that many civil libel suits brought by officials against newspapermen.[42] As there apparently are no appellate records of civil suits between officials and newspapermen in this country prior to the nineteenth century,[43] the private actions necessarily represent a major departure from past practices. Officials turned to civil suits as their success in criminal prosecutions dwindled.

An example of the more lenient attitude taken by the courts toward newspapermen came in the Massachusetts decision of *Commonwealth v. Child* in 1832.[44] The prosecution was against David Child of the *Massachusetts Journal*. He had printed an article claiming that a state senator had proposed, before bids were open, to award the state printing contract to the *Boston Statesman*, provided that newspaper's bid was no more than five hundred dollars higher than offers from other newspapers. "This was no more or less than a proposal to give $500 from the treasury of Massachusetts to that reprobated Jackson press," Child wrote.[45] The senator, John Keyes, claimed the article charged him with corruption. But the Massachusetts Supreme Judicial Court ruled that the senate did not have a duty to accept low bids. As no crime was alleged by Child's article, the court said the indictment was not good.[46]

Two years later, however, the Supreme Judicial Court upheld an indictment against William J. Snelling for an article in the *New*

England Galaxy that did impute a crime to a police court judge.[47] The article claimed the judge had disgraced his office by perverting the law to suit his personal feelings. The court said the article had to be proven true to escape a libel judgment. The words of the article had to be interpreted in accordance with their common and natural meaning, the court said, and they in effect charged the judge with a crime.[48] It would appear, then, that a charge of crime was necessary to sustain an indictment for libel in Massachusetts.

The doctrine of an unfettered press received an even greater boost in some jurisdictions prior to the Civil War. Perhaps this was nowhere more evident than in the 1838 ruling of *State v. Burnham* in New Hampshire.[49] Burnham, who printed some two hundred copies of a public proclamation calling the Strafford county solicitor intemperate, incompetent, and immoral, was indicted for criminal libel. Burnham claimed he intended the proclamation as a petition to be submitted to the legislature for the solicitor's removal. The jury, however, found this was not the purpose, that Burnham knew the charges were false, and that he made the publication maliciously. The verdict was guilty.

On appeal, the verdict was upheld. However, the Supreme Court of New Hampshire ruled that any publication concerning an official, if made on a proper occasion, could be justified by truth, regardless of malice.[50] Noting that many states required truth to be coupled with good motives and justifiable ends, the court said this "rule is too narrow." [51] Any effort to inform citizens, who had a right to know about their officials, was declared by the court as falling within occasions that were proper for publication.

The court did not stop with a defense of truth, however. It went on to say that when a proper publication could not be justified by truth, it still could be excused. The excuse would be that the publisher had proper cause for belief in truth and had acted with good motives.[52] However, the court stated that probable cause was not a sufficient defense for publishing falsehoods if motives were bad.[53] The New Hampshire decision, then, provided that it was not a crime for individuals to publish articles about officials "when they have a reason to believe the truth, if it is done with motives which will bear examination." [54]

Even this standard, however, was not so liberal as that in Kansas. When the Kansas Constitution was drafted in 1855, a provision was included similar to that in the New York Constitution, making truth published with good motives for justifiable ends a defense to libel. The same defense was provided for in the proposed Kansas Constitutions of 1857 and 1858. However, in the constitutional revision of 1859, the provision was changed. The guarantee stated that truth could be given in evidence in all libel trials, "and if it shall appear that the alleged libel was printed for justifiable ends, the accused party shall be acquitted." [55] The constitutional criteria in Kansas at the outbreak of the Civil War was the most liberal in the United States. Truth was not specifically demanded for acquittal; all that was necessary was that the publication be for justifiable ends.

Most states were not nearly so liberal as New Hampshire, and Kansas stood alone in the adoption of the "justifiable ends" doctrine. The views pronounced in these states, one in the courts and the other in the constitution, underscored a more liberal view toward criminal libel in all states. As a Tennessee justice said after the Civil War, a defendant was practically acquitted if he could prove he believed the truth of his publications, as such a plea was "sufficient to generate a reasonable doubt as to the defendant's guilt." [56]

SUMMARY

While there was a liberal view favoring newspapers in the libel prosecutions of some jurisdictions prior to the Civil War, the press generally had been granted a libel-free privilege only for truthful reports and comment on the conduct of elected officials and candidates. This privilege allowed considerably more freedom than prevailed at the beginning of the nineteenth century. At that time, under the common law, the privilege of discussion was marred by the English doctrine that any publication promoting an ill opinion of government or its officials was criminally libelous. The English doctrine was substantially altered, however, by a series of court holdings, new laws, and constitutional reforms in the various states.

The shift in the criminal law as it was applied in state courts began with the New York prosecution People v. Croswell. The case led to a statute in that state providing that a libelous publication could be defended if it were true and were printed with good motives for justifiable ends. Holdings in other states, under constitutions and at common law, strongly indicate that the requirements of good motives and justifiable ends were met if publishers had an honest intent to inform citizens about their government and elected officials.

It also was made clear that newspapers could comment about candidates for office with the same freedom that they could comment about officials already in office. However, in the Massachusetts case of Commonwealth v. Clapp, the precedent was set that the privilege of discussing elected officials did not extend to officials who were appointed. And, in Commonwealth v. Morris, decided in Virginia, the defense of truth was limited to inquiries into official, and not private, conduct of governmental officials.

This 1811 Virginia case held that the people have a right to know about the public conduct and character of their elected officials. Further, various state constitutions protecting press freedom to report with truth were based almost entirely on the people's right to investigate the affairs of their government. The people's right to know, then, was the primary reason for truth becoming a cloak of justification in state prosecutions for libeling elected officials and candidates for office.

A parallel development was the national government's withdrawal from criminal libel prosecutions. The United States Supreme Court decided in 1812 that the federal government had no common law jurisdiction to prosecute libel cases. And it appeared clear, in light of the experiences with the Sedition Law of 1798, that Congress would not pass another criminal libel statute. Criminal libel prosecutions, as a result, fell to the exclusive domain of the states, which also were increasingly recognizing the necessity of an unfettered press.

Before the War of 1812, then, in the so-called era of good feelings, the law of criminal libel had changed considerably. Truthful reports had become a guarantee against criminal restraints. With this guarantee, the number of criminal prosecutions dropped drastically between the War of 1812 and the Civil War. Even the defense of truth, however, was not considered sufficient in all jurisdictions. New Hampshire and Kansas advanced more liberal views, giving newspapermen even greater protection against criminal libel prosecutions. On occasion, even a newspaperman's belief in the truth of what he wrote was sufficient to free him from a charge of criminal libel.

6. The Transition

Public Officials Turn to Civil Libel Suits

With prosecutions for criminal libel becoming more difficult to support, public officials largely abandoned attempts to have newspapermen punished for printed defamation. Instead, they began filing libel suits in civil courts, seeking damages for character assassination. The trend was noticeable by the end of the first decade of the nineteenth century. Before mid-century, a definite change had occurred. Although criminal prosecutions were not completely replaced, civil suits began to account for the bulk of libel cases involving newspapermen and public officials.

In turning to civil libel suits, officials moved into an untried but inviting area of litigation. Because it was not a crime to comment truthfully on the character or conduct of public officials did not mean that officials could not collect damages in civil suits for such comments. This was especially true where officials' private reputations were concerned. Civil courts had drawn no line between an official's private and public character. The extent of privileged discussion had not been determined. There were few, if any, standards.

But standards, however jumbled, did evolve. They had to be hammered out case by case, state by state, and often without uniformity. As a result, the law remained hazy throughout the so-called period of the party press, which lasted until the Civil War.[1] By the close of this period, however, a number of precedents had been established by state appellate courts, and the civil law as it applied to libel against public officials was more clearly defined.

While the pattern of the law was slow in coming, civil court procedures were well established from the beginning, and these procedures gave public officials an advantage over newspapermen. For instance, officials did not need to present proof of a libel beyond a reasonable doubt as they did in criminal prosecutions. Their presentations could be aimed at a preponderance of the evidence, under which civil suits were and are decided.[2] Additionally, the burden of proof in civil suits was different. Instead of the public officials proving articles false, newspapermen normally had to prove them true.[3] Judgments also were different than in criminal actions as public officials who won their civil law suits received monetary damages to compensate them for libel. It is no wonder, then, that civil libel actions became the rule, and criminal prosecutions became the exception.

In New York, a shift to civil libel suits followed immediately on the heels of the Croswell trial and the 1805 state law providing that truth published with good motives for justifiable ends was a defense to criminal indictments. And it quickly became apparent, in an 1806 suit against James Cheetham, editor of the *Republican Watch-Tower*, that appellate courts would not overturn heavy damage awards by jurors. In a companion case, also involving Cheetham, it was ruled that newspapermen were legally responsible for each successive republication of a libel.

Cheetham had twice printed, in successive issues of his newspaper, that Secretary of State Thomas Tillotson was involved in bribery and intrigue in the incorporation of a bank. Tillotson sued on each publication. In the first case, the official won a fourteen-hundred-dollar verdict, and the Supreme Court refused to reduce it, ruling that the award was "a matter resting in the sound discretion of a jury."[4] Cheetham also appealed the second award, which was eight hundred dollars, on the basis that he already had paid Tillotson damages for the libelous statement and that the trial judge had erred in instructing jurors they could access punitive damages. The Supreme Court ruled that separate awards were proper for separate publications, even though the same language was used, and that punitive or exemplary damages were in order because Tillotson's character as a public official was at issue.[5]

More than ordinary damages also were approved in an 1807 Tennessee case in which a candidate for office had been falsely accused of committing a crime. In this case, *Brewer* v. *Weakley*, the

Supreme Court of Tennessee said it was immoral to slander or libel
a candidate for office. "Let his talents, his virtues, and such vices as
are likely to affect his public character be freely discussed, but no
falsehoods be propagated," the court said.[6] Truth, so long as it was
confined to an official's public life, was not libelous in Tennessee.
However, falsehoods could bring punitive damages there as well
as in New York.

Closely related to punitive damages was the degree of malice
involved in a publication. Newspapermen who could not prove the
truth of their publications attempted to mitigate damage payments
by pleading lack of malice. On the other hand, officials tried to show
malice in order to increase the probability of a larger award. Such
was the case in an 1808 civil damage suit filed against William
Duane of the *Philadelphia Aurora*.[7] Duane claimed he had published a letter about the plaintiff, Morris, after finding the letter in
the papers of the former editor, Benjamin Franklin Bache. He said
he published it in good faith, thinking it to be true. Morris's
attorney claimed, however, that malice was proved by the falsity of
the letter. Chief Justice William Tilghman did not accept this
argument. He ruled instead that any evidence which a defendant
offered could be reviewed by a jury to determine the degree of
malice and the amount of damages to be awarded.[8]

The Pennsylvania rule allowing a newspaperman an opportunity to disprove malice was not followed by the New York Supreme
Court a year later, in 1809. The New York court accepted the doctrine that a publication accusing an official of a crime was presumed
automatically by the law to be malicious if it was false. Governor
Morgan Lewis had brought a civil suit against William Few, chairman of a group of citizens who published in the *American Citizen*
an article that claimed Few had appointed his son to public office,
had encouraged bribery and corruption, and had unlawfully called
out the militia.[9] Few, in his defense, claimed a constitutional
privilege for electors to consider and communicate information concerning qualifications of officials and candidates. The court agreed
with the right, but added:

> There is a wide difference between this privilege, and a right
> irresponsibly to charge a candidate with direct, specific and un-
> founded crimes. . . . Candidates have rights, as well as electors:
> and those rights and privileges must be so guarded and protected,
> as to harmonize one with the other. . . . All that is required . . .

is, not to transcend the bounds of truth. . . . There is nothing upon the record showing the least foundation or pretence for the charges. The accusations, then, being false, the prima facie presumption of the law is, that the publication was malicious.[10]

The court, then, was balancing out the personal rights of officials and candidates as opposed to the discussion rights of electors. While there was a privilege for good faith publication of information believed to be true about the qualifications of these public men, the court said, such a privilege did not extend to charges of crime. Criminal charges had to be proved by truth.

Other rulings that followed soon after, moreover eliminated distorted or half truths as a defense to libel, especially as they applied to judicial or legislative hearings. In 1810 the New York Supreme Court held that editor Croswell of the *Republican Gazette* libeled Congressman David Thomas by printing a partial, though true, account of Thomas's trial for allegedly receiving counterfeit money. The jury had exonerated Thomas. Croswell's account, however, printed several years later in an attempt to keep Thomas from being appointed state treasurer, claimed the acquittal came because the only witness against Thomas was disqualified as a result of his being declared an accomplice.[11] The court ruled that Croswell's account, by suppressing the fact that the witness also was discredited, went against the trial and facts to insinuate that Thomas was guilty. "The inference of malice," the court said, "was inevitable." [12] While there appeared to be a privilege to report court proceedings, the decision held that reports had to be free of malice. This was stressed in a later suit filed after a newspaper article, combining a report made in the New York Assembly with rumors, accused a state land agent of fraud. The editor could prove only one of the six fraud charges he made, and the court stated this was not sufficient to excuse the libel as the proof was not as broad as the charge. The supreme court did rule that the press was privileged to report a true history of legislative or judicial proceedings with immunity from libel. However, the court ruled the particular article had no immunity, as privileged reports had to be fair, "not discolored or garbled, nor mixed with comments and insinuations calculated to asperse the character of those concerned." [13]

This concern with the character of public officials resulted in a review in 1824 of the doctrine announced in the Morgan Lewis case that publications concerning the qualifications of candidates or

officials were privileged. The occasion was a libel suit brought by
Lieutenant Governor Erastus Root against the *New York American*,
which opposed him for reelection. The *American* had printed an
article charging Root with presiding over the Senate while intox-
icated.[14] Though the newspaper presented witnesses to testify to the
truth of the claim, the trial jury determined the article false and
awarded Root fourteen hundred dollars.

The newspaper, claiming that the article was believed to be
true and that it was privileged, appealed all the way to the Court of
Errors and Appeals, the highest appellate court in the state. Chancellor Reubin H. Walworth, announcing the high court's decision,
replied to the contention of privilege as follows:

> If so, the defendants were under no obligation to prove the truth
> of the charge; and the party libeled had no right to recover unless
> he established malice in fact, or showed that the editors knew the
> charge was false. The effect of such a doctrine would be deplorable.
> . . . No man, who had any character to lose, would be a candidate
> for office under such a construction of the law of libel. The only
> safe rule to adopt in such cases is, to permit editors to publish what
> they please in relation to the character and qualifications of candi-
> dates for office, but holding them responsible for the truth of what
> they publish.[15]

The court also ruled that belief in truth did not constitute a defense,
as malice automatically was implied from falsity.[16]

The decision in the Lewis case had denied privilege for charges
of crime, and the decision in the Root case removed the protection
of privilege from publications commenting on the character and
qualifications of officials and candidates.[17] One authority has said
the cases left "no privilege of discussion whatsoever, as springing
from the relation of elector and candidate." [18] Still, there was no
limit to truthful discussions. The line was drawn in New York at
false reports, which were considered malicious in themselves.

The New York doctrine that false reports implied maliciousness
had been rejected by the Pennsylvania courts in the Duane case,
and in 1826 the doctrine also was rejected by the Massachusetts
legislature. The rejection came in a state law providing that when
truth was pleaded but not proved by a defendant in a libel suit,
it would not be "of itself proof of malice." [19] Jurors, according to
the law, would determine all issues in libel suits, including malice.

This law was in effect in 1828 when Daniel Webster brought

a suit for libel against Theodore Lyman. Lyman, editor of a newspaper favorable to the Jacksonian Republicans, accused the old Federalist faction of Massachusetts, singling out Webster, of conspiring
to break up the Union and to return New England to Great
Britain.[20] He based his article on a charge made several years before
by President John Quincy Adams, though Adams had referred only
to leading Massachusetts Federalists, not citing names. Lyman in
his article had asked why Adams previously condemned these men,
such as Webster, and now was seeking their political favor. Webster
sued, claiming he was not a resident of Massachusetts during the
period referred to by Adams and could not have been part of any
conspiracy.

At the trial, Judge Isaac Parker instructed the jury that truth
justified libel against officials when it was combined with good purposes and "honest view to expose or reform." [21] Further, he advised
jurors that if they believed Adams had meant Webster, then the
article was privileged and not unfair. Though it might have been a
libel by President Adams, he said, fair commentary on comments
made by the president were not libelous.[22] On the other hand, the
judge said that Lyman had no right to misrepresent Adams's remarks. He instructed jurors that the insertion of Webster's name in
the article, if not justified by Adams's comments, was not warranted and was libelous.[23] However, he added that if Webster's
name was inserted "by mere inadvertency or mistake, as has been
suggested, it is not so." [24] Additionally, he said malice could be
refuted by honest purpose, but that malice was to be inferred if
there was a tendency to create hostile feeling toward Webster.[25]

Questions of truth, intent, privilege, fairness and malice were
left to the jurors. However, the jury failed to bring in a verdict.
Members stated they disagreed on the facts.[26] Among other things,
there was a question as to whether Adams had referred to New
England Federalists or just those from Massachusetts, and Webster
had always been a New England resident. All the issues, then, were
left to jurors. And the criterion in the case for malice was not falsity,
as in New York, but rather a tendency to create hostile feelings.

New York was not alone, however, in holding that falsity imputed malice. As an example, an article published in a Maine newspaper, the *Kennebec Journal*, in 1834 accused the postmaster there
of opening a letter and taking money out of it. In fact, the postmaster had been arrested and charged with the offense, but he had

not been found guilty. The publisher could not substantiate the truth of his charge by proving the postmaster guilty, and the Maine Supreme Court ruled as a result that malice was implied. The fact that the publisher had later printed a retraction could not be given in evidence to show he believed the truth of the report or that no malice was involved. "We know of no authority for coupling two articles, not simultaneously published," Chief Justice Whitman said.[27] Despite the ruling that malice was implied from falsity, the court held that it was the jury's province to make the final determination.[28]

The relevancy of malice, then, in libel suits concerning public officials was not stabilized over the various states. There was a variety of viewpoints. In some states, malice was implied from falsity. In other jurisdictions, the lack of malice could be proven even though the article was false. Further, some states left the matter to the jury, while others adhered to the doctrine that malice was a decision for the judge. There was no uniform court procedure, and the applicable common law varied considerably among the states.

In some states, malice was not an issue. This was especially true in some of the western states during the period of Jacksonian ascendency and the spread of democratic principles. Both in Kentucky and Ohio, for instance, cases were determined entirely on the issue of truth or falsity.

The Kentucky case arose when a newspaper in Montgomery accused a judge of lacking judicial capacity, abandoning the principles of truth, and selling a clerkship in his office to the highest bidder.[29] The judge sued for libel, but he lost in the trial court because of the general belief of the townspeople in the truth of the charge. On the 1829 appeal, the court ruled, in *Robbins* v. *Treadway*, that belief in truth did not constitute a legal defense to libel. The newspaper charges implied corruption, the appellate court said, and constituted libel unless justified by truth.[30] The court stipulated, however, that a libel action would not be proper for articles that merely charged a judge with improprieties which would not be grounds for impeachment.[31] The doctrine of privilege here was somewhat broader than that set by the New York courts. Regardless of motives, the Kentucky press was privileged to discuss the character and qualifications of officials provided it skirted untruthful charges of crime or official misconduct that would lead to officials' removal.

Falsity, regardless of motives, also was the criteria for libel accepted in Ohio in 1833. When a candidate for sheriff was accused there of false swearing and perjury, the supreme court laid down this all-encompassing dictum: "We have no right to tell a lie of another, because he is a candidate for office, or is in office." [32] The decision did not limit its bar on falsity to imputation of crime. As in New York, defamatory statements about the public life of officials could be justified only by truth.

However, the question as to where the public life of an official ended and his private life began was soon at issue in an Ohio libel suit. The case reached the appellate court level in 1835 in a political squabble concerning Jackson's administration as president. Editor Benjamin Tappan was appointed by Jackson as a federal judge, pending confirmation by the Senate. While awaiting confirmation, another editor, James Wilson, printed an article concerning "Mr. Editor Tappan," in which Tappan was described as a "purse-proud aristocrat" who wanted to see the United States Bank fail so his stock in Ohio banks would become more profitable. The article also called Tappan the editor of a "mud-machine" devoted to political scandal and abuse.[33] Tappan sued. The Ohio Supreme Court ruled, however, that the article was about Tappan as a citizen, not as a judge, and that it did not "excite the passions to revenge" or lessen "his standing in the esteem of the world." [34] A newspaper article in Ohio, then, could discuss a public official as a private citizen without reflecting on his official conduct.

The New York Supreme Court soon ruled, however, that there was no immunity for discussing a private citizen's past character as a public official. The court in 1837 ruled that a private citizen could sue for libel if a newspaper claimed he was corrupt while previously serving as a member of the legislature. Such claims about official character reflected on the individual's private character, the court ruled, holding him up as "capable of like conduct if again trusted, thereby invoking upon him the odium and scorn of the public." [35]

In some jurisdictions, articles that heaped odium and scorn upon officials were libelous even though they were ambiguous and did not name officials directly. Other states, however, required that words in articles be understood by ordinary readers to libel specific officials. Cases in Connecticut and Alabama drew a contrast between the two doctrines.

The Supreme Court of Connecticut in 1837 ruled that an

official could relate an article to him by innuendo provided the innuendo was proved by averments. The case arose when the *Daily Herald* in New Haven, Connecticut, ran an article stating that an unnamed justice of the peace had been deprived of his "two-penny justiceship for malpractice in packing a jury." [36] The publisher was sued by Silas Mix, who along with two other justices of the peace had not been reappointed by the General Assembly. There was nothing in the ambiguous article singling out Mix, but he sued, using innuendoes to explain the original article.

The court allowed the innuendoes but held Mix to strict proof of them. He was allowed to show that when he asked for a retraction, the publisher, Thomas Woodward, had made fun of him in print.[37] Witnesses also testified that the publisher made oral statements after the original publication to the effect that Mix could "never pack another jury." [38] The court ruled these publications and actions were admissible because they pertained to the alleged libel.[39] It also ruled that publisher Woodward's showing that Mix did improperly select freeholders for jury panels did not justify the charge of packing individual court juries as such. A $591 verdict for Mix was upheld.

The decision in this case was considerably different from one in Alabama several years later in the case *Henderson v. Hale*, where it was ruled that an article "must receive the interpretation which an ordinary reader would put upon it." [40] The publication described how commissioners had turned some $1,949 over to the county treasurer, and the treasurer had accounted for only a portion when asked for a report. The court said the plain language of the article simply charged failure to disclose money and did not impute corruption, embezzlement, or misconduct in office. It was held not libelous. The publication was simply a factual account respecting the way the county treasurer of Cherokee County had made reports, and it was made to inform citizens about governmental operations.

Accounts of officials' operations in some jurisdictions, however, did not receive the same consideration as in Alabama. A line was not always drawn in libel suits between comments concerning the public character of officials and those concerning the character of private citizens. The lack of such a distinction was particularly noticeable in two appellate court decisions in the decade before the Civil War. In each of the decisions, one in Indiana and the other in Wisconsin, the courts made no allowance whatever for comment of a public nature. Instead, the courts based their rulings on general definitions of libel that applied to private citizens and officials alike.

The Indiana case, in 1854, involved an article in the *Spirit of the West*, which told about a fight in a Taylorsville, Indiana, post office in which pistols were fired. The article said the post office was maintained in such low character that a decent lady would not dare enter, and that it should be taken away from the postmaster. Benjah Johnson, the postmaster sued for libel. At the trial, editor Columbus Stebbins showed that intoxicating drinks were sold at a grocery maintained in the post office and that the premises were frequented by drunks, gamblers, and disorderly persons. He also pleaded that the publication was made without malice and for public information and that the trial should be stopped. The trial judge upheld Stebbins's demurrer and stopped the libel action. However, on appeal, the article was ruled libelous.[41] The appellate court declared:

> Any publication that tends to degrade, disgrace, or injure the character of a person, or bring him into contempt, hatred or ridicule, is as much a libel as though it contained charges of infamy of crime.[42]

No special privilege to discuss the public character of an official for the information of citizens was recognized. The demurrer was overruled, and the case was ordered back to trial.

The Wisconsin case, heard by that state's supreme court in 1859, established even more clearly that rules set down in private libel suits were being applied to suits involving public officials. An article in the *Daily Wisconsin Patriot* was at issue. It referred to a judge as a tool of special interests and called him "old habeas corpus Lansing." The article claimed that the judge released individuals held in contempt by the legislature for not testifying and that his actions warranted the abolishment of his office. The court said the article was "clearly libelous." [43] The article, the court said, had a tendency to injure the judge "in the business of his office, and we think these words are actionable within the rule relating to words spoken of a man in his trade or profession." [44] The relationship between an officeholder and a citizen, while recognized in the case, was relegated to the same status as the relationship between one private citizen and another. The court saw no more of a privilege to discuss the character and conduct of officials than businessmen.

While the privilege to discuss public officials appeared to be little more than the privilege to discuss private citizens, newspapermen did have, by and large, the privilege of giving a true history of legislative and judicial proceedings. This privilege was extended by the Massachusetts Superior Court in 1859. The extension was made to include quasi-judicial hearings, or hearings of public bodies other than the legislature or the judiciary.

The case involved, Barrows v. Bell, concerned the Massachusetts Medical Society.[45] A report of the society's legal proceedings, involving dishonorable conduct and a fraudulent transaction, was printed in the Boston Medical and Surgical Journal; and a libel suit resulted. In the supreme judicial court, it was ruled that the society received a charter from the state as a public institution to regulate "the important public interests of the practice of medicine and surgery."[46] The decision even advanced the idea that members were, in a sense, quasi-officials, as they had a status recognized by law to help regulate the practice of medicine. Specifically, however, the court ruled that the proceedings of the society were quasi-judicial and could be reported with privilege so long as a true and correct narrative was published.[47] The particular report was found not to be libelous as it was a true, just and fair statement of the transaction.

Generally, the court's holding in this case was much broader than the specific medical society case. It applied to the publication of quasi-judicial proceedings before all public bodies, stating that such proceedings were privileged "for the necessary information of the people."[48] The privilege extended to the giving of fair and impartial accounts of such proceedings, which presumably would include city and county governing boards as well as such public institutions as the medical society.

Prior to the Civil War, the determination as to whether an article was libelous frequently was made by the judge. This left the jury the task of determining the facts, whether there actually was a publication,[49] and, if so, whether it was justified. This practice was ruled invalid in an 1841 case, Dolloway v. Turrill, by the New York Court of Errors. The court in this case held that both civil and criminal juries had a right under the state constitution to consider the entire case, including whether the publication involved was libelous.[50] However, the decision was overruled by the same court in 1859.

The 1859 case, *Hunt v. Bennett*, arose when the *New York Herald* published an article that an applicant for appointment to the office of police justice had in the past been a police officer who had beaten a drunken woman with a cane and who had been involved in other acts of cruelty. In the trial court, the judge instructed jurors that the article was libelous and that Hunt was entitled to recover full damages and, if the jury desired, punitive damages. On appeal, publisher James Gordon Bennett claimed the judge should have defined libel and let the jury make the decision as to whether the article was libelous.[51] The court of errors did not agree. It quoted English cases and concluded it was the judge's duty to decide if libel was involved and to instruct the jury on the matter. The court said the New York statute stating jurors would be judges of both the law and the fact, as well as the constitutional guarantee, applied only to criminal cases.[52] The New York civil doctrine, then, was borrowed from English common law as had been the criminal doctrine before the *Croswell* case. The judge in civil suits could determine if a publication was libelous.

The case did not stop with defining the duty of judge and jury, however. It also ruled that an editor or proprietor was responsible for whatever was printed in the newspaper. Further, it held that appointed officials did not fall in the same category as elected officials so far as privilege was concerned. The court stated:

> If the defendant's opinions of the plaintiff's character and quali-
> fications as an officer had been contained in a remonstrance against
> his appointment to the office for which the defendant asserted he
> was a candidate, and had been presented to the appointing power,
> without an unnecessary publication in a newspaper, as in this in-
> stance, of wide circulation, the point [of privilege] would have
> been well made. As it is, he has been assailed through the columns
> of a public journal, as if he was a candidate for the suffrages of the
> people, and not of an appointing power, consisting of a few persons.
> It was not, therefore, a privileged publication.[53]

There was, then, no privilege to assail the character of an appointed official, other than to the board responsible for appointment. The case did imply that a privilege existed to comment on the character and qualifications of candidates for the people's votes. But this privilege, as determined in previous New York cases, extended only to truthful reports, regardless of motives or ends.[54]

SUMMARY

The extent to which the press had a privilege to report and comment on the character, qualifications, and conduct of public officials was the underlying theme of all these early civil libel suits. Though the arena of battle between newspapermen and officials had shifted from the criminal to the civil courts, the focal point was the same. Just how far could a newspaperman go in criticizing and discussing public officials? The answer to this question varied to an extent from state to state. Generally, however, the criterion during these formulative years was that pronounced in the 1807 case of Brewer v. Weakley in Tennessee: "Let his talents, his virtues and such vices as are likely to affect his public character be freely discussed, but no falsehoods be propagated." [55]

Other than the standard of justification by truth, there were few special privileges allowed in communicating information about officials. Some courts, such as those in New York, ruled that there was no privilege to impute crime to an official, or even to discuss the public character and qualifications of candidates officials, or, for that matter, former officials, unless true. And decisions in other states, such as Indiana and Wisconsin, allowed no greater privilege to discuss an official than a private citizen. It also was held, as in Kentucky, that to charge misconduct in office required proof of truth. However, the Kentucky decision emphasized that a libel action was not proper for merely charging improprieties against an official that did not amount to official misconduct or crime. A more liberal view also was taken in other states, such as Ohio, where it was held that an article was not libelous which did not excite passions to revenge or lessen the official's standing in the community.

At the most in any state, then, a newspaperman had a privilege to claim improprieties and to print articles that did not lessen an official's standing in the community. None of the civil judgments went so far as to adopt the criminal libel doctrine advanced by the New Hampshire court in State v. Burnham, that cause for belief in truth justified a libel. However, there was a liberal view in some states, such as Pennsylvania, that damages could be mitigated when a false article was not malicious. These privileges of publication and mitigation were not uniform throughout the states. The only uniform privilege was the communication of the truth.

There was, however, a recognition of the privilege to give a fair and impartial report of both judicial and legislative proceedings. But it was held in New York that this privilege did not extend to the suppression of facts in these proceedings that would lead to insinuations of an official's guilt. Nor did it extend to using official proceedings as a springboard for unsupported charges reflecting on the character of an official, regardless of belief in the truth of the charges. Proof of truth was necessary for any and all extraneous charges based on legislative or judicial reports. Privilege did extend, according to a Massachusetts case involving Daniel Webster, to comments on factual statements of a president. Also reports of quasi-judicial proceedings before all public bodies were declared privileged by Massachusetts in 1859, on the basis that such reports were necessary to inform the people. The privilege to fairly and impartially report a true history of official proceedings, then, was grounded not on the rights of the press, but on the right of the people to know.

The people's understanding of an article, however, was not always the criterion for libel. Connecticut, for instance, ruled in 1837 that an official bringing a suit could attach extraneous meanings, or innuendoes, to an article in which he was not named to show that it referred to him. It was required only that the official support his interpretation of the article's meaning. A court in Alabama, on the other hand, ruled in 1851 that the plain language of the article, as it was interpreted by the ordinary reader, determined whether it was libelous. Though it is hard to see how an official's reputation or integrity could be injured unless people understood such injury, there definitely were two schools of thought on the matter.

Other points of law, not always uniform among the various states, emerged in the libel suits of these formative years. As an example, it was held in Maine in 1834 that a printed retraction of a libelous article could not be used by a newspaperman in court to mitigate damages. Yet an 1837 judgment in Connecticut held that a newspaperman's intent could be shown in court by coupling the libelous article with subsequent publications. Libel suits also could be filed for each successive publication in which an alleged libel was repeated, according to a New York decision in 1806. That state's courts, as well as those of Tennessee, also held that verdicts calling for high damage payments were in the province of the jury and that the jury could levy extra damages as punishment when a public official was involved, because his public character was at stake.

Punitive damages often depended on malice, and both the New York and Maine courts adopted the doctrine that an article automatically was malicious if false. However, in Maine, it was the jury that made the final determination. The doctrine that false articles were in themselves malicious was rejected by both Massachusetts and Pennsylvania. Both states allowed newspapermen to produce evidence to show that publications, though false, were not malicious, leaving the determination to jurors. One Massachusetts jury was instructed that malice was inferred from the tendency to create hostility toward an official. In some states, such as Kentucky and Ohio, malice did not appear to be at issue in some of the early trials; libel and damages were determined on the basis of truth or falsity, regardless of motives. There was, then, a variety of viewpoints concerning malice and its place in libel trials. And where malice was relevant, some jurisdictions left the decision to the juries and others left it to the judge as a matter of law.

The respective duties of judge and jury in civil libel suits came to a head in New York in 1859. The ruling was that judges determined points of law, including whether libel was involved, and that jurors determined only the facts of the case. This was a major departure from the practice that had been established in early criminal prosecutions.

Other departures from the standards that had evolved in criminal prosecutions were few. Civil judgments generally had followed those of the criminal courts in holding that the privilege to comment on elected officials did not extend to appointed officials, although there were exceptions. Civil courts also adopted criminal holdings that equated candidates for office with elected officials. And while the civil courts in all states did not agree on points of law or the relevancy of malice in libel suits brought by officials, they generally accepted the criminal libel doctrine that truth justified newspaper reports of the public lives of those seeking and holding elective posts.

Truth was the focus of the entire law of libel in these formative years. Though it early was emphasized in our nation that elected officials had a right to be protected from newspaper attacks, it gradually was recognized that the people had a right to know the truth about their officials' public conduct, character and qualifications. This recognition of the people's right was only indicative of the times.

The entire period, from the birth of the United States until the Civil War, was one of political change in which individual rights under the law gained increasing recognition. With legal reforms, imprisonment for debt largely ceased, married women obtained more freedom, labor unions gained some recognition, and property qualifications for voting were gradually abolished.[56] The popular voice became a major force in politics, and the people's rights as such became important. The developing law of libel simply was keeping up with the times. And like other fields of law, the jurisprudence of libel made great strides. The precedents that had been set in the various state courts during the period touched on most of the problems that would face future jurists.

Still, these precedents had only defined the civil law of libel. It was not yet refined. Truth generally had been recognized as a justification for defamatory publications. Otherwise the courts had granted no real privilege to discuss officials. A more liberalized body of libel laws was yet to come.

THE GROWTH
OF
PRIVILEGE

---

7. Greater Privilege of Discussion

Belief in Truth

Sweeping changes in the law of libel came after the Civil War, allowing a greatly expanded privilege to discuss public officials. Prior to the war, newspapermen had no privilege other than that of printing the truth. But during and following the war, various state courts began to recognize new and liberalized doctrines that in many instances did not require strict proof of truth to defend libels against officials. Circumstances of publication became important, and allowances began to be made for good faith discussion of those seeking and holding office.[1] The privilege of criticizing officials and making comments about them, so long as publications were without malice, was adopted in state after state.

Even more important, perhaps, a number of states began to excuse published falsehoods about officials provided publishers had probable cause to believe that what they printed was true. In other states, belief in truth was accepted for mitigating damages. And substantial truth, as opposed to absolute truth, began to be recognized in some jurisdictions as a justification for libel.

The new libel doctrines did not spread uniformly over the nation. Courts in each state accepted or rejected the progressive views, or modifications of these views, as they saw fit. In some states, of course, all of the new doctrines were rejected. The only uniformly accepted standard by which a libel against an official could be excused was truth. Indeed, truth remained the primary defense in all states, regardless of other defenses. But by the beginning of the twentieth century, the privilege of reporting on and commenting about aspiring and elected officials had been broadened considerably.

The major changes in court decisions involving libel suits brought by officials came with the Civil War and the evolution in the social, cultural, and political life of the nation that followed. But these decisions were not without precedent. It is true that state appellate courts in their civil libel judgments prior to the Civil War had unanimously rejected any privilege to print false statements concerning public officials or candidates for office. Such a privilege was almost unheard of in civil suits.[2] However, it had been held in a New Hampshire criminal libel case in 1838 that a libel could be excused if the publisher had proper cause for believing in the truth of his publication and had acted with good motives.[3] And the Kansas constitution, adopted in 1859, provided for acquittal in a libel prosecution when it could be shown that a publication was for justifiable ends.[4] These liberal views were the forerunners of modifications in the law of civil libel.

Another stimulant for change was the pre–Civil War decision of the United States Supreme Court in the 1845 case of *White v. Nichols.*[5] This was not a newspaper case; it involved a letter to the President from a group of residents in Georgetown protesting political activities of the Georgetown collector of customs, Robert White, and asking for his removal. The Supreme Court held that since communications to masters about the character of servants in their jobs were privileged, letters to the President about government officials were privileged. Further, the court ruled that the writers of privileged communications could be held accountable for libel only if malice could be proved to the satisfaction of jurors.[6]

Malice could be shown, the court stated, by proving "falsehood and the absence of probable cause." [7] Under the decision, complaining officials not only had to prove communications false but also had to prove that probable cause for the statements did not exist.

The Supreme Court in this case also applied the rule that parties complaining of libel had to show malice for three other types of privileged communications: communications made in discharge of a public or private duty, either legal or moral, reports of judicial or legal proceedings, and reports of parliamentary proceedings.[8] While the Supreme Court decision was not binding on state courts at this time, since this was long before state infringement of the First Amendment guarantees of free speech and press was declared unconstitutional,[9] it was often cited by state appellate judges in later decisions. The national tribunal's judgment as to the law of privilege in libel suits could not be ignored. A standard had been set allowing privilege for reports of official proceedings. And while the letter in this case was to an elected official who appointed a customs officer, it was only one step removed from declaring that those who elect officials also should be communicated to with privilege. The importance of the Supreme Court decision was that privileged communications had to be malicious to be libelous, and that falsity and lack of probable cause had to be shown to prove malice.

The rigid civil libel doctrine of the nation's formative years remained undisturbed in state courts, however, until the Civil War and the reconstruction period. One of the earliest indications of civil court leniency for falsehoods about public officials came shortly after the war began, in 1862, with a decision in the Connecticut Supreme Court of Errors. The liberal doctrine advanced in this decision, which applied only to punitive damages, was extended by New Hampshire some six years later into a full-bloom recognition that a libel against a public official could be justified if the publisher had probable cause for believing it true.

The Connecticut decision held that punitive damages could not be assessed against a publisher for false articles unless it was proved that the articles were printed with malice.[10] The decision marked a definite departure from previous holdings in state courts. Prior to this time, states in which the relevancy of malice was considered had invariably ruled that malice was inferred from falsity or that the newspaperman had to prove lack of malice when false articles were published. The Connecticut judgment shifted the burden of proof from the newspaperman to the official.

Because malice on the part of a New Haven newspaper editor had not been proven, the trial jury in this case awarded only five dollars in damages. The small assessment was upheld in the appellate court on the basis of a new state law that prohibited more than actual damages for libel when publications were made with good intentions. One evidence of good intentions, the court stated, was when the publisher had no reason to doubt the truth of current news reports.[11] The court pointed out that the law controlling the decision was

> confessedly enacted to prevent editors of newspapers from being subjected to heavy punitive damages for articles which contained rumors, so generally circulated and credited as to constitute a part of the current news of the day, or proper and just criticism upon public men, public measures or candidates for office, or other matters of public interest.[12]

Where there was no malice, then, a newspaperman's only risk for printing false articles he believed true was paying actual damages that an official could prove.[13] The view allowed considerable latitude for public affairs reports and criticism.

Even more latitude was allowed, however, in an 1868 New Hampshire decision resulting from a Civil War newspaper publication charging the Union Army with cowardice and improper treatment of Southern noncombatants. The articles were printed in the *Democratic Standard* at Concord by Publisher John B. Palmer. Among them were the following poems:

THE LATE BATTLE-IMPROMPTUE

It frightened the federals to see them come,
They wheeled about and away they run,
They Run so fast to tell the news,
They left their knapsacks, guns and shoes.

EPIGRAM

To Manassas Junction
The Yankees thought was fun,
But greatly were mistaken
For They only took to Run.

CHANGING TUNE

Forward to Richmond, let us fly!
The Yankees shout, while blundering on,
But Davis changed their battle-cry
To "Backward, boys, to Washington." [14]

Five days after the articles and poems were printed, a mob of soldiers from the First New Hampshire Regiment Volunteers destroyed Palmer's newspaper. He filed a suit against the city under a
New Hampshire law making a city liable for property destroyed by
a mob. Since the law prohibited reimbursement if destruction
was caused by illegal or improper conduct, the question was raised
as to whether the articles were libelous and thus illegal. Libel, then,
became the central issue. And the New Hampshire appeals court
ruled that there was no libel so long as Palmer had probable cause
to believe the statements were true and had published them in good
faith so that citizens could act on the information.

New Hampshire, where the belief-in-truth doctrine had been
applied to criminal libel cases some thirty years before, apparently
was the first state to go so far in civil suits. The rationale behind
the decision is important. The court said:

> In this country, every citizen has a right to call the attention of
> his fellow-citizens to the maladministration of public affairs, or the
> misconduct of public servants, if his real motive in so doing is to
> bring about a reform of abuses, or to defeat the re-election or re-
> appointment of an incompetent officer. If information given in
> good faith to a private individual on the misconduct of his servant
> is "privileged," equally so must be a communication to the voters
> of a nation concerning the misconduct of those whom they are
> taxed to support, and whose continuance in any service virtually
> depends on the national voice. . . . If the end which Palmer had
> in view . . . was to inform the public of the manner in which the
> war was conducted, for the purpose of inducing citizens to use
> their influence with government to repress abuses, or to vote for
> members of congress and other elective officers who would check
> such abuses, reform the army, stop the war, or conduct it in a more
> humane manner, his end or motive was justifiable. If the end to be
> attained is "to give useful information to the community, or to
> those who have a right and ought to know, in order that they may
> act upon such information, the occasion is lawful." . . . If such

were Palmer's motives, *he is not guilty of libel if the facts he al-leged were true, or if he had probable cause to believe, and did believe, that they were true. But if he had no justifiable motive, in-asmuch as the natural and inevitable tendency of the publications is to injure and degrade, he is guilty of libel, even though the facts alleged in the article are true.* . . . It seems to us that, in order to settle whether the occasion was lawful, we must generally inquire into the motives of the publisher. There may be some cases where the occasion renders, not only the motive, but the truth of the com-munication immaterial. In a great many instances, and certainly in the present case, the lawfulness of the occasion depends upon the good faith and real purpose of the publisher. Most of what are called "privileged communications" are "conditionally," not "abso-lutely," privileged. The question is one of good faith or motive, and can be settled only by a jury.[15]

Whether articles were true or false, good motives clearly were pro-nounced as the primary consideration of a libel. Yet the court said an individual's motives were good and his statements privileged if his communications concerning the government and its officials were to inform the people so they could know and act. Informing the people, who had a right to know, was the only reason, then, for the newspaperman's privilege to publish good-faith falsehoods about public officials. And good faith could be shown by probable cause for believing the libel true.

The New Hampshire and Connecticut decisions were in the vanguard of liberal civil libel decisions that became prominent throughout the United States between 1870 and 1900, roughly the same period that one historian has described as marking the rise of the American city.[16] It was a time when the entire American way of life was being changed by the industrial revolution. The nation's population doubled, and urban residents tripled. At the same time, the number of daily newspapers quadrupled, rising from 489 in 1870 to 1,967 in 1900.[17] With this growth in the number of newspapers also came, almost by necessity, more articles and comment concern-ing government officials. And the progressive views in state courts concerning libel during this period allowed the press more freedom to canvass and discuss these officials.

Liberal views did not appear in state courts overnight, however. A period of development was required. For instance, in the Minnesota case of *Aldrich* v. *Press Printing Co.* in 1864, which decided that a newspaper could be sued as a corporation,[18] the only privileged communications recognized were those concerning legislative and judicial hearings. It specifically was ruled in this Civil War case that general articles about candidates and the officials were not privileged simply because of the citizens' interest in their rulers.[19] It was four years after this that a New Hampshire court in *Palmer* v. *Concord* adopted the view that articles about officials were privileged because of the people's interest. And the Minnesota Supreme Court in 1881, instead of relying on its own precedents, cited the New Hampshire case in extending the doctrine of privilege.

The 1881 case in Minnesota, *Marks* v. *Baker*, involved an article in the *Mankato Free Press* stating that the treasurer of that city, who was a candidate for reelection, had failed to account for all the money that had been entrusted to him. The treasurer sued for libel, and it developed that he had accounted for the money. The Minnesota Supreme Court ruled that even though false, the article was privileged if made in good faith, as a matter of public interest was involved.[20] The publisher was allowed to plead in his defense that he printed the article to inform the people, that the information came from official finance reports, and that he believed the official reports to be true.[21] These reports constituted proper cause for believing in truth and hence refuted malice. However, a later Minnesota case held that common talk did not constitute proper cause for belief.[22]

Considerably more leeway was allowed by the Kansas Supreme Court in interpreting proper cause. This became evident in an 1884 criminal case, *State* v. *Balch*. A handbill printed by George Balch accused C. H. Carswell, a candidate for county attorney, with fraud in counting votes during a previous election. The statements, without doubt derogatory to the candidate's character, were proven false. But the court, in ruling the handbill not libelous, said:

> Generally, we think a person may in good faith publish whatever he may honestly believe to be true, and essential to the protection of his own interests, or the interests of the person or persons to whom he makes the publication, without committing any public offense, although what he publishes may in fact not be true, and may be injurious to the character of another.[23]

Apparently even common talk was a sufficient base for a false article about an official in Kansas, as long as the publisher believed, in good faith, that it was true.

Courts in most states, however, were not willing to go as far as Kansas. An example was Texas, where courts adopted in 1885 the doctrine that belief in truth excused a libel against candidates for office provided "there were just and reasonable grounds for entertaining that belief." [24] The case arose when the *San Antonio Express* published an article stating that people should know that a candidate for mayor, who was to handle city finances if elected, had charged heirs $882 to settle a small $2,579 estate, and that the heirs were fearful that the remainder would have to go to administrator's fees. The trial judge ruled that malice was implied since truth was not proven. The jury returned a $2,500 judgment against the newspaper. On appeal, however, the trial judge was reversed. The ruling was as follows:

> Whatever pertains to the qualification of the candidate for the office sought is a legitimate subject for discussion and comment, provided that such discussion and comment is not extended beyond the prescribed limit. That is, all statements and comments in this respect must be confined to the truth, or what in good faith and upon probable cause is believed to be true, and the matter must be pertinent to the issue, *i.e.*, it must relate to the suitableness or unfitness of the candidate for the office.[25]

The Texas Supreme Court drew the line on privilege of communication in 1889, however. Probable cause for belief in truth was not accepted if the charge against an official, if true, could result in his removal from office for official misconduct.[26] In such cases, truth had to be proved.

Pennsylvania courts, however, even allowed charges of official misconduct when there was probable cause for believing them true. But the state's liberal view evolved slowly. Shortly after the Civil War, truth was the only defense in Pennsylvania for libeling officials.[27] Then, in 1874, a constitutional provision prohibited convictions for publications about the official conduct of public officers that were not maliciously or negligently made.[28] Four years after the provision was adopted, the Pennsylvania Supreme Court ruled it did not apply to civil suits.[29] Views had changed by 1886, however, when it was held in civil actions that statements were not libelous if there was probable cause for belief.[30] Finally, in the 1893 case of *Jackson* v. *Pittsburgh Times*, the Pennsylvania Supreme Court ruled that false statements imputing official misconduct to even an appointed official were privileged when there was probable cause for believing in truth and no proof of express malice.[31]

The 1893 case arose when the *Pittsburgh Times* carried an article about a national guardsman whose unit had been mobilized for flood control work. The article stated that the guardsman, an officer, was relieved because he had been drunk on duty and had started a fight with a deputy sheriff. The guardsman sued, and in the trial it was shown that he had not struck the first blow in the fight and had not been officially relieved. But the Pennsylvania Supreme Court ruled that the guardsman was in the service of the state at the time and was, as a result, a public official.[32] The court said:

> Such persons are amenable to public criticism in the newspapers without liability for libel, where there is probable cause for the criticism, and no proof of express malice, even though the published statements are not strictly true.[33]

The jury could determine, the court said, if the sensational or exaggerated accounts resulted from malice or if the publisher had reasonable cause to believe the statements true.[34] While this was a civil libel suit, two Pennsylvania criminal cases before the turn of the century held that public officials had to prove negligence and maliciousness as well as falsity to obtain libel judgments.[35]

Saying the same thing in a different way, the Georgia Supreme Court ruled in an 1893 civil case that public policy demanded that articles expressing distrust and contempt of officials could not be both false and unfounded.[36] The case arose when the *Augusta Evening News* claimed a constable had solicited business in magistrate courts simply to increase his fees. The foundation for the charges was important. The court ruled that the jury should determine whether the publisher had probable cause to believe in the truth of the information and whether he acted in good faith or with malice. It also was held in *Cox* v. *Strickland* in 1897 that lack of malice was a complete bar for recovery of damages on privileged communications.[37] However, in this case it was held that advertisements were not privileged. The court said, "As well might Judas Iscariot exhibit the price of his perfidy, as an excuse for his crime, as for a libeler to set up that he published the libel complained of for money." [38] The court said the payment aggravated rather than mitigated the libel. There was, then, no effective way in Georgia to plead lack of malice for paid advertisements.

But the privilege to communicate falsehoods in the news columns, without malice, about the conduct of public officials was recognized to some extent or another by a great majority of states before the twentieth century.[39] Publishers were not paid to print news articles, and good-faith publication of untrue statements in these articles often was accepted as justification.

This defense of good-faith publication existed, as was stated by the supreme courts of two widely separated states at the turn of the century, so that newspapers could give information to the people as to the conduct of public officers.[40] In one of the states, South Dakota, the case involved an article charging a candidate for sheriff with promising to place men on juries and to help others get elected in exchange for votes. In the other state, Maine, a newspaper had charged an official with being cruel to an insane pauper. Both courts held the articles privileged and stated publishers could not be held accountable for libel if they had reason for believing the articles true and honestly did believe them true.[41] Probable cause for belief in truth had become a reasonably complete defense for privileged comment. However, it was recognized that the privilege existed so that the public could be informed.

Courts in some states, however, did not allow so much freedom for examining officials in print as did others. For instance, it was made plain in the 1878 case of *Sweeney v. Baker* in West Virginia, that the privilege of criticism concerning officials was confined to acts and conduct, not character. The case arose when a candidate for the state legislature, Jim Sweeney, sued the *Wheeling Daily Register* for an article claiming he was a professional gambler, a bully, a confessed ignoramus, a thief, whoremaster, and a social leper. The supreme court of appeals ruled that a candidate's acts could be canvassed and his conduct censured, even unjustly. The only limitation to the right of criticism on the acts and conduct of a candidate or an official, the court said, was that the criticism be bona fide or made with good faith.[42]

"But as respects his person," the court stressed, "there is no such large privilege of criticism." [43] The inviolate nature of an elected official's private character was discussed by the court as follows:

The publication of defamatory language, affecting his character, can never be justified on the ground that it was published as a criticism. His talents and qualification mentally and physically for the office he asks at the hands of the people, may be freely commented on in publications in a newspaper, and though such comments be harsh and unjust, no malice will be implied; for these are matters of opinion; but no one has a right by a publication to impute to such a candidate falsely crimes, or publish allegations affecting his character falsely.[44]

The court ruled that the Sweeney article involved allegations concerning moral qualifications. As a result, malice implied, and it was not sufficient to prove that the publisher had good reason for believing the charges true.[45] The only justification in such a case, the court said, was truth.

While the West Virginia decision applied only to elected officials, it was held in New York in 1880 that the same doctrine of privilege applied to appointed as well as elected officers. The New York case, *Hamilton v. Eno*, was considerably more liberal than pre–Civil War cases in that state.[46] It, unlike the earlier cases, recognized a privilege to comment on and criticize acts of officials, with "everything but actual malice and evil purpose in the critic" being excused.[47] In such cases, the court said, it was the jury's duty to determine good faith, belief in truth of the statement and actual malice.[48] However, the court specified that privilege did not extend to attacks upon the character of officials. Such attacks required a defense of truth.[49]

The case arose when Allan Hamilton, an assistant inspector of the New York City Board of Health, published an article in the *City Record* recommending a specific kind of street pavement. Amos F. Eno, a private citizen, replied in the *New York Tribune* that Hamilton's report was fostered and dictated by individuals wishing paving contracts with the city. The court ruled that the report, as an act of an official, could be criticized with privilege. However, this criticism, the court said, imputed bribery and was an attack on Hamilton's private character which was not privileged. The charge concerning character required proof of truth. Similar decisions were common in New York throughout the remainder of the nineteenth century.[50]

It also was held in Illinois, Louisiana, and Oregon that criticism of a public official's character was not privileged. The Illinois case,

Rearick v. *Wilcox*[51] resulted from an article in the *Quincy Whig* that accused Frederick Rearick, a mayor who was candidate for police magistrate, of using petty disbursements for personal expenses. In Louisiana, the *Daily States* of New Orleans accused the mayor and council of being "thieves" who were fleecing building contractors by demanding kickbacks.[52] And in Oregon, the *Bold Beach Gazette* accused congressional candidate J. H. Upton of being a "perjured villain" who had deceived a court of justice by false swearing.[53] The courts ruled that all these articles were attacks on private character and that, if untrue, malice implied.

All three of the state supreme courts in these cases ruled, however, that if articles were published in good faith and with belief in truth, damages could be mitigated.[54] In both the Louisiana and Oregon cases it was held that it was no justification to claim articles were copied from other newspapers.[55] The articles involved in these two state cases, as well as that of Illinois, were similar in that they charged crimes to officials. And the decision of the Oregon Supreme Court specifically stated that attacks on private character or allegations of crime were not privileged.[56]

Character and crime were more closely linked in an 1885 Florida case, when it was falsely charged that a candidate for office was under indictment for felony. It was held that a charge of crime was an assault on private character.[57] Such charges were not privileged, the court said. However, both comments and acts of officials could be "freely commented on and boldly censured" with privilege. The injustice of comments, so long as privileged, made no difference, the court said.[58]

The Michigan Supreme Court in 1886 also ruled that neither attacks on character nor imputation of crime were privileged.[59] A newspaper, the *Big Rapids Current*, had falsely accused a candidate for Congress with being a forger, thief, and cheat. It was no defense, the court said, that the articles were published without malice and in an honest belief of the truth, though this would mitigate damages.[60] Character assassination required proof of truth. A similar ruling came a year later in the Michigan high court when a newspaper compared a candidate for city treasurer in Detroit to a moral graveyard. The court ruled this required proof of truth as it amounted to vilification and calumniation of character.[61]

It was an 1893 decision of the Ohio Supreme Court, however, that perhaps gave the clearest and simplest explanation for denying any privilege of false comment concerning the private character of an official. The court, in the case of *Post Publishing Co. v. Maloney,* recognized a privilege of free and full comment about official acts, provided there was a lack of malice. But the judgment stated, "A person who enters upon a public office, or becomes a candidate for one, no more surrenders to the public his private character than he does his private property." [62] The case arose when the *Evening Post* of Cincinnati published an article stating that it "was said" that policeman J. J. Maloney had a criminal record and had served time in the workhouse. The fact that the newspaper had qualified the charge by publishing what was said of the policeman did not make the charge any less libelous, the court said.[63] Further, the charge attacked the officer's private character and the court ruled that it could be defended in court only by proving truth. An Ohio court previously had ruled that proper cause for an honest belief in truth did not excuse a charge of larceny, a crime, against an official.[64]

While some states during this period did not allow any privilege of false comment when an official's private character was attacked or when crimes were alleged, still others denied privilege when articles claimed officials acted with corrupt motives. A Maryland court, for instance, held in 1883 that corrupt motives could not be ascribed to officials even though discussion was about official conduct.[65] The judgment sprang from a suit brought by a state senator over a newspaper article accusing him of voting against his party and receiving a profitable contract from the other party in return.

The senator admitted attending the rival party caucus and receiving a contract, but the vote and motives were disputed. The court said:

> There is a broad distinction between fair and legitimate discussion in regard to the conduct of a public man and the imputation of corrupt motives, by which that conduct may be said to be governed. And if one goes out of his way to asperce the personal character of a public man and to ascribe to him base and corrupt motives, he must do so at his peril.[66]

The decision would indicate that the only fair comment about officials in Maryland was good comment. As one historian has said, the decision in effect said that "you have full liberty of discussion, provided, however, you say nothing that counts." [67]

Nevertheless, decisions in several other state courts adhered to the doctrine that privilege did not extend to articles ascribing corrupt motives to officials. An early Pennsylvania case, in conflict with later decisions of that state, held the imputation of bad motives was not privileged "unless there is so much proof for the imputation that a jury shall find some foundation for belief in them." [68] And several Michigan Supreme Court decisions, including one in which a deputy sheriff was accused of arresting innocent men as tramps so his fees would increase,[69] did not recognize the imputation of bad motives as being privileged.

One of these Michigan cases, *Randall* v. *Evening News Association*, involved a cartoon as well as a news story. Cartoons were becoming more and more prominent during this period as a result of technological developments in metal engraving.[70] The newspaper article claimed that a member of the legislature, James A. Randall, had obtained passage of a bill to improve a boulevard in Detroit so that speculators, including himself, could be enriched at the expense of the taxpayers. It was claimed that he secured passage by keeping open house for legislators in which liquors were supplied. The cartoon, entitled "The Boulevard Napoleon," showed Randall standing with one foot on a cask of gin and the other hand holding a bag of money. The court held that the article and cartoon attributed bad motives and bribery to Randall and were justified only if true.[71]

An article questioning the honesty and integrity of a public weights and measures inspector was declared libelous by the Wisconsin Supreme Court in 1879. It was charged that the inspector "doctored" scales so that he could increase his fees. The court said the article brought the inspector into public hatred and contempt, and that such malicious attacks on character were not privileged.[72] The court did recognize, however, that privileged communications had to be both false and malicious.[73] The Wisconsin court also recognized that taunts and jibes could imply bad motives. When the *Oshkosh Times* in 1893 referred to state senator George H. Buckstaff as "his majesty Bucksniff," a "legislative god," and "dearly-beloved Bucksniff," the article was declared libelous because the appellations were "insulting." [74] The court said there was an undoubted reference to the fictional Pecksniff, one of the most contemptible characters of Charles Dickens's novels. Further, the court said that insulting phrases of a personal nature were not privileged, though they "might be privileged" if they concerned official conduct or Buckstaff's legislative duties.[75]

Many jurisdictions did extend privilege to include meaningful comment about officials, however. This was evidenced by an 1882 decision of the federal circuit court in Massachusetts, which quoted the "modern doctrine" as to how far people could go in discussing public conduct and qualifications. The court said:

> In such discussion, they are not held to prove the exact truth of their statements, and the soundness of their inferences, provided they are not actuated by express malice, and there is reasonable ground for their statements or inferences, all of which is for the jury.[76]

The emphasis was not on whether discussion was good or bad, but on lack of malice and on a basis in fact for discussion.

The factual base appeared to be extremely important in libel actions involving comment about officials, as was shown in an 1893 case before the Kentucky Court of Appeals. The case involved the *Louisville Courier Journal*, which ascribed corrupt motives to an election supervisor. The article described how the supervisor had interfered with Democratic workers at the polling place because he thought they were taking voters to another room and bribing them to vote their way. Yet he, too, took voters aside and talked to them. Further, the article said the supervisor would be arrested for violating his oath of office and for bribery. He was not arrested, and he sued, but the jury found for the newspaper. The appellate court, in upholding the jury's verdict, said that articles which were substantially true were not libelous.[77] More in point, the court ruled as follows:

> Animadversion on conduct of public officer, however severe, is not libelous, if it be confined within the limits of fair and reasonable criticism based on facts. It may be thought that the imputation of bribery was not supported in fact, but it will be observed, that he interfered with actions of opponents upon belief that it was evidence of bribery, therefore he cannot complain if his activity, exercised in the same manner, be taken as evidence of the same offense.[78]

One might question whether the newspaper actually was criticizing the election supervisor's conduct or was in reality making derogatory statements of fact concerning bribery. Nevertheless, it was clear that the court felt that the assigning of corrupt motives was not a factual allegation but rather legitimate criticism based on facts.

The difference between factual allegations and fair comment was cited by several state courts during this period as the difference between privileged and nonprivileged communications. In holding to this distinction, these states differed from most jurisdictions at this time. The majority of states appeared to deny privilege when publications dealt with private and moral character or with charges of crime and corrupt motives. One authority who examined these cases in detail, however, claimed that these various rules announced by the courts concerning character, crime, and motives were not the real distinction in liability for libel. Rather, he asserted, the difference was between statement of fact as opposed to comment.[79]

One decision differentiating between fact and comment was issued in Ohio in 1882. The *Cincinnati Gazette* carried an article, with the head "Conspiracy," which indirectly accused the governor of considering groundless charges against a subordinate officer. The governor sued, and the court ruled the article libelous. Legitimate criticism was not involved, the court said, because the article charged facts.[80]

A similar decision was issued by the Michigan Supreme Court in 1890. The case involved a suit brought by a candidate for Congress, Charles E. Belknap, against the *Daily Democrat*. The newspaper had printed a purported facsimile of Belknap's handwriting and signature with these words: "I don't propose to go into debate on the tariff differences on wool, quinine, and all the things, because I ain't built that way." [81] The publication was neither criticism nor opinion, the court said, but rather a statement of fact and not privileged.[82] The court said the statement was false and thus libelous, as showing Belknap to be ignorant, illiterate, and incapable of performing his duties. However, the publisher's intent and belief in truth, the court pointed out, could be brought out in a trial to minimize damages.[83]

There was no way to minimize damages in Massachusetts for false statements that were not privileged. This was evident in *Burt* v. *Advertiser Newspaper Co.*,[84] perhaps the leading case of the period ruling that factual allegations were not privileged comment. The case arose over articles in the *Boston Advertiser* charging fraud in the New York Custom House.[85] Charges made by the newspaper were believed to be true, having been based on an official report to the Treasury Department. But since belief in truth was justification only for privileged comments, and the statements were not considered privileged, the newspaper was not allowed to introduce evidence as to belief.[86] Further, belief in truth could not be introduced to mitigate damages, as Massachusetts required that no less than actual damages be awarded and allowed no punitive damages.[87] The only justification for matter not privileged and for damages was truth. Since truth could not be independently proved, the newspaper lost the case.

On appeal, Mr. Justice Holmes, then of the Supreme Judicial Court of Massachusetts and later a United States Supreme Court justice, said the articles were not privileged. They had stated that New York importers were paying tribute to Custom House officials to have below-value appraisals, cheating the government of more than twenty million dollars a year.[88] Justice Holmes said:

> What is privileged, if that is the proper term, is criticism, not statement, and however it might be if a person merely quoted or referred to a statement as made by others, and gave it no new sanction, if he takes it upon himself in his own person to allege facts otherwise libelous, he will not be privileged if those facts are not true. . . . What the interest of private citizens in public matters requires is freedom of discussion rather than of statement. . . . It is one thing to comment upon or criticize, even with severity, the acknowledged or proven acts of a public man, and quite another to assert that he has been guilty of particular acts of misconduct.[89]

The articles, containing factual assertions, had to be proved by truth. Justice Holmes did say, however, the official report to the Treasury Department should have been allowed in evidence, not to prove belief in truth but to prove the truth of the allegations. The jury, he said, upon review of the report might agree with the publisher and find that the allegations of the article were true.[90]

In a state that allowed truth only as a defense to libelous statements, as opposed to privileged comments, reasonable cause for belief in truth could influence a jury's decision. The jury, at least, could have the benefit of the evidence upon which the publisher based his article. The decision as to truth belonged to the jurors, and jurors as well as publishers could believe.

Publishers frequently found that probable cause for belief in truth was not a sufficient defense for libeling public officials.

Though probable cause showed good faith, the defense of good faith held only if the article was privileged. And there was no uniform definition from state to state, and often within the same state, as to privileged communications. Lines had been drawn variously denying privilege to statements of fact as opposed to comment, to criticism of private and moral character as opposed to criticism of acts and conduct, and to charges of crime, misconduct, and corrupt motives. When publishers stepped over these lines, their good faith might not be a justification, depending on the jurisdiction they were in. However, state appellate judges often recognized that good faith communications about officials, even though not privileged, were not subject to punitive damages.

As an example, the Michigan Supreme Court ruled in *Bailey v. Kalamazoo Publishing Co.* that newspapers had no right to transcend the truth in publishing articles about officials, in this case a candidate for congress. However, the court in this 1879 case stated:

> Damages for a libel upon a candidate for public office are reduced to a minimum if the libel results from an honest mistake made in an honest effort to enlighten the people as to his character.[91]

Publishers, the court said, could show that they honestly believed their articles true to defend against punitive damages. This rule was repeated in the same year by the court in *Scripps v. Foster*, when the *Detroit Evening News* printed a story that a city physician's improper vaccinations for smallpox had led to the death of a child. The story proved false, though it was believed true. The court ruled that good reason to believe in truth showed good faith and would refute exemplary damages.[92]

The Michigan high court ruled at various times through the remainder of the nineteenth century that comment, not fact, was privileged, and that privilege did not extend to attacks on private character, and that imputation of crime, corrupt motives, or misconduct in office were not privileged. The rule eventually evolved that newspapers could state "any fact which affects the fitness of a candidate" for the guidance of electors so long as the newspapers "observe an honest regard for the truth." [93] Still, all these decisions were consistent in that good faith communications, even if false, excused punitive damages. Publishers with cause for believing in the truth of articles about officials, even though the articles were not privileged, had to pay only actual damages.[94]

This practice, which can be traced back to the Civil War suit of *Hotchkiss* v. *Porter* in Connecticut,[95] was prominent in other states as well. It already has been noted how courts in Illinois, Louisiana, Oregon, and Florida denied privilege for attacks on the private character of officials. Yet all four states, in suits involving such attacks, allowed damages to be mitigated by reasonable cause for belief in truth.[96]

Publishers were allowed to mitigate damages because of lack of malice. This was made clear in an 1880 Nevada case, *Thompson* v. *Powning*. It arose when the *Reno State Journal* claimed that a former senator had been paid while in office to vote against his own resolution concerning fares and rates. Though the article was declared libelous, the court ruled that only actual damages could be awarded.[97] The court said:

> Where there is no ill-will or malice on the part of the defendant, no special damages, actual injury or pecuniary losses alleged, or proved, the jury may find a verdict for only nominal damages.[98]

Even though not privileged, the court said, all circumstances leading to publishing could be shown.[99] Good faith publications refuted malice and punitive damages.

Good faith was allowed for mitigation of damages even when states strictly adhered to the doctrine that truth was the only justification, as was shown in the 1893 California case of *Edwards* v. *San Jose Printing and Publishing Co.* The San Jose newspaper printed an article stating that a power company would attempt to buy voters in an election and that H. J. Edwards was in charge "of the sack." [100] The editor claimed that he had been contacted by dozens of individuals about the matter prior to publication and believed the information to be true. The California Supreme Court ruled that unless the editor named those who contacted him and presented reasons as to why they should be believed, the plea could not be allowed in mitigation.[101] The emphasis for mitigation was proper cause for belief, not belief itself. To excuse the libel as such, however, proof of truth was required.

Nothing short of the proof of truth would suffice in a number of states to justify a libel against an official, despite the accelerated movement toward the recognition of good faith communications for privileged occasions. As has been seen, Massachusetts allowed juries to consider a publisher's cause for belief in determining if articles were true, and California allowed cause for belief as evidence to refute punitive damages.[102] While both Kentucky and Michigan allowed privilege for comments, Kentucky required that factual statements be substantially true, and Michigan required that the publisher maintain an honest regard for truth.[103] Texas, though allowing privilege to discuss the fitness and qualifications of public officials, required proof of truth when charges were involved that would cause removal from office.[104]

While privilege was recognized under some circumstances, then, these states and others still retained the basic justification, that of truth, for all other articles concerning officials. Some states, though, did not recognize any kind of privilege as far as communications about officials were concerned. In these states, truth was the only defense.

One such state was Tennessee, where a court ruled in 1885 that neither the press nor the public could falsely discuss the conduct or character of officials or candidates for office.[105] The ruling came after the *Nashville Banner* had printed an article charging superintendent James E. Carter and other officials at the state penitentiary with dereliction of duty. The court said that even though the article was written without malice and upon probable cause, it was libelous unless true. Though this was a criminal libel case, in which the newspaper was fined fifty-one dollars, the Tennessee Supreme Court applied the ruling to civil cases as well. The doctrine of privileged communications was explored and rejected. The court said there was no uniformity in decisions on privilege and that conflict, discord, and uncertainty prevailed.[106]

The court recognized, however, that regardless of rulings by judges, juries would consider the circumstances involved. The court said that usually in a criminal case, when a publisher had grounds to believe the article true, it would be "sufficient to generate a reasonable doubt of the defendant's guilt." [107] Further, in civil cases, the court said, courts and jurors were not disposed "to be severe with the offender" when publications were made bona fide and without malice, even though the truth could not be proved.[108] So while not recognizing probable cause as a defense, the court in effect said juries would consider it.

Consideration was limited strictly to the truth in Missouri, however. The Missouri Supreme Court in 1872 ruled that publications which degraded or ridiculed officials were libelous, and that justification for such publications must "specifically allege conduct that would warrant the charge." [109] This was explained by saying that if a publication claimed a person was thought of as a horse thief, the justification must show that he had been guilty of horse stealing.[110] Malice automatically was considered from wrongful charges, the court said. Thus, good faith publications could not excuse a libel against an official, though the court said good faith "might" mitigate damages.[111]

The Indiana Supreme Court was another of the state appellate courts adhering to the same doctrine, as was shown in the 1889 case of *Prosser* v. *Callis*. Here the *Weekly Gazette* claimed that a financial report made by the county auditor was false in one respect and that it was suspected it was false in other respects. The court said bluntly that if a report in a newspaper concerning an official was false, it was libelous.[112] In a criminal prosecution two years later, the Indiana Supreme Court ruled that if there was a reasonable doubt as to the truth or falsity of an article, when considered in its entirety, the jury had to give the defending publisher the benefit of the doubt.[113] The burden clearly was reversed in civil suits, however, as was shown in the 1898 case of *Wintrode* v. *Renbarger*. Here the court said that to claim a sheriff was starving prisoners to death imputed crime in that it claimed official duties were neglected. There had to be "proof of truth beyond a reasonable doubt" for justification, the court said.[114]

SUMMARY

While proof of truth was adhered to more closely in some states than in others, it continued throughout the second half of the nineteenth century to be the primary justification for libels against public officials and candidates. Still, judges in state after state during this period began to recognize, in one form or another, that truth was not an absolute. In libel suits, they began to look at the circumstances under which so-called truths or falsehoods about officials were published. Allowances began to be made for libels against officials and candidates that were made in good faith, regardless of truth or falsity.

The novel view that a publisher should not be held accountable for the exact truth of articles concerning public officials, though not accepted in all states, was only indicative of the times. The entire period, from the Civil War through the remainder of the nineteenth century, was marked by a general overturning and reassessment of old values. This was not entirely due to the social upheaval caused by the industrial revolution. It was due in part to the introduction of new theories concerning life itself. These theories, which made a profound impression in the United States, included those of natural selection and survival of the fittest, springing from the works of Charles Darwin,[115] and that of economic determinism, fathered by Karl Marx.[116] It was an age of materialism, in which men began even to question the existence of a supreme being. Views changed, and values toppled; what appeared true before appeared false now. Truth became more elusive. And following the pragmatic philosophy of William James,[117] it began to be accepted that if an individual believed something to be true, it was true to him.

Belief in truth, so long as there was proper cause for that belief, also began to be accepted by many state courts during this period as a defense to libels against officials. The acceptance of this defense depended on whether the publications were privileged and whether the courts recognized privilege. The theory was that privilege extended to communications to the public about the acts and conduct of officials and candidates because the public had a right to know about those they were taxed to support. And when privileged communications were published without malice, even though they were false, they were not libelous. Newspapermen, then, attempted to prove lack of malice when published articles about officials or candidates turned out to be false. They could do this by showing they had probable cause for believing the articles true. Conversely, officials and candidates attempted to prove malice. This could be done by showing that newspapermen knew items were false at the time of publication. Privilege, then, was not all-inclusive. It did not extend to publications made in bad faith and with malice.

Some of the first libel suits in which the doctrine of privilege was expounded were decided during and shortly after the Civil War. But the doctrine did not become widespread until the mid-1880s. Between then and the turn of the twentieth century, some type of privilege was recognized in twenty-five of the twenty-eight jurisdictions in which appellate court decisions in public official libel suits were recorded. While truth remained the basic defense for factual statements in a number of states, courts in only three states, Tennessee, Missouri, and Indiana, recognized no privilege at all, adhering to the pre–Civil War standard that newspapermen published falsehoods about officials at their own peril, regardless of motives.

Even in jurisdictions where privilege was allowed, there was no uniformity. Judgments between and even within individual states differed as to what privilege encompassed. Some extended privilege only to comments about officials based on proven facts. A good many extended it to officials' public acts, conduct, and public character. Still others declared that any statements concerning the fitness of an individual to hold office were privileged. In several states, particularly Connecticut, California, and Oregon, privilege was recognized only to the extent that probable cause for belief in truth was sufficient to hold damages to a minimum.

It is difficult to categorize the exact doctrines followed by the individual state courts because of vacillation in judgments. Though states might recognize privilege, their courts often denied the protection of privilege when statements, as one authority has said, were "grossly in excess of what the occasion required." [118] Some courts denied privilege for published attacks on the private or moral character of officials and candidates. Imputation of crime seldom received the cloak of privilege, and frequently the ascribing of corrupt motives or misconduct in office was considered excessive of privilege. In instances such as these, in which courts denied the privilege they ordinarily recognized, a claim of libel could be defended only by proof of truth. Even then, however, newspapermen often could mitigate damages by showing they had probable cause for believing the truth of their publications. Still, no clear lines as to privilege could be drawn, even in individual states. Furthermore, there was no common policy from state to state as to what was excessive of privilege.

The doctrine of privilege, then, grew in accordance with the views of individual judges in separate states. In this respect, however, the growth of privilege was no different from the growth of any other body of laws. As was observed by Justice Oliver Wendell Holmes, Jr., in 1881, the law itself is always changing and never reaches consistency. He wrote that law constantly adopts new principles from the experiences of life, from what is believed to be public policy at a given time, or from what is in a given instance understood to be convenient.[119] But what was convenient or reflective of public policy in one state might not even apply in another. Human experience varied. As a result the doctrine of privilege was flexible, being bent to fit both strict and broad constructions of the law.

From an overall perspective, however, there was a much greater privilege of discussion concerning government officials and candidates for office during this post–Civil War era than in the early nineteenth century. And while there is no evidence to relate this expanded doctrine of privilege to the so-called new journalism of the later nineteenth century, there is no doubt that journalists were enabled to better canvass the affairs of government and those in it as a result of the protection of privilege in libel suits. Because of the people's right to know, many newspapermen in many jurisdictions could refute or mitigate claims of libel by proving that false articles were published in good faith. Despite disagreement as to individual policies of privilege, the broad confines of libel-free discussion had been established.

DEVELOPMENT
AND
DIVERGENCY

---

8. Crystallization and Conflict

The Jurisprudence of Libel Emerges

As publishers and public officials continued to fight their legal battles through the first half of the twentieth century, both the theoretical and procedural standards of libel became more clearly defined. At the same time there was and could be no national uniformity. Under the then interpretation of the Tenth Amendment to the United States Constitution,[1] each state was supreme in formulating, administering and interpreting its own laws of libel. And this established practice was sanctioned by the Supreme Court of the United States in 1931.[2] But while the states were free to determine their own libel policies, few in reality did. Instead they followed, both in policy and procedure, common-law precedents that had been established in well-reasoned court opinions elsewhere.

Judges began to accept the view that words had to be interpreted in accordance with their natural and obvious meanings to determine whether they were libelous. Further, differences between libel *per se* and libel *per quod* were formulated. The line between publications that were libelous and those that were not libelous became clearer. Rules were established for determining the extent to which unnamed officials could be libeled in articles referring to general groups. And some state courts even recognized a privilege to publish replies to officials and candidates without liability for libel.

Generally, however, the greatly broadened privilege to discuss, criticize, and comment on individuals seeking and holding government positions began to stabilize around two specific and conflicting doctrines. One doctrine extended privilege to false facts when they were communicated without malice and with probable cause for believing them true. The other limited privilege to comment and criticism based on established fact. Judges generally accepted one or the other view as controlling in their jurisdictions.

In the final analysis, each state had the prerogative to select its own doctrine of privilege. The decisions of the state courts of final jurisdiction could not be reviewed. Even the libel decisions of the United States Supreme Court at this time carried no force of law in the various states. Besides, in the early nineteenth century, the nation's highest court considered only one case in which a newspaper's privilege to discuss officials was an issue, and the decision in this case made no declaration as to the application of privilege to misstatements of fact.

The case went to the United States Supreme Court in 1912 from Puerto Rico because it involved a minister of the United States government. A Puerto Rican newspaper, *La Correspondecia*, had censured a United States district attorney, claiming his conduct was scandalous and immoral in serving as a public official while simultaneously acting as a private attorney for individuals suing the government. This practice was forbidden by law to Puerto Rican officials. The Supreme Court ruled, in *Gandia v. Pettingill*, that the newspaper comment did not go beyond the "permitted line" and was not excessive, as the acts were disapproved by the Puerto Rican community.[3] Stating that the newspaper discussion, though about the district attorney's private acts, pertained to his acts and conduct in office, the Court said, "Anything bearing on such acts was a legitimate subject of statement and comment. It was so at least in the absence of express malice."[4] The Supreme

Court held, in effect, that an official's private character was subject to scrutiny if that character affected fitness for office. However, there was no dictum in the case indicating whether privilege would or would not be extended to misstatements of fact. Only comments were involved. No issue was raised about the fact from which the imputations of immorality and scandalous conduct were drawn.[5]

This decision applied only to federal law, not to state law, because the Constitution of the United States, as interpreted at this time, did not give the United States Supreme Court appellate jurisdiction over state court libel decisions. The only possible avenue in the Constitution by which the Supreme Court could review a state libel decision was that avenue which many contended directly connected the Fourteenth and First Amendments. And the Supreme Court in the 1907 case of *Patterson v. Colorado*, while not denying that the avenue was there, refused to say it was open.

The 1907 case arose when the Colorado Supreme Court held a Denver newspaper in contempt for charging the court with participating in a scheme to seat Republican candidates. The court held this tended to interfere with the administration of justice in a pending case. The judgment was appealed to the United States Supreme Court on the basis that the privileges and immunities of citizens included freedom of the press and that the Fourteenth Amendment prohibited states from abridging the privileges and immunities. In sidestepping this issue, the Supreme Court issued the following dictum:

> Even if we were to assume that freedom of speech and freedom of the press were protected from abridgments on the part not only of the United States but also of the states, still we should be far from the conclusion that the plaintiff in error would have us reach. In the first place, the main purpose of such constitutional provisions is "to prevent all such previous restraints upon publications as had been practiced by other governments," and they do not prevent the subsequent punishment of such as may be deemed contrary to the public welfare.[6]

While the Court did not mention libel, it essentially sanctioned libel restraints as well as the power of courts to hold newspapers in contempt. These were not restraints prior to publication and, as a result, were not considered regulations that impaired press freedom.

Each state, then, was free to determine the extent to which libel against officials was confined by the American public's privilege to freely discuss those officials. This ideology was again under-scored by the United States Supreme Court in the 1920 case of *Prudential Insurance Co. v. Cheek*. While this suit concerned privacy, not libel, the decision again promoted state independence in determining controls on speech and press. In this case, the Court said that "neither the Fourteenth Amendment nor any other provision of the Constitution of the United States imposes upon the States any restriction about 'freedom of speech.' " [7]

The decision of the United States Supreme Court in the Prudential Insurance Company case was not long to stand. Five years later Supreme Court justices, in *Gitlow v. New York*, issued an opinion in which they stated that they did not regard the state-ment "in *Prudential Insurance Co. v. Cheek* . . . that the Four-teenth Amendment imposes no restrictions on States concerning freedom of speech, as determinative of this question." [8] The 1925 Gitlow case, in an opinion written by Mr. Justice Edward Sanford, assumed that freedom of speech and press "are among the funda-mental personal rights and liberties protected by the due process clause of the Fourteenth Amendment from impairment by the States." [9]

The Court, however, upheld conviction of Benjamin Gitlow for printing and distributing the *Left Wing Manifesto*. A state, the Court said, can take such action as a proper protection of public peace and safety. The publication, which advocated mass political strikes and militant revolution, violated New York's Criminal Anarchy Act of 1902. The punishment represented subsequent, not prior restraint. Mr. Justices Oliver Wendell Holmes, Jr. and Louis D. Brandeis disagreed with the decision but agreed that the "general principle of free speech . . . must be taken to be included in the Fourteenth Amendment, in view of the scope that has been given to the word 'liberty' as there used." [10]

Six years after the Gitlow decision, in 1931, the United States Supreme Court ruled specifically that the fundamental right of a free press was not violated by the restrictions of state libel laws. The ruling came in *Near v. Minnesota ex rel Olson*. [11] The primary holding of the Supreme Court was that states could not enact laws laying previous restraints upon publications, as this would destroy freedom of the press. [12] But it also was held that a state could punish publishers for abuse of press liberty. [13]

The issue of press freedom arose when an attempt was made to padlock the *Saturday Press* for publishing articles accusing officials of malfeasance, of connection with crimes, and of failure to suppress crimes.[14] The action was taken under what has been called the Minnesota Gag Law.[15] Under this law, a publisher of scandalous and defamatory articles could have his newspaper suppressed unless he could prove the articles were true and published with good motives for justifiable ends. After a judge ordered suppression, any further publication would be punished as a contempt.[16] The United States Supreme Court, in a five-to-four decision, held this censorship was "an infringement of the liberty of the press guaranteed by the Fourteenth Amendment." [17] The Court had this to say:

> The fact that for approximately one hundred and fifty years there has been almost an entire absence of attempts to impose previous restraints upon publications relating to the malfeasance of public officers is significant of the deep-seated conviction that such restraints would violate constitutional rights. Public officers, whose character and conduct remain open to debate and free discussion, find their remedies for false accusations in actions under libel laws provided for redress and punishment, and not in proceedings to restrain the publication of newspapers and periodicals.[18]

Previous restraints, the Court said, were "but a step to a complete system of censorship." [19] Subsequent punishment was held as the appropriate remedy so long as it was consistent with constitutional privilege.[20]

The Supreme Court did not explain what was consistent with constitutional privilege. However, it did make this statement:

> It is recognized that punishment for the abuse of liberty accorded to the press is essential to the protection of the public, and that the common-law rules that subject the libeler to responsibility for the public offense, as well as for the private injury, are not abolished by the protection extended in our constitution.[21]

The dictum was clear. States had no right to keep anyone from publishing defamatory matter about anyone else, including officials. But they did have a right to protect the public by libel laws that afforded punishment for irresponsible publications that abused liberty.

Not only did each state have the right to punish those who published scandalous and defamatory matter, all of them did. Every state had libel laws, either based on legislative enactment or court decisions. The other American jurisdictions, in Hawaii, Puerto Rico, Alaska, and the District of Columbia, also subjected libelers to court sanctions.

In a review of the state libel laws at mid-century, the United States Supreme Court found that eleven American jurisdictions through the years had accepted, with some variation, the following statutory version of libel:

> A libel is a malicious defamation, expressed either by printing, or by signs or pictures, or the like, tending to blacken the memory of one who is dead, or to impeach the honesty, integrity, virtue or reputation or publish the natural defects of one who is alive, and thereby to expose him to public hatred, contempt, ridicule, or financial injury.[22]

The laws of another twelve jurisdictions varied only slightly from the following formula:

> A libel is a malicious defamation of a person, made public by any printing, writing, sign, picture, representation or effigy, tending to provoke him to wrath or expose him to public hatred, contempt, or ridicule, or to deprive him of the benefits of public confidence and social intercourse; or any malicious defamation, made public as aforesaid, designed to blacken and vilify the memory of one who is dead, and tending to scandalize or provoke his suffering relatives or friends.[23]

Still another twenty jurisdictions followed common-law precedents that, in some instances, defined libel as consisting of publications that aroused "scorn" or "obloquy" and that impeached "virtue" or that held individuals up to public ridicule. And the remaining nine jurisdictions, the Supreme Court found, had definitions that did not fall into common patterns.[24] Regardless of what was encompassed in the laws of libel, these laws were well defined in each state.

Even with statutory or common-law definitions, however, libel depended, in the final analysis, on the meaning of words in articles that were published. And frequently such meanings were in dispute. In such cases, state courts generally followed the ruling of the United States Supreme Court in the 1913 case of *Baker v. Warner* to the effect that it was for the "jury and not the court to determine the meaning of ambiguous language in the publication." [25] The case involved a libel suit brought by a United States district attorney for Washington, D. C. The district attorney, who had been forced by court order to lift a warrant that had closed race tracks in the district, was closely associated with a candidate for Congress. And the candidate was asked, in a news article, if his campaign money was coming from the "race track." These words, the district attorney claimed, imputed that he, as an associate of the candidate, was taking a payoff from the race track to let it remain open. The Supreme Court said there was no such imputation in the words themselves; hence, the article was not libelous per se. However, the meaning was ambiguous, the Court said, and a retrial was ordered to give a jury an opportunity to determine what the words meant.

Jurors, though, needed guidelines to follow in making such determinations, and such guidelines, although established on a state-by-state basis, were remarkably similar. The general gauge became the reader's understanding of the words. The Wisconsin Supreme Court, for instance, declared that the criterion was the "plain and natural" import of words.[26] In Wyoming, words were interpreted in accordance with their "ordinary meaning as understood by readers." [27] And the Illinois Supreme Court held that the meaning intended by the writer and the meaning assumed by the aggrieved party made no difference, as libel stood or fell on the basis of the ordinary reader's understanding of the words.[28] The "ordinary understanding" rule also was adopted by Washington, Minnesota, and South Carolina.[29] In Oklahoma, the "most natural and obvious" meaning of the words determined libel,[30] and in Florida words were to be construed as "the common mind would." [31]

In interpreting words for their libelous import, courts generally held that words could not be taken out of context. The entire article had to be considered.[32] A somewhat typical rule, as announced by the Washington Supreme Court, was that articles must be "considered as a whole in the natural sense." [33] But in addition to determining the natural sense of words, jurors had to determine whether libel applied. The Massachusetts Supreme Judicial Court, for example, held that jurors had to find that words caused officials or candidates to be "discredited by a considerable and respectable class in the community" before they were libelous.[34]

Jurors, of course, did not make the determination in all cases as to whether words carried a libelous import. This was only, as the United States Supreme Court said in *Baker* v. *Warner*, when words were ambiguous.[35] Generally, officials bringing suits over ambiguous words had to prove, to the satisfaction of jurors, that those words were libelous when considered in the light of extraneous events. Jurors in such cases were concerned with libel per quod. This was and is a form of libel requiring allegations of fact to show the defamatory nature of words where libel is not readily apparent.[36] Conversely, libel per se statements are those libelous in themselves. As the Maryland Court of Appeals put it, "libel per se requires no innuendo to make the defamatory nature apparent." [37] And when statements in articles were not ambiguous, when they could be interpreted in only one way, it was the duty of judges, as a matter of law, to determine if they were libelous per se.[38]

Standards followed by judges in determining libel per se varied slightly from state to state in suits brought by public officials. Examples of this deviation can be seen in decisions of Washington, Wyoming, Oklahoma, and Wisconsin courts. One decision of the Washington Supreme Court, for instance, held that statements about officials were libelous per se if they imputed misconduct in office, want of fidelity to public trust, or want of official integrity.[39] While the Wyoming Supreme Court included articles imputing want of integrity, it added articles that claimed lack of qualifications or dereliction of duty.[40] In Oklahoma, articles charging neglect of official duty, malfeasance in office, or incompetency were libelous per se.[41] And the Wisconsin Supreme Court held that libel per se extended to anything which caused an officer to be looked on with distrust or which brought him into disgrace.[42]

A specific example of libel per se was a charge in Nebraska that a candidate for Congress, when previously serving as a county clerk, had not accounted for all his money.[43] In another case, the New York Court of Appeals held that an article was libelous by charging a congressman with introducing legislation requiring that a privately owned commissary system be continued on Ellis Island for the benefit of former clients. The court said this showed the official was serving the interests of private parties rather than the interest of the public.[44] In Michigan, libel per se was ruled on charges that a superintendent of schools was lax in paying bills, that a sheriff was drunk when making an arrest, that a county clerk was dishonest in office, that a village attorney was a pettifogger, and that someone must have stopped "putting up" to cause slot machine gambling to be stopped.[45] The Minnesota Supreme Court said that a publication charging a candidate with not being a citizen was libelous *per se* because citizenship was a requisite of eligibility for office.[46] And a charge that a member of a county bond committee sold a bond issue for several thousand dollars less than he could have was held to constitute libel *per se* in Wisconsin.[47]

Charges of crime against officials consistently drew rulings of libel *per se*. And sometimes these charges were not readily evident. For instance, the Wyoming Supreme Court held in one case that a newspaper article entitled "Dive Reopens" was libelous *per se*; the article asked the mayor if he had misrepresented his actions in regard to closing the club. The court said the article at least implied the mayor was not sincere in his duties and could imply that he was partial in the protection of unlawful conduct.[48] Somewhat more evident was the imputation of crime that the Oregon Supreme Court said was contained in an article about a school board member. The article, ruled libelous *per se*, said school contractors were required to buy hardware and materials from the board member or face trouble in obtaining approval of their work.[49] Then there were the most obvious charges of crime, such as published claims that a prosecuting attorney was shielding criminals by delay and inaction in trial or that a police chief stole papers while in a building illegally. The Washington Supreme Court, ruling on these two separate claims, found both to be libelous *per se*.[50]

Even though a judge might declare an article to be libelous *per se*, a newspaperman still might not be liable for damages. The same was true in cases in which juries found libelous import in ambiguous articles. Even after the declaration of libel, newspapermen could defend themselves by proving truth of the statements, or possibly by proving truth and good motives. And when public officials were complainants, newspapermen also could attempt to justify libels by showing fair comment or privilege.

Though the general rule was that trials would be held if articles were reasonably susceptible of defamatory interpretations,[51] libel suits brought by officials occasionally were dismissed on the basis that libel was not involved. Generally, published statements that particular groups supported public officials or candidates were declared not libelous. Even a charge that criminal elements supported a candidate for sheriff in Illinois was declared not libelous *per se*, it being presumed that no criminal agreement had been made.[52] And the Georgia Court of Appeals held that an article stating a group of Negroes had endorsed a candidate for sheriff was not libelous.[53] Similarly, the Minnesota Supreme Court ruled that no libel attached to a publication stating a candidate was backed by corporations.[54] Even a charge that a legislator was working to put breweries in control of the legislature was found not to be libelous by a Minnesota judge, who held such efforts were not illegal and were not dishonorable "from the viewpoint of practical politics." [55]

Politics certainly was the issue in a 1941 Tennessee case, one of many across the United States brought by Congressman Martin L. Sweeney of Ohio for articles stating he was seeking to prevent the appointment of a foreign-born Jewish judge. The Tennessee Supreme Court held simply that a person must be damaged to be libeled and that Sweeney was not damaged.[56] Frequently, judges also were lenient in considering publications concerning official actions. For instance, the North Carolina Supreme Court held that a publication accusing a police chief with refusing to cooperate with a citizens' committee was not libelous because he was not obliged by law to serve or cooperate with anyone.[57] And the Alabama Supreme Court decided that an article claiming the city clerk had made an error in the city commissioners' minutes was not libelous as it did not charge incompetency.[58] There were, then, a number of suits filed by officials in which no bona fide issue of libel could be raised.

Even unnamed officials could raise a bona fide issue of libel, however, if they could show that defamatory articles specifically pertained to them. This was not difficult when an official was a member of a small group of persons referred to in an article. To illustrate, a county commissioner in Alabama in 1901 was allowed to bring suit for a newspaper article claiming the commissioners court awarded a contract to the highest bidder because the bidder's politics was the same as theirs.[59] And the charge was held libelous per se as an imputation of corruption.

When a Boston newspaper carried an article in 1914 claiming the city benefited "tax title sharks" by conducting "quickie" public sales of property seized in lieu of delinquent taxes, the Massachusetts Supreme Judicial Court allowed the city tax collector to bring a suit for libel. The court said he was the only one authorized by law to sell the property, so the article could refer to no one else.[60] There were several instances in which individual jurors were allowed to bring libel suits for publications impeaching their integrity and conduct.[61] Though the jury, as such, was referred to in the publications, courts ruled that any one member of the jury could be damaged. Similarly, the West Virginia Supreme Court of Appeals said in 1943 that when restricted groups were defamed, any member may maintain a libel action.[62] This case, based on a claim that a city council refused to insure honesty by instituting a new system of bookkeeping, was brought by an individual councilman. An individual member of a state board of medical examiners also was allowed to bring a suit in Minnesota for an alleged libel concerning the entire board.[63]

Individual members of large groups, however, generally were not able to claim libel over defamatory articles about their groups. An example of this was the decision of the Virginia Supreme Court of Appeals in the 1924 case of *Ewell* v. *Boutwell*. The case arose when an advertisement was printed in the *Virginian-Pilot* claiming there was a "scheme" in the state House of Delegates to change pilotage laws to make whisky and dope smuggling easier. The court held that the article was subject to libel action by those referred to in the article; however, those not referred to could not claim they were libeled, the court said. The House of Delegates consisted of too many members for an individual unnamed legislator to claim the article meant him.[64] The court said that if the inference had been to a small group, any member could have sued.

Also in the twentieth century some states established a privilege to publish nonmalicious replies to public officials without being held responsible for libel. As far as could be determined, only one appellate court decision in the nineteenth century dealt with a libel that was published in answer to an official's similarly libelous attack. In this case, in Indiana, it was ruled that an answer to one libel did not justify another libel.[65] The fact that it was a reply was allowed in mitigation. By the turn of the century, however, the privilege of reply was recognized in New York. It was ruled that a school financial adviser could answer a school trustee's misrepresentations as to finances without fear of libel.[66] Similar decisions in other states followed over the years.

While the Washington Supreme Court recognized a right to answer attacks, it held in 1905 that the answer could not be in excess of normal fair comment and criticism rules.[67] And the Louisiana Supreme Court ruled in 1918 that when a candidate suggests matters for public discussion, he cannot complain when questioned about those matters, as such questions constituted fair comment.[68] In Texas, it was ruled in 1928 that a district attorney who had criticized a grand jury could not successfully maintain a suit over a newspaper's publication of the grand jury's reply.[69] Further, newspapers that published articles or letters, on request, could without fear of libel publish simultaneous counterattacks, the New York Supreme Court held in 1943.[70]

One of the more unusual cases in which the right of reply was upheld concerned a controversy over a law professor who was dismissed from the University of Missouri. He wrote a letter for publication in the *St. Louis Post-Dispatch*, giving his version of the controversy, and the other members of the law faculty replied, stating his dismissal was based on good ground and that in their opinion he was not fit to continue teaching at the school. The dismissed professor sued. The Missouri Supreme Court in this 1923 case held that as a professor, the dismissed teacher had held "a public position of great responsibility" and was subject to comment in the public press about his fitness and qualifications for the position.[71]

He was placed in the same position as a public official because, the court said, the University of Missouri was established by law, governed by the legislature, and supported by taxpayers. Further, his letter to the newspaper implicitly invited an answer, the court ruled, and the reply of other professors was qualifiedly privileged as they had a direct interest to protect.[72] The privilege to reply, then, was based partially on the right to discuss public issues and partly on the right of self-protection when a direct interest was involved.

Judges also began to crystallize their views concerning a general immunity from libel for those discussing public officials and candidates for public office. Two basic concepts emerged. One, which had come to the fore in the post–Civil War period, was that the importance of public discussion about officials and candidates far overshadowed any inconvenience or injuries that might result to them by an occasional and honest falsehood. Those holding to this view felt that privilege of discussion should be extended to falsehoods when there was probable cause for believing them true and when they were communicated without malice.

But a second, more restrictive conception of privilege became especially prominent in the opening years of the twentieth century, possibly as a reaction to the widespread and exaggerated attacks that typified the reform literature in this "age of the muckrakers." [73] This concept, which also had been advanced in the closing years of the previous century, held that an official's right to a good name could be destroyed even by the best-intentioned falsehoods. As a result, it was believed that any privilege for discussing officials should be limited to comment and criticism based on facts.

These two views, one narrow and the other liberal, began to serve as rallying points for judges from state to state. The uncertainty and confusion concerning privilege that had prevailed through the last half of the nineteenth century began to give way. In the twentieth century, judicial pronouncements concerning privileged communications, despite the two major conflicting doctrines, began to be more uniform.

The rule that privilege extends only to comment and criticism, not to facts, appears to have been borrowed from English common law. The two leading cases in which this view was promulgated, *Burt v. Advertiser Newspaper Co.* in 1891 and *Post Publishing Co. v. Hallam* in 1893, based their holdings on English decisions.[74] The rulings in these two United States cases, written by two judges who later became justices of the United States Supreme Court, were particularly influential. The Burt decision, written by then Massachusetts Supreme Judicial Court Judge Oliver Wendell Holmes, Jr., and discussed in the previous chapter, specified that "what is privileged, if that is the proper term, is criticism, not statement." [75] At the time, this was just another state court decision. But when United States Circuit Court of Appeals Justice William Howard Taft, who later became president, arrived at the same conclusion two years afterward in the Post Publishing Company case, the rule took on added importance.

The Post Publishing Company operated the *Cincinnati Post*, which printed an article claiming that Theodore F. Hallam had sold his influence in a Kentucky political convention to a rival candidate for party nomination to Congress. Hallam, after a number of ballots at the convention, had asked his supporters to vote for Albert S. Berry, and the newspaper claimed that Berry in return had paid the group's food and drink bill, totaling $865.[76] This published claim could not be proved at the trial, which was in federal court because Hallam was a Kentucky resident and the newspaper was published in Ohio. In his decision, Taft rejected the theory that untrue statements printed without malice were privileged. Instead he relied on the English doctrine that statements of fact had to be proved, leaving only fair comment and criticism privileged.[77] Judgment was for Hallam.

In his opinion, Taft also upheld the right of Hallam to show in court that the newspaper failed to publish the fact that the libel suit had been filed. The "intentional omission" of such an article, the decision stated, reflected on the publisher's good faith.[78] Testimony also was allowed concerning an agreement between all Cincinnati newspapers not to print the news of the suit being filed. This showed an indifference on the part of the publisher, and Taft stated that "a reckless indifference to the rights of others" was equivalent to malice.[79]

The reasoning used by Taft in limiting privilege to fair comment and criticism was particularly important. He wrote:

> The existence and extent of privilege in communications are determined by balancing the needs and good of society against the right of an individual to enjoy a good reputation when he has done nothing which ought to injure it. . . . We are aware that public officers and candidates for public office are often corrupt, when it is impossible to make legal proof thereof, and of course it would be well if the public could be given to know, in such a case, what lies hidden by concealment and perjury from judicial investigation. *But the danger that honorable and worthy men may be driven from politics and public service by allowing too great latitude in attacks upon their characters outweighs any benefit that might occasionally accrue to the public from charges of corruption that are true in fact, but are incapable of legal proof. The freedom of the press is not in danger from the enforcement of the rule we uphold.*[80]

In weighing an official's right to a good name against society's right to a free press, Judge Taft refused to rule that the press could print false statements that it believed true. It was not the publisher's intent, but the charges printed that were at issue, he said.[81] The crux of the case, however, was his unproven theory that any greater privilege than comment and criticism would prevent better citizens from seeking office. This view was accepted in at least twenty-one states before the end of World War II.[82]

The leading decision of the early twentieth century for expanded privilege came in the 1908 Kansas case, *Coleman* v. *Mac-*

Lennan.[83] In this case, Kansas Supreme Court Justice Rousseau A. Burch rejected the rationale of *Post Publishing Co.* v. *Hallam*, stating that Justice Taft's "sole reason" for his holding was the hypothesis that worthy men would be driven from politics.[84] This had not been the experience in Kansas, Justice Burch said, and privilege in that state for years had extended to untrue statements that were made in good faith, without malice, and with an honest belief that they were true.[85] "Here, at least, men of unimpeachable character from all political parties continually present themselves," he stated.[86]

The Kansas case arose when the *Topeka State Journal*, edited by F. P. MacLennan, published an article concerning the attorney general, C. C. Coleman, who also was a candidate for reelection. As attorney general, Coleman was a member of a commission that controlled state school funds. The article included facts and inferences about a questionable school fund transaction. Coleman sued for libel. The supreme court decision stated that the matter may have been false and injurious to Coleman's character, but that false statements were privileged if publishers honestly believed them true and if publications were made in good faith to inform voters.[87] For MacLennan to be held liable, the decision stated, there had to be proof of actual malice. This could be shown by proving bad faith and reckless disregard of the truth.[88]

Justice Burch made it clear that his decision was based on a belief that people were entitled to know about and discuss public officials. He wrote:

> It is of the utmost consequence that the people should discuss the character and qualifications of candidates for their suffrage. The importance to the state and to society of such discussions is so vast and the advantages derived are so great that they more than counterbalance the inconvenience of private persons whose conduct may be involved, and occasional injury to the reputations of individuals must yield to the public welfare, although at times such injury may be great. The public benefit from publicity is so great, and the chance of injury to private character is so small that such discussion must be privileged.[89]

The opinion also stated that private character, in so far as it affected a candidate's fitness for office, was subject to public scrutiny under the "liberal rule" of privilege.[90] "It should always be remembered," Justice Burch wrote, "that the people have good authority for be-

lieving that grapes do not grow on thorns nor figs on thistles." [91]
His theory of privilege was followed by at least sixteen state jurisdictions before the end of World War II.[92]

SUMMARY

Both theoretical and procedural standards, then, became more
firmly established as the number of libel suits between newspapermen and officials grew. The libel laws of the various states, by the
accepted practice of the time and by official pronouncement of the
United States Supreme Court, did not impair liberty of the press.
Each state was at liberty, as it had been since the dawn of the
nation, to follow its own convictions and preferences in the formula-
tion of its public policy of libel. The only exception was that there
could not be suppression prior to publication. Everyone had the
liberty to print his sentiments and views without restraint, being
subject to sanctions if that liberty was abused. Definitions of abuse,
as well as the defense of privilege, belonged to the individual state
legislatures which made the law and the individual state courts that
interpreted that law.

    Courts throughout the United States recognized that libel
basically is determined by the interpretation of words. And it was
generally held that words must be interpreted in their plain and
ordinary sense. When words could be interpreted in only one way,
it became the duty of the judge to rule whether they constituted
libel per se. But if words were ambiguous or could, in the light of
extrinsic facts, be interpreted in more than one way, it was the job
of jurors, in finding fact, to determine if they constituted libel
per quod.

    Quite frequently officials found upon filing suits that they did
not have a bona fide issue of libel. But in some instances officials
not named in articles could successfully raise an issue of libel provided they could readily be identified as members of small groups

that had been defamed. Either libel per se or libel per quod could apply.

But simply because an article was declared libelous did not mean that a publisher was liable for it. The publisher could defend the libel on the basis of truth, or possibly truth and good motives, or he could justify it on the basis of fair comment or privilege. Privilege, in effect, granted immunity from libel. And there was a parallel growth of several types of privilege, including that of replying to officials when a direct interest was being protected.

Two major decisions near the turn of the century, however, had a profound effect on the definitions of privilege that were adopted in the various states. One of these decisions, in the case of Post Publishing Co. v. Hallam,[93] held that privilege to discuss officials extended only to comment and criticism based on facts. Publishers in libel suits, under this rule, were held strictly accountable for the truth of factual statements. The other decision, in the case of Coleman v. MacLennan,[94] held that privilege extended to the facts themselves. Publishers were not held accountable in libel suits for false statements about officials, provided those statements were communicated in good faith, without malice, and with an honest belief that they were true.

While these two cases did not originate the rules of privilege they adopted, they did become the opinion leaders in defining the privilege of discussing public officials without liability for libel. Perhaps because of ther deliberately careful and studied reasoning, Post Publishing Co. v. Hallam and Coleman v. MacLennan were later cited in case after case by state courts accepting one or the other of the two rules of privilege.[95] The first, in promoting the doctrine of fair comment and criticism, presented a most logical case for limiting privilege to protect officials' right to a good name. The second, in advancing the doctrine of honest belief in truth, just as forcefully promoted a wide privilege of discussion to protect the public's right to know. Judges in each state had meaningful precedents upon which to balance the two interests that were being protected.

9. The Evolving Law

Majority v. Minority View

The development of the law as it concerned libel against public officials and candidates for office was primarily centered, through the first half of the twentieth century, on the extent of privilege. Libel itself had been well defined, both by state statutes and by common law decisions of the state courts. But it generally was recognized in most states that the freedom to discuss officials was somewhat broader than the freedom to discuss private citizens. As a result, doctrines were formulated to excuse or justify ordinarily libelous statements about public officials. These were the doctrines of privilege. And they generally fell within two broad formulas, grounded in what was referred to in the previous chapter as the narrow or liberal view.

The narrow rule, that privilege was confined to comment and criticism based on actual facts, eventually was adopted by the largest single group of state courts. It became known as the majority view.[1] The liberal rule, that privilege extended to misstatements of fact when made without malice, was adopted by the second largest single group of state courts. It was referred to as the minority view. Both rules were qualified. Ordinarily libelous criticism concerning officials could be excused under the narrow rule only if that criticism was based on true facts. Libelous statements about those seeking or holding office that were false could be justified under the liberal rule only if those misstatements were communicated in good faith, without malice.

As neat as these two doctrines of qualified privilege appeared, many judges found it impossible to reduce them to set formulas that would cover all libel cases. Some judges would excuse falsehoods concerning officials' acts and conduct, but not falsehoods concerning crime or private character. Further, the division between fact and comment was not always clearly evident. Circumstances, then, often dictated judgments that varied slightly from the two main doctrines. Basically, however, most state courts had adopted one or the other of the major doctrines by the end of World War II.

The Majority View: *Fair Comment and Criticism*

From 1900 to the end of World War II, the narrow rule of privilege was adopted by decisions in twenty-one states and the territory of Hawaii. These jurisdictions firmly rejected, as had Mr. Justice Taft in the *Post Publishing Co. v. Hallam* decision, the doctrine that privilege extended to false statements made without malice in the belief that they were true. Instead, the courts held to the standard of truth for statements of fact, allowing privilege only for fair comment and criticism concerning the acts and conduct of officials. Jurisdictions accepting this rule were Alabama, Arkansas, Florida, Hawaii, Illinois, Kentucky, Louisiana, Maine, Maryland, Massachusetts, Mississippi, New Jersey, New York, North Dakota, Ohio, Oregon, South Carolina, Tennessee, Vermont, Virginia, Washington, and Wisconsin.

ALABAMA

In some states, such as Alabama, the fair comment rule was adopted in piecemeal fashion. For instance, the Alabama Supreme Court partially accepted the narrow rule in the 1901 case of *Wofford v. Meeks*. Citing Justice Taft's decision in the Hallam case, the court said a newspaper publisher had to prove the truth of a charge that county commissioners were manipulating tax funds to favor political associations. This requirement of truth, the court said, was because the character of officials was attacked.[2] Otherwise, as in the 1910 case of *Advertiser Co. v. Jones*, the court appeared to lean toward the more liberal rule, stating there was a privilege to discuss officials so long as there was no malice.[3] Privilege, however, was not allowed in this case because corruption was charged. A newspaper had claimed a city street superintendent was using city crews and equipment to sell gravel for personal gain. It was not until 1913 that a decision specified, without qualification, that privilege extended only to comment or criticism on admitted or proven facts.[4] The ruling was in *Parsons* v. *Age-Herald Publishing Co.*, a suit brought by a constable who had been accused by a Birmingham newspaper, on the strength of a grand jury report, of preying on the poor.[5]

ARKANSAS

A newspaper claim that a county gravel commissioner was preying on the taxpayers led to a ruling on privilege by the Arkansas Supreme Court in 1910. And the Arkansas court rejected a plea that false statements about an official were privileged because they were communicated in good faith, with no malice and with belief in their truth.[6] The suit involved, *Murray* v. *Galbraith*, was filed after a Pine Bluff newspaper accused the commissioner of overcharging neighbors seven thousand dollars for gravel used in street paving. The article stated if such a profit was made in this transaction, it was reasonable to assume that there were other overcharges to the people by the gravel district. The overcharge claim proved false, and the case went to the state supreme court twice for consideration.

The court's second look at the case concerned the publisher's plea of honest belief in the facts published and lack of malice. While it was ruled that privilege did not extend to falsehoods, the court said belief in truth and good faith publication without malice could be considered in mitigating damages.[7] It was ruled, however, that motives could not be justification for libel. "Publication of a false article calling into question the integrity of another implies malice," the court said.[8] It was pointed out that the publisher could have waited on publication until his facts were verified and that the publication of false facts was at his peril.[9]

FLORIDA

Florida courts, too, had denied privilege for false statements in the nineteenth century, but there appeared to have been a reassessment of this view in the 1917 case of *McClellan* v. *L'Engle*. The Florida Supreme Court here held that an article ridiculing and ascribing distrust to a member of the United States House of Representatives was privileged unless both false and malicious.[10] The *Florida Metropolis* had called the representative a "grand stand player," a "turncoat" to Florida, and the "laughing stock" of Washington. While the court recognized the article as privileged, it said determination of malice was the job of the jury.

The privilege to communicate nonmalicious falsehoods, however, did not prevail. This was shown in a 1928 habeas corpus proceeding brought by a Florida newspaperman who had been arrested without charges for an alleged criminal libel against a candidate for the city commission. The supreme court, while releasing the newspaperman for lack of charges, made some pertinent observations concerning libel and the defense of privilege. The opinion stated that privilege to discuss officials and candidates did not give a right "to make false statements of fact, to attack the private character of public men, or falsely impute to them a want of loyalty or misconduct in office." [11] This more narrow rule of privilege continued to be expounded from the Florida bench, as was shown in the 1941 case of *Metropolis Co.* v. *Croasdell*. Here the court defined "libel per se" as a false and unprivileged publication, but it made it plain that false articles about officials were not privileged. A newspaper article falsely stating an assistant county engineer had been "cashiered" was held to be "libelous per se." [12]

ILLINOIS

In Illinois, it was consistently held that false charges affecting private character were without the realm of privilege. For instance, in 1876 it had been held in *Rearick* v. *Wilcox* that a charge of criminal action or moral delinquency reflected on private character and was not privileged.[13] On this basis, the Illinois Supreme Court declared in the 1909 case of *People* v. *Fuller* that a false article in the *Dixon Daily Sun* claiming a county treasurer had illegally "filched" public money was not privileged.[14] The case did uphold the right to fair comment and criticism of officials. But fair and reasonable criticism, it was ruled in a 1917 circuit court case involving William Randolph Hearst's *Chicago Examiner*, did not extend to any false statement of fact.[15] And the Illinois Supreme Court in

1919 substantiated the lower court decision that privilege did not extend to misstatements of fact. The case involved here, Ogren v. Rockford Star Printing Co., concerned newspaper advertisements that claimed a mayor on the Socialist ticket favored blowing up tenement houses. The court held that this was a malicious attack, going beyond the right of citizens to freely comment on and criticize officials' actions and conduct.[16] The law in Illinois defined libel as a malicious defamation. To refute malice, the court said facts had to be true and had to be published with good motives for justifiable ends.[17] It was no defense that the charges were mistakenly and honestly made.

The supreme court also ruled in 1943, in the criminal case of People v. Doss, that false charges of malfeasance made against a state's attorney were libelous.[18] The court again said that truth and good motives had to be proven or that privilege was abused.[19] Once more, in 1944, an Illinois appellate court for the fourth district held that false allegations of dishonesty made against an election canvassing board constituted facts that were not justified as fair comment and criticism.[20]

KENTUCKY

Despite a ruling of the Kentucky Court of Appeals shortly after the turn of the century that comment and criticism of an officer's conduct had to be based on facts, a plea of honest mistake was accepted as a defense. The requirement that facts be true was announced in Evening Post Co. v. Richardson in 1902, but the decision in the case extended privilege to a newspaper article that falsely charged an election officer with corruption in counting ballots.[21] The court declared the article privileged because it had been sent to the newspaper by an experienced journalist who was known for prudence and accuracy, leading the publisher to believe it true.[22] The election supervisor had to prove the publication was printed with malice, the court said, and this was a question for the jury.[23]

By 1918, however, with the decision in Democrat Publishing Co. v. Harvey, the Kentucky doctrine of fair comment was firm. The case arose after the Paducah News-Democrat severely criticized a state legislator for supposedly being in a fight in which a knife and gun were drawn. The court of appeals ruled that privilege extended to fair and reasonable criticism of public men's acts only if the factual statements were true.[24] A similar ruling came in a 1928 criminal case, which arose when the *Louisville Leader* and the *Louisville News* claimed a judge had become an active prosecutor in his court to bring about a "legal lynching" of Negroes being tried for rape.[25] The court held the articles accused the judge of gross misconduct and were false and libelous. While it was plain that privilege did not extend to misstatement of fact, the court in the very next year, 1929, stated the privilege did not extend to criticism unless it too was "bottomed on truth." [26] A newspaper had asked the removal of motorcycle policemen on the grounds that they were loafing each day at a particular corner. It was shown at the trial that the loafing charge was false, as the men had been assigned to the corner. The newspaper article was ruled libelous.

LOUISIANA

A similar imputation of corrupt motives, this one that public lands had been leased through official favoritism, brought the ruling in Louisiana that privilege extended to criticism but not to false facts. The favoritism charge was made by the *New Orleans Daily States* against the board of administrators of Tulane University, which had leased land others offered to buy to the son and nephew of the board president. The court in this 1909 case, *Levert v. Daily States Publishing Co.*, said there may have been an error in judgment but that the charge of favoritism was false.[27] Privilege was denied, and the article was declared libelous. Criticism, however, was upheld as privileged several times in the Louisiana Supreme Court. An article describing a detective as a "fly cop" and stating he pulled a "bonehead stunt" in an arrest was held in 1916 to be legitimate comment and criticism if printed without malice.[28] And in 1917, the Louisiana Supreme Court held that the *Daily Signal* of Crowley was within the bounds of proper criticism when it called the mayor the "self constituted champion of the red light." [29] The publication dealt with the mayor's action in vetoing a bill to abolish the red-light district, the court said, and his acts and their effects were open to criticism.[30]

Two World War II cases, both in 1943, also stressed that there was no "qualified privilege" to extend the discussion of officials to false statements of fact. The first, *Cadro v. Plaquemines Gazette*, denied privilege for a false statement that a member of a levee board had fled during a hurricane, leaving volunteers to strengthen the levee and protect property.[31] The second case arose when a deputy sheriff sued a woman who wrote a letter to a newspaper saying she saw the deputy shoot and kill a Negro who was surrendering. Though the Louisiana Supreme Court issued a split decision, it was held in *Martin* v. *Markley* that she had to justify the facts.[32] Comment on known or admitted facts was different than assertion of unsubstantiated facts, the court said, and privilege did not extend to false statements of fact.[33]

MAINE

While the Maine Supreme Judicial Court ruled in 1900 that the privilege of discussing public officials extended to falsehoods when there was probable cause for believing them true,[34] such a privilege was denied in 1915. In that year, in the slander case of *Pattangall* v. *Mooers*, the court refused to extend privilege to a voter's statement that a candidate for congress had received pay-offs to both pass and defeat a pending bill.[35] The court ruled that the law of privilege did not justify "a false charge of specific acts of culpable dishonesty against a candidate for office." [36] One can only speculate, from this limited decision, whether general charges of dishonesty would be privileged. Still there was an apparent switch, though perhaps not total, to the narrow rule of privilege.[37]

MARYLAND

The only specific rule concerning privilege in Maryland during the period through World War II was that announced in the 1883 case of *Negley* v. *Farrow*, that the imputation of corrupt motives to an official was not privileged.[38] In this case, the court had said that if anyone defamed the character of another, "it is no answer to say he did so in good faith, and without malice, honestly believing it to be true." [39] While the dicta were applied in this nineteenth-century case only to imputation of corrupt motives, it apparently was interpreted by Maryland judges in the twentieth century to mean that misstatements of facts were not privileged.

The Maryland Court of Appeals, however, in the 1902 case of *Kilgour* v. *Evening Star Newspaper Co.* said it was not libelous for a newspaper to state that citizens were aroused because a state's attorney had stifled an investigation of a baby's suspicious death. The article, which stated the official would not recommend payment of expenses for an autopsy, did not injure the official in his public position because it was not his duty to sanction autopsy payments, the court said. It was ruled that to be libelous, the article would have to contain statements that, if true, would disqualify him from office or render him less fit to fulfill his duties.[40]

Following this, in 1925, the court of appeals held that a libel action was appropriate for an article that falsely stated a judge rebuked a sheriff for an increase in "bootlegging" and for allowing a witness to be tampered with. The court said the statements imputed that the sheriff was unfit to hold office.[41] In this case, *Bowie v. Evening News*, the court declared that libel was any "unprivileged, false, and malicious publication" that held one up to public scorn, hatred, contempt, or ridicule.[42] There was no privilege for false publications concerning the official acts or conduct of public officials.

MASSACHUSETTS

The same rule, that privilege extended only to comment and criticism of officeholders, not to erroneous statements of fact, was upheld time and again by the Massachusetts Supreme Judicial Court. Following the precedent set in *Burt* v. *Advertiser Newspaper Co.*, privilege was denied in 1906 to a factual assertion in the *Boston Sunday Telegram* that the police superintendent there had five thousand dollars to "buy" an election for a city street superintendent candidate.[43] And in the case of *Commonwealth v. Pratt* in 1911, the court rejected a claim that false statements about candidates were privileged if there was probable cause for belief in their truth.[44] The rule of fair comment applied to officials and candidates alike, the court said.

MISSISSIPPI

Unlike the Massachusetts courts, the Mississippi Supreme Court was silent on privilege until 1910. But in that year, in the case of *Oakes* v. *State*, the court ruled that the privilege of commenting about officials did not extend to published falsehoods imputing crime or moral delinquency in the discharge of their public duties.[45]

The case arose from the publication of a handbill charging a circuit court judge with crimes. Such charges, the court said, had to be proved by truth and good motives.[46] Privilege was recognized, but false facts were libelous regardless of motives.

NEW JERSEY

Fair comment and criticism on true facts also was the doctrine of privilege followed by the New Jersey Court of Errors and Appeals, though this court at one time, in the World War I period, did switch to the liberal rule. The rule that prevailed through most of this period, however, was that which the court adopted in 1897, that falsehoods were not privileged. The 1897 decision came in *Benton v. State*, a criminal libel action brought when a newspaper article falsely accused a policeman of pocketing money he received from a prisoner's family to pay a fine. The court ruled that misstatement of fact, as opposed to criticism, could not be privileged even if published accidentally and with an honest belief in the truth.[47] But the privilege of criticism did extend to imputation of bad motives, the court ruled in a 1911 civil suit, if the criticism was based on actual conduct of officials. The court in this case, *Merrey v. Guardian Printing and Publishing Co.*, said that jurors determined when fair comment was exceeded.[48]

The court's World War I change in view came in 1917, in a criminal libel action brought against a newspaper for accusing a grand juror of protecting a swindler. The article was declared privileged provided it was published in good faith and in belief that the facts were true. The court said:

> The truth of the words is ordinarily a complete defense, and the doctrine of privilege rests usually, if not always, on the assumption that the words were untrue but excused.[49]

The doctrine of belief in truth apparently was upheld again in 1925 in the criminal libel case of *State v. Dedge*, when the court said libel, either civil or criminal, could be defended on the truth of the statement or on privilege.[50] A second switch in doctrines occurred in 1933, when the New Jersey Supreme Court held that a false charge of official misconduct was not privileged as fair comment and criticism.[51] Privilege, the court said, did not extend to inferences not based on actual facts. The case arose when the *Jersey Journal* claimed voters were being disenfranchised because they did not "bow to the knee" of a political leader.

NEW YORK

One of the more enlightening decisions concerning privilege during this period was issued by the New York Court of Appeals in 1911. The case involved, *Bingham* v. *Gaynor*, arose when a citizen wrote the mayor of New York City asking for the removal of a police commissioner on the grounds the commissioner was incompetent, corrupt, a despot, and lawless. The letter by itself, the court ruled, was privileged even if false, provided it was sent to the commissioner's superior officers in good faith with belief in truth.[52] But copies of the letter had been sent to the New York press before the mayor got it, and the court stated the resulting general circulation destroyed the qualified privilege the letter had as a private communication.[53] Facts in letters as well as articles published in newspapers had to be true, the court said, though there could be reasonable and justifiable comment and criticism based on facts. Even then, there was no privilege to make unjust inferences concerning private character, the court ruled.[54] Only the acts and public conduct of officials were subject to fair comment, not personal attacks on private character.[55]

Still, criticism of public acts was not libelous, no matter how severe or ridiculous, if not written maliciously, the New York Court of Appeals ruled in a 1930 case concerning a high school football coach. The court applied the public official privilege rules to the coach, stating that he was "paid out of the public treasury, holds a semi-official position and trains the boys for public exhibits and contests." [56] The suit had been brought by the coach because of a newspaper article condemning him. The article claimed he apparently lacked fundamental knowledge of football, judging from outmoded plays used by the team. Though the newspaper attack was alleged by the coach to be malicious, the court said malice could be shown only if the coach proved "personal spite or ill will" or "culpable recklessness or negligence" on the part of the reporter.[57] The court made it plain that it felt the article was honest criticism, but it stated the jury did have a right to determine whether the article abused privilege by attacking the coach's professional capacity as a physical education teacher.[58]

In 1939 the New York Supreme Court, in the case of *Cohalan v. New York Tribune*, again upheld the fair comment and criticism rule so long as facts stated were true and there was no imputation of corrupt motives.[59] The case involved severe criticism of a judge. And in the 1941 case of *Hall v. Binghamton Press Co.*, it was held that everyone had a right to criticize the acts of officials so long as there were no attacks on private character or imputation of unworthy motives. Heavy criticism of Congressman Edwin A. Hall's vote against the lend-lease bill prior to World War II was excused as opinion. The criticism included a charge that he had misrepresented his district and was not acting in the best interests of the United States. Instead, the article said, he represented "weak-kneed, jelly bellied . . . parasited . . . mugwumps who are merely using the country." [60] The court, in saying that no libel was involved, pointed out that the division of sentiment on national policy during this war period warranted wide extension of the fair comment doctrine.

NORTH DAKOTA

The narrow rule of privilege was upheld in three early twentieth century decisions by the North Dakota Supreme Court, but in each the justices were split three-to-two in their opinions.[61] The decisions came in the immediate post–World War I period and were climaxed by the 1920 case of *Langer v. The Courier-News*. In this case, the court denied a newspaper publisher's plea of privilege for false charges that the state's attorney general asked to be custodian of a voting group's "slush funds." The majority of the court held that the term "slush funds" has the connotation of evil and that the false charge along with other false statements of fact were not privileged.[62] The two judges issuing minority opinions did not discuss privilege, but they claimed the decision was destructive of press freedom. Nevertheless, the majority view became recognized law in North Dakota.

In World War II, the court refused to consider a claim of privilege on a review of a requested demurrer. A taxpayers group, which had accused a sheriff of taking money for travel he did not do and for prisoners' meals he did not serve, had asked that the suit be dismissed because of honest belief in the accuracy of the statements, which were taken from city and county records. The court said this was not a proper subject for demurrer, however, as privilege was a matter of defense in the trial itself.[63] The last ruling of the court, then, was that misstatements of fact were not privileged.

OHIO, TENNESSEE, AND HAWAII

Though there were no Ohio Supreme Court decisions on privilege during this period, lower courts in the state continued to hold that privilege did not extend to factual allegations.[64] The rule of law in Tennessee also was dated, having been expressed in the 1885 case of *Banner Publishing Co. v. State.*[65] While this case denied privilege to false statements, the court had voiced an inclination not to be severe with publishers when publications were bona fide and made without malice. Still, the limit was fair comment, not false charges. And in the territory of Hawaii, it was held at the end of World War II, in 1945, that the privilege to make critical comments did not include the right to make false statements of fact.[66]

OREGON

The Oregon Supreme Court, in the case of *Peck v. Coos Bay Times Publishing Co.*, also held that fair comment could not be used as an excuse to charge facts that defamed.[67] A newspaper article identified a political boss as a member of the Ku Klux Klan and stated he was a "double-crosser in politics" who built his power on hate. The court, upholding the right of comment, said that when a man "enters the political arena, even though not a candidate, he must not be sensitive about criticism." [68] One could question whether comment, as opposed to factual allegations, was involved; however, the article also charged the politician with a vicious assault. The court said truth was the only defense for the factual charge as privilege ended where defamation began.[69]

SOUTH CAROLINA

Defamation began in South Carolina with false statements of fact, the supreme court there ruled in 1935. The case arose because of a report in the *Columbia Record* about a political rally in which rival candidates for the state legislature were critical of each other.

One candidate, after referring to two incumbent members of the county delegation to the legislature, said the county had failed to get roads and bridges and asked: "Who got the money?" [70] He also said one of the members of the delegation had organized a "gigantic steal" from women and children and that one was "hogging" a water power company.[71] One of the candidates for senator, Tillman Jackson, brought the suit, claiming the charges were false and imputed that he bargained away the rights of the county. The South Carolina Supreme Court ruled that the newspaper was reporting a public meeting, making the occasion quasi-privileged.[72] The report, the court said, was substantially correct. Further, there was no proof of express malice, so there was no libel. However, the court did say that privilege did not protect false charges or statements volunteered by the newspaper that imputed crime or brought officials into the public's hatred, contempt, or ridicule.[73]

VERMONT

A charge of bribery resulted in the adoption of the narrow view of privilege by the Vermont Supreme Court. The charge was made in a circular, distributed to voters during an election, that claimed a state's attorney had been paid off. In the resulting criminal libel case, *State* v. *Colby*, the court held in 1924 that false charges of criminal misconduct against a candidate could not be justified on the grounds they were made in good faith. The court added that it adopted the "narrow view" that freedom of discussion did not extend to "false facts," in either civil or criminal cases.[74]

VIRGINIA

Money also figured in the 1912 case of *Williams Printing Co.* v. *Saunders*, in which the Virginia Supreme Court of Appeals rejected privilege for misstatements of fact. This case resulted from a charge in the periodical, the *Idea*, that a candidate for the Democratic Executive Committee was buying votes. The court ruled that statements had to be true, though there was a qualified privilege to comment on both the character and qualifications of candidates for office.[75] This privilege did not extend, the court said, to imputation of bad motives or to reflection on private character not associated with the office.[76] Further, the court stated that jurors determined when privilege was abused, though it was the job of the court to first decide if privilege existed.[77]

Despite this 1912 ruling, it was not until 1918 that the Virginia Supreme Court of Appeals specifically declared that it accepted the "narrow view" concerning privilege. The statement came in *Carpenter v. Meredith*.[78] The suit arose when a county treasurer was accused of bribery and theft, and the Virginia court said this imputation of criminal dishonesty was not privileged.

WASHINGTON

The Washington Supreme Court in 1909 refused to extend privilege to false statements in the *Spokesman-Review*, which charged a city inspector with favoritism in allowing some contractors leeway in meeting sidewalks specifications.[79] And in 1914 the court said that in addition to charges of improper conduct in office, charges of crime and nonfeasance in office were not privileged.[80] Four years later, in *McKillip v. Grays Harbor Publishing Co.*, the court said that in all cases comments, not false facts, were privileged.[81] The case involved an advertisement wherein a candidate for county superintendent of schools was charged with waging a campaign of lies. Such advertisements were the responsibility of newspapers printing them, the court ruled, and charges of moral depravity had to be proven by truth.[82] Proof of truth also was necessary for charges of crime, as was shown in a 1925 suit brought by a policeman. A newspaper, apparently by mistake, had listed the officer as being involved with other policemen in criminal conduct. The court in this case, *Graham v. Star Publishing Co.*, declared the article libelous, stating that privilege "ends where falsity begins." [83]

WISCONSIN

The Wisconsin Supreme Court held to the same rule, though there appeared to be some maneuverability as to the point where falsity began. For instance, in 1912, the court held that factual conclusions were qualifiedly privileged as discussion, provided the conclusions arose from more serious charges that were true.[84] The court again stated in 1916 that privilege applied when the substance of the charge proved true.[85] It was this 1916 decision, *Putnam v. Browne*, that overruled a lower court decision allowing privilege for factual accusations that a county judge candidate administered a "slush fund" and sold his political influence for money.[86] The supreme court said privilege did not extend to statements of fact or to insults and jibes. Later decisions of the court consistently held to this view.[87] But it perhaps was best summed up in the 1929 case of *Lukaszewicz* v. *Dziadulewicz*, which was brought by a candidate for alderman. A newspaper had accused him of growing fat selling bakery goods at wartime prices while his opponent lay on the battlefield wounded. The court stated:

> It is thoroughly established that discussions of the qualifications and fitness of candidates for public offices are conditionally privileged. Such discussions, however, must be confined to truthful statements. They must not malign, falsify, insult, or hold up to public hatred, contempt, or ridicule, but comment may be caustic and severe when confined to facts.[88]

The court, in saying that criticism could be severe, apparently meant just that. In 1932, a highway commissioner sued a newspaper for allegedly libeling him in an article claiming drainage ditches had been built beside the highway for murder.[89] The article referred to the "highwayman" who "dug killing ditches beside the road." It was declared privileged, though the court said it was a borderline case. "We feel that in doubtful cases, the doubt should be resolved in favor of free criticism and discussion," the court said.[90] Along this line, the court held in the 1941 case of *Hoan* v. *Journal Co.* that it was not libelous to blame a mayor for the lack of control on repeated bombings in Milwaukee.[91] This was criticism based on facts.

The Independent View: A *Middle Ground*

Many jurisdictions, in allowing the greatest possible freedom of discussion about public officials, deviated in some measure from the strict doctrine that privilege did not extend to falsehoods. Some state courts accepted the narrow rule of privilege where charges of crime were involved, but they apparently left room for a more liberal interpretation of privilege in other cases. Additional jurisdictions adopted what has been referred to as the public officer's rule,[92] refusing to extend privilege to misstatements of fact only when the false charges were grounds for removal of the officials involved.

Courts in two states presumed articles about officials were true until proven false. And the decisions of still other state courts simply did not clearly define privilege. The jurisdictions falling into this middle area included Delaware, the District of Columbia, Georgia, Indiana, Missouri, Oklahoma, Texas, and Wyoming.

DELAWARE

The Delaware Supreme Court in 1904 rendered a judgment that was typical of those issued by state courts that did not fully subscribe to the narrow rule of privilege. The judgment came in *Donahoe v. Star Publishing Co.*, a suit brought by legislator John P. Donahoe against the *Wilmington Star*. The newspaper charged in an article that Donahoe had joined a "disgraceful conspiracy" to trade his vote for United States senator for a cash payment from the gas interests. The court said this was a charge of bribery.[93] And false charges alleging a criminal offense, the court said, were not privileged even if made in good faith and on probable cause.[94]

The court, however, restricted the decision to allegations of crime. Stating a charge of crime was the only question to be determined, the court said:

> If . . . we were asked to hold that no allegations of fact charging a candidate with disgraceful acts, whether criminal or not criminal, are privileged . . . we might deem it necessary to extend the discussion further, and analyze the whole subject exhaustively.[95]

The court, then, left in question whether false statements concerning matters other than criminal charges would be privileged. The narrow view, restricting privilege only to comment and criticism but not false charges, was accepted only when officials were charged with crime. There were no other appellate court cases on the subject of privilege in Delaware through World War II.

DISTRICT OF COLUMBIA

A middle course between the two rules of privilege also was taken by the United States Court of Appeals for the District of Columbia. But the decision to do this was delayed until World War II, and it varied considerably from the court's 1936 holding in *Washington Times Co.* v. *Bonner* that privilege did not exist for misstatements of fact.[96] This 1936 case arose when the *Washington Times* printed charges of misconduct against an executive secretary of the Federal Power Commission, stating he had taken commission files relating to his appointment. The newspaper charges, which claimed the missing files showed the secretary was "slipped" into the post by power companies, were based on a complaint made to the secretary's superiors by a file clerk. The court declined to rule whether proceedings of a federal executive department hearing were privileged, but said even if they were, the newspaper had no right to enlarge on the charges as it did.[97] Quoting the *Post Publishing Co. v. Hallam* case, the court said the great weight of authority favored the "majority view" that privilege did not extend to misstatements of fact.[98] And this rule was affirmed, at this time, for the District of Columbia.

Six years later, however, in the 1942 case of *Sweeney v. Patterson*, the court changed its view. The suit was brought by Congressman Martin L. Sweeney against the *Washington Times Herald* as a result of a Drew Pearson column stating Sweeney opposed appointment of a federal judge because he was "a Jew, and one not born in the United States." The court of appeals said the claim was not "libelous *per se*" even if false. It added:

> In our view it is not actionable to publish erroneous and injurious statements of fact and injurious comment and opinion regarding political conduct and views of public officials, so long as no charge of crime, corruption, gross immorality or gross incompetence is made and no special damage results.[99]

Falsehoods, then, were privileged when discussing officials and candidates except when crime or "gross" immorality and incompetence was involved.

The rationale of the court in this case, which occurred in the midst of World War II, perhaps showed the feelings of the time. The opinion included the following words:

> Cases which impose liability for erroneous reports of the political conduct of officials reflect the obsolete doctrine that the governed must not criticize the governors. . . . The interest of the public here outweighs the interest of appellants or any other individual. The protection of the public requires not merely discussion, but information. . . . Errors of fact, particularly in regard to a man's mental state and processes, are inevitable. Information and discus-

sion will be discouraged, and the public interest in public knowledge of important facts will be poorly defended, if error subjects its writer to a libel suit, even without a showing of economic loss. Whatever is added to the field of libel is taken from the field of free debate.[100]

This decision, at least partially, rejected Justice Taft's reasoning in *Post Publishing Co. v. Hallam*, that too much liberality in publications would keep good men from seeking office. Still, the rule adopted did not fully subscribe to the liberal doctrine that all facts were privileged if communicated without malice and with probable cause for belief in truth.

GEORGIA

The Georgia courts also switched back and forth in their opinions. For instance, Georgia Supreme Court decisions in the 1890s clearly held that false statements were privileged when published without malice or in belief that they were true.[101] In 1911, however, a lesser court of appeals in Georgia, in *Lowe v. News Publishing Co.*, ruled that statements of fact had to be true.[102] The appeals court decision apparently had little influence on the supreme court, however, as was shown in that court's 1925 opinion in the case of *McIntosh v. Williams*. This suit was brought by a county commissioner who had been accused in a circular of spending county money to hire mules when mules were available free and of depositing county money at less interest than could be obtained. The supreme court ruled that the circular was privileged. A taxpayer in protecting his interest, the court said, could make statements about officials that were either true or that were made in good faith without malice.[103]

Despite the supreme court's ruling, the court of appeals in the 1928 case of *Kirkland v. Constitution Publishing Co.* denied privilege for a nonmalicious newspaper charge that a state oil inspector had not paid fee collections to the state treasury when due. The newspaper claimed good faith since the article was based on a statement made by Governor Herman Talmadge.

But the appellate court said repetition of Governor Talmadge's statement was libelous as it charged the inspector, a woman, with misconduct in office. Further, the court, citing the 1910 civil code, stated privilege did not extend to libelous statements, as distinguished from comment, about a "public official as respects his conduct in office." [104] The decision was reviewed by the state supreme court but justices were divided evenly.[105] As a result, the court of appeals judgment was automatically approved.

Other than in the split decision of the Kirkland case, the Georgia Supreme Court during this period was consistent in holding that privilege extended to nonmalicious falsehoods about officials. The court of appeals regularly held to the narrow view, that misstatements of fact were not privileged. It would appear from the 1928 case, the last on the subject during this period, that the more narrow rule prevailed. Still, this could not be asserted with assurance because of the court's inability to reach a consensus. The law of privilege in Georgia was left uncertain.

INDIANA

The Indiana Supreme Court without doubt entered the twentieth century adhering to the doctrine, in both civil and criminal cases, that false reports about officials were libelous.[106] However, the supreme court included dictum in the criminal libel suit of *Cummings* v. *State* in 1929 as follows: "Any false publications maliciously made, when imputing official dishonesty and corruption in office, constitutes criminal libel." [107] This would indicate that statements, even those claiming corruption, had to be both false and malicious before the publisher could be found guilty of libel.

But the case did not turn on this point. It involved an article in a Chicago newspaper based on an affidavit that had been meant for an attorney. The affidavit stated a judge and prosecutor led a mob consisting of Ku Klux Klansmen into a man's house, threatened to shoot the man's son, and left the son's wife in shock, from which she died. The court ruled that these statements could not be the basis of a libel charge and that the individual given the affidavit could not be held responsible for libelous statements made by the Chicago newspaper.[108] While the opinion pointed to the liberal rule requiring proof of malice as well as falsity in statements concerning officials, there was no mention of qualified privilege. Nor was there precedent concerning privilege in Indiana cases.

MISSOURI

Precedents for privilege were many in Missouri. The right to comment and criticize allowed inferences as to motives, whether "right or wrong, reasonable or unreasonable, provided they are made in good faith and based upon the truth." [109] But unlike other states denying privilege for falsehoods, Missouri required that public officials prove statements false rather than requiring newspapermen to prove them true. This was an independent view.

The privilege of making fair comments and criticism about the acts and conduct of officials first was approved by the Missouri Supreme Court in 1909. The judgment, in *Branch v. Publishers: George Knapp & Co.*, came as a result of a suit brought over an interpretative article in the *St. Louis Republic*. The article asserted that State Assemblyman Grover C. Branch switched his support to a candidate for United States senator because of hospitalities offered by the candidate. The court said this was fair comment as Branch had spent two nights in St. Louis as the candidate's guest prior to the announcement.[110] The same doctrine of fair comment was extended a year later to the chairman of a Democratic Central Committee in Missouri, a man described by the court as a "quasi public official." [111] Then, in 1913, the court, in *Walsh v. Pulitzer Publishing Co.*, ruled that while a "lie is never privileged," newspapers have both a right and duty to discuss the fitness of candidates "either by analysis of . . . individual qualifications or by comparison with other candidates." [112] It was not libel, the court said, for the *Post-Dispatch* to claim an attorney engaged in criminal law practice could have no proper motive for seeking the circuit attorney's post.[113]

The fair comment doctrine in Missouri was best summed up, however, in a 1919 case brought by the warden of the state penitentiary, Dickerson McClung, against the *St. Louis Post-Dispatch*. The newspaper, after printing a convict's letter stating prisoners were being whipped and tortured, criticized McClung's policies and asked for reforms. It carried one article about a prisoner being hung by his hands for hours in an attempt to get information from him. The court, noting that testimony showed statements in the articles to be substantially true, ruled that McClung and the prison were matters of public interest to be commented on with privilege.[114] Privilege, it was ruled, was a question for the court, not a jury.

Further, when articles were privileged, the court said, officials bringing suit had to prove them either false or malicious.[115] The warden claimed the prisoner had not been hung by his hands to get information but rather for punishment. But the court said either good or bad motives could be attributed to officials when several motives were warranted by the facts.[116]

In 1927 and again in 1944, the Missouri Supreme Court reasserted that the burden was on officials to prove either falsity or express malice when privileged publications were challenged. And in each of these cases, *State ex rel Zorn v. Cox* and *Kleinschmidt v. Johnson*, substantial truth of statements was deemed sufficient. In the 1944 Kleinschmidt case, the court said that it was not necessary that the article, accusing a candidate for circuit judge of permitting gambling while serving as prosecuting attorney, be literally true as slight inaccuracies were immaterial.[117] Officials and candidates, the court said, were not entitled to the presumption that comments or criticism was based on false information. Falsity had to be proved.[118]

OKLAHOMA

The Oklahoma Supreme Court in 1923 followed the Missouri precedent by placing the burden on officials to prove the falsity of articles about their acts and conduct. The decision came in a case brought against the *Oklahoma City Times* by the superintendent of state institutions for the feebleminded. The newspaper had printed an article claiming that the superintendent instructed his employees to herd inmates like hogs and that imbeciles "die of influenza, inadequately treated." [119] The court ruled that the privilege to criticize public officials' acts did not extend to the publication of false statements. However, if officials could not prove statements in privileged articles untrue, the court said, publishers could not be held responsible for libel.[120]

The same rule was announced in the 1927 case of *Oklahoma Publishing Co. v. Tucker.*[121] This case concerned newspaper criticism of a peace justice's conduct in fining traffic violators. But the justice of the peace proved that the charge around which the criticism was built, that he had pocketed a fine, was false. He collected a one-thousand-dollar judgment.

The Oklahoma Supreme Court did not stop with requiring

public officials to prove falsity. In *Holway* v. *World* in 1935, the court made the following statement:

> In regard to matters of public interest, all that is necessary to render the words spoken or published privileged is that they should be communicated in good faith, without malice, to those who have an interest in the subject matter to which they refer, and in an honest belief that the communication is true, such belief being founded on reasonable and probable ground.[122]

The court made it clear, however, that the privilege did not extend to false imputations of crime.[123] In the case at issue, the court allowed the privilege for criticism of an engineer hired by a municipal water district because he was claiming the confidence of the public and seeking possession of public funds for services rendered.

Oklahoma, then, had a rather wide freedom of discussion. Public officials had to prove that allegedly libelous statements were false. And falsehoods about public officials even then were privileged, provided there was no charge of crime and provided publishers had probable cause for believing the falsehoods true.

TEXAS

The Texas courts during this period definitely shifted from their more liberal view of the nineteenth century but finally settled on a rule of privilege similar to that of Oklahoma. Though there was much contrary dictum in the lesser courts of civil appeals concerning privilege in Texas, the judgments of the courts of final jurisdiction were fairly consistent in granting considerably leeway for false statements concerning officials. Both the Texas Supreme Court and its special auxiliary, the Texas Commission of Appeals,[124] held to the doctrine that only those false statements which would be grounds for an official's removal were not privileged.

The doctrine that proper cause for belief in truth excused falsehoods about fitness of candidates and officials, promulgated in *Express Printing Co.* v. *Copeland* in 1885, was supplanted by the more narrow rule of privilege in the 1923 Texas Supreme Court decision in *A. H. Belo & Co.* v. *Looney.* The suit resulted from an article in the *Dallas Morning News* accusing the attorney general of bringing antitrust suits to drive some oil companies out of Texas, leaving others untouched.[125] The court ruled that imputation of corrupt motives to the attorney general was not fair comment but rather a statement of fact that was not privileged.[126]

However, the Texas Commission of Appeals, sitting as a court of final jurisdiction in 1924, said in the case *Webster* v. *Nunn* that misstatements of fact, so long as they were not cause for an official's removal, were accepted as privileged. The case arose when a newspaper, the *Amarillo Daily News*, stated a city secretary "robbed" his chief clerk, a woman, of a job to make way for a man. The court said this was privileged, even though false, because it was not such a charge, that, if true, would be the cause of the secretary's removal. Because it was privileged, the court said, the burden was on the plaintiff official to show actual malice. The case reversed a lower civil appeals court decision that statements made in the body of the article had to be true. Truth, the commission said, was a perfect defense, and a perfect defense was not necessary for a defense of privilege.[127]

Following this decision, two of the intermediate courts of appeals held that statements of criticism had to be grounds for removal from office before actionable without privilege.[128] The doctrine was reaffirmed by the Texas Commission of Appeals in 1929, in *Ferguson* v. *Houston Press Co.*, though this case did deal with charges of nepotism that were grounds for removal.[129] Additionally, the commission in 1932 held again that imputation of corrupt motives could be considered a statement that was grounds for removal.[130]

Even if statements were grounds for removal, substantial truth was sufficient to defeat libel.[131] For instance, a charge that an official had wasted $80,000 of the taxpayers' money on useless projects was not considered libelous when it was proved that only $17,500 had been spent.[132] This was considered substantial truth. Still, the court of criminal appeals, the court of final jurisdiction on criminal matters in Texas, held in 1941 that publishers have a duty to investigate to determine if information is true.[133] In this case, *Yecker* v. *State*, a circular falsely claimed a candidate for constable had a criminal record. The man with the record was someone else with a similar name. Though the publication apparently was made in good faith, the circular was declared libelous.

The defense of privilege in Texas for this period was best described in a 1941 decision of the federal district court for the southern district of the state. The case involved, *Sweeney v. Caller-Times Publishing Co.*, was one of the many libel suits brought by Ohio congressman Martin Sweeney over a Drew Pearson column. The column stated Sweeney was a spokesman for Father Charles E. Coughlin and was leading an effort to prevent the appointment of a foreign-born Jew to a federal judgeship in Cleveland.

The decision, based on Texas law, was rendered by Federal District Judge James Allred, a former governor of Texas. He held that articles which hurt officials' feelings were not libelous, as officials were legitimate subjects of news and comment.[134] Further, he said Texas law gave newspapers freedom to criticize and comment about government officials or candidates so long as there were no false charges that were grounds for removal from office.[135] The fact that the congressman opposed the proposed appointee did not make the congressman guilty of misconduct in office, Judge Allred said, as a representative has no duty to appoint a federal judge. He also said it was never libel to accuse an official of favoring or opposing legislation where opposite views prevailed.

More important, perhaps, he ruled that while newspapers could not ascribe corrupt motives to officials, they did not have to wait for facts to be established before there was a privilege to report on and comment about officials' acts "and other matters of public concern for general information." [136] There was, then, liberality concerning false charges in Texas. The state had adopted, in effect, the public officer's rule, which meant that falsehoods about an officer's public conduct that would cause removal were not privileged. Still, some falsehoods were sanctioned. The privilege of comment and criticism was somewhat different in Texas from that in states adhering strictly to either the liberal or narrow rules of privilege.

WYOMING

Wyoming, too, modified the doctrine of privilege. The Wyoming Supreme Court accepted the liberal rule in the 1915 case of *Kutcher v. Post Printing Co.* The suit was filed when the *Sheridan Post* printed an article entitled "Dive Reopens" that was critical of the mayor. The article asked the mayor whether he had misrepresented his actions in regard to closing the club, whether he was not sincere in his duties, or whether he was not partial in protection of someone in unlawful conduct. The Wyoming court held that the article imputed want of integrity or dereliction of duty and was libelous per se.[137] The court ruled, however, that false publications were privileged when made in good faith and without malice.[138] Limitations to this rule were announced in *Nicholson* v. *State*, a 1916 criminal case. The court here held that false charges of crime or malfeasance in office, even though they were made in good faith, were not privileged.[139] Wyoming, like Texas, apparently stabilized its doctrine of privilege around the public officer's rule.

The Minority View: *Honest Belief in Truth*

Courts in sixteen states adopted the liberal rule of privilege before the close of World War II. Courts in these states excused false statements about officials that ordinarily would be libelous, provided the statements were published without malice and with probable cause for believing them true. The states following this doctrine, so forcefully advanced in the Kansas case of *Coleman* v. *MacLennan*,[140] included Arizona, California, Colorado, Connecticut, Iowa, Kansas, Michigan, Minnesota, Montana, Nebraska, New Hampshire, North Carolina, Pennsylvania, South Dakota, Utah, and West Virginia.

ARIZONA

Like the courts in many of the other states adopting the liberal rule of privilege, the Arizona Supreme Court originally did not extend privilege to falsehoods. This was shown in the 1919 case of *Arizona Publishing Co.* v. *Harris*, which resulted when the *Arizona Republican* claimed the state's adjutant general's resignation would be asked because he had made strike reports that had been characterized as seditious. The governor testified at the trial that he asked for the resignation only because there was no need for an adjutant general after the First Arizona Regiment went into federal service during World War I.[141] The court held that the newspaper could not escape liability for libel on the plea that the false statement was made in good faith and without malice.[142] While officials and candidates were subject to fair comment and criticism, the court said, "it is the truth when published, and not falsehood, that is privileged." [143] A definite shift came in the 1934 case of *Conner* v.

Timothy, when the Arizona Supreme Court embraced the more liberal view of privilege. The case was brought by a school teacher who had been accused of taking school dance money for his personal use and of drinking with a student. The court said:

> It is true that statements respecting political affairs, public officers, and candidates for office are in a measure privileged, for one who seeks public office waives his right of privacy, so that he cannot object to any proper investigation into the conduct of his private life which will throw light on the question as to whether the public, which bestows upon him the office which he seeks, shall elect him or not, and a charge made in good faith against such candidate, which affects his fitness for the office which he seeks, is privileged even though untrue.[144]

The rule, the court said, did not apply to the teacher, who was not a candidate nor in a job depending on the vote of the people. It did apply to one of the teacher's supporters, who was a candidate for the public office of school trustee.

CALIFORNIA

California, too, adhered to the narrow view of fair comment and criticism until after World War I. It was in 1921 in the case of *Snively v. Record Publishing Co.* that the California Supreme Court held that falsehoods about officials and candidates were privileged if communicated in good faith and without malice. The suit was brought against the *Los Angeles Record* by Police Chief C. E. Snively as a result of a cartoon showing the chief speaking with his hand at his back receiving money. The court said the cartoon was "clearly libelous," but remanded the case for retrial to determine if it should be excused by privilege.[145]

Privilege, the court said in this case, consisted of communicating without malice. It added that since newspapers have a right and duty to inform the people about officials, there are reasonable grounds for supposing the motive of publication to be innocent.[146] It also was ruled that privilege was not diminished because the chief was appointed. Denial to privilege for newspaper articles concerning appointed officials, the court said, was the "result of ancient decisions made before the effect of popular government became fully appreciated." [147] Later decisions of the California Court of Appeals emphasized that privilege did not extend to officials' private lives and that newspapers and citizens had the same right of privileged discussion.[148]

This was clarified in a 1943 decision which held that newspaper and magazine articles about public officials were privileged because they were communicated by interested individuals to other individuals who also were interested. The ruling came in *Harris* v. *Curtis Publishing Co.* after the *Saturday Evening Post* had printed an article about the Laguna Beach school board president's reasons for not having a students' savings bank system in school. There was no malice, the court said, as the publishers had cause for believing the false statements true.[149] Further, the court said, no one associated with the magazine publication even knew the officials, and there could not have been ill will or actual malice.[150]

COLORADO

The privilege to discuss the public lives of public officials and candidates for office was considered by the Colorado Supreme Court in 1944, when a libel case was brought by a candidate for governor, George J. Knapp, against the *Denver Post*. The court's decision in this case, *Knapp* v. *Post Printing and Publishing Co.*, indicated that it adopted the liberal rule, that privilege extended to falsehoods if uttered without malice. The newspaper had listed all the candidates for governor and stated that Knapp was not qualified. The court said the statement was not libelous in itself and added:

> It is one of the hazards which a candidate for public favor must face that he is exposed to critical, and perhaps unjust, comments, but these, unless they transcend the bounds of what the law permits, must be born for the sake of maintaining a free press.[151]

As to the bounds of what the law permitted, the court quoted the liberal precedent in the Kansas case of *Coleman* v. *MacLennan* in asserting specifically that falsehood and malice had to be shown.[152] Candidates and officials, according to the opinion, were different from private individuals. They invited public trial of their qualifications, honesty, integrity, and fitness for service. Still, privilege itself was not an issue in the case. The court simply stated that it subscribed to the liberal rule.

CONNECTICUT

The liberal rule of privilege, even with a charge of crime, was recognized by the Connecticut Supreme Court of Errors in the 1918 case of *Moynahan v. Waterbury Republican*. The court said, however, that the publisher had to prove the "occasion of privilege." This could be done by showing that false information about an official was obtained in the regular course of business and published in good faith and without malice, in honest belief that it was true.[153] When privilege was shown, the court said, the official bringing the suit had the burden of proving malice in fact.[154] The decision came in a suit brought by the superintendent of a city poorhouse because a newspaper printed a nurse's charge that he unlawfully appropriated public funds for his own use and gave unwholesome food to indigents. The trial court found that the publisher had acted with malice and consequently did not successfully prove an "occasion of privilege." The finding was upheld by the supreme court, which said evidence of malice warranted the decision, as the false article apparently was "made recklessly and without sufficient excuse."[155]

IOWA

There was absolutely no excuse for attacks on the private character of officials the Iowa Supreme Court ruled in the 1913 case of *Ott v. Murphy*. This case resulted when the *Dubuque Telegraph Herald* published an article about a past political figure, stated beer "flowed like water" in his last campaign, and claimed that if he was elected mayor there would be a tax increase. The court, noting that the onetime politician was not even a candidate for the mayor's office, stated that he was not subject to comment or criticism for "all time in the future" simply because he once was a candidate.[156] Perhaps this 1913 case prohibiting attacks on private character was more notable, however, for the adoption of the narrow rule that comment and criticism had to be based on truth.[157] But the narrow rule held for only two years.

Iowa's supreme court ruled in 1915 in *Children v. Shinn* that a newspaper article about a county supervisor running for reelection was privileged, even if false, provided it was published without malice, solely to inform voters, and with belief in its truth.[158] The article, in the *Oakland Acorn*, had accused the official of violating the law in constructing a bridge. While this case concerned a man seeking election, the court ruled in 1922 that the same privilege applied to discussion of officials who were not candidates. The 1922 case, *Salinger v. Cowles*, involved a statement in the *Des Moines Register* that a supreme court justice, B. I. Salinger, had forced a railroad with a suit pending before the court to hire a particular person. Evidence showed the publisher's belief was based on rumors, but the supreme court ruled that there was no liability for libel unless express malice was shown.[159] The criticism was so closely related to the judge's public office that it was qualifiedly privileged, the court said. But the supreme court again ruled in 1928, when a newspaper article referred to a town marshall as ignorant and as being a ruffian, that attacks on private character transcended the right of legitimate criticism.[160]

KANSAS

The Kansas case of *Coleman v. MacLennan*[161] in 1908 was followed by a number of other Kansas Supreme Court cases holding to the liberal rule of privilege. In 1919, for instance, it was ruled in *Carver v. Greason* that privilege extended to an article charging a county attorney with failure to fulfill his duty of investigating the records of accused criminals.[162] Officials had to show express malice when defendants claimed false articles were published in good faith, the court said. Another case involving a woman county attorney, *Steenson v. Wallace*, resulted when the *Larned Tiller and Toiler* reported that she had refused to approve mileage allowances for other county officers but had sanctioned these "illegal fees" for her own transportation.[163] The Kansas Supreme Court held the article did not impute commission of a crime by the use of the word illegal, that the article was privileged, and that the official had to prove express malice before the newspaper article could be found libelous.

MICHIGAN

Malice, defined in Michigan as "willful injury without just reason," also had to be shown in that state before damages could be collected on privileged communications. This rule was announced by the Michigan Supreme Court in the 1909 case of *Lawrence v. Herald Publishing Co.* The case arose when a mayor of Grand

Rapids was quoted in the press as accusing a former police commissioner of establishing a license control system for saloons so that money could be extorted for election purposes. The court ruled that the mayor's statement was privileged unless it was false and malicious and made without good motives. If there was no foundation for the belief of the statements, the court said, there could be no privilege.[164] Three years later, in 1912, the court said:

> Qualified privilege extends to all communications made *bona fide* upon any subject matter in which the party communicating has an interest, or in reference to which he has a duty, to a person having a corresponding interest or duty.[165]

Bona fide publications already had been ruled as those communicated in good faith, without malice and with reason for believing them true.

But a more narrow view of privilege appeared to be sanctioned by the Michigan Supreme Court in 1921. The occasion was a suit brought by a mayor for a newspaper article which claimed he wasted one hundred thousand dollars of city money on a rush contract after he was defeated for election and before he was replaced. The court ruled in this case, *Moore v. Booth Publishing Co.*, that the publication was not libelous. Still, the opinion included dictum that privilege to discuss public officials was limited and did not extend to false statements or imputations of unworthy motives.[166] Despite this declaration, the court returned to the more liberal rule in 1931, with the decision in *Poleski v. Polish American Publishing Co.* The suit was filed by a candidate for community council. A newspaper article called him a political swindler who conspired with the Ku Klux Klansmen against his Polish public. The court said:

> Where, as in this case, the publication is qualifiedly privileged, it is not actionable unless made in bad faith, or with actual malice, or without reasonable cause to believe it true.[167]

The court, however, found that the publication was malicious and made in bad faith, since the newspaper, the *Polish Daily News*, was published by a rival candidate for the community council post.

MINNESOTA

Falsehoods about officials also had to be malicious in Minnesota to be libelous, and the Minnesota Supreme Court said in 1901 that malice could be defeated by a publisher's belief in truth. The decision in this criminal libel case, *State* v. *Ford*, specified that neither rumor, suspicion, nor gossip was proper cause for a publisher to believe in the truth of a false article he published about a mental institution superintendent.[168] The liberal rule of privilege was clarified and crystallized in the 1925 case of *Friedell* v. *Blakely Printing Co.* The case, involving a libelous article about a candidate that was written for the *Rochester Daily Post* by a part-time worker, went to the state supreme court solely on the question of privilege. The court held that communications to the public, which had an interest, were privileged, qualified to the extent that they were made in good faith, without malice. But in this case, malice on the part of the writer defeated privilege, and it was ruled that the publisher was liable for the action of the writer.[169]

The reasoning of the court on privilege was meaningful. The opinion stated:

> The benefit of the liberty of the press is a myth, if dishonesty or questionable loyalty of candidates for public office must be handled with delicacy and discussed with such choice of words as to make it appear that the publicity is a matter of indifference. No public good could come from a rule making every publisher answerable for the literal truth of every word in his columns.
>
> Good faith and absence of malice is a good standard where there is a qualified privilege. If the liberty of the press must be exercised under a responsibility that is always threatening, it will never be used effectively for the public good. Under such a rule the dishonest man and the cheat would never be exposed. In a case of this character good faith and bad faith are as easily proved as in any other branch of the law. Malice is important in libel cases only to affect damages and to overcome a defense of privilege.[170]

The court added that malice could be shown by proving the publisher knew the facts were false, by showing actual ill feeling existed, and by the exaggerated character of language used. Further, it could be shown that the publisher took advantage of an otherwise privileged opportunity to malign a candidate unjustly and that the extent of publication was not warranted.[171]

The burden of showing malice was on the official bringing suit, the state supreme court ruled in the 1938 case of *Clancy* v. *Daily News Corp.* The case arose when the *St. Paul Daily News* attempted to defeat the reelection of James E. Clancy to the municipal council. Articles were published about an unnecessary trip costing thousands of dollars. The purpose of the trip, the newspaper stated, was to buy an unneeded fire and police alarm system. The court, stating its decision was in "accord with what the authorities call the minority rule," said the article was privileged if the publisher believed it to be true.[172]

MONTANA

A newspaper charge of favoritism or graft against a county commissioner had to be both false and malicious before the publisher was liable, the Supreme Court of Montana ruled in 1914. This case, *Cooper v. Romney*, was filed when the *Western News* said the commissioner let the county printing contract without bids to deflect all possible graft of public money to a favored publisher. The court said the charge was libelous if false and unprivileged. But the court said privileged matters were concerned, and no malice was shown.[173] Under this liberal rule of privilege, there was no liability.

The rule was still in effect nearly thirty years later, when the supreme court of the state heard the 1943 case of *Griffin v. Opinion Publishing Co.* A city treasurer brought this suit against the *Chinook Opinion* after the newspaper commented on his being hired as an attorney to sue the city for payment of improvement bonds. "This in itself," the newspaper stated, "is a new wrinkle in civic affairs as few men can both serve and sue the city at the same time." [174] The supreme court ruled that the statement was privileged.

Further, the court said both officials and governmental employees of all levels were subject to articles of general interest to the public. Such articles, the court said, could contain untrue information that the publisher had reason to believe true.[175] This included information as to private conduct and character in so far as it affected public conduct. And it extended to articles describing how elected officials and appointed employees carried out both discretionary and ministerial functions.[176] This particular article was neither false nor unprivileged, the court said.

NEBRASKA

The Nebraska Supreme Court held in several cases shortly after the turn of the century that privileged communications were not libelous if they were not published maliciously. Some restrictions were placed on privilege, however. As an example, in the 1903 case of *Bee Publishing Co. v. Shields*, the court said there was no privilege to impute bad motives or criminal offenses to officials.[177] The article at issue, in the *Omaha Evening Bee*, had questioned how much money was "put up" to keep a county attorney from prosecuting gamblers. Another limitation on privilege was announced the following year in *Mertens v. Bee Publishing Co.*, brought about by an article in the same newspaper claiming a candidate for county treasurer was a "chronic deadbeat." The court said privilege did not extend to statements injurous to reputation or character.[178] And in 1905 the court refused the defense of privilege for an article falsely stating a candidate for reelection as sheriff had padded his expenses by drawing money he never spent. The court said there was a privilege to call attention to illegal charges made by the sheriff as a reason why he should not be reelected. But this pirvilege was "recklessly" abused because the facts had not been checked.[179] The ruling would indicate that newspapers had an obligation to check their facts before there could be probable cause for believing them true.

Despite the Nebraska Supreme Court's preliminary skirmishing, the doctrine of privilege was not firmly established until the 1916 case of *Estelle v. Daily News Publishing Co.* A candidate for reelection as district judge brought the suit when the *Omaha Daily News* printed a story stating he was associated with the "third ward crowd" of ballot stuffers and thieves and that he was involved in a "frame up" to send a man to prison. The article was proven false at the trial for libel. On appeal, however, the supreme court said statements on candidates' qualifications were qualifiedly privileged. And there was no liability for publications informing voters of any well-grounded belief about candidates' fitness.[180] However, the articles were libelous, the court said, if false statements were made maliciously and not for good motives or justifiable ends.[181] In this case, the jury held that the statements were malicious and as a result libelous.

NEW HAMPSHIRE

A New Hampshire jury also found that the privilege of discussing officials had been exceeded when the *Berlin Reporter* claimed, falsely, that a police officer admitted he was guilty of lewd conduct with two juvenile girls he arrested. The girls had filed charges against the officer, and he had been prosecuted, but he had pleaded *nolo contendere*, which did not admit guilt but did subject him to fine.[182] When the officer was awarded damages in the trial court, the newspaper appealed. But the New Hampshire Supreme Court, in *Lafferty v. Houlihan*, upheld the verdict. The court said that while the occasion was privileged, the jury determined if privilege was a defense.[183] Not only was a lawful occasion required, the court said, but there had to be probable cause for the belief that an article about an official was true. The actual belief in truth, without probable cause, was no defense. There was no doubt that New Hampshire adhered to the liberal rule, as it had since the Civil War,[184] but the criterion for privilege was that there be a reasonable basis for accusations.

NORTH CAROLINA

The lack of a reasonable basis for charges also prevailed in a 1919 North Carolina case in which the liberal view of privilege was announced. The case, *Lewis v. Carr*, involved an affidavit printed in a newspaper, written by a bank cashier, that charged the chairman of the county board of education with using public school funds for his personal business. The North Carolina Supreme Court said the article was libelous though protected if privileged. But privilege, the court said, was qualified to the extent that the article could not be both false and malicious. Further, falsehood was not enough to establish malice, the court said.[185] However, the charge was that the chairman used the money without legal authority, and neither the newspaper nor the bank cashier had checked the school vouchers, which were public record, before making the charge. This was sufficient evidence, the court ruled, for an issue of malice.[186] The case was remanded for retrial.

The liberal doctrine that privilege extended to misstatements of fact was again applied by the North Carolina Supreme Court in a 1920 criminal case. The case, *State v. Greenville Publishing Co.*

followed a newspaper publication claiming a sheriff was negligent in enforcing the law as to deserters. The court said the publisher could not be found guilty of criminal libel unless it was shown beyond a reasonable doubt that the article was both false and malicious.[187] Malice could be shown, the court declared, by proving an ulterior motive for the article, by showing the publisher knew it was false, or by showing there was no fair ground for believing it true.[188]

PENNSYLVANIA

The Pennsylvania Supreme Court, which adopted the liberal rule of privilege in 1893,[189] continued it into the twentieth century. As an example, in the 1927 case of *Stevenson v. Morris* it held that statements claiming a city employee was incompetent was qualifiedly privileged if made without malice and if efforts to determine the truth had been made. The court in 1935, however, ruled that belief in truth could not be justified by hearsay. The decision came in *Weglein v. Golder*, resulting when a banker during a political campaign sent written statements to newspapers and radio stations claiming that a political candidate was insolvent. The court said that merely sending the written statements to the media was libelous. Further, the court said the nature of the article showed that the charge was "studied and deliberate," justifying the jury's finding that it lost the protection of privilege by being malicious.[190]

The Pennsylvania Supreme Court also ruled in 1945 that malice could be shown when a deliberate effort was made, without a proper occasion, to publish an official's long-past association with criminals. The ruling was in *Bausewine v. Norristown Herald*. The newspaper article cited by the official, a chief of police, recounted his involvement in an automobile accident eleven years before, as the passenger of a man with a record. It also insinuated unlawful activity in Florida during prohibition days. The court ruled that malice defeated privilege and that there was evidence of malice.[191] Not only did there have to be reasonable or probable cause and a proper motive for privilege, the court said, but there also had to be a proper occasion. While the article was capable of libel, the court ruled that it still was the job of the jury to determine if the eleven-year-old record was printed on a proper occasion.[192] It would appear, then, that the wide privilege sanctioned by the Pennsylvania court could be defeated if efforts were not made to determine the truth, if charges were deliberate, and if they were not made on a proper occasion.

SOUTH DAKOTA

Lack of malice and probable cause for belief in truth also constituted a successful plea of privilege in South Dakota, as was shown in early twentieth-century cases involving a sheriff, a candidate for mayor, a state's attorney, a county auditor, and a candidate for the legislature.[193] However, a suit brought by a candidate for governor caused the Supreme Court of South Dakota to reappraise the rule of privilege in 1915. The *Sioux Falls Daily Press* had carried an article claiming that George W. Egan, a candidate for governor, had been accused of raping two women in Iowa some years before. His license to practice law in that state was revoked, the newspaper said, and he moved to South Dakota to practice. The court found, in *Egan v. Dotson*, that the statements were false and that there was a definite intent to injure the candidate. As a result, the rules of privilege were explored in depth. Still, the court discarded the narrow view that false statements were not privileged, though it admitted this was the rule of the majority of states.[194] The intent to defeat Egan's candidacy, the court said, did not show express malice. The article was declared privileged so long as there was belief in the truth of the facts and there was probable cause for the belief.[195] But privilege would be defeated, the court held, if jurors found that the publisher did not make a proper investigation as to the truth of the charges.

UTAH

It was not until 1933 that the Utah Supreme Court accepted probable cause for belief in truth of defamatory statements as a defense to libel. The case involved, *Williams v. Standard-Examiner Publishing Co.*, drew a line of distinction between the doctrine of fair comment and the doctrine of privilege.[196] The public acts of public men were open to comment and criticism by newspapers and citizens alike, the court said. But it was only when defamatory untruths were published that privileged communications became an issue.

The suit was filed by the city water commissioner of Ogden,

Utah, after a newspaper article, based on a state bacteriological report, accused him of dereliction of duty by turning a polluted water
supply into the city system, causing a typhoid epidemic. The commissioner's resignation was demanded in the article. The court ruled
that the occasion, the moral or social obligation to communicate
information to people who had an interest, made the article qualifiedly privileged.[197] As a result, the court said, actual malice had to
be proved. The following words were used:

> Courts do not draw fine distinctions as to the kind of language
> that may be used in the criticism of a public officer who has appar-
> ently been derelict in the performance of the duties of his office.
> The comments and criticisms declared on may not be said to give
> rise to civil liability in the absence of proof that they were pub-
> lished with malice in fact or actual malice.[198]

Though the burden of proving malice was on the official, there had
to be probable cause for believing the truth of the charges, the court
said.[199] Probable cause in this case was the state bacteriological
report, and the court in its opinion stated that allegations of fact
based on other facts fell within the realm of privilege.[200]

WEST VIRGINIA

An article based on a state report, this one a financial audit, also
was involved when the West Virginia Supreme Court of Appeals
adopted the liberal rule of privilege in 1943. The case, *Swearingen v.
Parkersburg Sentinel Co.*, was brought by an incumbent candidate
for mayor after a newspaper article claimed irregularities in city
finances. The article cited the state report and stated the city council refused to institute a new bookkeeping system to insure honesty.[201] The court noted that the report was a basis for believing the
truth of the charges and said that anything connected with the
official duties of city councilmen was proper for discussion. Newspapers, the court said, had a duty to discuss matters relating to government.[202] Further, it was ruled that there could be no libel unless
the official proved malice.[203]

Prior to this World War II decision, the law in West Virginia
had been that set in the 1878 decision of *Sweeney v. Baker*, that
while bona fide criticism was privileged, facts had to be proved.[204]

This decision had not been overruled in the Swearingen case, but it was the next year in the case of *Bailey* v. *Charleston Mail Association.*[205] This 1944 case was brought by a member of the state road commission after the *Charleston Daily Mail* called a state bridge purchase a scandal. It was falsely claimed the state spent extra money for the purchase by going through an agent. The newspaper, in defending the suit, made what the court called a "rolled up plea" to the effect that the facts were privileged and that the rest was fair comment. The court admitted that it was extremely difficult to draw a line between fact and opinion.[206] Noting, however, that the publisher had made an honest inquiry to obtain facts, the court said:

> The official acts of a public officer are of such concern and importance to the public generally that a misstatement thereof is qualifiedly privileged if made in good faith and in a reasonable and honest belief that the statement is true. We restrict this rule . . . to official acts done in the performance of a public officer's official duty.[207]

The decision was made after a careful review of privilege, which the court said extended to candidates for office only in so far as mental and physical qualities and moral character were involved.[208] Noticeably implicit in the court's decision was the fact that privilege did not extend to personal attacks on officials.

Privilege Undefined: *Category Elusive*

The privilege to discuss, criticize, or comment on public officials and candidates for public office was not raised as a court issue in all jurisdictions prior to the close of World War II. As a result, courts in four states—Idaho, Nevada, New Mexico, and Rhode Island— failed to define any doctrine of privilege or fair comment. Nevada and New Mexico decisions were completely silent on privilege, and discussions by the Rhode Island and Idaho Supreme Courts were inconclusive.

The Rhode Island Supreme Court did rule in 1897, in the case of *Tiepke* v. *Times Publishing Co.*, that a plea of privilege could not be considered on the question of demurrer because the official bringing the suit had alleged malice as well as falsity.[209] Indications were that the plea would be considered under other circumstances, and that privilege might be granted for falsehoods in the absence of malice. Still, the question of privilege was left in doubt.

The Idaho precedent concerning privilege involved a charge made to city officials about a police officer. In this 1917 case, Dwyer v. Libert, the Idaho Supreme Court ruled that private publications to those with the power for removal were qualifiedly privileged if they were not made maliciously.[210] There was no mention of discussion about public officials in public publications, such as newspapers, and the law of privilege on this issue was left open.

The defenses for libel against public officials in Idaho, Nevada, New Mexico, and Rhode Island, then, could not be categorized by the end of World War II. These states had built up no body of law to excuse libelous publications about the public conduct of public officials. They were pledged neither to the narrow nor the liberal rules of privilege.

Privilege in Federal Courts

Public officials always have been able to sue in federal courts if they live in a state other than the one in which an allegedly libelous newspaper article was published.[211] And frequently, out-of-state officials filed libel suits in federal courts on the basis of this diversity of citizenship. Further, the federal courts during the early part of the twentieth century were not required to follow state precedents in determining common law principles.[212] In determining privilege to discuss public officials, the federal courts usually followed the 1893 decision of Post Publishing Co. v. Hallam,[213] rendered by Mr. Justice Taft while serving on the United States Circuit Court of Appeals for the Sixth District. Privilege was extended to fair comment and criticism but not to misstatement of facts.

This narrow rule of privilege, for example, was followed by another United States Circuit Court of Appeals in a 1924 Nevada case, Nevada State Journal Co. v. Henderson. The court upheld a federal district court ruling that drew a distinction between comment and factual charges, holding that there was no privilege for facts charging crime or disgraceful conduct.[214] The article at issue had imputed both bribery and murder to a candidate for the United States Senate. The circuit court said there had been an "entire absence of inquiry or investigation to ascertain the truth of the charges before publication." [215] Further, there was a refusal by the newspaper to retract the story. Clear malice was shown, the court said, by the reckless disregard of the rights of others. While the case turned on the issue of malice, the circuit court left no doubt it subscribed to the narrow rule of privilege.

Federal courts, however, were not free to determine their own rules of privilege by World War II. The United States Supreme Court held in 1938 that state law, common or statutory, had to be applied in all cases other than those involving constitutional matters or acts of congress.[216] This meant that federal judges had to conform to the common law doctrines of privilege in states where the alleged libels were published, and differences in federal court decisions became noticeable in the war years.

These differences perhaps were best shown by a series of judgments in libel suits filed by Congressman Martin L. Sweeney. It has been estimated that he filed from sixty-eight to seventy-five different court suits over the United States, seeking damages in excess of $7,500,000.[217] He claimed he was libeled by a syndicated column which stated he opposed the appointment of a foreign-born Jew as a judge of a federal district court. Many of the cases were filed in federal courts, and in all but three trials—two in Illinois and one in New York—courts declared the articles either not libelous or privileged.[218] However, the New York decision, rendered by a federal circuit court of appeals on the basis of that state's law, held that the article was false and libelous.[219] The column had been circulated in the *Schenectady Union Star* in an area of New York in which a number of Jewish people lived, and the court said this held the congressman up to hate and scorn before the Jews who read the article.

The circuit court's judgment was not unanimous. Justice Charles E. Clark wrote a dissenting opinion stating that there should be no libel against public officials unless statements were both false and unfair and unless the aggrieved official proved special damages.[220] Otherwise, he wrote, freedom of comment would be stifled.

On the basis on Justice Clark's dissent, the Supreme Court of the United States granted certiorari to review the decision.[221] The Supreme Court justices, however, were equally divided, with Mr. Justice Robert H. Jackson taking no part.[222] As a result, the lower court's decision was affirmed; and the Supreme Court was, thus, deprived of the only opportunity in its history to render an opinion determining the constitutional limitations upon the power to award libel damages to public officials.[223] The justices of the Supreme Court, like the judges in the various states, were not agreed on whether privilege should extend only to fair comment or to non-malicious falsehoods as well. The question of privilege again was left to individual states to answer.

Overview Through World War II

The individual states through World War II were not agreed on the extent of privilege to discuss public officials without responsibility for libel. Most adhered either to the narrow rule, limiting privilege to comments based on facts, or to the liberal rule, extending privilege to include nonmalicious falsehoods. In a few states, however, these rules were modified. The doctrine of privilege adopted in each state depended on the individual determination of that state's court of final jurisdiction.

Even though courts in several states might adopt the same broad rule of privilege, they often interpreted that privilege differently. As an example, states accepting the liberal rule were not consistent in qualifying privilege. Dicta in Iowa, Arizona, and Kansas cases indicated that the privilege to communicate falsehoods was allowed if there was an honest belief in the truth. This belief refuted malice and justified libel. But honest belief was not enough to refute claims of malice in most of the liberal rule states; generally there had to be probable cause for that belief. At least four state court decisions—in Pennsylvania, West Virginia, Nebraska, and Texas—placed a burden on newsmen to investigate or make efforts to determine whether facts were true prior to publication. When facts were not checked, privilege was considered to be recklessly abused, and in at least one state, Connecticut, a court held that recklessness without sufficient excuse constituted malice.

The liberal rule states were generally agreed that an official had to show actual malice on the part of a publisher before the publisher could be held accountable in a libel suit for a privileged communication. But again, definitions as to actual malice varied. A Pennsylvania decision stated a "studied and deliberate charge" constituted malice. In a Michigan decision, malice was referred to as "wilful injury without just reason." And in South Dakota, malice was defined simply as "intent to injure," though it was held there that intent to defeat a candidate was not malicious. Few courts, however, attempted to define malice. Rather, they explained how it could be proved. It was stated in a North Carolina decision that malice could be shown by proving that a publisher had ulterior motives, that he knew an article was false, or that he had no fair ground for believing an article true. A Minnesota case held malice could be proved if the publisher knew the article was false, if there was ill will or feeling, or if there was exaggeration in presentation. Lack of a retraction was cited as evidence of malice by a federal circuit court in Nevada. And a number of courts elaborated on the word "reckless" as showing abuse, disregard, and malice. In a somewhat related vein, both New Hampshire and Pennsylvania courts stressed the importance of a proper occasion for the communication. Digging into facts that were a number of years old, as an example, begged the question as to whether a proper occasion existed. And one case in Minnesota indicated that there was no lawful occasion of privilege when publications circulated in areas where people had no direct interest in the officials involved. Further complicating the picture was the opinion of jury members, who generally determined whether malice was involved and whether privilege was abused.[224]

Inconsistencies in interpretation of privilege also could be found in states adhering to the narrow rule of fair comment and criticism, not allowing false statements of fact. Most of these state courts required publishers to prove the truth of statements officials claimed were libelous. But courts in at least two states, Mississippi and Illinois, took a more conservative view and demanded proof of truth and good motives. And privilege in Wisconsin was considerably broader than in some of the other states following the narrow doctrine. The supreme court there, despite its purported adoption of the rule that privilege did not extend to facts, held that substantial truth was sufficient[225] and that fair comment extended to factual conclusions drawn from other facts.

The fine line between fact and opinion obviously caused considerable difficulty for judges who tried suits in this turbulent period. The Oregon Supreme Court, for instance, ruled that a factual statement accusing a politician of building power on the hate of the Ku Klux Klan and of being "a double crosser in politics" was an opinion and fair comment.[226] And the Missouri Supreme Court held that the fact a prisoner was hung by his hands warranted the false conclusion that it was torture to get information from him. This was considered fair comment drawn from an established fact. Further, while imputation of corrupt motives frequently was regarded by the courts as severe criticism, courts in some states—among them Virginia, New York, and Maryland—held that such imputations were allegation of fact and not privileged.

Whether state courts limited privilege to comments based on fact or extended it to nonmalicious falsehoods did not determine the degree to which publications could delve into the private lives of public figures. There were differences of opinion among judges, regardless of the rule of privilege followed, as to discussions about the personal affairs of public officials and candidates for public office. Courts in some of the liberal rule states, such as California, Iowa, and West Virginia, as well as in some of the narrow rule states, including New York and Illinois, were very specific in holding that privilege did not extend to attacks on officials' private lives. But articles about private character that affected a candidate's or official's fitness for office were recognized as privileged in some of the states following the narrow rule, such as Virginia and Wisconsin, as well as in most of the states following the liberal rule.

Despite many inconsistencies, there was unity of opinion within each rule concerning published charges of crime. States adhering to the narrow rule of privilege commonly held that imputation of crime was not fair comment and criticism but rather was a factual allegation that had to be proved. Conversely, states that adopted the liberal rule commonly held that charges of crime against officials were privileged if not made maliciously and if communicated with good motives and with honest belief or probable cause for belief in their truth.

The liberal rule perhaps was not adopted by other states solely because privilege was extended to charges that officials committed crimes. For instance, the Delaware Supreme Court denied privilege for charges of crime but indicated it might allow the liberal rule of privilege where disgraceful acts were charged. Oklahoma did allow the liberal rule except where charges of crime were published. Further, Texas and Wyoming, following the public officer's rule, extended privilege to false charges except when they would be cause for officials' removal. Such charges would include crime and malfeasance in office, which also were denied privilege in the District of Columbia courts. These courts, along with those in Missouri, which assumed published articles about officials were true until proven false, advanced independent views of privilege.

But not all of the courts which adopted neither the minority nor majority view *in toto* had their own individualistic outlook on privilege. In five states—Indiana, Idaho, Nevada, New Mexico, and Rhode Island—cases involving privilege were either nonexistent or inconclusive. And in one state, Georgia, the courts switched between the two views, leaving its doctrine confused. Vacillation concerning privilege, however, was not uncommon. Court decisions within individual states between 1900 and the end of World War II noticeably shifted from one doctrine to another.

The vacillation in decisions concerning privilege, however, was consistent with the many changes in social, economic, and political conditions of the period.[227] The century opened with a spirit of reform, with the mood of criticism being typified by the work of the muckrakers. Then came the conflicting strains of imperialism and isolationism, accompanied by the growth of Woodrow Wilson's new freedom, the surge of progressive democracy, and the expansion of women's suffrage. This peaceful progress came to an end in 1917 with the United States' entry into World War I. Simultaneously, freedom of expression was drastically reduced by wartime restrictions.[228] Following the war came the age of the flapper, prohibition, racketeering and crime, and even corruption in high government circles, as was shown by the scandals in President Harding's administration.[229] There also was a wave of prosperity, with emphasis on mass production and inventions, such as the automobile, radio, refrigerator, and finally the airplane.

But "normalcy" ended abruptly with the stock market crash of 1929. Industries reduced production, unemployment rose, and millions were thrown out of work. The resulting dissatisfaction was shown at the polls, and the long period of Republican rule was replaced in 1932 by that of President Franklin D. Roosevelt and his "New Deal." The nation started its struggle to rise from its economic stagnation through such governmental programs as the National Recovery Act, the Works Progress Administration, and the Social Security Act. Living standards rose, as did international tension. And again in 1941 the United States found itself in another world conflict. But during World War II there was noticeably less suppression of information. A highly informed populace joined the war effort,[230] and the resulting industrial development and peak output carried through to peace.

The social, economic, and political changes during this lengthy period were accompanied by modifications in court views as to the privilege for discussing government. There appeared to be, perhaps because of the suppressive measures of World War I, a growing belief that freedom of speech and press should not be violated. This, to an extent, was exemplified by the United States Supreme Court decisions in 1925 and 1931 which held these freedoms were protected against state infringement by the due process clause of the Fourteenth Amendment.[231] At any rate, during World War I, nearly one thousand individuals had been convicted for utterances or publications considered disloyal or seditious.[232] But only one such case came before the United States Supreme Court during or after World War II, and the court then found that the alleged offender was not guilty of a crime.[233] There was an implicit recognition that citizens had a right to discuss, verbally disagree with, and even harshly criticize their government.

Similarly, there appeared to be a growing trend toward greater privilege to discuss officials themselves in this period between the two world wars. Most, though not all, of the state courts adopting the narrow rule of privilege had done so before World War I.[234] And it was after this war, despite the shifts of view in courts of individual states, that the liberal rule of privilege attracted approximately half of its adherents.[235] Further, two states—West Virginia and Colorado—endorsed the liberal rule during World War II. It also was in these World War II years that the District of Columbia partially adopted the privilege to publish nonmalicious falsehoods about officials and candidates.

By the end of World War II, the numerical difference between the so-called majority and minority views of privilege was not so great.[236] Sixteen states had adopted the minority view, following the liberal rule that extended privilege, on a qualified basis, to misstatements of fact. Also, this view was partially subscribed to by the District of Columbia and to some extent by the states of Delaware, Oklahoma, Texas, and Wyoming. These four states were among the twelve following independent views or whose rules of privilege were uncertain. Meanwhile only twenty-one states, the territory of Hawaii, and some federal jurisdictions could definitely be said to adhere to the majority view, holding that fair comment and criticism were negated by false statements. And the United States Supreme Court appeared to be evenly divided on the issue of privilege.

Simply listing states by the specific views of privilege that they followed, however, does not give an overall perspective. Upon close examination, some geographical patterns emerge. The inland states to the northeast and the so-called southern states generally limited privilege to fair comment and criticism. A different and more liberal pattern became evident around the Great Lakes, and a variety of views persisted on the eastern seaboard. The western states, however, appeared to allow a much greater privilege to discuss officials and candidates than the bulk of those in the east. In fact, most of the states west of the Mississippi River followed the more liberal views.

The doctrine that privilege extended to false statements had been unequivocally adopted by courts in the western states of Minnesota, Iowa, South Dakota, Nebraska, Kansas, Montana, Utah, Arizona, and California. Missouri, while not granting privilege to false statements, allowed considerable privilege of discussion by refusing to presume that articles about officials were false until proven so. In fact, both Missouri and Oklahoma placed the burden of proving falsity upon officials. Oklahoma in addition followed a doctrine similar to that adopted by Texas and Wyoming, extending privilege to falsehoods except when those falsehoods charged officials with the commission of acts that were either indictable or cause for removal from office. In three western states, Nevada, New Mexico, and Idaho, the issue of privilege had never been raised. In only five other states west of the Mississippi River —Arkansas, Louisiana, Washington, Oregon, and North Dakota— did decisions of the courts follow the narrow view. And in one of these, Oregon, courts were extremely liberal in accepting factual assertions as comment. There is no doubt that at the conclusion of World War II, newspapermen west of the Mississippi River generally had a much wider privilege to discuss public officials and candidates than did newspapermen to the east.

This defense of privilege in libel suits was not limited to publications discussing elected officials or candidates for elective offices. Courts in many states, regardless of the rule of privilege followed, had recognized the defenses of privilege or fair comment in libel cases involving appointed as well as elected officials. A New York decision had declared a football coach a "semi-official," [237] and several state courts had dealt with privilege in cases involving political bosses or political party functionaries. In a Missouri case, a party chairman had been referred to as a "quasi-official." Among the appointed officials discussed with privilege were a grand juror, city inspector, city street superintendent, prison warden, policeman, mental institution superintendent, poorhouse manager, federal agency secretary, and a state oil inspector. The Montana Supreme Court went so far as to say, during World War II years, that the defense of privilege was appropriate for articles discussing either elected officials or employees in performing either discretionary or ministerial functions.

Courts throughout the nation, then, had during this first half of the century extended publishers greater immunity from libel liability via the defense of privilege, regardless of the rule followed. Generally a plea of privilege was just as valid in a libel suit brought by an appointed government officer as in one brought by an elected official or candidate. By allowing libels against government employees to be defended under the doctrines of fair comment or privilege of discussion, the courts had rejected, in the words of the California Supreme Court, "ancient decisions made before the effect of popular government became fully appreciated." [238]

There is no doubt that popular government in this turbulent half-century had become more fully appreciated. Events had propelled people toward change; much of the mystery of government had been swept away. And many judges, those who say what the law is, had been persuaded to change their ideas as to the people's relationship to their governors. Perhaps this was nowhere more directly shown than in 1942 when the United States Court of Appeals for the District of Columbia declared obsolete the doctrine that people must not criticize those who govern them.[239]

State courts everywhere appeared to agree, by the end of World War II, that the governed had a right to criticize the governors with some immunity from libel. This right was shared by citizens and newspapers alike, varying somewhat from one state to another. The largest single group of states followed narrow court precedents requiring that criticism be based on truth or established fact before libelous publications could be excused. But a growing number of state courts followed liberal precedents, allowing publishers to justify false and defamatory statements about officials and candidates if those statements were printed without malice, with good motives, and with honest belief or reasonable cause for believing them true.

10. Public Proceedings

Privilege to Publish Fair and Accurate Reports

The privilege of publishing fair and accurate reports of public proceedings without liability for libel, like the privilege of discussing public officials, was expanded greatly during the first half of the twentieth century. The fair and accurate report privilege existed, of course, as the century opened. In fact, fair and accurate reports of judicial proceedings had been granted libel immunity in some of the earliest of court clashes between newspapermen and public officials.[1] Further, the United States Supreme Court in the 1845 decision of White v. Nichols, which carried no force of law in the various states, declared that publishers had to act with malice before parties complaining of libel could collect judgments for reports of judicial, legal or parliamentary proceedings.[2] It was not, however, until the 1859 Massachusetts case of Barrows v. Bell that the privilege of reporting judicial affairs was actually extended by a state to other official and quasi-official hearings. Such an extension, the Massachusetts Supreme Judicial Court said in that case, was "for the necessary information of the people."[3] In following this rationale, courts in other states through the years, especially in the twentieth century, recognized a privilege of publishing accurate and impartial accounts of the official reports and proceedings for practically all levels of government.[4]

A problem did exist, however, as to what information was essential for the people's knowledge. Perhaps the accepted view at the beginning of the twentieth century was that voiced by Mr. Justice Oliver Wendell Holmes, Jr., in Cowley v. Pulsifer. He had declared that the fair and accurate report privilege had been granted in this country, not because controversies between citizens at official proceedings such as court trials were of public concern, but because the public had a right to scrutinize the way officials performed their public duties.[5] However, twentieth-century court decisions began to hint broadly that, in addition to officials' activities, people had a right to know about the public issues discussed in official proceedings.[6] And during the post–World War II period, with the growing emphasis of free discussion, the libel-free privilege of publishing fair and accurate reports was extended in some jurisdictions to include reports of unofficial public meetings, such as political rallies and even civic gatherings.

Despite the direct interest of citizens in official meetings, libel cases in the late nineteenth century indicate that the privilege to make fair and accurate reports of these meetings was given begrudgingly. An example of this came in an 1882 Louisiana case. A newspaper told how city aldermen at a town council accused the mayor of awarding an overly expensive verbal contract for a "pet job" in which the mayor's son had an interest. The article ended with the comment: "There is something rotten in Denmark." [7] Jurors found that the article was not libelous though it was "ungentlemanly in tone, and beneath the dignity of correct and honorable journalism." [8]

The jury verdict was upheld by the state supreme court, which said that giving the substance of town council proceedings for citizens who were interested "cannot be regarded by us as being in itself malicious and libelous." [9] The court agreed with the jurors, however, that the article was not "the highest culmination of taste and refined journalism." [10] But no matter how reluctantly, bad journalism, if not malicious, was sanctioned in Louisiana to allow reports of proceedings to be communicated to citizens.

The Wisconsin Supreme Court in 1896, however ruled that voluntary and unofficial reports given in official city council meetings were not privileged when the conduct of individuals was discussed.[11] The case was brought by a state senator after critical remarks about him had been made in the council meeting. The court also indicated the privilege was limited because the newspaper circulated outside the city, where citizens who lived in the senator's district had no vested interests in the council activities.

At the turn of the century, privilege also was denied by the Kentucky Court of Appeals to the publication of statements made to a United States commissioner at the time charges were filed. The charges were against a collector of internal revenue. Despite the public interest, the court said only the records of the commissioner's office showing the charges were privileged, not the substance of the charges obtained from the individual making them.[12] In New York, the privilege to report public proceedings was ruled in 1899 to extend only to what was said and done in the meetings. The decision was based on a New York statute declaring public proceedings privileged, but the court said this did not extend to inferences and insinuations outside the factual occurrences.[13]

The privilege to give fair and accurate accounts of public meetings became more widely recognized, both by statutes and common law proceedings, in the early years of the twentieth century. Dicta outlining the privilege can be found in a number of cases involving public officials.[14] A typical delineation of the privilege, perhaps, was that of a 1913 Wisconsin decision holding that it extended to judicial, legislative, or "public official proceedings." [15]

As a general rule, courts denied any privilege to comment on court proceedings, but comments about public officials in court proceedings were somewhat different. Frequently newspapermen coupled the privilege to publish true and impartial reports of court proceedings with the privilege to criticize and comment on officials and candidates. Such a case arose in Texas when the fitness of a candidate for county judge was questioned in a newspaper. The discussion was based on a $1,000 court fee charged by the candidate for settling a $4,070 estate. When the candidate sued for libel over the article, the Texas Court of Civil Appeals held that the candidate's fitness was of public interest and that a fair and reasonable report of the past court action had been given.[16] There was no libel.

The privilege of making judicial reports was defined differently from state to state, but it distilled down to fairness and accuracy. As an example, it was held in a 1903 Rhode Island case brought by the state's governor that judicial reports had to be based on good motives and could not prejudge decisions or misstate facts.[17] More typical was a New Mexico Supreme Court decision in 1919, holding simply that every impartial and accurate report of law court proceedings was privileged.[18] And often it was held that even accurate reports had to be published without malice. Comments or facts outside the trial record, the California Court of Appeals ruled in 1923, could show malicious publication.[19]

Still, fair and just criticism of officials' actions in trials, so long as character or integrity was not attacked, normally was allowed. In South Carolina in 1921, criticism of jurors' trial work was ruled free of defamation.[20] And the Missouri Supreme Court in 1941 held that a double privilege extended to a *St. Louis Globe-Democrat* article asserting that a state's attorney would question a justice of the peace for an explanation as to why taxes were paid in his court. It was ruled that the article could be construed first as a report of a court proceeding and, secondly, as fair comment.[21]

Even more freedom has been granted newspapermen in reporting judicial proceedings in recent years. This is exemplified by a 1956 decision of the Virginia Supreme Court of Appeals, in which it was held that a "substantially correct" report of a trial record as well as the trial itself was privileged.[22] The suit involved a newspaper story that a domestic relations court judge had acted as an attorney in his own court. A New Mexico Supreme Court decision in 1964 also held that the compression of a city employee's lengthy testimony into one paragraph was privileged as it in substance fairly represented what he said.[23] The first paragraph of the article quoted the employee as saying he "carried $225 in city funds around for eight months in his wallet out of loyalty to the city." It was explained later in the article that the employee said he felt the money would buy the city more goods than could be obtained by official bids. Not only testimony, but also judges' remarks were ruled to be covered by privilege. The Indiana Supreme Court in 1957 said even judges' offhand remarks were privileged if made from the bench in the exercise of judicial functions.[24]

This Indiana case, *Henderson v. Evansville Press, Inc.*, pointed out that newspaper reports of judicial proceedings are protected by privilege because of the public's interest in proper administration of justice.[25] And in a 1964 case before the Georgia Court of Appeals it was held that since the privilege of court reports is for public interest, it cannot be used as a cloak for publishers to vent private malice.[26] In language similar to that used by other courts, the Georgia court declared that malice was the determining factor in all privilege for reporting court proceedings.[27] Malice, then, was a deterrent to the privilege of making fair and accurate reports of judicial proceedings as well as to the separate privilege of discussing or criticizing public officials.

A number of libel suits have been brought by public officials through the years as a result of newspaper reports concerning matters more or less on the periphery of official judicial proceedings. Perhaps the more common rule throughout the nation has been, as the United States Court of Appeals for the District of Columbia stated in 1952, that qualified privilege does not arise until official action on the matter is taken by a magistrate.[28] In this case, the court denied privilege for a newspaper article repeating a woman's statement to a district attorney to the effect that a police sergeant took $1,225 from her home when searching it. This could be privileged only after charges were filed with a magistrate, the court said. The policeman had a valid libel case.

Once charges have been filed with a magistrate, however, it generally has been held that privilege attaches to accusations so long as publications do not themselves state the accused person is guilty. Such a decision was rendered by the Oregon Supreme Court in a 1930 case that arose over the arrest of a school principal. He was charged with theft before a magistrate. The officers' reasons for suspecting the principal were published by a newspaper, though care was taken not to accuse the school official otherwise. The principal, after acquittal, sued the newspaper for libel; however, the court said the article was privileged as a report of judicial and public proceedings and hence not libelous. The paper had a right to publish the article, it was held, so the public would know the reasonable circumstances for the arrest.[29]

Several states do not require that the magistrate act on a case prior to the granting of privilege. New York law, as pronounced in a 1927 fraud case, extends privilege to the pleadings filed in a law suit regardless of whether the judge has acted on them.[30] Further, the Nebraska Supreme Court held in 1962 that a newspaper account of a sheriff seeking an attorney who defaulted court bond was privileged as an extension of a fair and accurate report of court proceedings.[31] And the Kansas Supreme Court has extended the privilege to include "reasonably fair comment" on reports it receives about Bar Association disbarment proceedings.[32]

Another major area of concern to newspapermen through the years has been the extent of privilege to publish articles on grand jury reports. Decisions in this area have not always been consistent. Generally, a ruling of the Michigan Supreme Court in a libel suit brought by a state prosecuting attorney is followed. The court in this case said a grand jury has no authority to make a report not followed by an indictment, and that there is no privilege for statements in such a report that reflect on public officials.[33]

An Alabama Supreme Court ruling declared that privilege does not extend to publications concerning grand jury reports about officials, in this case a constable, when the facts are not proved and indictments are not returned.[34] Turning this around, the Texas Commission of Appeals held that editorial comment on grand jury reports about a tax collector's conduct in office was privileged provided the report was justified by proven facts.[35] It has been the burden of newspapermen in such cases to prove justification.

Still, there have been more favorable cases from the newspaperman's standpoint. The Missouri Supreme Court, for instance, pointed to grand jury reports as the basis for rejecting the contention of a children's home superintendent that he was libeled. A St. Louis newspaper had criticized operations at the home following four grand jury reports about the conditions there. The court said this made the articles qualifiedly privileged.[36] Also the Wisconsin Supreme Court in a 1933 decision held that when a grand jury report is received in court, even erroneously, there is a qualified privilege to publish a fair report of it. Though the grand jury report in this case, concerning a special assistant city attorney, was later stricken from the record, it was made as a "public statement . . . in a judical proceeding" and was privileged.[37]

Generally, the privilege of publishing reports about legislative and governmental executive proceedings has carried the same conditions as reports about judicial proceedings.[38] And when public officials have been involved, there appears again to have been a merging of two privileges:

1] to make a fair and accurate report and
2] to criticize and discuss without malice.

In Texas, for instance, it has been held that privilege extended to newspaper editorial comment relating to libelous statements of a legislator on the floor of the state House of Representatives. The legislator in a privileged speech had made specific charges against the Texas Cotton Cooperative Association of conspiracy, malfeasance, deception, and embezzlement. And the *Houston Chronicle*, in an editorial, repeated the charges to claim the legislator had misused his immunity from prosecution. When the legislator sued for libel, the Texas Commission of Appeals ruled that the editorial related to a fair, true, and impartial account of the legislator's libelous statements on the floor and, in addition, constituted fair and reasonable criticism.[39] Even accounts of legislative committee activities were subject to publication with qualified privilege, the court said.

Similarly, the New Jersey Supreme Court in 1959 held that the qualified privilege to report on public proceedings extended to statements made in a "conference room" session of a city council.[40] The *Passaic Daily News* had quoted the city manager in this special session as saying two police officers were insubordinate and should be fired. One of the policemen brought suit, but the state supreme court said it was a fair and accurate report and privileged in absence of actual malice. Further, the distribution of the majority of newspapers outside the city did not constitute an excessive publication that would defeat the privilege. The court said newspapers could not be required to publish special editions for each community.

Erroneous statements made before a city council, though libelous in themselves, still could be published by newspapers with qualified privilege, the Louisiana Supreme Court held in 1924. This suit was brought by a court recorder who had been accused at a council meeting of canceling fines to let thieves go free. Even though the charge was later proved false, the *New Orleans Item* had the privilege of fairly and accurately reporting what was said at the meeting. This was true even with slight inaccuracies in the headlines.[41]

Inaccurate reports of the public proceedings themselves, however, generally destroyed any immunity from an action of libel. This was shown in a 1959 Maryland case when the *Salisbury Times* erroneously quoted an auditor's report to county commissioners as saying the sheriff kept incomplete records for booking prisoners. The report had said he kept complete records. The Maryland Court of Appeals held that the published report was subject to libel damages as it was protected only to the extent that it was fair and substantially correct.[42] Newspaper employees had caught the error before all copies of the first edition were printed, and the presses were stopped to make a correction. Still, a few copies were sold. The court held that this constituted a publication but that the attempt to stop the libel could mitigate damages.[43] Even distribution to employees alone would be a publication, the court ruled.[44]

Publications concerning the proceedings of college and school board meetings also have been held privileged, and the privilege has been extended to statements made by members of the boards at such meetings.[45] Public officials' libel suits against newspapers also have been defeated because of privilege granted to reports of public museum board meetings and to the minutes of a municipal water board.[46] In addition to board minutes, the privilege of making fair and accurate publications has been extended in many instances to reports of officials. This has included the report of an official committee to investigate a county treasurer,[47] the report of a governor's commission concerning a judge,[48] a fire marshall's report concerning firemen,[49] an auditor's report to county commissioners,[50] a city audit reflecting on a councilman,[51] a state audit reflecting on a former assistant attorney general,[52] and an adjutant general's report to a governor reflecting on a judge.[53]

However, the *New York Times* failed in a 1961 attempt to apply the privilege of making a fair report of an official proceeding to the administrative action of an assistant city attorney. The official fired two subordinates whose only offense, the newspaper said, was being "zealous in prosecuting slum landlords." The court said this was the publisher's own view, not the report of a public proceeding.[54] The court did say that the newspaper still could defend the case on the basis of truth or on fair comment of a public official's act.

A number of state court decisions, especially in recent years, have extended the privilege of making fair and accurate reports to include reports of political rallies. For instance, the *Columbia Record* was absolved of libel against a member of the South Carolina legislature in 1935 because it had printed a substantially correct account of a political rally where charges were made against the official. The court held that the rally was "quasi-privileged" as a public meeting.[55] So long as the newspaper did not add charges or statements not made at the meeting, the court said, it had a privilege to report what happened. The court added, however, that privilege did not apply if a newspaper printed such reports with express malice.

After World War II, additional jurisdictions extended privilege to include political gatherings. For instance, the Florida Supreme Court in 1956 said newspaper accounts of political rallies were protected by a "qualified privilege to publish matters of great political interest." [56] This court, as did the Arizona Supreme Court in a similar case in 1957, held that only malice in fact could make such reports libelous. The Arizona case resulted from an article about a junior chamber of commerce forum in which one slate of candidates asserted the city would be open to prostitution and gambling if the other slate was elected. The Arizona Supreme Court said the discussion was of public interest and that the matter was "communicated by one whose right it was to inform the public of such matters." [57]

Closely related to political forum reporting is the routine news coverage of political speeches. And the United States Court of Appeals for the Fourth Circuit ruled in 1955 that privilege extended to publication of statements by a candidate for the presidency during a political campaign. The suit was filed after General Dwight D. Eisenhower, then a Republican presidential candidate, had referred to a "sort of crookedness" in Washington, specifically outlining the "five per cent" profits being received by some Democrats on government contracts. The court said:

> The right and duty of newspapers to publish for the benefit of the public matters of this character is well recognized, and, in the age in which we are living, popular government could hardly function if this were not true. Of course, newspapers should be held strictly accountable where they maliciously or recklessly publish false statements for the purpose of injuring candidates or their supporters.[58]

There was no false statement or recklessness in the Maryland newspaper account, the court said, as the report accurately depicted the statements of Eisenhower.

The fair report privilege also has been extended by some courts, especially since World War II, to include other civic meetings that have no official governmental connection. One such instance was a holding of the United States Court of Appeals for the Ninth Circuit in which privilege was extended to a newspaper account of a meeting of the Good Government Association of Moscow, Idaho. Those attending the meeting asked for a grand jury investigation of a justice of the peace for dismissing a complaint. The peace justice filed a libel suit against both those making the statements and the newspaper that published them. The court, however, held that the proceedings of a public gathering, like those of a judicial hearing, were privileged. It was pointed out that the state constitution gave the people a right of assembly and that the gathering was similar to the old New England town meetings to which everyone was invited.[59]

The court went on to say that the conditional privilege to speak on or print matters concerning public officials was limited in that no attacks could be made on the private character of officials and that the subject matter could not go beyond public concern. This was not violated, the court said; hence the newspaper could not be held responsible for libel as an accurate report of the privileged proceedings was published.[60] Interestingly, the court refused to speculate on whether "false facts" or comment were involved at the meeting, stating there was no evidence at this time that Idaho courts had ruled on whether privilege extended to false statements or comment.[61] Again the privilege of fair and accurate reports was merged with the privilege of discussing the acts of officials without malice.

The privilege of publishing true and impartial accounts of proceedings in the United States Congress without liability for libel was established beyond a doubt in a series of 1923–24 court cases. All were filed by Charles C. Cresson, who had been an army prosecuting attorney. He objected to newspaper stories on a congressional committee report. The newspaper stories, which were supplied by news services, said the majority report of the committee named Cresson as playing a leading part in a conspiracy to help convicted draft dodger Grover Bergdoll escape to Germany. State courts in Pennsylvania and Texas and federal courts in Kentucky and Minnesota held that while the charge was libelous, the stories in the newspapers were privileged as fair and accurate summaries of the official report.[62]

Even secret congressional committee proceedings, if officially released by a committee member, were held to be privileged by the New Jersey Supreme Court in 1959. The decision was made in a suit that arose after Senator Joseph McCarthy released information on an investigation of purported Communist activities at Fort Monmouth, New Jersey. He asserted that the chief of the systems section of Evans Signal Laboratory, an ex-Marine, had been the roommate of convicted atom spy Julius Rosenberg and may have been the direct link to Rosenberg. The systems section official, McCarthy claimed, had kept forty-three classified documents in his apartment at a time Rosenberg and several other known Communists had keys and access to the apartment. The officer claimed all of this was false. But the New Jersey Supreme Court said it was privileged and not subject to libel so long as it was communicated without actual malice.[63] Actual malice existed, the court said, only if the publisher had full knowledge of falsity or used the occasion to justify anger without just cause.[64]

The New Jersey Supreme Court went even further. McCarthy said after one of the closed committee meetings that the Justice Department had decided the systems section officer could be brought to trial, and that evidence was being forwarded to a grand jury. This too was privileged, the court said. To hold matter in excess of the committee proceedings as evidence of malice would defeat the protection granted by privilege. The subject matter was of public concern, the court said, and the people had a right to know about matters "substantially related to national security and defense."[65]

Further clarification of privilege concerning congressional reports came in a 1960 decision of the United States District Court for the District of Columbia. The case was brought by Congressman George S. McGovern over a syndicated newsletter. The news report, by reprinting only a portion of a United States House of Representatives' official report, falsely claimed that McGovern had sponsored a "Communist Front" known as the American Peace Crusade. A counter claim of libel was filed against McGovern by the publisher. Here it was claimed that McGovern had inserted matter in the Congressional Record, not spoken on the floor of the House, to the effect that the publisher had been employed to defame the Farmers Union.

In determining the libel suit, the court held that the United States Constitution gave congressmen an absolute privilege for immunity to libel for any matter discussed in Congress. This privilege, it was ruled, did not depend on purpose, motive, or reasonableness.[66] Further, it was held that legislative privilege extended to material not spoken on the floor but inserted in the Congressional Record with consent of the House.[67] As a result, the counter claim of libel was dismissed; however, the court did say that if a congressman republished portions of the *Congressional Record* for unofficial dissemination, the congressman could claim only a qualified privilege for these reprints. The dictum was as follows:

> Congressmen have responsibility to inform constituents, and circulation of *Congressional Record* is a convenient method of doing so, but then action in republishing material in *Congressional Record* is only qualified by privilege and thus they are protected in their unofficial dissemination of defamatory matter in *Congressional Record* only if they do not act maliciously.[68]

As far as the publisher's partial account of the report concerning McGovern, the court ruled that a jury, in determining fact, would have to determine if the report was fair and accurate.

A day after this decision, however, the United States Court of Appeals for the District of Columbia ruled that fragmentary references to proceedings of Congress could not be considered fair and accurate reports and hence were not privileged. The decision was in a suit brought by Harry H. Vaughan, who had been military aide to President Harry S Truman, against the *Saturday Evening Post*. In an article about columnist Drew Pearson, "Confessions of an S.O.B.," the magazine had printed Vaughan's picture as one of those whom Pearson had exposed. The picture carried a caption claiming many charges against Vaughan had been confirmed by testimony before a Senate committee. Vaughan sued for libel and won a ten-thousand-dollar verdict in trial court, and the verdict was upheld in the appeals court. The fact that an investigation by a Senate committee was made did not give any privilege to publish false matter on one's own authority, the court said.[69] Immunity from libel required a fair and accurate report and could not center on a portion of a proceeding to leave a false impression.

The Vaughan decision split the court two to one. Mr. Justice Henry W. Edgerton stated that the court had previously declared in *Sweeney v. Patterson* that false statements about public officials were privileged if there were no charges of crime or gross immorality. Though Vaughan claimed the magazine article imputed malfeasance, Judge Edgerton's dissenting opinion claimed there was no more than a charge of impropriety. The article should have been privileged, he said, because it was discussion of a public official.[70] This again underscored the possibility of a double defense in suits brought by public officials for libel in reports concerning public meetings. One was the privilege of discussion, and the other was the privilege of making fair and accurate reports.

SUMMARY

Courts through the years have been faced with a parallel growth of separate doctrines of privilege. One of these doctrines provided that publishers cannot be held responsible for fair and accurate reports of official transactions and public meetings. This doctrine grew slowly. But twentieth-century cases have allowed this libel-free privilege for newspaper reports on the proceedings of the legislative, executive, and judicial branches of practically all levels of government. It generally has been held that publishers were not liable for any false and defamatory matter in these official reports and proceedings unless their articles were published with actual malice.

After World War II, there was a noticeable trend toward expansion of the fair and accurate report privilege. In some instances, state courts extended the privilege to include the proceedings of political rallies and other unofficial civic meetings as well as political speeches. It was held that newspapers have a duty to publish such material to inform the people. Even secret proceedings of a congressional committee and a city council have been declared privileged because the people had a right to know about the matters involved.

Frequently cases arose in which there was no clear line between a report of a proceeding, as such, and separate discussion of an official or candidate. When public officials and candidates for office claimed they were libeled in articles about public proceedings, there was a possibility of a double defense. Newspapermen could claim either that fair and accurate reports of the proceedings were published or they could claim privileged discussion. The best defense consistently was the privilege to make a fair and accurate report. This privilege, in all states, could be defeated only by an aggrieved official or candidate showing actual malice in publication.

And actual malice generally required, in such cases, that the publisher knew material he published was false or that he published the report to gratify anger without cause. There was no such uniformity in the doctrine of privileged discussion. Through the years some states extended this to fair comment based on facts while other states allowed privilege for any nonmalicious publication so long as there was probable cause for believing it true.

11. Shift to Liberalism

Greater Tolerance of Discussion

Libel battles between public officials and newspapermen after
World War II were fought in courts reflecting rapidly changing
public policies.[1] Frequently the parties to these libel actions found
that the established rules of fair comment and privilege were no
longer appropriate. Judges began to bend the rules in seeking what
the United States Supreme Court referred to as a "ground for a
rational compromise between individual rights and public welfare." [2] The general tendency was toward wider tolerance of discussion concerning government, government officials, and candidates
for government office.

Perhaps this liberal movement was led by the Supreme Court
itself. Immediately after World War II the Court refused to hold
two newspapermen in contempt of court for harsh, unfair, and even
partially untrue condemnations of judges. Instead, it stated that
"freedom of discussion should be given the widest range compatible
with the essential requirement of a fair and orderly administration
of justice." [3] And in 1959, the Supreme Court declared federal
officials were absolutely immune to libel for statements made about
their official duties. In another case, it ruled that state libel laws
did not apply to television and radio stations for defamatory political speeches made on equal time broadcasts.[4]

This liberal judicial trend was noticeable in a variety of decisions rendered by judges throughout the nation, even in states that
retained the narrow view of privilege. Courts in many of these
states, while holding to the doctrine that criticism had to be based
on facts, began to give newspapermen more leeway with facts in

190

discussing the public lives of both officials and candidates. And courts in at least three states shifted outright to the liberal rule of privilege, joining other courts that prohibited libel judgments for nonmalicious falsehoods about the public conduct of those seeking and holding public office.

There were, of course, many state courts that reaffirmed and strengthened their adherence to the narrow rule. But even in these courts, dissenting opinions stressing a free press and the right to discuss public affairs became more common. And the libel judgments awarded were largely confined to cases that involved specific charges of misconduct, crime, or dishonesty.

In many instances after World War II, public officials found difficulty in keeping libel actions before the courts. While the appellate judges in each state continued to interpret their laws of libel in their own way,[5] they began to look more favorably upon newspapermen's pleas that public officials' libel claims were unfounded. Many gave newspapermen the benefit of doubt if published words were capable of innocent construction. And a growing number of suits after World War II were dismissed by appellate judges before trial, on the grounds there were no bona fide issues of libel.

Judges in both California and Colorado, for instance, dismissed separate but similar defamation suits brought by officials because of statements which charged them with accumulating more money than their salaries afforded.[6] The judges said that specific charges of dishonesty were not made and could not be inferred. An Illinois appeals court also held in 1955 that no libel existed in a newspaper article quoting an investigator as saying he saw a county commissioner receiving money from a dogcatcher.[7] An ordinary reader, the court held, would not understand this to be a charge of embezzlement as claimed.

Perhaps the rationale for these decisions was best explained in another Illinois appeals court decision, which stated that published words would be given an innocent construction if they were susceptible of it.[8] In this case, the court said a police magistrate had not been libeled by a newspaper article which claimed he refused to file monthly reports unless he was forced to do so by the city council. Similarly, a legislator was not libeled, a Texas civil appeals court said in 1955, by a newspaper article stating his investigation of gambling resulted from a convicted murderess' affidavit. There was nothing reflecting on him personally or indicating that he solicited false affidavits.[9]

Judges, too, seemed to have particular difficulty in obtaining libel judgments in the post–World War II years. The Wisconsin Supreme Court ruled in 1946 that it was not libelous for a newspaper to state a judge spent most of his time in a building containing his office and a tavern.[10] It also was held in Georgia that since a judge has a legal duty to instruct and direct grand jurors, he could not be libeled by a newspaper article claiming he instituted or directed a grand jury investigation.[11] In Michigan, it was ruled that an article stating that a judge went to a police station to post bail for two men was not libelous. The judge claimed the article imputed that he, as a judge, was obligated to certain persons; but the Michigan Supreme Court said he was acting as an individual in posting bond, not as a judge.[12]

Criticism which simply caused injury to the feelings of officials and candidates normally was found not to be defamatory. The Massachusetts Supreme Judicial Court, for instance, held in 1951 that it was not libelous to charge that an official acted in his own interests rather than in the interest of taxpayers.[13] And the court said a political advertisement asking eight rather pointed questions did no more than claim that a city councilman was working officially in his own behalf. The Oklahoma Supreme Court also ruled in 1958 that a cartoon advertisement showing a candidate taking money from a man labeled "taxpayer" was not libelous. The advertisement may have hurt the candidate's feelings, the court said; but since officials could legally levy taxes, there was no charge of breach of trust and consequently no libel.[14]

Judges, then, frequently dismissed suits brought by officials and candidates on the grounds that no libel existed. They were looking at the innocent construction of articles and bending the old rule that trials would be ordered if articles were reasonably susceptible of being construed as libel.[15] The rulings were made strictly on the basis of libel or no libel and did not impinge on such defenses as truth, privilege, or fair comment. Judges, it appeared, were beginning to tolerate a wide degree of freedom in discussion of public servants.

The shift in attitude concerning libel perhaps was nowhere more pronounced than in a 1958 decision of Judge Nathan R. Sobel of the Kings County Court in New York. Judge Sobel dismissed a criminal libel indictment with a ruling that libel in itself was not a public offense.[16] He said that libel was a special kind of crime, originally having been made punishable because of its tendency to provoke individuals to revenge. Stressing that this breach-of-the-peace basis for criminal prosecutions was no longer valid, he held that criminal prosecutions for libel should be sought only when there was a flagrant public wrong.[17]

The decision, perhaps, reflected the practicalities of the law of libel. While the number of civil suits had grown steadily during the years, the number of criminal prosecutions had dropped drastically. One study indicates that in the half-century ending in 1965, there were only half as many libel prosecutions as in the previous half-century. And of the twentieth-century criminal libel cases, only thirty-one involving public officials reached courts of final jurisdiction or were tried by federal judges. Nine of these involved newspapers,[18] and one could not say that the prosecutions against newspapers were to prevent aggrieved parties from taking revenge. It would be closer to the truth to state that the prosecutions themselves constituted a form of revenge. In this context, it would appear that Judge Sobel's decision was timely.

The infrequency of criminal libel prosecutions was nowhere more emphasized than in a 1946 Alabama case. During an election campaign, a man was indicted for libel after circulating a political dodger accusing the town mayor of Warrior of "pocketing" more than one thousand dollars in city funds. He was convicted of libel on the basis of malice, without being given a chance to prove the truth. And the Alabama Court of Appeals, citing cases from early common law, ruled that the publication did not have to be false to be criminally libelous. Truth was no defense at common law when there was a tendency to breach the peace, the court held.[19]

This antiquated decision was reversed by the Alabama Supreme Court on appeal. This court of final jurisdiction, perhaps to excuse the lower court's decision, stated that Alabama appellate courts had not previously determined a criminal libel case.[20] The state supreme court then turned to the 1804 *Croswell* case in New York as determinative of the issue. It was held by the Alabama court that a jury had the right to consider both the facts and libel, along with privilege, and that truth was a complete defense.[21]

The rarity of criminal libel cases[22] and the inertia in the growth of the law in this area is demonstrated by the fact that the judges of the Alabama Supreme Court felt compelled to rest a 1946 decision on an 1804 precedent. This rigidity was most unfortunate. By still holding to the ancient doctrine that publications tending to create disturbances of the peace were criminally libelous, courts were ignoring the conditions of the times. In this context, again, Judge Sobel's 1958 decision in New York, discounting the view that a libelous article would bring revenge that would disturb the peace, represented an attempt to adapt the law to the modern environment.

Modern thinking also influenced post–World War II decisions dealing with privilege. This was true even in narrow-rule states that denied privilege for misstatements of fact about the public acts of public officials and candidates. In some of these states, judges began to excuse libel against officials on the basis of fair comment where there was merely a substratum of fact, or a foundation of fact. Emphasis began to be placed on free comment instead of fair comment, and honest mistakes were excused, along with occasional errors that came with the rapid handling of news. The thrust was toward more freedom of discussion.

For example, the Florida Supreme Court, one of those adhering to the narrow rule, in 1950 excused erroneous statements in a critical editorial about a former city attorney who filed a mandamus action against his city to force a tax increase. The court said:

> When it is recalled that a reporter is expected to determine such fact in a matter of hours, it is only reasonable to expect that occasional errors will be made. Yet, since the preservation of our American democracy depends upon the public's receiving information speedily—particularly upon getting the news of pending matters while there still is time for public opinion to form and be felt—it is vital that no unreasonable restraint be placed upon the working news reporter or the editorial writer.[23]

The Florida Court of Appeals in 1961, however, made it clear that false imputations of crime, or malfeasance, were not privileged as fair comment.[24] A one-hundred-thousand-dollar libel judgment was upheld against the Miami Herald for claiming a state's attorney muzzled a grand jury in an attempt to protect someone. The decision carried by only one vote, and the dissenting opinion contended freedom of the press was being impaired.[25]

In a case the next year, the court unanimously refused to hold the same newspaper responsible for falsehoods in an article claiming the Internal Revenue Service had seized a city councilman's pay checks to satisfy tax liens. While this was not true, the pay checks were being given to the service by the councilman, and the court said the ultimate effect of the published falsehood was no different than the truth.[26] The newspaper could not be held to exact facts or minute details, the court said.[27]

Further, the Florida courts held publishers liable only for actual damages if mistakes were made honestly, with grounds for believing truth. Publishers making mistakes could show good faith by printing retractions.[28] Retractions also delimited the award of punitive damages in New Jersey. However, the New Jersey Supreme Court ruled in 1956 that a retraction, to be effective, had to be frank and full, "without insinuations or hesitant withdrawals." [29] A retraction also had to be given space and prominence equal to the original charges.[30] The suit at issue had been brought by a city councilman falsely accused by the *Passaic Daily News* of being in a political fist-fight with the dog warden of the city of Clifton. The court ruled that the newspaper's publication of the councilman's denial was not a retraction.[31] There had to be an honest endeavor on the part of the newspaper itself to repair the wrong.

In 1957, the New Jersey Supreme Court reasserted its acceptance of the narrow rule of privilege, that fair comment must be based on facts. But the decision, in a case brought by a member of the Bergen Board of Freeholders over a news release, allowed considerable freedom with facts. The news release stated the official served as director of the board when it condemned some property to give him a "windfall profit." The property condemned belonged to a corporation of which the official was a stockholder. He sued for libel, claiming that he did not direct the condemnation as the article indicated, that the condemnation was to gain park land and not to give him a profit, and that the records showed he voted against condemnation. However, the court declared the article was fair comment and not libelous.[32] He was the director of the board, which was claimed by the article, and he did receive a profit. The court said this constituted a "sufficient substratum of fact" to justify the article.[33] This decision and one in 1959 greatly broadened the fair comment doctrine in New Jersey. In the 1959 case, it was held again by that state's courts that all that was required for fair comment was a sufficient substratum of fact.[34]

Criticism also appeared to be privileged in Mississippi so long

as it was based on a substratum of fact. There was evidence of this
in a 1955 slander suit that arose when a sheriff claimed his opponent
had attempted to influence an election by shooting at his own car
and then claiming he was attacked. The car had been shot at, and
the Mississippi Supreme Court said the sheriff's opponent would
have to prove the statement both false and malicious before he
could obtain a judgment.[35] And the court specifically ruled in 1957
that conditional privilege was not abused when statements of fact
had some foundation in truth.[36] Privilege was extended on this
basis to an editorial in the *Delta Democrat* stating a public figure
had distorted facts in a liquor election.

The Mississippi Supreme Court held in 1963, however, in the
case of *Henry* v. *Collins*, that privilege did not extend to a statement issued to newspapers by a civil rights worker charging a county
attorney and a police chief with plotting his unlawful arrest. The
charges were made recklessly without regard to the truth, the court
said, and privilege did not extend to malicious charges of crime.[37]
This decision was criticized as a threat to the civil rights movement
in the South,[38] and it eventually was overruled by the United States
Supreme Court.[39] Still, the holding, that there was no privilege for
charges of crime, was no different from those holdings in other states
following the narrow rule of privilege. Except for charges of crime,
the Mississippi Supreme Court appeared to tolerate a wide degree
of freedom. All that was necessary for privilege, it would appear,
was a foundation for truth, not necessarily the truth itself.

The Washington Supreme Court in 1955 also appeared to
relax its narrow rule of privilege, that no misstatement of fact was
privileged.[40] Perhaps this was because of pressure from some of the
court's judges who wanted to shift outright to the liberal rule of
privilege. The case involved was brought against the *Tri-City Herald*
by a school board member accused of furnishing supplies and materials to school construction contractors. The article was published
prior to a state auditor's investigation concerning the disposition of
school surplus property. Four of the judges wanted to apply the
liberal rule, excusing the libel because of sufficient cause for believing the charges true.[41] But it was held by a bare majority of five
judges that probable cause for belief was not sufficient justification
for defamatory publications charging officials with crime, misconduct, or improper motives.[42] The case was remanded for retrial,
however, because the jury had improperly multiplied the circulation

of the newspaper by one dollar to arrive at a forty-thousand-dollar damage award.

In a later case, in 1961, the court held that only compensatory damages could be allowed public officials in Washington libel cases.[43] A similar rule was in effect in Massachusetts, where Senator Owen Brewster was able to win only a one-cent libel judgment against the *Boston Herald-Traveler* in 1960.[44] He claimed that a newspaper story accusing him of using wire taps prevented his appointment as counsel to the Congressional Committee on the District of Columbia, headed by Senator Joseph McCarthy.

Senator McCarthy's "witch hunts" for Communists in government were having their effect in libel suits during this period. In at least two occasions after World War II, the New York Court of Appeals held that it was libelous to falsely call officials or candidates either Communists or Communist sympathizers.[45] In other respects, however, a more liberal trend was noticeable in New York as elsewhere. As an example, the appellate division of the New York Supreme Court held in 1961 that a newspaper editorial which inaccurately charged a district attorney with improper conduct in excluding the press from a pretrial hearing was not libelous. The official's action was proper, the court held, but inaccurate criticism was not libelous.[46] In arriving at such a decision, the court explained that consideration had to be given to a newspaper's right of "free comment" when public officials were involved.[47]

In the following year, 1962, the New York Supreme Court again reiterated its stand that false statements about public officers went beyond the point of fair comment. An article in the *Rockland County Citizen* claiming a candidate for supervisor was a "fast-buck" artist who attempted a raid on the "public till" was declared libelous.[48] This was a charge of crime. However, the court stated that otherwise the communication media were not confined to weak, passive or queasy words.[49] It added that libel decisions had to give reasonable latitude to the communication media in discussing the record and qualifications of all candidates.

Despite the growing emphasis placed by courts on free comment, libel against officials still was common, especially when specific charges of misconduct or crime were charged. As an example, an Illinois appeals court held in 1946 that a judge was libeled by an article in the *East St. Louis Journal* which accused him of selling jobs in his office.[50] Factual allegations were not privileged, the court said, even when one of the judge's employees signed an affidavit for the Illinois Attorney General claiming she had to give the judge a portion of her salary each month. No charges were ever filed, and the court said malice in fact was shown by the lack of investigation into the facts and the sensational play given the article.[51] A twenty-thousand-dollar libel judgment was upheld.

A libel judgment against *Colliers* magazine also was upheld in a United States Circuit Court of Appeals in 1947 on the basis of malice. The magazine carried a story quoting part of a letter written by Florida Governor Millard F. Caldwell which made it appear that he sanctioned the action of a mob that took a Negro from jail and shot him to death. The governor heard of the story prior to publication and called the publisher's attention to the entire letter. But the excerpt was printed anyway and resulted in the libel suit. The court of appeals held that there was a qualified privilege to discuss and criticize official records of public men, but that facts could not be perverted.[52] A false imputation resulted from the partial statement, the court said, and malice was shown by the circumstances.[53] The qualified privilege that existed, it was held, could not be a "cloak for malice." [54]

The North Dakota Supreme Court in 1955 clarified its somewhat hazy position on privilege, stating it extended only to fair comment based on factual foundations.[55] In doing so, it held that a state dairy commissioner had a legitimate libel case against a union newspaper that had stated he was a "tool" of large dairy corporations, from which he solicited expense funds, and was working against small dairy farmers. The newspaper had compared the official to a police chief who solicited funds from tavern operators. Such a charge cited a specific instance of dishonesty and could not be fair comment, the court said.

An insinuation of impropriety concerning the governor of Maine also was held libelous by the Maine Supreme Judicial Court in 1956. An article printed in three newspapers stated the governor had asked two members of the state liquor commission to grant licenses to three individuals. In view of the tenor and insinuations of favoritism, the court said the article was libelous per se. While the court was ruling only on a question of demurrer, it added that the privilege of fair comment did not extend to false statements.[56]

The Ohio Supreme Court also denied privilege for false statements in a 1947 case involving the *Cleveland Press*. The newspaper printed an article entitled "Blood on our Judges," with pictures of several judges, in which it was charged that they had been influenced by political pressure and inducement from lawyers to grant continuances of an underworld figure's trial. While free awaiting trial, the man had killed a prostitute and stuffed the body in his car trunk. When apprehended, both he and an officer were killed in a gun fight. The newspaper claimed the blood of the victims was on the hands of judges because the continuances provided the man an opportunity to commit murder. A judge of municipal court named in the article brought suit. She had given a continuance in the trial, but at the request of the prosecutor, not the defense. The court held that the allegations of misconduct and want of integrity were libelous and not privileged.[57]

A false implication of dishonesty concerning the president of a city library board also was declared without the bounds of privilege by the Louisiana Supreme Court in 1955. The suit was brought over an editorial stating a library board president had sold some of his land to the board for more than he paid. The court said the official had bought the land eight years before, that the value had gone up, and that the record clearly showed the land was desired by the board for a library building. Fair comment did not extend to charges that an official violated public trust for private gain, the court said.[58] In 1960, the court again denied privilege for false statements claiming a candidate for Congress had taken off his wings and refused to fly when recalled to active duty in the Korean War.[59] Evidence showed that the candidate had requested and received a transfer to legal duties in the Air Force because he had graduated from law school.

One decision, issued by the Maryland Court of Appeals in 1961, held that an editorial was libelous because it referred to a police officer as infamous. The editorial belittled a legislative investigation of a police commissioner; and in doing so, it criticized the police officer conducting the legislative inquiry. The majority of the court held that facts had to be set out in the editorial itself to warrant the charge of infamous.[60] A forty-five-thousand-dollar libel judgment was upheld despite a strong dissent.[61]

Different views concerning privilege also were prevalent in Texas. A false allegation that a county attorney had fired shots at the feet of several Negroes was declared privileged in 1950 by a Texas Court of Civil Appeals.[62] But on review, the Texas Supreme

Court held the statement to be libelous per se. The charge constituted grounds for the official's removal, and the Supreme Court
said:

> The liberal rule relating to the privilege of newspapers to a
> reasonable and fair comment of the official acts of public officials
> does not apply to the publication of an article not true which would
> subject a public official to removal from office.[63]

The Texas courts, then, continued to abide by both the narrow
and liberal rules of privilege. The liberal rule, allowing untrue condemnations of officials, prevailed except when charges constituted
a basis for removal.[64]

An example of this was a 1959 suit filed by a candidate over
an advertisement which stated he was a "radical" backed by "big
shot labor bosses." The Texas Court of Civil Appeals said it was
"no libel, erroneous or otherwise, to say a person supports political
views where citizens differ." [65] There was nothing in the charge to
cause removal from office.

The Texans' double view of privilege appeared to be followed
to some extent by a number of other state courts which formally
subscribed to the strict version of the narrow rule prohibiting privilege for misstatements of fact. While libel against officials in these
states still was not unusual, the range of permissible discussion
seemingly had been expanded considerably. The bulk of the libel
judgments sustained by their courts of final jurisdiction after
World War II resulted from newspaper charges of crime or misconduct or dishonesty.

Meanwhile, the number of states following the liberal rule of
privilege increased after World War II. As an example, the privilege
to communicate nonmalicious falsehoods about the public actions
of officials again was condoned in Georgia, where the law had been
uncertain since 1929.[66] And courts in three other states—states that
previously had not followed the liberal rule—rendered decisions protecting published untruths about the public acts of officials when
there was probable cause for believing them true. These states,
Idaho, Nevada, and Virginia, joined the list of older liberal rule
states, many of whose courts during this postwar period again reasserted a privilege for misstatements of fact.

The uncertain doctrine of privilege in Georgia was clarified
in 1956 by the decision of the Georgia Court of Appeals in Camp v.
Maddox. The case involved an imputation of crime. While an offi-

cial was not involved, the question of privilege was, and the court quoted the public official rule in the 1925 decision of *McIntosh v. Williams* as determinative of the law. This case had extended privilege to charges of misconduct against officials so long as the charges were true or were made in good faith and without malice.[67]

In Idaho, the liberal rule was announced in the 1954 case of *Gough v. Tribune Journal Co.*, filed by a county commissioner after the *Idaho State Journal* printed a taxpayer's letter asking for a recall election because of commission budget transactions. The commissioner alleged that the letter falsely claimed that a public meeting was not held on the budget. But the court ruled that false statements made in discussions concerning the official acts of public officers were not libelous if there was ground for believing them true.[68] The privilege, the court said, extended to newspapers and taxpayers alike.

The liberal rule of privilege was applied in Nevada by a United States district court in 1954. The decision was in the case of *Reynolds et al v. Arentz*, which involved a charge that a public hospital administrator was practicing medicine in a county hospital even though he was not a doctor. The court found that any practice by the administrator was under a doctor's guidance. But it held that the statement was privileged because it was communicated in good faith with reasonable grounds for believing it true.[69] The decision was based on Nevada law. The court recognized that it was changing that law, however, as the narrow rule had been announced in another federal court case in 1929.[70] It was pointed out that the earlier decision was made by a federal judge from Idaho sitting in the Nevada district.

A letter to the editor of the *Virginia Pilot* sparked the libel suit that led the supreme court of appeals in Virginia to rule in 1956 that qualifiedly privileged publications can be libelous only if malicious. The letter stated school children were suffering from a decision of unscrupulous school officials who repaired buildings only to vacate them so they would become surplus and could be purchased by a private school concern. The action was blamed on the South Norfolk school superintendent, who sued for libel. The supreme court of appeals held that the article was not libelous; but that even if it were, it was protected by qualified privilege. The court said, "It is not a question of whether the imputations are true, but whether the words are such as the author might have honestly used under the circumstances." [71] Malice in fact had to be proved to defeat the privilege of discussing officials in their public capacity, the court said.[72]

Many state courts reasserted the liberal rule of privilege after World War II. For instance, the Pennsylvania Supreme Court ruled in 1950 that malice in fact did not exist if privileged publications were made with belief or reasonable grounds for belief in truth.[73] The ruling admitted that an article was misleading in quoting a county treasurer's deputy as saying "we all have to have a little Communism today" because it did not disclose that the statement was in answer to a charge that Communists were in the Democratic party. But the court said "not every lie is a libel." [74]

The North Carolina Supreme Court held again in 1955 and 1962 that all falsehoods about officials were not libelous. Privilege extended to false articles, the court said, unless publishers knew articles to be false or had no probable cause for believing them true.[75] This included one charge in a newspaper's letter column that election officials had fraudulently certified vote returns. Evidence did show that poll books had not been properly maintained, which was considered cause for belief in the charge.[76] Another case involved an editorial claiming the purchase of land by a city council "smelled." The court said this was a charge of wastefulness, not corruption.[77]

A pamphlet that accused a city councilman of taking a bribe to make a zoning change was declared privileged by the Minnesota Supreme Court in 1962. The court said the charge could not be both false and malicious, but that the burden was on the official to prove that the publisher was actuated by malice.[78] And in New Hampshire, the privilege of making misstatements of fact was extended to articles about state committeemen in political parties, who the state supreme court said were public officials.[79]

The Kansas Supreme Court in 1959 ruled that a court of common pleas judge would have to prove that the *Wichita Beacon* acted with malice in naming him as the leader of a gang of burglars. The newspaper article was based on official reports of police officers. As a result the court said it was immaterial whether the judge was involved with burglars or not.[80] Though the article reflected on the judge's private character, the court said it also concerned his public performance and was privileged. Both falsity and malice had to be proved.

That there could be abuse of the liberal rule of privilege, however, was shown in two West Virginia cases in 1958. Each was brought against the *Charleston Gazette* by legislators because of an editorial claiming, in effect, that they sold their votes for allotment of state insurance business to their firms. The supreme court of appeals in each case held to the view that both malice and falsity had to be proved before the privileged editorial could be libelous. But malice, it was ruled, could be found from unreasonably violent or vehement language that showed willful imputation of wrongdoing.[81] Further, the court said there was no basis for believing the legislators sold their vote simply because their firms, along with others, were selected for a portion of the state's insurance business.

Jurors in each of these cases found that publications were made with malice, and the libel judgments were upheld. Even with a privilege to make misstatements of fact about public officials, then, it was possible to publish a libel, especially when there was a charge of crime based on no more than supposition. The liberal rule of privilege required that there be probable cause for believing in the truth of statements made.

The growth of radio and the subsequent establishment of nationwide television networks after World War II required that the rules of privilege formulated for the printed media also be applied to broadcast libel. Evidence of this was in a 1951 case involving commentator Drew Pearson. In a radio broadcast originating in California that reached several adjacent states, Pearson charged a candidate for California office with accepting a bribe. A United States district court held that the charge was either libelous or slanderous per se, but privileged nonetheless. In determining the extent of privilege, the court ruled that libel and slander takes place where it is communicated, not where it originates.[82] As a result, privilege applied in California, Arizona, and Utah even if the broadcast was untrue, the court said.[83] But the liberal privilege did not apply in the other states reached by the broadcast as they allowed only fair comment based on true facts.[84]

The trial pointed to three problems. One was the extensive coverage of the broadcast media over several states, providing ever increasing circulation for libels. The second was the disparity in the law concerning privileged communications. And the third was the question as to whether defamatory remarks in broadcasts constituted libel or slander.

While the federal court judge in California was not certain whether a radio broadcast was libel or slander, it was ruled by the United States District Court for the Eastern District of Kentucky that a false and defamatory television broadcast was libelous because it was read from a written script.[85] This too was a bi-state broadcast. A West Virginia television newscaster claimed a Kentucky county attorney had been accused of corruption in trying to "take over" city rackets and "shake down" gamblers and bootleggers. Trial evidence showed there had been no official governmental charge levied. The county attorney had been reported to the Kentucky State Bar Association because he had used underworld figures as "stool pigeons," and one of these men had testified under an assumed name before a grand jury about gambling, only to be arrested himself at a later date. A trial jury found that the television report was both false and malicious and hence libelous.[86]

The federal district judge in this case stated evidence showed the newscast had been made without knowledge of what the charges were. He said:

> The public is entitled to know the truth about those who are conducting public business. . . . We jealously guard our right of freedom of speech, and courts should not, by their judgments, hamper or discourage full and free discussion of public business or circumstances connected with it. . . . Nevertheless, it is equally true that the law should respect and protect the rights of individuals. . . . Freedom to gather and broadcast news does not give a license to defame character, and the dissemination of news must be held within the bounds of reason and justice.[87]

He further said that news agencies have a minimum requirement of using a reasonable degree of care in gathering and broadcasting news. Television station newsmen, then, were now facing the same balancing test that newspapermen had faced long before. The rights of officials to a good name were opposed to the public's right to know.

A decision favoring the public's right to know was rendered in 1955 by the Connecticut Supreme Court of Errors in another case involving libel by radio. In upholding the liberal rule, the court said privilege extended to nonmalicious falsehoods about officials, candidates, and even issues involved in a campaign.[88] Consequently, a manufacturer could not collect damages for false charges made by a candidate for mayor. The candidate had claimed over the air that his opponent's neglect while mayor had caused the manufacturer to reduce production by 90 percent. Though false, it was privileged as an issue in the campaign.

Further, the radio station broadcasting the speech was exonerated of libel on the basis of the Federal Communications Act of 1934. The court held that the station's officials, under the act's equal-time allotment rule, had no power to censor speeches by candidates and could not be responsible for libel in them.[89] The case clearly demonstrated a new problem of jurisdiction in disposing of electronic libel suits brought by officials and candidates. The laws of Connecticut applied to statements broadcast by the candidate, and yet the laws of the federal government protected the electronic media.

The unusual libel problem presented by Federal Communications Commission control of the electronic media eventually had to be resolved by the United States Supreme Court. And the Supreme Court, in the 1959 case of *Farmers Educational & Cooperative Union of America, North Dakota Division v. WDAY, Inc.*, held that state libel laws did not apply to equal-time statements over the electronic media.[90] The decision was made on the basis of federal law, not the constitution. The court said that Station WDAY was not liable for defamation, regardless of state law, because the Federal Communications Act forced the station to allow the equal opportunity speech without power of censorship.

The case arose when a North Dakota candidate for the United States Senate took advantage of the equal-time provision of the Federal Communications Act to reply to opponents on WDAY. In his broadcast, he accused the Farmers Educational & Cooperative Union of America in North Dakota with conspiring to "establish a Communist Farmers Union." [91] The statement was libelous per se, but the broadcasting station could not be held responsible.

The Supreme Court's ruling in some respects placed the electronic media in a preferred position so far as libel against officials and candidates was concerned. Only seven years before, in *Beauharnais v. People of the State of Illinois*, the Supreme Court had ruled that state libel laws did not violate the United States Constitution.[92] And the printed media still were subject to these state libel laws. There was, then, a double standard. Television and radio stations could not be held responsible for libelous statements in equal-time appearances by any candidate or official. Yet, if newspapers or magazines printed these libelous statements, they did not have the same federal protection.

This lack of protection did leave newspapers at a disadvantage. While newspapers, and even magazines, did not have the electronic media's legal responsibility to allow political rebuttals, they nevertheless did have an ethical responsibility to print opposing views of candidates. And they also had a moral responsibility to provide competing voices in the marketplace of ideas.[93] Still, newspapers were not afforded the libel-free protections given the competing electronic media for disseminating antagonistic views.

Further disparity in the law resulted from the Supreme Court's 1959 decision in *Barr v. Matteo*. Here public officials were given an immunity from libel not shared by the common citizen. The decision provided that federal officials could not be held responsible for libel for any statements about their duties or the "outer perimeter" of their duties.[94] The court stated that officials should be "free to exercise their duties unembarrassed by the fear of damage suits." [95] The suit was brought by several government employees who claimed the acting director of the Office of Rent Stabilization had libeled them in a press release.

In another decision the same day, *Howard v. Lyons*, the Supreme Court held that statements by a military officer also were absolutely privileged.[96] A navy captain had been sued because he had voiced dissatisfaction in an official report about an employees' group at the Boston Naval Yard. The report was circulated in the Massachusetts legislature, but under the doctrine of absolute privilege, claims of libel were denied. The net effect was that federal officials could criticize citizens with an immunity to libel, but citizens had no similar immunity to criticize them.

The Supreme Court of the United States, then, had rendered decisions in 1959 that allowed a wide freedom of discussion, but on a select basis. Federal officials could not be subjected to libel judgments for statements made concerning their official duties. And television stations were not to be held responsible for libelous statements made by candidates whose speeches were immune from censorship. For the first time in history, the Supreme Court had held that a state libel law was not applicable. This in itself marked a turning point in the law of libel.

Another turning point perhaps came with a 1963 decision of a United States Court of Appeals in a Connecticut case involving the

New York Times. The court ruled that the newspaper libeled two police officers in an overly fictional account of a police raid on a Connecticut dice game. The published article claimed that, in the resulting melee, one officer struck another, four police night sticks were lost, and only four of ten gamblers were arrested. The raid was compared to a "Keystone Comedy" script. The policemen, in suing for libel, alleged both falsity and malice.

The trial jury was told that under Connecticut law, privilege could be abused if a publisher acted with malice. Malice could be shown, the jury was instructed, if a publisher knew an article was false or if there was "reckless disregard" for facts.[97] In determining reckless disregard, the court held that consideration could be given to whether efforts had been made prior to publication to learn the truth, possibly by contacting the officers involved. The jury found that privilege had been abused and awarded damages of $12,145. The judgment was upheld in *Hogan v. New York Times Co.* by the United States Court of Appeals for the Seventh Circuit, which ruled that reckless disregard for facts was a question for the jury.[98] Further, the court said that the degree of care that should be taken by an experienced reporter in ascertaining facts was higher than that expected from a candidate during the heat of a campaign.

In some respects, the case departed from previous holdings under the liberal rule of privilege. The criterion for malice was not the absence of a probable cause for believing an article true. Instead, the stress in this 1963 case was on knowledge of falsity and on reckless disregard of facts. It was a standard of malice that only a year later was to be modified by the United States Supreme Court in establishing a libel rule for the entire nation.[99]

SUMMARY

The latitude that was allowed for discussion in post–World War II years was not so unusual when one considers the very real emphasis being placed on individual liberties.[100] The war had changed society's entire frame of reference. In the wake of the war, the atomic and hydrogen bombs were developed, nuclear power was harnessed, and space probes were launched. And it had ended with the world divided into two great armed camps, each maneuvering for power. There was a new diffusion of cultures, a diffusion that was heightened by the electronic age, an age in which instant information and awareness could be provided to virtually everyone through the medium of television. Educational opportunities were expanded, standards of living rose, and society became more affluent.[101] At the same time, there were strains of social ferment and political fear. The menace of communism as opposed to democracy was preached. Racial unrest was stirred and grew. And through it all, there was an emphasis on human rights and freedom.

Among those emphasizing individual rights was President Harry S Truman. In vetoing the Internal Security Act of 1950,[102] President Truman said the act's attempt to stifle communism would come closer to destroying the basic liberties of American citizens. He said:

> We need not fear the expression of ideas—we do need to fear their suppression.
> Our position in the vanguard of freedom rests largely on our demonstration that the free expression of opinion, coupled with government by popular consent, leads to national strength and human advancement. Let us not, in cowering and foolish fear, throw away the ideals which are the fundamental basis of a free society.[103]

Here, then, was recognition that free discussion was necessary to government in a democracy. The statement reflected a libertarian philosophy. And despite the conflicting strains of conservatism during the administration of President Dwight D. Eisenhower, the United States Supreme Court under Chief Justice Earl Warren continued to promote a libertarian view. And after later appointments by President John F. Kennedy, who was pledged to the protection of human rights,[104] the Court consistently supported basic liberties.[105]

The views of the United States Supreme Court had a direct effect on state courts everywhere.[106] These courts had to take special care with decisions concerning liberties guaranteed by the United

States Constitution or face possible Supreme Court reversal. And the Supreme Court, through a broad interpretation of the due process clause of the Fourteenth Amendment, persistently prohibited state infringement of basic rights.

The right of discussion, therefore, was often emphasized in judicial decisions dealing with libel against public officials. One judge even ruled that libel itself was no longer a crime. And there was a noticeable drop in the already dwindling number of prosecutions for the offense of libeling public officials. Freedom of discussion frequently was stressed in judgments on civil libel suits as well. As the Supreme Court of New York ruled in 1961, consideration had to be given to the right of "free comment" in libel suits brought by officials and candidates. Still, civil libel judgments for officials and candidates were common, especially when publications charged crime, misconduct, or dishonesty. But even in these cases, courts in both narrow and liberal rule states allowed freedom for discussion.

In fact, a generous measure of privilege for discussion was allowed by state courts after World War II. Courts in the narrow rule states continued to hold that immunity extended only to fair comment and criticism, not to misstatements. In some instances, however, narrow rule courts granted immunity from libel if there was a hidden substratum of fact or if there was an honest mistake. Allowances were made for occasional errors in routine news handling. Some of these decisions, in allowing wide freedom with facts, began to resemble the holdings of liberal rule courts. State court decisions in general, then, were more favorable toward newspaper discussion of public officials and candidates.

Meanwhile, the liberal rule of privilege, allowing immunity from libel for misstatements of fact about the public lives of officials and candidates, gained wider acceptance. Idaho, Georgia, Nevada, and Virginia courts, by rendering liberal rule decisions, swelled the number of states following the so-called minority view to nineteen by the end of President Kennedy's administration.[107] In the same period, the number of state courts limiting privilege to criticism based on facts decreased by one, leaving twenty-one states following the so-called majority view.[108]

While figures alone showed a more even balance between the majority and minority views by the end of the Kennedy admin-

210   DEVELOPMENT AND DIVERGENCY

istration, the figures in themselves were misleading. One reason was the course taken by the District of Columbia, Wyoming, and Texas, jurisdictions which generally subscribed to the liberal or minority view except when charges of crime or misconduct were involved. Another reason was the status of Oklahoma and Missouri. While courts in these states did not allow privilege for misstatement of facts, they placed the burden on officials and candidates to prove falsity when misstatements were claimed. Their standard, then, was considerably more liberal than that of the other courts limiting privilege. Oklahoma courts, especially, granted leeway with facts where crime was not involved.

Further, several of the states following the majority view, such as Florida, New Jersey, Mississippi, and New York, were beginning to allow more freedom with facts, so long as the foundation or substratum of fact remained. The majority view, then, was no longer pure. Moreover, the minority view, in some instances was becoming more liberal. Knowledge of falsity and reckless disregard of facts had been claimed as the standard in one case for determining malice. The trend definitely was toward more freedom in discussing public officials and candidates for office, toward more immunity from libel.

Actually, one could say there was no longer any majority or minority view. The minority had for all practical purposes caught up with the majority. Still, there was discord. Courts in the majority of states west of the Mississippi River and those in a growing number of states on the East Coast either made officials and candidates prove statements false or granted immunity from libel if falsehoods were not published maliciously. The remainder allowed no immunity from libel for misstatements, permitting privilege only for fair comment and criticism. The United States, to paraphrase Abraham Lincoln, was like a courtroom divided. The law as it pertained to libeling public officials and candidates was being administered differently in one part of the courtroom than in another.

Not only was the law being administered differently, it also was being applied differently. Public officials, for instance, had an immunity in making libelous statements that the communication media and the private citizen did not have. Further, as a result of the United States Supreme Court decision in the WDAY case, television and radio stations could not be held responsible under state libel laws for statements made by political candidates in equal-time broadcasts. Yet this libel-free guarantee did not apply to newspapers. If they printed rebuttals made by political candidates, they were subject to state libel laws. Despite the shift to liberalism and a greater tolerance of discussion, then, the need was for uniform administration and application of the laws of libel.

ORDER
AND
COHESION

---

12. A Nationwide Libel Standard

The United States Supreme Court Speaks

On March 9, 1964, the Supreme Court of the United States declared that state courts could not award public officials damages for nonmalicious libels about their official conduct. And in making this declaration, in the case of *New York Times* v. *Sullivan,* the Supreme Court brought order and cohesion to an area of libel jurisprudence that had long suffered from dissonance. It established a new federal rule that prohibited a public official from recovering damages for defamatory falsehoods about his official conduct unless he could prove they were published with knowledge of falsity or with reckless disregard of falsity.[1] The decision, based on the free speech and press guarantees in the First Amendment to the United States Constitution, was made binding on state courts through the Fourteenth Amendment.[2]

Eight months after this decision, in the case of *Garrison* v.

Louisiana, the Supreme Court stipulated that a publisher did not have to have probable cause for believing statements he published about an official's conduct were true. The Court was not talking about the same doctrine of privilege that had so sharply divided the courts of the nation. It was talking about a new constitutional privilege. And in doing so, it came close to saying that an official could not be libeled unless a "calculated falsehood" was published.[3] Further, this case held that the Constitution protected publishers from criminal libel prosecution as well as civil libel judgments. A new and uniform standard for the entire nation had been born.

While the standard was conclusively defined, those to whom it applied were not. The Supreme Court, however, met this issue in the 1966 case of *Rosenblatt* v. *Baer.* Here it held that the term "public official" did not apply to elected officials alone. The Court said public officials included governmental employees, at least those believed by the public to have substantial responsibility for governmental affairs.[4] In the following year, the Court even ruled that public figures, including those who thrust themselves into public view, could not obtain libel damages for nonmalicious falsehoods.[5] In this series of rapid-fire decisions, the Supreme Court had committed itself and the nation to an unfettered press, free to debate and discuss public issues.

New York Times v. Sullivan

It was the discussion of a public issue, the civil rights movement in Montgomery, Alabama, that produced the libel suit of *New York Times* v. *Sullivan.* The public was asked in a full-page advertisement in the *New York Times* to help Southern Negroes achieve human dignity. Funds were requested to support Negro students in nonviolent protests, to help Negroes gain the right to vote, and to assist in defending civil rights leader Dr. Martin Luther King, Jr., against a perjury indictment. It was signed by the "Committee to Defend Martin Luther King and the Struggle for Freedom in the South." [6]

Montgomery Commissioner of Public Affairs L. B. Sullivan, who supervised the police and fire departments, claimed that two paragraphs in the text of the advertisement libeled him. They were as follows:

In Montgomery, Alabama, after students sang "My Country, 'Tis of Thee" on the State Capitol steps, their leaders were expelled from school, and truckloads of police armed with shotguns and tear-gas ringed the Alabama State College Campus. When the entire student body protested to state authority by refusing to re-register, their dining hall was padlocked in an attempt to starve them into submission.

. . . .

Again and again the Southern violators have answered Dr. King's peaceful protests with intimidation and violence. They have bombed his home almost killing his wife and child. They have assaulted his person. They have arrested him seven times—for "speeding," "loitering" and similar "offenses." And now they have charged him with "perjury"—a *felony* under which they could imprison him for ten years.[7]

Though Sullivan was never mentioned by name, he claimed that since he was in charge of the police department, he was accused of ringing the campus with police. Further, he said, the imputation was that police under his direction had padlocked the dining hall. He also claimed that the reference was to him, as police supervisor, when it said "they" had arrested Dr. King seven times, and that the "they" who arrested would be equated by readers with the "they" who bombed Dr. King's home and assaulted him. In effect, he claimed that he and police were accused of intimidation and violence in bombing Dr. King's home, in assaulting him, and in charging him with perjury.

To complicate the picture, many statements in the advertisement were inaccurate.[8] Students had not been expelled for the demonstration on the capitol steps but for demanding lunch counter service at the Montgomery County Courthouse on a different day. While most students protested the expulsion, it was not the entire student body. Nearly all the students reregistered, and the campus dining hall was never padlocked. Further, police had not been called for the capitol-step demonstration. They had never ringed the campus, though on several occasions they had been deployed near the campus. Dr. King had been arrested four times, not seven. And though he claimed to have been assaulted when arrested for loitering outside a courtroom, it had been denied by an officer making the arrest.

In alleging that he had been falsely and maliciously defamed,

Sullivan asked libel damages of five hundred thousand dollars. He was awarded the full amount by an Alabama jury, and the judgment, the largest in the state's history,[9] was sustained by the Alabama Supreme Court. And for the first time in the history of this nation, the Supreme Court of the United States issued a writ of certiorari to review a state judgment in a civil libel suit.

Though there was precedent for the move,[10] the review was unusual. A private law suit was involved, not a state prosecution. And the Fourteenth Amendment guarantees only that states will not abridge citizens' privileges and immunities or deprive individuals of life, liberty, or property without due process of law. Of this, the United States Supreme Court in the New York Times v. Sullivan opinion stated:

> Although this is a civil lawsuit between private parties, the Alabama courts have applied a state rule of law which petitioners claim to impose invalid restrictions on their constitutional freedoms of speech and press. It matters not that law has been applied in a civil action and that it is common law only, though supplemented by statute. . . . The test is not the form in which state power has been applied but, whatever the form, whether such power has in fact been exercised.[11]

A judge in rendering a civil libel judgment, then, was exercising state power. And state power could not be used to abridge freedoms guaranteed by the United States Constitution. This holding, which applied specifically to the New York Times case, had a much wider impact. It marked a turning point in the jurisprudence of libel. It meant that any civil libel judgment in any state could be scrutinized by the nation's highest court to see that freedom was not abridged.

In reviewing the New York Times case, the Supreme Court said that it made no difference that the allegedly libelous statements were in a commercial advertisement. The decision stated:

> Any other conclusion would discourage newspapers from carrying "editorial advertisements" of this type, and so might shut off an important outlet for the promulgation of information and ideas by persons who do not themselves have access to publishing facilities —who wish to exercise their freedom of speech even though they are not members of the press. . . . The effect would be to shackle the First Amendment in its attempt to secure "the widest possible dissemination of information from diverse and antagonistic sources."[12]

The only question at issue, the Court said, was whether the advertisement lost its constitutional protections because of false and
allegedly defamatory statements. It then ruled that neither falsity
nor defamation nor a combination of the two was enough to forfeit
these protections.[13]

The defense of truth, which was allowed in Alabama, was not
a proper standard in libel suits filed by public officials, the Court
said. There had to be an allowance for honest misstatement of facts.
The opinion stated:

> A rule compelling the critic of official conduct to guarantee the
> truth of all his factual assertions—and to do so on pain of libel
> judgments virtually unlimited in amount—leads to a comparable
> "self censorship." . . . Under such a rule, would-be critics of
> official conduct may be deterred from voicing their criticism, even
> though it is believed to be true and even though it is in fact true,
> because of doubt whether it can be proved in court or fear of the
> expense of having to do so. . . . The rule thus dampens the vigor
> and limits the variety of public debate.[14]

The Alabama rule of law, then, did not provide the protection for
the freedoms of speech and press which the Supreme Court of the
United States felt was required by the First and Fourteenth Amendments. Hence, the Alabama judgment was reversed.[15]

But the Supreme Court was not content with the simple reversal of the Alabama libel judgment. The opinion, written by Mr.
Justice William J. Brennan, Jr., specified that it was limiting the
power of all states to award libel damages for statements about the
official conduct of public officers.[16] The crux of the decision came in
these words:

> The constitutional guarantees require, we think, a federal rule
> that prohibits a public official from recovering damages for a
> defamatory falsehood relating to his official conduct unless he
> proves that the statement was made with "actual malice"—that is,
> with knowledge that it was false or with reckless disregard of
> whether it was false or not.[17]

Noticeably, the holding was limited to defamatory statements about
official conduct and did not apply to a public official's private conduct.[18] But if articles concerned their official conduct, public officials
could not collect libel damages unless they proved publishers knew
articles were false or that they recklessly disregarded whether they
were true or false. The decision placed the United States Supreme

Court squarely behind the growing number of states that subscribed to the liberal rule of privilege.[19]

Still, the privilege granted under the new federal rule was conditional. And three Supreme Court justices, while basically agreeing with the majority decision, took exception to the conditions. Mr. Justice Arthur Goldberg, in his concurring opinion, stated there should be "an absolute, unconditional privilege to criticize official conduct despite the harm which may flow from excesses and abuses." [20] In a separate concurrence, Mr. Justice Hugo Black stated the press should be granted an "absolute immunity for criticism of the way public officials do their duty." [21] Both opinions, which were subscribed to by Mr. Justice William O. Douglas, stated the Constitution afforded an absolute right of discussion in this area. Both opinions also expressed fear that the conditions—knowledge of falsity or reckless disregard of truth or falsity—would not stop future juries from awarding libel damages to officials.[22]

Perhaps it was for this reason that the majority opinion served notice that the Supreme Court would review evidence independently of jury findings in similar suits to assure there was no erroneous finding of malice.[23] And in doing so, it held that even if there were a new trial of the New York Times case in Alabama, evidence would not constitutionally support a libel judgment on the basis of the new federal rule of privilege. The opinion stated that those who signed and printed the advertisement had no knowledge of falsity and had not acted recklessly in that regard.[24]

And it was here that the Supreme Court shed light, to some extent, on the boundaries of its criteria for malice. The New York Times had published the advertisement even though news stories in its files would have shown some of the statements to be false. But this did not prove that the newspaper personnel knew the statements were false, the Court held.[25] It was pointed out that those handling the advertisement relied on the good reputation of the sponsors. The failure to check the files showed at most, the Court said, that the newspaper was negligent in not finding errors. And it was ruled that this was "constitutionally insufficient to show the recklessness that is required for a finding of actual malice." [26] Recklessness was, then, something more than mere negligence. And the Supreme Court appeared to be saying that if there was no reason for believing statements false, there was no reckless disregard of falsity in not checking those statements.

Not only was there no reckless disregard of falsity in the publication, but the Court added one final touch by saying that in reality there was no libel against Mr. Sullivan. He originally had been awarded a libel judgment on a holding of Alabama courts that criticism of governmental bodies reflected on those in control. In attacking this holding, the Supreme Court said:

> Raising as it does the possibility that a good-faith critic of government will be penalized for his criticism, the proposition relied on by the Alabama courts strikes at the very center of the constitutionally protected area of free expression. We hold that such a proposition may not constitutionally be utilized to establish that an otherwise impersonal attack on governmental operations was a libel of an official responsible for those operations.[27]

The Court held, in effect, that a public official cannot convert criticism of government into personal criticism for the purposes of a libel suit. Further, the Court made it clear that criticism of government was not only not libelous but was a *duty* of citizens everywhere.[28] In this respect, it said the infamous Sedition Act of 1798, which made it a crime to falsely libel government, had been shown by the "court of history" to be unconstitutional.[29]

By holding, in effect, that seditious libel was unconstitutional, the Supreme Court was not adding color to its decision. It was facing the issue involved. The case could not be separated from its reason for being. And that was an effort by a Negro minority to gain constitutional rights under a government by a white majority.[30]

What's more, there was evidence that Alabama was using its libel laws to suppress Negroes and their supporters in the civil rights movement. Sullivan, in suing the *New York Times*, also had sued four of the eighty-four individuals who signed the published advertisement. Interestingly, the only four sued were Alabama Negro clergymen, including Dr. Martin Luther King's chief lieutenant, the Reverend Mr. Ralph D. Abernathy.[31] The $500,000 state libel judgment had been brought against all the defendants, the newspaper and the clergymen. And an Alabama newspaper, the *Montgomery Advertiser*, carried a headline at the time that "State Finds Formidable Legal Club To Swing At Out-of-State Press." [32] This was no idle boast. When the Supreme Court overturned the *Sullivan* case, there already was another $500,000 libel judgment awarded to a second commissioner on the same advertisement. And

Alabama officials had eleven additional libel suits pending against the newspaper for a total of $5,600,000.[33]

This was ample evidence that an attempt was being made to suppress discussion of Alabama government by making it appear that the discussion reflected on individual officials. Seditious libel was an issue as well as libel against officials. There is scant wonder then, that the Supreme Court of the United States inserted these words in the *New York Times* v. *Sullivan* decision:

> We consider this case against the background of profound national commitment to the principle that debate on public issues should be uninhibited, robust, and wide-open, and that it may well include vehement, caustic, and sometimes unpleasantly sharp attacks on government and public officials.[34]

The entire decision, then, was based on the First Amendment guarantees of free speech and press. The issue was libel, but the foundation was the right to discuss public issues.

Because of this right, and the attempts to suppress it, a new libel law was formulated for the entire nation. A new legal principle was drawn from the experiences of life, or as Mr. Justice Oliver Wendell Holmes, Jr., said years ago, from what is "understood to be convenient." [35] In guarding the individual liberties of all citizens, the Supreme Court expanded the legal freedom of the nation's newspapers to discuss public officials. Under the new federal rule, neither the communications media nor individuals could be held responsible in civil libel suits for nonmalicious falsehoods about the official conduct of public servants.

Garrison v. Louisiana

That the Supreme Court of the United States was firmly committed to the new federal rule became evident eight months later when it decided the case of *Garrison* v. *Louisiana*. This was a criminal libel action, but the Supreme Court said the rule announced in the *New York Times* case for civil libel suits still applied.[36] The Court said that states could not impose criminal sanctions for falsehoods about the public conduct of public officials unless actual malice was proven. And to prove actual malice, it had to be shown that statements were made with knowledge of falsity or with reckless disregard of whether they were true or false.[37]

The decision overturned a criminal libel conviction of New Orleans District Attorney Jim Garrison. He had been prosecuted because of angry accusations he made at a press conference about eight district judges in New Orleans. He accused them of taking overly long vacations, of laziness, of inefficiency, and of hampering his vice investigations by refusing to authorize expenses. In addition, he questioned their motives in refusing the funds and said it raised "interesting questions about the racketeer influences on our eight vacation-minded judges." [38]

The Supreme Court, again in an opinion written by Mr. Justice Brennan, said it made no difference that the judges' private character had been impeached in the attack upon their performance of official duties. The opinion stated:

> Any criticism of the manner in which a public official performs his duties will tend to affect his private, as well as his public reputation. The *New York Times* rule is not rendered inapplicable merely because an official's private reputation, as well as his public reputation, is harmed. The public-official rule protects the paramount public interest in a free flow of information to the people concerning public officials, their servants. To this end, anything which might touch on an official's fitness for office is relevant. Few personal attributes are more germane to fitness for office than dishonesty, malfeasance, or improper motivation, even though these characteristics may also affect the official's private character.[39]

In effect, the Court said that an official's right to a good name is not as important as the public's right to know. Even charges of corrupt motives, dishonesty, or malfeasance in office did not lose their constitutional protections under the new "public-official" rule.

What's more, the Court said the Constitution even protects discussion about the public conduct of officials that stems from hatred, anger, or ill will.[40] This was not actual malice as defined by the newly adopted public-official rule. Criminal or civil sanctions were possible under the new rule, the Court said, only when public officials proved there was a knowing or reckless falsehood.

Elaborating further, the Court said that truthful discussion of public affairs could never be subjected to libel sanctions. The opinion stated that "only those false statements made with a high degree of awareness of their probable falsity . . . may be the subject of either civil or criminal sanctions." [41] The Constitution does not protect the "calculated falsehood," the Court said.[42] And a

calculated falsehood was defined as a "lie, knowingly and deliberately published." [43]

The second condition under which the privilege of discussing
the official conduct of public officers could be defeated, proof of
reckless disregard of the truth, also was explained by the Supreme
Court, to some extent. This did not mean, the Court said, that
public officers could prove that there was no reasonable belief in
the truth of statements published.[44] This would require simply a
showing that ordinary care was not taken by the publisher to find
out whether the statement was false. Of this the Court said:

> The test which we laid down in New York Times is not keyed
> to ordinary care; defeasance of the privilege is conditioned, not on
> mere negligence, but on reckless disregard of the truth.[45]

Even a publisher who did not take ordinary care to determine
whether statements were false, then, could not be held responsible
for libel. Mere negligence in checking facts was not enough for a
civil libel judgment or a criminal libel conviction. The Supreme
Court had set specific guidelines as to what did not constitute reckless disregard for the truth.

These guidelines, along with those defining a knowing falsehood and extending the boundaries of the "official conduct" concept, were of extreme importance in determining the limits of
public discussion about public officials. Perhaps it is just as well
that a specific definition for reckless disregard of the truth was not
proffered. It was clear that falsehoods about the official conduct of
public officials, to be libelous, had to be published with more than
normal awareness that they were likely false.[46]

In both New York Times v. Sullivan and Garrison v. Louisiana,
the Supreme Court had pointed out that privilege granted to the
public to discuss public officials was analogous to the immunity from
actions for libel already enjoyed by public officials.[47] And in each
case, the Court made the following statement:

> It would give public servants an unjustified preference over the
> public they serve, if critics of official conduct did not have a fair
> equivalent of the immunity granted to officials themselves.[48]

In effect, the Court said, there was freedom for mutual criticism.
But the Mississippi courts did not have this view when a county

attorney and police chief were accused of a "diabolical plot" in fabricating a charge of assault against a worker for the National Association for the Advancement of Colored People. Though the charge could be made, the criticism of the charge was held libelous. And the judgment against the worker, Aaron E. Henry, was upheld by the Mississippi Supreme Court in 1963.

The Mississippi judgment was reversed in 1965, however, by the United States Supreme Court in a per curiam opinion. It held that there was no showing that Henry made a knowingly false criticism or that he recklessly disregarded the truth.[49] Though the Supreme Court did not elaborate, it made clear that the new federal rule of privilege, protecting nonmalicious discussion about public officials, was not to be modified.

Further, in *Garrison v. Louisiana,* the Supreme Court had strongly hinted that modern conditions made criminal prosecution for libel inappropriate.[50] It cited the "paucity of prosecutions" and stated state criminal libel statutes would have to be narrowly drawn. And in early 1966, the Supreme Court had occasion to state that the broad Kentucky criminal libel statute was unconstitutional.[51]

The case came to the Court after a labor agitator had been convicted of libel for a "writing calculated to create disturbances of the peace." He had published a pamphlet accusing the Hazard, Kentucky, police chief of deputizing mine operators to stop a mining strike and of blinding a boy. The pamphlet further accused the newspaper publisher in Hazard of withholding money and food sent to strikers, in care of the newspaper, from all over the nation. At the trial, the agitator was found guilty, fined three thousand dollars, and sentenced to jail for six months.

But the Supreme Court overturned the conviction because it was based on a publication "calculated to disturb the peace." Such a standard required a calculation as to the "boiling point" of the groups discussed, the Court said, and did not require an appraisal of the publication itself.[52] The Court said that when a First Amendment right was involved, as here, the law had to be very carefully and narrowly drawn. As the criminal libel law had not been redefined in Kentucky, it was held that it should not be enforced as a penal offense.[53] In this case, then, the Supreme Court again, in effect, put states on warning that criminal libel statutes had to conform to the constitutional guarantees of free discussion.

Rosenblatt v. Baer

One major question still had not been explored. It was the question as to who was a public official, as to who could be discussed with the latitude allowed by the Supreme Court in *New York Times* v. *Sullivan* and in *Garrison* v. *Louisiana*. One of these cases was filed by an elected city commissioner, and the other was a prosecution for statements pertaining to district judges. All were without doubt public officials. Still, clear lines had not been drawn as to the extent of the "public official" designation. This was left until the case of *Rosenblatt* v. *Baer*, decided by the Supreme Court early in 1966.

The suit arose because of a newspaper column written by Alfred D. Rosenblatt about a public ski resort in New Hampshire. At the time he wrote the column, the resort was operated by the state. But six months previously, Frank P. Baer was the appointed supervisor, being directly responsible to three elected county commissioners. The column claimed there had been a huge increase in cash income under the new state management. It further asked what had happened "to all the money last year? and every other year?" and wondered what "magic" the new managers had performed. On the strength of these statements, Baer sued for libel and obtained a $31,500 judgment. After the judgment and before the New Hampshire court affirmed it, the *New York Times* v. *Sullivan* decision was issued. And it was on the principles of the *New York Times* case that the Supreme Court of the United States granted certiorari.

At the outset, the Supreme Court stated that Rosenblatt's column was no more than an "impersonal discussion of government" and contained no clearly libelous statement.[54] It was not enough, the Court said, for Baer to prove that a large part of the community understood the column to charge dishonest manipulation of funds at the resort. The opinion, again written by Mr. Justice Brennan, stated:

> A theory that the column cast indiscriminate suspicion on the members of the group responsible for the conduct of this governmental operation is tantamount to a demand for recovery based on libel of government and therefore is constitutionally insufficient.[55]

Baer was responsible to three county commissioners for the operations, and he could not be libeled unless he showed evidence that the column was made "specifically of and concerning him." [56] On this basis alone the case was reversed.

But there still was a question as to whether Baer, in his position as a public ski resort supervisor, was really a public official. And the Supreme Court had asked attorneys on both sides to brief and argue this point. The purpose clearly was to establish a national, uniform standard for defining the term "public official." The Court said that state standards were insufficient as there could be no state jurisdictional variance on the limits of constitutionally protected expression.[57]

In setting a uniform standard, the Supreme Court said that to assure uninhibited debate on public issues, the new public-official rule would of necessity have to apply to individuals in a position to influence the settlement of those issues. More specifically, the Court held that

> the "public official" designation applies at the very least to those among the hierarchy of government employees who have, or appear to the public to have, substantial responsibility for or control over the conduct of government affairs.[58]

A precise line, then, was not drawn by the Supreme Court. But the definition did include employees as well as officials, and it did provide a guideline for judges in all states and federal jurisdictions.

In the *Baer* case, the Supreme Court said there was a "substantial argument" that he was a public official since he had claimed in his suit that the public regarded him as responsible for ski resort operations.[59] However, the Court did not make a final decision. The issue was sent back to New Hampshire for retrial because the case originally was tried before the *New York Times* decision.[60] In the original trial, Baer had proved only that Rosenblatt's column contained negligent misstatements of fact. The Supreme Court stated that if Baer was determined to be a public official, he would have to prove that the column was published with knowledge of falsity or with reckless disregard of whether it was true or false. Possibly, the Court said, Baer could prove he was not a public official. Then he would not have to show a knowing or reckless falsehood.[61] Still, he would have to show he had been libeled.

This was the first of the three public-official rule cases in which all justices did not concur. There was a division of thought, obviously, as to Baer's status. Mr. Justices Douglas and Black, for instance, concurred as to the reversal but dissented as to the retrial. Both said there should be no limit on discussion as to the way any agent of government does his job.[62] Douglas said this should also include discussion of individuals contracting to do government work.[63] On the other hand, Mr. Justice Potter Stewart wrote a separate concurring opinion in which he cautioned that the New York Times rule did not apply to libel of private citizens.[64] A dissent on the portion of the opinion that dealt with impersonal libel came from Mr. Justice John Marshall Harlan. The Rosenblatt column, he said, was not aimed at such a wide group as the "police" that had been cited in the Sullivan case. He felt it was aimed at a group so small that a jury could legitimately make a direct connection to Baer.[65] A complete dissent was lodged by Mr. Justice Abe Fortas on the ground that the writ of certiorari should not have been granted as the trial was before the New York Times v. Sullivan decision.[66]

Noticeably, none of the dissenters questioned the newly formulated public-official rule that prohibited civil or criminal libel sanctions for nonmalicious falsehoods about the public conduct of public officials.[67] There was concern for protecting private individuals from defamation, and there was concern lest the concept of libel on government would be over expanded. Two justices even wanted to make the definition of public officials more encompassing. The majority held, however, that the term public official applied only to those employees thought by the public to have substantial responsibility for governmental operations.

The Supreme Court's definition of a public official in Rosenblatt v. Baer was grounded on the thesis that the public should have wide freedom to discuss those in positions to influence the resolution of public issues.[68] Since all public issues are not governmental issues, it stood to reason that individuals other than public officials could influence public issues. If so, did the federal libel rule promulgated in the New York Times case apply to these public figures as well as to public officials? This question was presented to the Supreme Court in the 1967 case of Curtis Publishing Co. v. Butts, which incorporated Associated Press v. Walker.

Wallace Butts, former athletic director at the University of Georgia, sued the Saturday Evening Post over an article that claimed he had secretly outlined Georgia's football plays for the University of Alabama football coach about a week before the 1962 Georgia-Alabama football game. Former Major General Edwin A. Walker sued the Associated Press for a 1962 article claiming he had "assumed command of the crowd" and had "led a charge of students against federal marshalls" at the University of Mississippi during riots that followed the admission of a Negro student. Though at the university, Walker claimed the charge was not true. Butts won a Georgia federal court verdict of $460,000 in 1964,[69] and Walker won a Texas court verdict of $500,000.[70] He also had filed fifteen other libel suits, in various stages of completion, in which he was asking total damages of $33,250,000.[71]

In reviewing the cases, simultaneously, the Supreme Court unanimously held that the two men were public figures—Butts as a result of his position and Walker as a result of "thrusting his personality" into the center of controversy.[72] Further, the Court held, nonmalicious discussion about public figures, as well as public officials, was protected by the Constitution. There was a division of thought, however, as to the extent of this protection.

All nine justices agreed in reversing Walker's judgment on the basis that there was "no evidence of even ordinary negligence" in the processing or publishing of the Associated Press story.[73] The *Saturday Evening Post*, however, had published a completely unsubstantiated article without the pressure of an immediate deadline. It was based on the story of a man who said he picked up a telephone and overheard another telephone conversation between Butts and the Alabama coach. The man had a record of passing hot checks, and his notes on the conversation had never been seen by any *Post* employee. The story had not been investigated, nor had the football game itself been scrutinized. The published story was based on the word of a questionable character respecting an unverified telephone call which he said had been inadvertently intercepted. And the majority of the Court held that this exceeded the area of freedom protected by the Constitution.

Butts won his $460,000 libel judgment on a five-to-four vote of the Supreme Court. Four justices, in an opinion written by Mr. Justice Harlan, upheld the judgment by modifying the New York Times rule. They stated a public figure did not have to rely on a "calculated falsehood" but could collect libel damages for falsehoods when there was an extreme departure from responsible standards of reporting.[74] They were joined by Chief Justice Earl Warren in sustaining the judgment, but on the basis that the magazine had recklessly disregarded the truth.[75]

Warren was in the middle of an otherwise equally divided Court. While the remaining four justices would not agree that they should declare the *Saturday Evening Post* article libelous, they did join the chief justice in stating that the *New York Times* rule applied to public figures as well as to public officials.[76] Warren in his opinion stated that the "attitudes of public figures are as much of concern to the citizens as attitudes of public officials with respect to the same issues." [77] In protecting the public's right to know, then, the majority of the Court held that a public figure could not collect libel damages unless he offered the same proofs of malice that were required of a public official.

The decision perhaps has particular import, though it was never mentioned, on the status of candidates for public office. Candidates certainly are public figures. Like General Walker at the University of Mississippi, they thrust their personalities into the midst of controversy. And without doubt they too could not collect damages for libel unless they could prove that articles about their public lives were published with actual malice. In their opinions, Justices Warren, Brennan, and Bryon R. White were specific in stating the standard applied to "public men" as opposed to simply public figures.[78] This again would be applicable to candidates for public office, if they are not indeed considered the same as public officials. The great freedom to discuss any issue that was allowed by this decision, however, greatly enlarged the federal public-official rule of libel announced in *New York Times* v. *Sullivan*.[79]

SUMMARY

The 1964 decision of the United States Supreme Court in New York Times v. Sullivan marked a turning point in the jurisprudence of libel as it was known in this country. It was in this decision that the Supreme Court assumed authority to review state court judgments in civil libel suits to ascertain whether those judgments violated First Amendment guarantees of freedom of speech and press. A series of similar reviews followed. In all it was held that truth was not a valid legal criterion for the discussion of public issues. And the result was a severe modification of the law, both civil and criminal, as it pertained to libeling public officials and public figures.

The modifications began in the New York Times case. Here the Supreme Court ruled that state courts could not award civil libel judgments to public officials for statements about their official conduct that were not made with actual malice. Further, the Court said that officials had to prove malice. To do this, they had to show that statements were false and made with knowledge of falsity or with reckless disregard of whether they were true or false. Unless this was proved, both the communication media and individuals had an immunity to libel. The Supreme Court said this was a constitutional standard of privilege that was binding on the state courts through the Fourteenth Amendment.

In Garrison v. Louisiana, the Supreme Court ruled that state courts also had to allow this newly announced constitutional privilege in criminal prosecutions resulting from statements critical of the official conduct of public officials. And a public official, it was held in Rosenblatt v. Baer, meant not only those elected to office but also those government employees who were in positions of substantial responsibility. The Court did not stop here, though. In Curtis Publishing Co. v. Butts, it was ruled that the privilege to discuss public officials also extended to discussions of public figures. Presumably this would include candidates for public office, if, per chance, they should not be considered in the same category as public officials. In this series of cases, the Supreme Court had formulated a federal rule, binding on all states, that allowed a libel-free privilege to publish nonmalicious falsehoods about the public lives of public officials and public figures.

This constitutional privilege was different from that allowed by state courts. The more strict state jurisdictions allowed a privilege only for fair comment based upon truth, and the more liberal excused libelous falsehoods only if there was cause for believing them true. Neither of these rules of privilege allowed the latitude of the New York Times rule. This was made clear by the Supreme Court in Garrison v. Louisiana, in which it ruled that the new constitutional privilege did not depend on reasonable belief in truth. Even those who did not take ordinary care to determine falsehoods were not responsible for libel. The Supreme Court stated that only false statements made with a more than normal awareness of probable falsity, such as the "calculated falsehood," could be subjected to civil or criminal libel sanctions. In effect, the law as it pertained to libeling public officials and public figures had been liberalized for the entire nation.

The law was left confused, however, as to the extent to which the personal and public lives of public officials and public figures could be segregated. The Supreme Court made it clear that personal defamation was not within the realm of constitutional protections. Even so, the Court recognized in the Garrison case that criticism of public conduct would affect private reputation. And the Court stated that in such cases there still would have to be proof of a knowing or reckless falsehood. Even false charges of corrupt motives, dishonesty, and malfeasance in office were privileged unless made with knowledge of falsity or with reckless disregard of truth or falsity. The Court further said that anything affecting an official's fitness for office was relevant to discussion.

Obviously, the Supreme Court had both reduced the area of libel and enlarged the area of free discussion. In all these Supreme Court libel cases, whether they involved public officials or public figures, the common denominator was the right to discuss public issues. It was this right of discussion that the Supreme Court said was protected by the First and Fourteenth Amendments from infringement. And in finding that state libel laws infringed upon the freedom to discuss public issues, the Supreme Court sharply curtailed those laws.

Perhaps state laws would not have been curtailed, at least not at this time, if there had not been a civil rights protest movement in Montgomery, Alabama. It was a discussion of this movement that led to the Supreme Court's decision in New York Times v. Sullivan. There was evidence that Alabama officials were using state libel laws in obtaining prohibitive judgments to penalize Negroes and their supporters for discussing governmental actions in relation to the movement. The effort appeared to be toward legal suppression of discussion about government itself. Clearly, this application of the law was inconsistent with constitutional guarantees of free speech and press. As a result, the Supreme Court stated there could be no libel against government, and that public officials could not obtain libel damages for impersonal criticism of government. Still, if state libel laws could be manipulated to violate constitutional liberties, they needed to be changed. This the Supreme Court did in formulating a new federal rule for libel that allowed "uninhibited, robust, wide-open debate on public issues." [80]

The constitutional privilege to discuss public officials and public figures, then, was a product of its time. It stemmed from a clear effort to suppress the discussion of a Negro minority in a government controlled by a white majority. While the issues were not so clear in the other cases, there is no doubt that the central concern of the Supreme Court was on the right to discuss public issues. The Garrison case focused on heated discussion of a thwarted vice investigation, and the Rosenblatt case involved statements critical of a public ski resort operations. A publication about a campus riot and the participants in that riot led to the Walker decision, and elaboration on an alleged football fix resulted in the Butts case. The basis for all these decisions, despite the issue of libel, was the freedom to speak and write about public issues.

That this freedom was not unlimited was shown in the Butts case. While part of the court felt the Saturday Evening Post had incurred responsibility for libeling a public figure by drastically departing from standards of responsible reporting, Butts could not have obtained his judgment unless at least one justice felt the magazine had recklessly disregarded the truth. The magazine had published a completely unverified charge of wrongdoing based on a questionable informant whose information was obtained under highly improbable circumstances. This was more than mere negligence; it came close to being gross negligence. It would appear that it also came close to what the Supreme Court meant when it said there had to be more than normal awareness of probable falsity before there could be any Court sanctions for libel. Civil and criminal sanctions, then, still were available for malicious calumniation. The Supreme Court standard had made it extremely difficult for a public official or a public figure to obtain redress for defamatory falsehoods, but it had not made it impossible

Perhaps, however, it was the jury system that remained the greatest hope of public officials and public figures in obtaining libel judgments. Despite the Supreme Court's expressed authority to review libel cases anew, the issue of the knowing or reckless falsehood was in the first instance to be determined by a jury. And juries, in making inferences from testimony, could render widely varying verdicts. This was one variable in libel trials that could not be standardized by the new constitutional rule of privilege.

Still, there were few variables left. The constitutional rule of privilege promulgated by the Supreme Court superseded the conflicting rules of privilege followed in state courts, thus providing a national standard for uniform administration of the law. Additionally, the new federal standard did much to eliminate the inequality in the application of privilege. It gave the public a fair equivalent of immunity from libel already enjoyed by public officials. And for all practical purposes, the new privilege to discuss public officials and public figures did away with the preferred privilege of discussion that previously had been granted the electronic media as a result of the Federal Communications Commission regulations.[81] So long as no knowing or reckless falsehoods were printed, newspapers could now compete with the equal-time immunity enjoyed by television in disseminating antagonistic views during political campaigns.

It was an effort to assure such public debate, the free discussion of public affairs, that had caused the Supreme Court to develop the libel-free privilege for nonmalicious falsehoods about public officials and public figures. This privilege was not a right reserved solely for the media. It had been extended to the public generally, including those who spoke, wrote, or advertised. It was an all-inclusive, nationwide standard for civil and criminal libel alike. The Supreme Court had expounded a constitutional privilege of law to be applied with uniformity and conformity in all courts of the United States.

13. State Conformity

Unity Under a Developing Law

The classic decision of the United States Supreme Court in *New York Times v. Sullivan* was assimilated rapidly into state laws. Appellate courts in a number of states began to prohibit libel judgments for public officials, candidates for office, and public figures unless it was proved that the allegedly libelous statements were made with knowledge of falsity or with reckless disregard of falsity. There were, of course, new legal questions raised as to what constituted a knowing or reckless falsehood. Since no infallible definition could possibly be given, this was only to be expected. Still, there were few hostile decisions in the state courts and, so far as could be determined, no outright attempt to circumvent the Supreme Court's mandate. Generally, the judges in the state courts of final jurisdiction attempted to comply.[1]

In conforming to the new constitutional standard of privilege, state appellate judges dismissed a number of libel actions on the basis that knowing or reckless falsehoods had not been proven. Libel judgments for public officials and public figures were few; nevertheless, the law was in a developmental state. And by 1968, four years after the *New York Times* decision, judges appeared to be ruling more frequently that issues of reckless falsehood existed and should be determined by juries. Furthermore, a few juries found that publications were made with reckless disregard for the truth. Nationwide uniformity under a constitutional rule of law, then, did not mean that liability for libel against public officials and public figures had been eliminated.

The immediate effect of the *New York Times v. Sullivan* ruling

in 1964 was a general liberalizing of the law of libel as applied to discussions of public issues. Lower courts did not limit this liberaliza-
tion to actions brought by public officials. Proof of actual malice—
knowledge of falsity or reckless disregard of falsity—was required by
some courts to sustain judgments in other areas of libel as well.

As an example, it was decided by a United States Circuit Court
of Appeals in 1964, shortly after the New York Times case and long
before the Butts-Walker case, that the federal rule of law could not
be limited to public officials.[2] Public figures also were required to
prove actual malice, the federal court of appeals stated. This included Nobel Prize-winning Linus C. Pauling, who had brought the
suit. He was asking a five-hundred-thousand-dollars judgment
against the New York Daily News, which had called him a "loud-
mouth" and had suggested he had pro-Communist leanings. The
suit was dismissed.

Two other suits brought by Pauling were dismissed in 1966 on
the basis that he was a public figure and had not proved publications about him were made with reckless disregard of falsity. One
was against the St. Louis Globe Democrat, which concerned an
editorial that criticized Pauling's antinuclear testing stand. The
federal appeals judge stated that the then new New York Times rule
applied to lobbyists, political party officials, heads of pressure
groups, and any leader in a position to guide public policy, such as
Pauling.[3] In the other case based on a National Review article which
associated Pauling's actions with those of the Communists, a New
York Supreme Court justice said Pauling had made himself a public
figure by thrusting himself into the vortex of discussion upon a public issue.[4]

Interestingly, these cases were all determined prior to the
United States Supreme Court decision stating that public figures
had to offer the same proofs as public officials in libel cases. And at
that time, in 1967, the Supreme Court borrowed the words of the
New York jurist by saying that General Edwin Walker had made
himself a public figure by thrusting himself into the vortex of a controversy at the the University of Mississippi.[5] The expansion of the
public-official rule by the lower courts, then, may have influenced
the Supreme Court and had a direct effect on shaping the law for
the entire nation.

Lower court decisions following the New York Times decision
even reflected tolerance for discussion about private individuals who

became involved in governmental affairs. For instance, the Delaware Supreme Court in 1965 held that a taxpayer had no recourse for libel as a result of a false publication stating his property had been seized for delinquent taxes. A federal employee as a result of federal privilege granted in *Barr* v. *Matteo* had absolute immunity from libel in releasing the defamatory material to the press. And the counter policy of qualified privilege, the court said, protected the newspaper that published a fair and accurate account of the press release.[6] Here the court adopted the *New York Times* standard of malice by saying the newspaper's privilege could not be defeated in absence of knowledge that the release was false.

In a similar case in New York, the court of appeals there held that a press release of a borough president was absolutely privileged even though it charged an appraiser working for the borough with possible misfeasance. Further, the court said, the account in the press also was privileged.[7] A wide measure of privilege was also promulgated by a California Court of Appeals in 1965. The California case resulted when a street contractor sued a newspaper for an article about a city council meeting in which he was criticized for being late in his street work. The court pointed out that the contractor's work was an issue of public interest. Further, the court said, fair and accurate reports of city council meetings and other lawful public meetings were absolutely privileged, not simply qualifiedly privileged.[8]

Even an account of a meat market owner's difficulties with a city health department were declared qualifiedly privileged by the Illinois Supreme Court in 1966. A newspaper had listed the department's findings of the market's sanitary code violations, and the court said the article was a fair and accurate report and was actionable only if there was actual malice. The court further quoted the *New York Times* rule that actual malice consisted of a knowing or reckless falsehood, but it declined to rule whether this new standard of malice applied specifically in the meat market owner's case. Constitutional questions, the court said, would not needlessly be determined.[9]

It was evident, however, that the constitutional rule of privilege announced in the *New York Times* case was affecting state court decisions in libel suits based on reports of government action. Even private individuals caught up in the whirl of government red tape could not collect libel damages, in some instances, unless they

proved publications were made with actual malice. Obviously, the
rule of malice set down by the nation's highest court was having an
impact that reached beyond the discussion of public officials. Not
only had state courts anticipated the Supreme Court in ruling that
the New York Times decision applied to public figures, but in many
instances they appeared to be extending the rule to cover the discussion of public issues as well.

Within four months after the New York Times ruling, it had
been held that the law partner of a mayor was subject to criticism
as a public figure because he represented clients before the mayor
and council. In a city election campaign, a New York newspaper had
accused the mayor with a conflict of interest in determining issues
submitted by his partner. The partner sued. However, the Appellate
Division of the New York Supreme Court said that the attorney had
"entered the fray" and made himself part of the local political
campaign.[10] As a public figure, he could not collect libel damages
unless he submitted the same proofs of actual malice required of
a public official.

The Alaska Supreme Court in 1966 also extended the public
figure designation to political columnist Drew Pearson. The court
said he had made himself a public figure by commenting on matters
of public concern; therefore he had to prove reckless disregard of the
truth to collect libel damages. He had been accused by the Fairbanks News-Miner of being a "garbage man" of journalism, which
the court said was not reckless.[11]

Perhaps neither the mayor's law partner nor Pearson felt they
would have to do any more than prove that statements made
about them were false. The decisions in these two libel suits were
handed down prior to the United States Supreme Court's holding,
in Curtis Publishing Co. v. Butts,[12] which extended the public-
official rule to include public figures. The two men were, however,
participants in public affairs. For that matter, so are public employees, regardless of the level of their employment. And their status in
the courts, so far as libel suits are concerned, also appears to have
been altered somewhat by the Supreme Court's public-figure ruling.

For instance, the New York Supreme Court held that an auditor of a county water works would have to prove that a letter to the
editor which reflected on him was written with knowledge of or
reckless disregard of falsity. He was a public figure, the court said,

because he voluntarily became involved in the water works contro-versy.[13] And the Delaware Supreme Court held that the chairman of a county Republican committee who was an employee of the state highway department was a public figure. Hence, a false news-paper statement that he had kept money collected for the highway department was declared privileged because the publisher did not know it was false.[14]

The implication was that a government employee, involved in any way in public affairs, must prove malice to collect damages for defamation. Though his status as a public official might be ques-tioned, he could be considered a public figure. And as a public figure, he could not collect libel damages without proof of actual malice in publications concerning him.

A further example of this is the case of *Rose* v. *Koch*, decided by the Minnesota Supreme Court in 1967, four months after the *Butts-Curtis* case. The suit arose when a special interest publication referred to State Legislator Arnold Rose as a Communist collabora-tor. The charge was repeated after he left the legislature to resume his post as a college professor. He sued for libel and won a trial court judgment, but the jury was allowed to consider the ill will of the publisher as well as knowledge of falsity and reckless disregard of the truth. As a result, the state supreme court reversed the judgment. It held that since Rose was a public figure as a college professor and participant in public affairs when the charge was repeated, the only basis for libel was a knowing or reckless falsehood.[15] The court added that since Rose was a public figure, it was not necessary to determine whether he was a public official by virtue of being a state university professor.[16]

The indication was that, for the purpose of proving libel, it made no difference whether the professor was a public official or a public figure. The Texas Supreme Court crystallized this view in December 1969, in the case of *El Paso Times Inc.* v. *Trexler*. A pro-fessor who led an anti-Viet Nam War demonstration was declared by the court to be a public figure. His status as a possible public official was not considered. However, despite the contradictory dicta in the *Butts-Curtis* case, the Texas high court ruled that no distinc-tion should be made in the proofs required of public figures and public officials in libel cases.[17] Because of this, the professor was required to prove that a letter to the editor of the *El Paso Times* which accused him of treason was written and published with knowledge of falsity or with reckless disregard of falsity. This he failed to do.

Police and firemen, for the purposes of libel cases, also have been declared public figures rather than public officials. For instance, the Washington Supreme Court in 1969 held that newspaper criticism of police and firemen supporting a municipal charter election was not criticism of the officers' official conduct. On this basis, then, the officers who thought they were defamed did not have to prove actual malice. However, the court said the firemen and policemen in this instance were public figures because they had thrown themselves and the weight of their Public Safety Council into the issues of a political campaign.[18] As public figures they had to prove the article was written with knowledge of falsity or with reckless disregard of falsity. Involvement in public affairs, then, required government employees to make court proofs in a libel suit that they ordinarily would not have been required to make.

Individuals being investigated by police officers also have found themselves subject to the more stringent libel proofs. For instance, a federal district court in California ruled in 1969 that an individual referred to as head of a Cosa Nostra family could not obtain a libel judgment from a magazine without proving with "convincing clarity" that statements were made with knowledge of falsity or with reckless disregard to falsity.[19] The court said that the public has an interest in organized crime and has a right to know about it.

It also has been held that an editor who publishes views on political and public affairs is endowed with such public interest that he is a public figure. As a result, the Washington Appeals Court has held that an editor would have to prove a knowing or reckless falsehood to collect damages for broadcast statements that he is "our leading American local Facist and Jew-baiter." [20] But political activity does not have to be limited to the United States. For instance, a federal appellate court in Florida has ruled that an individual who supported and directly influenced political elections in a foreign country is subject to public-figure libel rules because of the public's interest in foreign political involvement.[21]

Regular political party workers also have been declared public figures in Michigan and federal courts. The Michigan Supreme Court, ruling on a news story claiming improper political activities in various state political organizations, stated that individuals acting in furtherance of party politics must, as public figures, prove actual malice in seeking libel damages. This, the court said, included routine party workers.[22] The United States Court of Appeals for Washington, D.C., modified the words of the Michigan court only slightly by stating that individuals taking an active role in political parties were public figures. These people, the court said, have a role in determining public questions; hence the actual malice standard applies.[23] The particular case, *Thompson v. Evening Star*, involved a newspaper article about the founder of a group promoting a slate to take over party machinery. He was accused of conducting a "racist appeal" campaign and of being chief spokesman for Malcolm X and the Black Muslims. The court made it clear that the public-figure designation stemmed from the public issue of politics that was involved.

With individuals on the fringe areas of politics being forced to prove actual malice in libel suits, it would be strange indeed if candidates for public office were exempt. It was quickly shown, however, that they were not exempt. Proof of actual malice also was required by state courts before libel damages would be awarded candidates. But it was not because they were public figures. State appellate judges left no doubt that they placed candidates in the same category as public officials. The constitutional privilege of discussion announced in *New York Times v. Sullivan* was assumed to apply to both.

Seven months after the *New York Times* decision, the coequal status of public officials and candidates was proclaimed by the Pennsylvania Supreme Court. The case had been filed after one candidate for the United States Senate accused the other of having a voting record with Communist tendencies. The state supreme court said the charge was derogatory but not libelous. More specifically as to candidates, however, the court stated:

> Criminations and recriminations made against candidates for public office are privileged under the theory that the people are entitled to know and discuss the life, the character and qualifications, the finances, and the innermost thoughts, motives, connections and associations of public officials and candidates for public office, as well as the likely or inevitable result of the offiical's or candidate's action, connections, statements or votes.[24]

The court quoted at length from the *New York Times* decision and stated that it applied to individuals in public life, such as the candidates, who argued and debated controversial issues. The decision pointed out that the candidate was not charged with being engaged in Communist activities and that there was no way to prove the truth or falsity of the tendency charge as people disagreed as to what Communist tendencies were or were not.[25]

The Michigan Supreme Court in 1964 also granted immunity from libel to the *Detroit News* for an editorial stating a candidate represented the thinking of the ultra old guard "which complains that President Eisenhower has made socialism respectable." Privilege applied, the court said, because fitness for public office was at issue.[26] Another Michigan decision, this one by the court of appeals, held that there was no proof of actual malice in a newspaper publication that intimated that two candidates joined in a "phony" attack on a third candidate. The character, habits, and mental and moral qualification of candidates were privileged in the absence of actual malice, the court said.[27]

Another decision which conformed to the *New York Times* ruling was that of an Illinois appeals court in the 1965 case of *Wade v. Sterling Gazette Co.* The editor of the newspaper had written an editorial calling a candidate for mayor of Rock Falls an "unadulterated liar." The uncomplimentary appellation referred to a specific incident, and the court said it was pertinent to the candidate's qualification for office.[28] There could be no libel, the court said, without actual malice.

The same ruling, in effect, was given in a California District Court of Appeals in 1966. Here a candidate for Congress published a tabloid in which he accused his opponent of not being a bona fide Republican, stating instead that he was a left-wing Democrat attempting to drive part of the party into Democratic ranks. The court quoted *New York Times v. Sullivan* in stating that unless it could be proved that the statements were false and made with knowledge of falsity, there was no valid libel action.[29]

The primary application of the new constitutional rule of privilege was to libel suits brought by public officials. As far as could be determined, all judgments in state appellate courts adhered to the federal public-official rule promulgated in *New York Times v. Sullivan.* As a result, public officials generally failed in their attempts to obtain libel damages.

In two of the earliest cases considered after the *New York*

Times decision, however, state appellate courts held for officials. The Louisiana Supreme Court, for instance, held that an article in the *New Orleans Times-Picayune* about a candidate had been published with actual malice. The article stated that the candidate, a state legislator then running for a court constable post, was unfit for office because he had been guilty of irregularities while previously serving as New Orleans airport manager. It said he had retained money received for airport materials and that he had ordered airport workers to repair his mother's house. But the article failed to mention that a grand jury had exonerated him of the charges; the court said this showed reckless disregard of falsehoods.[30]

A forty-five-hundred-dollar judgment awarded a city policeman also was upheld by the Kentucky Court of Appeals in 1964. The policeman had been assigned to duty at a convention of a private fraternity, of which he was a member, and he had been asked to eject a representative of the Congress of Racial Equality. The CORE official later attacked the policeman in a handbill, claiming the officer would not know a fraternity's Greek letter if he saw it in box-car letters. The handbill stated the policeman not only lacked culture but also bummed money. The officer sued, and the court said the attack was personal, not falling under the ruling of *New York Times v. Sullivan*.[31] The judgment contained the following dictum:

> The freedom of "uninhibited, robust, and wide-open" debate on public issues guaranteed by the First Amendment cannot sensibly be turned into an open session to shoot down the good name of any man who happens to be at a public event.[32]

The court thus drew a distinction between discussion of official conduct and discussion of private character. The decision was that private defamation was not protected by the federal rule of privilege.

Decisions in these two early cases were the exception rather than the rule, even when accusations of a personal nature were made in publications. As an example, the New York Supreme Court ruled in 1966 that privilege extended to a newspaper article accusing a school board member of trying to get a teacher to upgrade the scholastic marks of her son. Proof that the publication was made with knowledge of or reckless disregard of truth was required for a libel judgment, the court said, because the discussion was in the "periphery of the area" protected by the United States Constitution.[33]

First Amendment guarantees of freedom also were cited by the Pennsylvania Superior Court in 1964 when it said a school board member would have to prove that a breach of trust charge was made with actual malice.[34] A newspaper had accused the school official with conspiring to pay a friend an excessive price for land needed by the schools. The same proof of malice was required of a county commissioner in Kansas who was charged in a television newscast with collecting illegal mileage fees and buying delinquent tax land through his father-in-law.[35]

Libel suits filed by judges themselves fared no better. As an example, the Ohio Court of Appeals in 1965 dismissed a libel action brought by a municipal judge who had been accused in the *Toledo Blade* of meting out sentences to the workhouse when no such sentences were prescribed by law. The court said that under the *New York Times* rule, the article was privileged.[36] And a police judge in Kentucky must have realized that he could not sustain a libel judgment over a newspaper article criticizing his judicial performance and claiming he was delinquent in personal and property taxes. He sued for both libel and invasion of privacy. But the Kentucky appeals court said the article was not libelous and that the judge, as a public official, had no right of privacy. "One who holds public office," the court said, "subjects his life to the closest scrutiny for the purpose of determining whether the rights of the public are in safe hands."[37]

Just as the Kentucky court ruled that public officials could not obtain judgments for libel by suing for invasion of privacy, the New Jersey Superior Court ruled in 1965 that officials should not bypass civil libel remedies in attempts to obtain criminal libel indictments. The court dismissed a libel indictment that resulted from inflammatory statements about a city councilman. It was held that written defamation may be a crime, but private individuals should seek civil damages.[38] Further, the political flyer was a reply to a charge originally made by the councilman, and the court said it automatically was privileged as a defensive declaration in addition to being privileged as discussion of a public officer.[39] The court quoted the *New York Times* rule of privilege, which could be defeated only if a knowing or reckless falsehood was proved.

The *New York Times* decision also was quoted by the Ohio

Common Pleas Court in 1965 when it dismissed a libel suit brought by a water board member against the *Mansfield Journal*. An article in the newspaper had quoted city council members as wondering if the water board was getting a "kickback" from an engineering firm it hired. None of the water board members were mentioned by name, and the Ohio court said:

> To hold that such a statement constitutes libel would seriously encroach upon the constitutional guarantees of free speech and the freedom of the press, which are among the fundamental bases for the preservation of our personal liberties. Under such circumstances, the public welfare outweighs that of an individual who claims that his public image may have been impaired thereby.[40]

Since the article had dealt with water district procedures for letting contracts, the issue was closer to libel on government than to libel upon an official. Neither the city councilmen discussing the water board nor the newspaper publishing the statements were accountable for libel, the court said.

The New Hampshire Supreme Court held in 1966, however, that privilege did not apply to a newspaper editorial about a former governor. The editorial implied that the ex-official had attempted to embarrass his old political party, which had rejected him, by inducing three of his former associates, state senators, to vote for a sweepstakes bill the party opposed. The *New York Times* rule applied only to public officials, the court said, and the former governor was removed from political life and not a public official. Though the former official may have been a public figure, he did not have to prove a knowing or reckless falsehood to obtain a libel judgment.[41] This decision was issued one year before the United States Supreme Court extended the public-official rule of libel to include public figures, and it likely would not be good law today.

Though the *New York Times* rule of privilege could not be evoked for an article about a former governor in New Hampshire, it could be for an article about a student government officer at the University of Arizona. The university newspaper, the *Wildcat*, published an editorial calling a student senator a campus demagogue who attempted to "hamstring" the student newspaper much as Stalin, Hitler, and Mussolini had when they killed the free press in their countries. The student senator sued for libel. The Arizona Appeals Court in this 1966 case said that the editorial was within the bounds of free criticism of public officials as laid down by the United States Supreme Court in the *New York Times* decision.[42] On the basis that the student was a government official to the student body served by the newspaper, the suit was dismissed.

A state legislator in Wisconsin faced the same difficulties as the student senator in trying to obtain a libel judgment in 1966. The *Milwaukee Journal* had been critical of his efforts to promote a rally, at which he said civil rights leader Dr. Martin Luther King, Jr., would speak. Dr. King did not appear, and the newspaper stated that he had never been booked. The state legislator claimed the article was libelous because it questioned his competency. At the trial, it was disclosed that Dr. King's brother had pledged that the leader would speak, but Dr. King's office said the brother had nothing to do with such arrangements. The Wisconsin Supreme Court said there was evidence that no booking had been made; but even if the charge were false, it was not libelous as the *New York Times* ruling protected all but knowing and reckless falsehoods about public officials.[43] The court recognized that the legislator's official duties were not involved, but a public issue was.

The public issue of race relations was at the center of another libel suit against the *New York Times* that was dismissed in 1966. This suit had been brought by Eugene (Bull) Connor, who had been city commissioner at Birmingham, and it was one of the suits that had been pending when *New York Times* v. *Sullivan* was determined. The article that was asserted to be libelous was one by Harrison Salisbury which stated that Connor was running on a platform of race hate. It quoted the councilman as saying: "Damn the law. Down here we make our own law." Salisbury had written the article without interviewing Connor, though testimony showed that an attempt to interview him had been made. Instead, Salisbury had relied on several individuals actually involved in Birmingham race incidents for his information, and the United States Court of Appeals for the Fifth District stated this was not "reckless" and hence not libelous. In fact, Salisbury was able to trace every statement in the article to an identifiable source, and the court said high standards of reporting had been practiced.[44]

Actually, it was never proven that the information in the story about Connor was twisted or misstated in any way. However, the article represented a point of view. In this regard, the court said:

Although accuracy and objectivity in reporting are goals for which all responsible news media strive, the protection of the first amendment is not limited to statements whose validity are beyond question or which reflect an objective publication of the reported events. While verification of fact remains an important reporting standard, a reporter without a high degree of awareness of their probable falsity may rely on statements made by a single source, even though they reflect only one side of the story, without fear of libel prosecution by a public official.[45]

Lack of impartiality, then, did not make an article libelous. The court was holding, in effect, that reporting with a viewpoint did not mean falsity, knowledge of falsity, or reckless disregard of falsity.

Another viewpoint, this one expressed in an editorial highly critical of a policeman's action in chasing a motorist at high speeds through heavy traffic, also was declared not to be libelous by the South Carolina Supreme Court in 1966. The automobile being chased had crashed into another vehicle, killing the occupant. The editorial stated police radios should have been used to communicate with other officers in order to establish roadblocks to stop the automobile. The policeman sued, but the court said he had to prove the publication was made with actual malice since he was a public official. Further, the court held, the criticism centered on his acts, fitness, and qualification for the work he did and was a matter of public concern.[46] He lost his suit.

A libel suit over another newspaper editorial, this one critical of a West Virginia court clerk, went all the way to the United States Supreme Court in late 1967. And the Supreme Court, in a per curium decision, restated the dictum of the *Garrison* case to the effect that a publisher's ill will or actual desire to injure an official could not be grounds for awarding a libel judgment. Such a standard, the court said in *Beckley Newspapers Corp.* v. *Hanks,* was "clearly impermissible." [47]

The editorial, obviously designed to injure the official, stated that the court clerk and a woman official stood alone on a controversial issue, that he had made unsuccessful threats about the newspaper's coverage of the issue, but that "perhaps his blustering threats were able to intimidate the lady." Both the woman official and the court clerk denied that she had been threatened, and the jury found that the false statement, which stemmed entirely from supposition, was both libelous and malicious. A five-thousand-dollar award was made to the clerk. In reviewing the case, the United States Supreme Court said it was making an "independent examination of the record" to assure that the publisher's rights were not impaired.[48] And the judgment was overturned. The Court said there was no "convincing clarity" that the statement was made with actual malice, which in this case was defined as a high degree of awareness of probable falsity.[49]

Adopting the Supreme Court's "convincing clarity" standard, the New Jersey Superior Court six months later overturned an eighty-thousand-dollar libel judgment against the *Philadelphia Inquirer*. The state court held that it had not been shown by convincing clarity that actual malice existed in the publication of a false article. The newspaper, obtaining distorted information from courthouse employees, reported that a court clerk had ordered a woman jailed for disorderly conduct in his office and had threatened to fire a critical employee. The court said that negligence in failing to get correct information was insufficient to show reckless disregard of falsity.[50]

Neither was there reckless disregard of falsity, according to the Arizona Supreme Court, when the *Arizona Republic* tied statements of the state's attorney general to Communist ideology. The newspaper ran a critical editorial stating the official's call for a people's council to represent his constituents at the legislature was typical of left-wing ideas that came "straight from the writings of Karl Marx." The court said there was no actual malice as defined in *New York Times v. Sullivan*.[51] The official lost his libel suit.

A city councilman in Illinois also lost a libel suit against a newspaper in 1967. The newspaper said the councilman was indebted to the city for tax liens totaling sixty-four thousand dollars. At the trial it was disclosed that he had paid all but sixteen thousand dollars of the total, but the liens had not been released. An Illinois appellate court ruled that the records showed sixty-four thousand dollars, and that there was no requirement for a reporter to exhaustively investigate each news story.[52] Again the *New York Times* rule of privilege was quoted, and the court said there was no reckless disregard of the truth.

Illinois appellate courts, incidentally, have extended the "public official" designation quite far. It has been determined there that a juvenile officer had substantial responsibility for public affairs and is a public official,[53] that the lowest patrolman is a public official because the public is interested in "on-the-street" level policemen,[54] and that an architect for a public building is a public official when embroiled in a controversy over the building or furnishings.[55] The Illinois Appeals Court even held in 1968 that a nursing home licensed by the state housing wards of state is a "public official." [56] Courts held that all of these officials could not sustain libel suits unless they proved falsehoods about them were printed either with knowledge or reckless disregard of falsity. The same proofs were required of an appointed director of public welfare in a Louisiana parish,[57] of an appointed supervisor of a branch post office in New York,[58] of a private garbage collection agency serving an Arizona city,[59] of a manager of a community center,[60] and of a deputy marshall in Missouri.[61] They too were considered public officials.

There was no doubt, of course, that Senator Thomas J. Dodd was a public official when columnists Drew Pearson and Jack Anderson published information obtained from his office files without his knowledge. But there was a question of libel, and Dodd brought suit both for libel and for abstraction from his files. The United States District Court for Washington, D.C., held in late 1967, however, that Dodd could recover for libel only if he could prove the publication was false and made with knowledge of falsity or reckless disregard of falsity.[62] As the documents came from Dodd's files, it was virtually impossible for him to prove that the columnists knew the information was false. The court further said the documents were of public interest and not subject to a suit for invasion of privacy.[63] The material had been secreted from Dodd's files by an employee and given to Pearson and Anderson, who later returned them. The court said the only recourse Dodd had was a suit seeking damages for conversion, and this too eventually failed. The court in this case held, in effect, that the method of obtaining information does not change the actual malice criterion for libel.

Similarly, a United States Court of Appeals held in 1968 that the particular timing of a publication could not alter the actual malice standard. A county commissioner in Pennsylvania brought the libel suit because of a false advertisement printed in a newspaper the day before an election. The advertisement claimed he was instrumental in spending $127,000 on a radar site without competitive bidding, in paying $10,000 to an out-of-town architect for plans never used, and in paying attorney fees to fight the county's own attorney. The commissioner claimed he lost the election because of his inability to publish an answer to the advertisement before the polls opened the next day. However, the federal appellate court held that when issues are public, they can be discussed at any time so long as there is no actual malice.

The particular advertisement, the court said, was believed by the editor to be a response to two advertisements previously published by the commissioner. Further, the editor knew three people who signed the advertisement as being responsible individuals. And while failure to check the accuracy of the statements in the advertisement may have constituted negligence, the court said, such negligence was not sufficient to show recklessness.[64] Here again, as in the New York Times case, the responsibility for determining accuracy in public issue advertisement was not placed upon the publishing newspaper. Public discussion, the court held, can constitute libel only when there is reckless disregard of falsity.

Public officials, then, were finding it extremely difficult to prove that publications about their official conduct were made with knowledge of falsity or with reckless disregard of falsity. With the exception of two cases immediately following the Supreme Court's mandate in New York Times v. Sullivan, decisions in state and federal appellate jurisdictions generally favored newspapermen. Even discussions of the public lives of officials, as opposed to their official conduct, were in many instances held to be immune from libel in the absence of actual malice. And biased reporting was held not to be malicious reporting. There indeed appeared to be a new charter of freedom for discussing public officials.

Still, Supreme Court libel decisions did not leave public officials totally unprotected from defamatory falsehoods. This has been shown by the several appellate courts which held that legitimate question existed as to whether publications were made with knowledge of falsity or with reckless disregard as to falsity. One of the questionable suits involved a Chicago police officer, Captain Frank Pape. He sued Time magazine over an article discussing a report of the United States Commission on Civil Rights. The official report stated that it had been alleged that Pape exercised brutality in arresting a Chicago family. The magazine, however, did not report that the brutality was claimed. It stated without qualification that brutality was involved. Pape sued for libel in federal court, but his action was dismissed. He appealed.

Upon appeal, the United States Court of Appeals for the Seventh Circuit on two reviews stated that the magazine article was not absolutely privileged even though the Civil Rights Commission report was. The magazine's privilege, the court said, depended on comments being fair and accurate.[65] Still, Pape, as a public official, was not entitled to a libel judgment even if the report was not fair and accurate because *Time* had a constitutional privilege to discuss public officials. Pape had to prove that statements about his official conduct were made with knowledge of falsity or with reckless disregard of the truth, the court said.[66] The court, however, pointed out that in departing from the fidelity of the official report, *Time* possibly did act with reckless disregard for the truth. It was held that a determination would have to be made in a jury trial.[67] Pape's lawyers filed petition for certiorari with the United States Supreme Court, alleging the constitutional privilege in libel had been misinterpreted.[68] The nation's high court granted a review in April 1970,[69] and the case was still pending at the time this book went to press.

A jury trial also was ordered in a two-million-dollar libel suit brought by United States Representative Eugene B. Keogh of New York against the late syndicated columnist Drew Pearson. Pearson wrote a column appearing in the *Washington Post* which Keogh said accused him of being influential in attempting to bribe a federal judge. The United States District Court for the District of Columbia held that there was a legitimate issue of actual malice for a jury to consider.[70] At the time both Pearson and the *Post* were defendants. But on review the United States Court of Appeals dismissed the newspaper as a party to the suit. The newspaper had claimed its editors had no reason to believe the column was false. The appellate court accepted this and stated that public comment of public affairs would be hindered if newspapers had to check into the facts of syndicated columns, as verification is a time-consuming process. In a decision that would appear to be of extreme importance to newspapermen, the court ruled that no liability existed against a newspaper for libelous statements about a public officer that was printed in syndicated columns unless the newspaper had reason to believe the facts untrue.[71] Keogh filed an appeal petition with the United States Supreme Court, but that court in 1967 refused to

disturb the decision.[72] Only columnist Pearson was left as a defendant to the action for libel, and he died in 1969 while the case was
pending.

A decision somewhat similar to that in the *Washington Post*
case was issued by the South Dakota Supreme Court in 1969. The
state court held that a wire service could not be held liable for libel
for failing to investigate the allegedly defamatory contents of a
press release from a secretary of state. This did not show knowledge
of falsity or reckless disregard of falsity, the court said.[73]

Another jury trial has been ordered by the Appellate Division
of the New York Supreme Court in a five-million-dollar libel suit
brought by a police officer against the Congress of Racial Equality.[74]
The policeman sued after "wanted for murder" signs with his picture on them were circulated in Harlem, a section of New York
City. The signs were circulated after the officer, while off duty, shot
and killed a Negro youth. The officer claimed self-defense, stating
he shot only because the youth was charging him with a knife.
Although the officer later was cleared of wrongdoing, the incident
triggered six nights of riots. Meanwhile, the case lingered in courts
for several years until in was ruled in 1968 that a jury trial was in
order. The posters, design and play on words all were subject to
jury interpretation, the court said, as to whether there was a knowing falsehood or reckless disregard of the truth.[75]

These cases, while not determinative, clearly pointed to the
fact that the constitutional privilege of discussing public officials
could be abused. The actual malice standard set by the Supreme
Court in the *New York Times* case had not placed an impossible
burden on public officials after all. This became even more apparent
in 1968 when at least five juries found that publications about
public officials were made with actual malice, with knowledge of or
reckless disregard of falsity.

Perhaps the most publicized of the 1968 trials was that involving 1964 Republican presidential candidate Barry Goldwater. He
won a $75,001 jury verdict against *Fact* magazine and its publisher,
Ralph Ginzburg, as a result of an article published in the magazine
during the 1964 campaign.[76] The article, purportedly based on replies to 12,356 questionnaires mailed to psychiatrists, claimed that
Goldwater was mentally unbalanced, a dangerous lunatic, and unfit
to be President.

Goldwater, who originally sued for one million dollars found that he too had to go through preliminary court hearings to oppose *Fact* magazine petitions for dismissal. But it was ruled in 1966 by a United States District Court in New York that there was enough in the published article to raise a jury question as to whether publication was actual malice.[77] The trial was held in May 1968, and a federal court jury found that the article had been printed with reckless disregard of the truth, that publisher Ginzburg had deliberately assassinated the character of Goldwater by printing falsehoods.[78]

Such a finding deserves examination to determine specifically what, in the minds of jurors, constituted reckless disregard of the truth. Testimony showed that psychiatrists based their replies on a claim in Ginzburg's questionnaire that Goldwater had suffered a mental breakdown. Yet Ginzburg, according to trial records, obtained this information from only one source and did not have personal knowledge that it was so.[79] Goldwater and his family doctor testified at the trial that the candidate never had suffered a mental breakdown, and pollster B. W. Roper testified that the facts in the questionnaire were "loaded" and slanted.[80] Further, before Ginzburg published the article, he was notified by the director of the American Psychiatric Association that his survey was invalid because responses were sought from psychiatrists who had not made personal examinations. Ginzburg was, in effect, made aware of the probable falsity of the poll results even before publication.

Perhaps further evidence of recklessness was shown by the way the psychiatrists' replies were compiled and published. The trial record showed that only selected portions of the replies were printed. The out-of-context passages selected for publication were frequently altered, abridged, and combined with other statements from other replies. Statements contradicting the stand taken by the magazine were omitted from the article. It is no wonder, then, that the jury found that Ginzburg deliberately set out to libel Goldwater.[81]

The jury verdict was upheld by a United States Court of Appeals for the Second Circuit in 1969, and the United States Supreme Court in 1970 denied certiorari to review the decision.[82] However Mr. Justice Hugo Black, joined by Mr. Justice William O. Douglas, dissented, stating the judgment against Ginzburg was "repressive" and "ominous." Black's dissent stated:

The public has an unqualified right to have the character and
fitness of anyone who aspires to the presidency held up for the
closest scrutiny. Extravagant, reckless statements and even claims
which may not be true seem to be an inevitable and perhaps essential part of the process by which the voting public informs itself of
the qualities of a man who would be president.[83]

The dissenting justices also took a verbal slap at the punitive damages awarded in the case, stating punishment for exercising privileges of speech in public affairs was "incomprehensible." Their
views obviously were not those of the Court's majority, which by
failing to grant review in effect upheld the jury verdict.

When evidence of actual malice is presented at the trial level,
appellate judges of all types likely would find it extremely difficult
to overturn jurors' libel awards to public officials. As an example,
the Minnesota Supreme Court in 1968 upheld a four-thousand-
dollar libel verdict for a police captain because evidence was sufficient for the jury to find that actual malice existed. The case arose
when the St. Paul Dispatch printed a completely unverified charge
that a police captain in Minneapolis had refused to arrest a man
accused of molesting a child. The source of the story was a Catholic
priest, who said the officer's refusal was related to him by the child's
mother, who was very upset at the time.

As it developed, the story was false; the captain, though faced
with legal technicalities, had arranged to arrest the man. However,
the story was published without ever contacting the captain, the
mother, or two other policemen actually involved in the incident.
Testimony showed that all were available for interviews. The writer
did contact the police chief by telephone, and the chief told him
before the article was published that there was a misunderstanding.
This statement, the state supreme court held, placed the newspaper
on notice that facts were erroneous. The court also stated that if
any of the actual participants rather than the outside party—the
priest—had been contacted, the needlessly false story could have
been corrected and probably would not have been published.[84]
Despite the shaky secondhand source, the court said, the story was
given the most controversial view possible. All this was held sufficient to show reckless disregard of falsehood.

One candidate who recklessly called his opponent a Communist during a political campaign also had to pay a forty-five-hundred-

dollar libel judgment in Louisiana. The opponent was noted for his anti-Communist activities and proved that the candidate knew this at the time the Communist statement was made. As a result the jury found that the candidate knew he was telling a falsehood, and the appellate court in 1968 upheld the verdict on the grounds the evidence was sufficient to satisfy the *New York Times* rule of malice.[85] The privilege of discussion had been abused.

The United States Supreme Court in April 1968 also made it clear, in *St. Amant v. Thompson*, that the new constitutional privilege to discuss the official conduct of public officials could be abused. In this decision, the Court recognized that there could be no single infallible definition for the term "reckless falsehood." The Court did state, however, that "inevitably its outer limits will be worked out by case-to-case adjudication." [86] By using the word adjudication, the Court left no doubt that judges, and more specifically the justices of the Supreme Court, would determine exactly what reckless falsehood meant. Still, the Court said the burden rested with juries to determine if and when knowing and reckless falsehoods had been published. "The finders of fact," the Supreme Court said, "must determine whether the publication was indeed made in good faith.[87]

By the time the Supreme Court rendered its decision in *St. Amant v. Thompson*, the case already had a long and varied history in Louisiana courts. It originally was filed in 1962 by sheriff's deputy Herman A. Thompson against Phil A. St. Amant, a candidate for the United States Senate in opposition to Russell B. Long. St. Amant, in a television equal-time broadcast, criticized labor union activity in Louisiana politics. In doing so, he repeated a labor union official's accusation that the president of a Teamsters Union local had passed money to Deputy Thompson and that there was no way to tell how much influence the union president had with the sheriff's office.

Thompson, who was in no other way connected with the political campaign, won a five-thousand-dollar verdict for libel. St. Amant appealed, and meanwhile the United States Supreme Court rendered the *New York Times v. Sullivan* decision. The Louisiana Court of Appeals held, as a result, that Thompson as a deputy sheriff was a public official who had to prove that a knowing or reckless falsehood had been broadcast. The court said he had not, and the decision was reversed.[88] It also was held that the television station could not be held responsible under the equal-time provision of the Federal Communications Commission regulations.

However, the Louisiana Supreme Court then reviewed the case. The television ruling was not disturbed, but the state's high court reversed the decision of the court of appeals in other respects. It stated that evidence did show that the broadcast was made with reckless disregard of the truth and that the trial court judgment was not inconsistent with the constitutional guarantees.[89] The case then went to the United States Supreme Court.

The nation's highest court held in an eight-to-one decision that St. Amant's broadcast could not be held libelous.[90] It was admitted that he falsely charged a sheriff's deputy with a crime by relying only on the word of a union official without trying to verify the charge. But the Court said that the standard of actual malice could not be measured "on what a reasonably prudent man" would publish.[91] The Court stated:

> There must be sufficient evidence to permit the conclusion that the defendant in fact entertained serious doubts as to the truth of his publication. Publication with such doubt shows reckless disregard for truth or falsity and demonstrates actual malice.[92]

The Court stated that the Supreme Court of Louisiana had misunderstood the actual malice standard, and the decision was reversed again.

St. Amant's statements had been declared not libelous by the United States Supreme Court because there was no evidence that he seriously doubted their truth. The Court pointed out that Montgomery Commissioner Sullivan had failed to prove that the New York Times was aware that it was circulating false information.[93] Further, the Court said, in Garrison v. Louisiana, it was held that there had to be a "high degree of awareness . . . of probable falsity" before there could be libel. And Mr. Justice Harlan's opinion in Curtis Publishing Co. v. Butts was quoted to the effect that "evidence of either deliberate falsehood or reckless publications 'despite the publisher's awareness of probable falsity' was essential to recovery by a public officer." [94] These were the boundaries of the actual malice standard as defined, but not the outer limits that would be determined case by case.

In addition to stating that juries would have to determine if publishers acted with actual malice or in good faith, the Supreme Court provided limited guidelines.[95] A jury likely would not be persuaded of good faith, the Court said, if a publisher used a highly imaginative story indicating an article had been fabricated or if he based a publication "wholly on an unverified anonymous telephone call." Further, the Court said a publisher's pleas of good faith likely would not be believed by juries if charges alleged to be libelous were "so inherently improbable" that they would be published only by a reckless man. "Likewise recklessness may be found," the Court said, "where there are obvious reasons to doubt the veracity of the information or the accuracy of the reports." [96]

These observations of the Supreme Court were not necessary to the determination of the case at issue. They were needed only to clarify the evolving law as it pertained to libeling public officials. While stressing that the law was developing, the Court was careful to emphasize the role of juries in that development. It specifically outlined situations in which juries could determine that the privilege to discuss public officials had been abused. Here was implicit recognition that the constitutional standard, prohibiting libel unless there was a knowing or reckless falsehood, rested in the first instance on the findings of trial court juries. Further, there was the implication that the findings of juries, as well as the rulings of judges, were subject to review by the Supreme Court to assure that the constitutional right of discussion would not be abridged.

Since the ruling in the *St. Amant* case, the Supreme Court has been very selective in the cases it accepts for review. For instance, as previously discussed, the jury award of $75,001 to presidential candidate Barry Goldwater was left undisturbed in 1970 when the Supreme Court refused to grant certiorari for a review. Mr. Justice Hugo Black in his dissenting opinion was roundly critical of the court's policy of "case-to-case adjudication." [97] This policy, however, still is in effect, and the *Goldwater* case is evidence that a jury award to a public official or candidate for office can hold up under Supreme Court scrutiny.

However, one jury award to a public official in Illinois fell with the Supreme Court's refusal to grant a review in 1970. In this case, a jury had found that the writer of an editorial in the *Edwardsville Intelligencer* had recklessly disregarded whether statements written about a city attorney were false. The editorial stated: "Rumors are that the city attorney is working to break the law."

The law was opposed by the mayor, and testimony showed no effort was ever made to enforce it. Yet the writer testified that no one had ever told him the city attorney was going to break the law. Further, testimony showed the official had not been contacted by the writer, no effort had been made to determine if the rumor even existed, and no attempt had been made to discover the official's intent concerning the law at issue. The jury awarded a thirty-five-thousand-dollar judgment to the city attorney.

The circuit court trial judge set the jury verdict aside and ruled for the newspaper, but an Illinois appellate court in late 1968 reversed the trial judge and upheld the jury. The appellate court held that since the jury had the job of finding fact, it would not disturb a finding that the writer had recklessly disregarded falsity.[98] The jury's decision, however, did not sway the Illinois Supreme Court, which reversed the appellate court and again held for the newspaperman. The state high court said the editorial writer's statement was sufficiently close to the facts to prevent a holding that he was disseminating information which he knew to be false or which he seriously doubted to be true. The court said the law was repugnant to the mayor, that there was a question of interpretating the law, and that it would not be uncommon for one to place the responsibility of enforcement with the city attorney.[99] The Illinois court then quoted the St. Amant case to the effect that editorials do not have to be written by reasonably prudent men. A petition for certiorari was filed with the United States Supreme Court but was denied in mid-1970 with no opinion.[100]

Also in late 1969 the Supreme Court refused to review a Hawaiian judge's summary judgment favoring a newspaperman. The newspaperman had seen county equipment at work on a county official's property, and he wrote a critical article about it. A libel suit followed, but the newspaper involved filed an affidavit that the publication was made "without deliberate falsification and without a high degree of awareness of probable falsity." [101] In issuing a summary judgment without trial, the judge held that the newsman at most was negligent in not making a telephone call to discover the official had contracted to pay for the work. The judge further stated there could have been no actual malice on the part of the newsman when he had actually witnessed the equipment being used as it was. The United States Supreme Court apparently did not see anything wrong with the summary judgment, as the petition for certiorari was denied.

These cases which the Supreme Court refused to review offered no really new questions of law. Furthermore, the lower courts had in each instance attempted to follow guidelines previously outlined by the Supreme Court. Still, several cases were slated for review by the Supreme Court in 1970, and all dealt with questions which have been left somewhat hazy or untouched by past Supreme Court decisions. For instance, one, which involved allegedly libelous broadcasts about the distributor of nudist magazines, centered on whether a purely private citizen involved in a matter of public interest would be required to prove actual malice to collect libel damages.[102]

A closely related case which the Supreme Court decided in mid-1970, involving a public figure as opposed to a purely private individual, gave the press wide freedom to report activities at public meetings. In *Greenbelt Cooperative Publishing Association, Inc. v. Bresler*, the Supreme Court held that the reprinting of heated public debate about a public figure was not libelous unless actual malice—a knowing or reckless falsehood—could be proven.[103] Such debate about public issues, the Court said, could include exaggerated charges, "rhetorical hyperbole," or "vigorous epithet." Specifically, the case involved an article about a city council meeting in which a landowner was accused of practicing blackmail by demanding rezoning on his property before selling other property to the city for a school. The Court said the word blackmail could not be understood by even the most careless reader to charge a criminal offense. It would appear by this decision, then, that the libel-free privilege granted the media to report governmental meetings and proceedings is conditioned on lack of actual malice rather than on the traditional fair and accurate report. Perhaps, however, the two standards are not so different. In fact, this is a central issue in the previously mentioned case of *Pape v. Time*, which the Supreme Court in mid-1970 slated for summary review.[104] Pape, a detective and public official, claimed he was libeled by an inaccurate and hence unfair report of a public document. The central question of the case is whether juries can infer from inaccurate or unfair reports that publications were made with knowledge of or reckless disregard of falsehood.

Another important question concerns the period of time an official's past life is open to scrutiny. The Supreme Court is faced with such a question as a result of a New Hampshire jury, which awarded a United States Senate candidate a ten-thousand-dollar libel judgment after he had been called a "former small-time bootlegger" in a Drew Pearson column. The judge in this case allowed the jury to choose whether private or public libel was involved, and the jury found that the charge, based on alleged activities twenty-six years before, was "purely private libel" outside the constitutional protection rule of actual malice.[105] The New Hampshire Supreme Court refused to overturn the verdict, stating that in its opinion the small-time bootlegging, if any, occurred so long ago that it could be found by a jury to have lost its relevancy in a political election today. The newspapers that were sued, the Concord Daily Monitor and the New Hampshire Patriot, filed a petition for certiorari with the United States Supreme Court, which granted a review in 1970.[106] The question pending is whether, by addition of a "relevancy" criterion, the newspapers were deprived of their First Amendment rights to discuss candidates short of publishing knowing or reckless falsehoods.

The Supreme Court in May of 1970 granted another review that could help clarify the extent of constitutional protection in discussing the private lives of officials.[107] The case arose when a newspaper falsely accused a garage owner of having been indicted for perjury. As it developed, it was the garage owner's brother who had been indicted. The garage owner also was a public official, but this was not mentioned in the article. Hence the judge directed the jury that the actual malice standard required by the Constitution for officials did not apply.[108] Official conduct, he said, was not the issue. This instruction is the central issue slated for review.

Several Supreme Court decisions were pending, then, at the time this book was published. Still, all indications were that these decisions would do no more than help define the existing law. The major decision, that public officials cannot collect damages for libel for publications concerning their official conduct unless they prove actual malice, appeared to be firmly entrenched. The problem remaining, as was stated in St. Amant v. Thompson, is to work out the outer limits of the law on a case-by-case basis. It is to this problem that cases docketed for review by the Supreme Court have been addressed. They should help determine more precisely what this new constitutional freedom to discuss public officials actually entails.

SUMMARY

The Supreme Court of the United States in New York Times v. Sullivan had indeed established a new charter of freedom for discussing public officials. Within a four-year period after this extraordinary decision, judges in both federal and state jurisdictions generally had modified their old doctrines of libel to conform to the new federal rule of law. This rule prohibited public officials of all levels from obtaining libel judgments for defamatory falsehoods about their official conduct unless they could prove actual malice. And actual malice was knowledge of falsity or reckless disregard of falsity.

This constitutional standard of actual malice had an impact in lower courts that reached far beyond the discussion of public officials. Several state and federal judges anticipated the United States Supreme Court in holding that public figures as well as public officials had to prove actual malice to obtain libel judgments. And the term "public figures" was used in a broad sense to include such people as government employees involved in public affairs, political party workers, or, as one federal judge said, lobbyists, political party officials, and heads of pressure groups. Another interpretation has included "artists, athletes, business people, dilettantes and anyone who is famous or infamous because of who he is and what he has done." [109] In some instances, even private individuals falsely defamed in reports of routine governmental affairs or proceedings were unable to obtain libel judgments unless they proved actual malice. Thus the new Supreme Court standard of libel was being applied in many jurisdictions whenever public issues were involved.

Candidates for public office obviously were involved in public issues. As a result, they were required in all jurisdictions to prove actual malice to obtain damages for libel. However, judges generally followed historical precedent in making it clear that such a requirement did not rest on the candidates' status as public men or public figures. As their fitness for holding office was at issue, they were placed in the same category as public officials themselves.

Public officials, meanwhile, fared badly in their libel suits during the period immediately following the establishment of the federal rule of law. Prior to 1968, only two cases can be found in which they were able to sustain judgments in state appellate courts. In one, a newspaper had declared an official guilty of misconduct for which he previously had been exonerated by a grand jury. In the other, a personal attack against a policeman, not comment on official conduct, was involved.

Accusations of a personal nature, however, were declared not libelous in some courts. And several lower courts after the New York Times decision required that public officials prove actual malice for defamatory falsehoods concerning their public lives as well as their official conduct. Even charges of Communist tendencies or collaboration were held not libelous in the absence of proof that statements were made with reckless disregard of falsity.

Interestingly, one appellate court struck down what appeared to be an attempt by an official to circumvent the new standard of libel. The official had sued also for invasion of privacy. Officials, the court said, had no right of privacy. Another court, in New Jersey, stated aggrieved public officials should sue for civil libel damages and not seek criminal libel action.

Cases were heard in which the public official designation was applied to individuals ranging from policemen to members of Congress. Even a director of county welfare, a supervisor of a branch post office, an architect on a public building, a private garbage collection agency serving a city, a manager of a community center, and a nursing home licensed by the state were declared public officials in libel trials. One state appellate judge in Arizona held that a college student serving as a student senator was a "public official" who had to prove actual malice in his attempt to recover libel damages against a student newspaper.

Decisions generally gave newspapermen wide leeway for covering and writing news without fear of libel. One federal court, faced with a libel suit brought by an official because of the publication of information stolen from his files, held that the method of obtaining facts could not alter the requirement that public officials had to prove a publication was made with knowledge of or reckless disregard of falsity. Another court decided that the actual malice standard could not be defeated simply because a political advertisement was published on the last possible day before election, leaving no time for a reply.

Three United States Court of Appeals decisions appeared to be particularly significant, though it is too early to speculate on the effect they may have on law in other jurisdictions. One of these decisions held that biased newspaper reporting, presenting only one side of an issue and based on one or two sources actually involved in the event, could not be considered actually malicious in the sense of being reckless disregard of the truth. Another court held that newspapers are not liable for defamatory falsehoods in syndicated columns unless editors have a reason prior to publication for believing them false. The third decision indicated that unfair and inaccurate reports of governmental proceedings might constitute such reckless disregard of the truth that a public official could be libeled. Specifically the court held that a magazine, in departing from the fidelity of a governmental report, raised a jury issue as to whether a public official was libeled by reckless disregard of falsity.

While this last decision was pending for review before the United States Supreme Court at the time this book was published, the initial holding made it clear that federal and state courts would allow public officials the benefit of jury determination in questionable cases. In fact, since 1968, a number of appellate judges have declared the existence of bona fide jury issues as to whether publications were made with knowledge of falsity or with reckless disregard of falsity. Further, several judgments since 1968 indicate that jurors as well as judges are not opposed to giving libel damages to public officials and candidates for office. Former presidential candidate Barry Goldwater was awarded $75,001 in damages by a New York jury, and the judgment stood on appeal even to the Supreme Court of the United States. A city councilman in Florida received $3,500,[110] and a political candidate in Louisiana won a $4,500 judgment. In Minnesota, a police captain got $4,000. An Illinois city attorney, in a decision later overturned, got an initial award of $35,000 from a jury. And a New Hampshire candidate for the United States Senate, in a case pending before the United States

Supreme Court at the time of this publication, won a jury award of $10,000.

What did jurors consider to be reckless disregard of the truth? The article about Goldwater was based on a slanted survey, and the publication included only selected statements that had been altered, abridged, and combined with other statements. Published charges were made about the police captain without checking with people involved. The article was based on hearsay—on what a priest said was told to him. The city attorney won his case at the jury level because an editorial writer, with questionable bases, manufactured a "rumor" to get his views across. And the candidate for senator obtained a judgment because a newspaper article discussed events that allegedly happened twenty-six years before and that the jury considered irrelevant in the campaign being conducted.

It is hard to see how some of these jury awards can stand in light of the Supreme Court mandate that a public official must prove a high degree of awareness of probable falsity before obtaining a libel judgment. For instance, how can a jury decide a statement about a twenty-six-year-old event in a candidate's life is not relevant and hence does not have the protection of the new constitutional standard of libel that supposedly covers all discussion? Also acceptance of a priest's story about a police captain certainly was not good journalism, but it did not mean that the writer was aware that the story was false. The sin here would appear to be no greater than in the precedent-setting New York Times case, when the United States Supreme Court said there was no reckless disregard in failing to check the facts in a public issue advertisement that had been submitted by a reputable source. And surely a priest is a reputable source.

That jury awards are vulnerable was shown when the award to the Illinois city attorney was overturned by the Illinois Supreme Court. The high court said there was lack of evidence that the writer knew the so-called rumor was false or that he seriously doubted its truth. The validity of this Illinois Supreme Court decision perhaps was supported when the United States Supreme Court refused to review it. After all, the editorial comment based on rumors was not much different than another editorial accusing a court clerk of making "blustering threats" against a woman. The latter comment, also made without a factual base, was declared not libelous by the United States Supreme Court in Beckley Newspapers Corp.

v. Hanks, also because there was no "convincing clarity" that it had been published with reckless disregard of falsity.

No doubt the United States Supreme Court has favored free and sometimes irresponsible expression. The Goldwater case, however, presents clear evidence that the nation's highest court will not disturb a proper verdict for a candidate or an official. Perhaps, however, the most important of the recent Supreme Court libel decisions was that of St. Amant v. Thompson. This case, decided in mid-1968, overturned a five-thousand-dollar libel award to a Louisiana sheriff's deputy. But the Court did more than reverse the decision. It recognized that the law as it pertains to libeling public officials had greatly evolved since the 1964 decision in New York Times v. Sullivan and that it would evolve further as time continues. In restating the law in the St. Amant case, the Court again said there could be no libel for discussing the official conduct of public officials unless there was actual malice. But actual malice, the Court said, required evidence that a deliberate falsehood had been published or that a publication was made recklessly despite a high degree of awareness of probable falsity. Additionally, the Court pointed out that juries had to find if evidence in fact did show actual malice. Guidelines were offered here, too. Jurors could find that publishers acted with actual malice, the Court said, if the inherent improbability of articles clearly showed recklessness or if the articles were published despite obvious reasons to doubt their truthfulness.

In establishing guidelines for jurors to follow in determining whether publications were made with actual malice, the United States Supreme Court was reaching to the grass-roots level in the law of libel. Moreover, the Court in this decision indicated it would tolerate verdicts for public officials only under specific circumstances. Both the verdicts of jurors and the decisions of judges remained subject to review by the Supreme Court to assure that the constitutional standard for free discussion would not be violated.

Still, the Supreme Court was not offering its restatement of the law as the final word on its public-official rule of libel. It had only defined that rule as it existed by mid-1968. Further development of the law on a case-by-case basis was predicted. During 1969 the only developments were in state courts and in the lower federal courts. By 1970, however, the Supreme Court again had a rather sizeable backlog of libel cases to look into. Despite uniformity of the law under a nationwide standard, then, there is no permanence. Future court holdings, perhaps even at the jury level, will determine the course of the evolving law and the limits of the constitutional standard to discuss public officials without liability for libel.

THE LAW
YESTERDAY, TODAY,
AND TOMORROW

---

14. Public Officials and Libel

An Overview

Throughout the history of the United States, from the settlement of New England colonies until the present, the laws for libeling public officials have been narrowed consistently as the people's right to know about their government and to discuss their governors has been broadened. In colonial days, when the people were subject to English common law, any criticism of the government or government officials, whether true or false, was considered malicious and seditious and hence libelous. Today, with a recognized freedom to discuss public issues, there is no libel on government. And even false criticism of the public conduct of public officials is not considered malicious or libelous unless it can be proved that it is made with a high degree of awareness that it is probably false. Between these two extremes lies three centuries of struggle for the liberty

265

to discuss public officials without fear of libel. The conflict began in the American colonies.

New England colonists, when they came to America, brought with them a heritage of seditious and schismatical libel. It long had been established in England, as a result of Star Chamber trials, that publications promoting an ill opinion of either the governors or the government were libelous. This included publications about prelates and the established church, as religion and government were closely entwined. Furthermore, Star Chamber justices had declared in the 1606 *Case de Libellis Famosis* that it was immaterial whether libels were true or false. This decision, considered the formal beginning of libel prosecutions in England, declared that the circulation of ill opinions about magistrates was a breach of the peace and punishable as libel. The colonial government in Massachusetts Bay followed this law. Roger Williams, a colonial minister who circulated letters critical of theocratic government, was prosecuted for libel only six years after the Puritans landed in America.

However, as the colonies grew, and as reason began to take the place of theology and tradition, colonial courts began to administer the law of libel differently than did the English courts. Judges in England, despite some inconsistencies, generally did not allow juries to consider evidence of truth or to determine if publications were libelous. The judges themselves determined libel on the basis of malice, which, although undefined, included criticism of government. Juries determined only the factual issue as to whether the libels, as declared by judges, were published by defendants. In the colonies, these principles were modified. Starting with the seditious libel trial of printer William Bradford in 1696 and continuing through trials of Thomas Maule, Gerald Sly, and finally John Checkly in 1723, the colonial law of libel had two threads of consistency. One was jury determination as to whether libel existed; the other was justification of libel by truth. Additionally colonial court cases reflected a definite reluctance to convict individuals for public-affairs libels, whether they resulted from religious statements or from publications critical of government.

Still, it was not until the 1735 trial of New York newspaperman John Peter Zenger that colonial differences with English law were well publicized. Zenger was accused of a political libel against New York's unpopular governor, who was appointed by an unpopular king. The explosive political situation created considerable interest in the trial. The judge asserted the right to determine libel in accordance with English common law, which held that opinions against the government were seditious and hence malicious and, as such, libelous. But Zenger's attorney, Andrew Hamilton, argued that principles of nature and law "in these parts of the world" had given the people the right to truthfully oppose arbitrary power. The jury acquitted Zenger, finding his publication was true and not libelous. The trial established in the colonial mind that jurors, not judges, determined libel on the basis of truth or falsity.

This colonial concept of the law of libel continued to prevail and was widely promoted by the press when attempts were made by Crown officers to prosecute phamphleteers and newspapermen shortly before the War of Independence. The ideas that truth justified libel and that truth was to be determined by a jury of peers, not English puppet judges, pointed to still another difference with England at this time of heightened feeling. Such ideas of justice were consistent with the ideals of liberty and independence that were being expressed prior to the revolution. After the revolution and independence, however, it was found that the law of libel as practiced in America could not be separated so easily from the English common law that gave it birth.

Immediately after independence, newspapers in the United States had what amounted to an unrestrained freedom to discuss and criticize both governors and government. Many, however, felt that criticism was excessive, that press freedom was abused; and by 1791 criminal libel prosecutions had been revived. In that year, Massachusetts editor Edmund Freeman was prosecuted for maliciously criticizing a legislator. His trial, which ended in acquittal, is believed to have been the first in the new nation for libeling a public official. Other states, however, also began to indict newspapermen for libel. The English common law of criminal libel was revived. And in 1798, as a result of vehement press criticism over an expected war with France, Congress passed the Sedition Law to allow federal court prosecution for libel against government.

The Sedition Law, by declaring that it was a crime to publish ill opinions of government or governors, adopted the old English common law of seditious libel; however, it also embodied the libel standards of colonial America. Truth was declared by the law to be a defense for libel, and jurors were given the right to determine if libel existed. Despite these safeguards, federal judges refused to afford Sedition Law defendants the moral and perhaps even legal rights to which they were entitled. The law drew extreme opposition and died in political controversy two years after it was enacted, leaving federal courts without statutory authority to prosecute for alleged criminal libels against either the governors or government. Additionally, the United States Supreme Court decided in the 1812 case of *United States v. Hudson and Goodwin* that the federal government had no common-law jurisdiction to prosecute libel cases. Criminal libel prosecutions, as a result, fell to the exclusive domain of the states.

Perhaps the Sedition Law did have one benefit. It promoted the idea that juries determined if public officials had been libeled by considering if publications were true or false. At the beginning of the nineteenth century, however, the criterion of truth was not in complete accord with standards set in state courts that followed the old English common law of libel. The defense of truth was either questionable or nonexistent in state courts. In some instances, truth appeared to be allowed in evidence only to refute malice, which was implied from criticism itself.

Starting with the New York case of *People v. Croswell* in 1804, defense standards changed. In this case, Alexander Hamilton, noting that truth had been allowed as a defense in the Sedition Law, argued there should be a right to defend charges of libel by showing that truth was published with good motives for justifiable ends. The New York legislature in 1805 incorporated these standards into law as a defense to criminal libel. Other states, by statutes and by constitutional reforms, rapidly adopted similar provisions. Many states went further and stated that since the people were free to investigate the affairs of their government, truth was a defense to libel in all instances where publications were proper for public information.

The people's right to know about their government also was stressed by state judges in a series of criminal libel cases before the War of 1812. Because of this right, the judges held, truthful publications which honestly intended to inform citizens about the public conduct of their public officials or candidates for their public offices could not be libelous. The judges in effect held that informing the citizens was both a good motive and a justifiable end. Truth, then, for all practical purposes, became a complete defense to a criminal prosecution for libeling a public official or a candidate for office.

One New Hampshire case in 1838 even held that belief in truth was sufficient to free a publisher from a criminal libel charge.

Coincidental with state court acceptance of truth with honest intent to inform the citizenry as a defense to criminal libel, the number of criminal prosecutions for libeling officials declined drastically. Public officials largely abandoned attempts to punish newspapermen for printed defamation. Instead, the officials began to file civil libel suits seeking damages to compensate them personally for defamation. In the civil court trials, officials did not have to prove beyond a reasonable doubt that articles were false; in fact, newspapermen had to prove articles were true. The burden of defense shifted with the move from criminal to civil courts, a move which became noticeable shortly after the Croswell decision. As a reflection of this change, state appellate courts between the War of 1812 and the Civil War rendered decisions in ten civil libel suits for every criminal libel action filed by officials.

Though new rules of law had to be determined in civil libel suits, the defense standard of truth remained the same. Judges generally followed the criterion for discussing public officials that was announced in the 1807 case of *Brewer v. Weakley* in Tennessee: "Let his talents, his virtues and such vices as are likely to affect his public character be freely discussed, but no falsehoods be propagated." [1] Other than the right to make truthful reports, however, there were no special privileges to either discuss or comment on the character, qualifications, or conduct of public officials and candidates for office without liability for libel. Some states did begin to recognize a libel-free privilege to make fair and accurate reports of judicial, legislative, and even quasi-judicial proceedings. One state judge even held that comments on the factual statements of a president were privileged. But there was no uniformity from state to state on these judgments.

In fact, court proceedings varied considerably. In some state courts, false articles automatically were considered malicious; in others, juries determined malice. In some states, jurors could consider malice in assessing punitive damages against newspapermen. In others, jurors considered only truth or falsity and awarded compensatory damages alone. Some state courts allowed damages to be mitigated by retractions or good intentions; others did not. There also was disagreement over whether libel should be determined by innuendoes or the plain language of the publications. The law, then, was varied and somewhat hazy in this period before the Civil War.

Still, the decisions in these pre–Civil War cases set precedents that touched on most of the problems that would face future jurists. Broad outlines for the law of libel, both civil and criminal, had been established. As political changes brought increasing recognition of the people's right to know about their government, courts in turn had recognized the right to report truthfully on the activities of those seeking and holding elective office. In the formative years of the nation, therefore, truth had become the standard by which newspapermen could defend libels against public officials.

Although truth continued to be the only uniformly accepted standard for defending libels against public officials, a greatly expanded privilege of discussion was recognized by state courts during and following the Civil War. Starting with the New Hampshire case of *Palmer* v. *Concord* in 1868, many judges began to excuse libelous falsehoods about public officials when publications were made in good faith and without malice. Newspapermen in these jurisdictions were granted a libel-free privilege if they could show they honestly intended to inform the people about government and had probable cause for believing the truth of the communications published.

Judges in all jurisdictions, of course, did not allow this libel-free privilege. Some went only as far as to allow good-faith falsehoods to mitigate damages. Others allowed a privilege for comment and criticism but not for misstatement of fact. And those state courts which allowed privilege for nonmalicious falsehoods often made exceptions. Some required strict proof of truth for attacks on officials' private or moral character. Others granted no privilege for imputations of corrupt motives or misconduct in office. And some continued to hold that newspapers published falsehoods at their peril. There was, then, no common policy, no conformity to any one view.

Despite disagreement as to individual policies, the broad confines of libel-free discussion had been established. Truth and in some instances probable cause for belief in truth had been defined as defenses to libel against public officials. The basic format of the law had evolved. By the end of the nineteenth century, as a result of the general acknowledgment of the people's right to know about government, the privilege to discuss public officials and candidates for office, though inconsistent, had broadened considerably.

In the first half of the twentieth century, both the theoretical and procedural standards of libel were more clearly defined. Each state continued to formulate, administer, and interpret its own laws of libel, but a number of broad, general principles began to emerge. For instance, libel itself was reduced to a formula. State statutes or common-law interpretation generally declared libel to be either a malicious defamation that impeached the honesty, integrity, virtue, or reputation of an individual or a malicious defamation that exposed one to public hatred, contempt, or ridicule. Furthermore, state courts generally held that publications could not be libelous unless the words in the publications, as ordinarily understood, imported defamatory meanings.

However, two types of printed defamation evolved. When words were ambiguous, public officials had to prove to the satisfaction of jurors that those words were libelous when considered in the context of relevant circumstances. This was libel *per quod.* When words in articles could be interpreted in only one way and the defamatory nature was apparent, it was the duty of the judge to declare them libelous *per se* and the duty of jurors, in the case of public officials, to determine if they could be justified by truth, fair comment, or privilege.

Meanwhile, in the early part of the twentieth century, courts began to center their views of privilege around two specific doctrines. By World War I, in a period noted for widespread and exaggerated attacks in muckraking literature, the majority of state courts had rejected the doctrine that libelous falsehoods about public officials could be excused if there was probable cause for believing them true. Instead, these courts followed the view expressed by Mr. Justice Taft in the 1893 decision of *Post Publishing Co.* v. *Hallam,* that even the best-intentioned falsehood could destroy a public official's right to a good name. The only privilege they allowed was to make fair comment and criticism about the public conduct of public officials. There could be no misstatements of fact.

Some courts, however, continued to grant a libel-free privilege for falsehoods if there was probable cause for belief in truth. These courts followed the views expressed by Mr. Justice Burch in the

1908 case of *Coleman v. MacLennon*, that the importance of public discussion overshadowed any inconvenience or injuries that might result to public officials by occasional falsehoods. Interestingly, the number of states adhering to this minority view of privilege approximately doubled between World Wars I and II, during a period in which constitutional protections were extended to state action abridging freedom of speech and press and in which the idea that the governed must not criticize the governors became obsolete.

The United States Supreme Court had ruled in 1925, in *Gitlow v. New York*, that the First and Fourteenth Amendments to the Constitution prohibited the states from impairing freedom of speech and press. But the Court also held, in the 1931 decision of *Near v. Minnesota ex rel Olson*, that the individual state libel laws did not impair press freedom. Consequently, privilege or the lack of it had no constitutional significance at this time. Each state was free to do as it chose, and decisions seemingly were influenced by conditions of the times. While state judges drew lines between the people's right to know as opposed to public officials' right to a good name, those lines often varied. Vacillation as to what constituted privilege within and between individual states was common throughout the first half of the twentieth century.

By the end of World War II, twenty-two states followed the doctrine limiting privilege to fair comment based on true facts, and sixteen states extended privilege to nonmalicious falsehoods, those published when there was probable cause for believing them true. There were doctrines that varied slightly from these two main views. For instance, Missouri did not grant privilege for falsehoods, but Missouri, along with Oklahoma, did require that public officials and candidates for office prove statements false rather than requiring that newspapermen prove them true. Three other states and the District of Columbia allowed a privilege for falsehoods provided charges of crime or corruption in office were not published.

After World War II, there was no stabilization in the law of libel, but more and more jurisdictions granted wider freedom for the governed to criticize their governors. Courts were faced with rapidly changing public policies. There was an increased emphasis on constitutional rights and individual liberties, and the emphasis on free discussion was reflected in public official libel judgments. There even was an extension of the now universal privilege to make fair and accurate reports of public proceedings. State courts began to grant the fair and accurate report privilege for newspaper articles concerning political rallies, speeches of presidential candidates, unofficial civic meetings, and even press releases based on secret congressional hearings.

Public officials began to find it much harder to obtain libel judgments except when publications specifically charged misconduct, crime, or dishonesty. And even then, there were frequent dissenting opinions alleging freedom of the press had been impaired. Many state courts that required a factual base for comments and criticism started making allowances for honest mistakes and occasional errors. Some held that there could be no libel for criticism as long as there was a substratum of fact. Furthermore, the number of criminal prosecutions had dwindled almost to nonexistence. And the privilege to discuss public officials and candidates for office, whether limited to fair comment or extended to falsehoods that were honestly believed, also was extended to discussions of appointed public employees of practically all levels of government.

Court tolerance for discussion of government and government officials had widened considerably. The United States Supreme Court in 1959 ruled that federal officials were not subject to libel judgments for statements concerning their official duties and concerning people affected by those duties. Additionally, the Court held that television stations were not subject to state libel laws for defamatory statements made in equal-time political broadcasts.

By the end of President John Kennedy's administration, terminated by his 1963 assassination, there also had been an increase in the number of states granting a libel-free privilege for nonmalicious falsehoods about the public conduct of public officials. Twenty states had set court precedents for the privilege, and four other states and the District of Columbia allowed a partial privilege for nonmalicious falsehoods when charges of crime or misconduct were not published. Meanwhile, twenty-one states allowed privilege as a defense only for fair comment and criticism based on truth. One other state, Missouri, did not allow privilege for falsehoods, but it required officials and candidates to prove that articles were indeed false.

There were, for all practical purposes, no longer majority and minority views concerning privilege. The states were about equally divided. The net result was that statements about those seeking and holding public office could be libelous in one part of the nation and not libelous in another. Other disparities in the law also had evolved. Television stations could not be held responsible by the states for defamatory remarks in their equal-time broadcasts, but newspapers could be held liable for defamatory replies that were published. Furthermore, federal officials had an immunity from libel in discussing citizens that citizens did not have when discussing the officials. All of these things pointed to an inequality in the right of discussion that could be remedied only by a uniform application of the law throughout the nation.

THE LAW TODAY

A national charter of freedom to discuss public officials was issued by the United States Supreme Court in early 1964, and the autonomy of states in administering their individual laws of libel ended. In New York Times v. Sullivan, the Supreme Court held that constitutional guarantees of free speech and press prohibited any state from awarding damages to a public official unless he could prove actual malice. To prove actual malice, the Court ruled, the official had to show that statements were published with knowledge that they were false or with reckless disregard as to whether they were false. This was a new standard; moreover, it was a constitutional standard that had to be applied with uniformity and conformity in state and federal courts throughout the United States.

The nationwide standard of libel admittedly was designed by the United States Supreme Court to protect the public's constitutional right to discuss public issues. The facts surrounding the law suit of New York Times v. Sullivan clearly showed that the right of discussion had been threatened. State libel laws were being used to penalize individuals who discussed the civil rights of a Negro minority in a government controlled by a white majority. Basic liberties were being abridged by claims that public officials had been libeled. As a result, a new constitutional principle of law was formulated to limit the power of states to award libel damages to public officials.

Shortly after the New York Times case, in Garrison v. Louisiana, the Supreme Court ruled that the new constitutional standard of law also applied to criminal libel actions. Even further, the Court said that publishers did not have to show probable cause for believing articles they printed were true. Public officials in both civil and criminal actions had to prove that libelous falsehoods about their official conduct were published with a more than normal awareness of probable falsity or that the falsehoods were calculated. Additionally, public officials, the Court said in Rosenblatt v. Baer, included government employees believed by the public to have substantial responsibility for governmental affairs.

The federal rules declared in these cases were assimilated rapidly into the common laws of the various states. They were applied to both public officials and candidates for office. As a result, the divergent views on privilege and fair comment in state courts were eliminated. And for all practical purposes, the public and the printed media were granted fair equivalents of the privilege of discussion previously enjoyed by public officials and the electronic media. The legal freedom to discuss public officials had been expanded for all citizens and all media alike. Moreover, in the 1967 case of Curtis Publishing Co. v. Butts, the Supreme Court held that the freedom of discussion included public figures. They, like public officials, could not collect libel damages unless they proved that knowing or reckless falsehoods had been published. Since then, a number of state courts have indicated that anyone involved in public affairs, including government employees, could be considered public figures. Furthermore, in mid-1970, the United States Supreme Court held that publication of stories on governmental proceedings, including debate containing heated accusations about individuals involved in public issues, is protected from libel judgments unless publications are made with knowledge of or reckless disregard of falsity.

Since the New York Times v. Sullivan mandate in 1964, only a very few public officials or candidates for office have been successful in obtaining judgments for libelous falsehoods. But by 1968, four years after the mandate was issued, judges appeared to be ruling more frequently that jury issues of reckless falsehood existed. Since then, both judges and juries have found more frequently that publications were made with reckless disregard of the truth and hence libeled public officials and candidates.

Meanwhile, perhaps the most enlightening statement concerning libel against public officials was made by the United States Supreme Court in April, 1968. In St. Amant v. Thompson, the Court repeated that a public official could not obtain a libel judgment for defamatory falsehoods about his official conduct unless he proved actual malice. To do this, the Court said, he had to present evidence of a deliberate falsehood or of reckless publication despite a high degree of awareness of probable falsity. The Court said jurors must weigh evidence to find whether actual malice, and hence libel, exists. Jurors, the Court said, could find actual malice if the inherent improbability of the false publications showed recklessness. Or they could find actual malice if publishers had obvious reasons, prior to publication, for doubting the truth of articles.

Though this is the law of libel today, the Court made it clear that these guidelines are not static. Situations under which public officials can and cannot be libeled are expected to be determined in the future on a case-by-case basis. Meanwhile, every time a public official or a candidate for office files a libel suit for a defamatory falsehood, he is battling the constitutional rights of the individual who published that falsehood. The Supreme Court, as guardian of constitutional rights, has become the final arbiter of the law in public-official libel suits throughout the United States.

15. The Future

Alternatives and Consequences

Predictions concerning developments in the law of libel as it pertains to public officials must take into consideration the constitutional guarantees of free discussion. Libel law has become constitutional law. A federal rule, based on the United States Supreme Court's interpretation of the First and Fourteenth Amendment guarantees of freedom for speech and press, has been established as the supreme law of the land. And that rule limits state authority to use libel laws for interfering with discussion of public issues and public officials.

Still, the federal rule for libeling public officials is subject to change. It was formulated by the Supreme Court on the basis of current views of liberty; it can be either reformulated or discarded on the basis of future views of liberty.[1] It can change as the interpretation of the United States Constitution changes[2] or, perhaps, as the Constitution itself is changed. It can vary as the opinions of the Supreme Court vary.[3]

There is, of course, another source of variance. It is in the rule itself. This rule, as promulgated by the Supreme Court, simply prohibits states from awarding libel judgments to public officials unless these officials can prove that defamatory falsehoods about their official conduct are made with actual malice. Actual malice is defined as knowledge of falsity or reckless disregard as to whether publications are true or false. In explanation, the Supreme Court has said this means publication of a deliberate falsehood or reckless publication despite a high degree of awareness of probable falsity.

277

Within the broad confines of this definition there is considerable room for differences of opinion.

Perhaps it was for this very reason that the Supreme Court in perhaps its most enlightening decision on defamation, *St. Amant v. Thompson*, was careful to establish guidelines for public-official libel suits. The standard for libel was repeated, and public officials were told, in effect, what type of evidence they would have to present before they could obtain a libel judgment. Further, jurors were given examples as to when they could find publications libelous. This is about as far as the Supreme Court can go in establishing procedural safeguards at the grass-roots level to prohibit libel judgments that might curtail constitutional liberties.

Procedural safeguards, however, do not necessarily mean that the same procedures will be followed in all state and federal courts. Circumstances likely will dictate different procedures, at least until the scope of the terms "public official" and "official conduct" is more clearly determined. While the Supreme Court has dealt in part with each of these terms, the results have not been definitive. Consequently, judges and perhaps juries in various jurisdictions have choices to make. Depending on the point of view, the public-official rule of law can be applied or rejected at the trial court level.[4] Procedures undoubtedly will vary.

This would appear to be particularly true in libel suits brought by public employees. The Supreme Court in *Rosenblatt v. Baer* ruled only that public employees were considered public officials if they "have, or appear to have, substantial responsibility for or control over the conduct of government affairs."[5] Under this rule, there can be no uniformity. Decisions from state to state have differed in the past, and there is nothing in the Supreme Court guideline to prevent divergent views in the future.

Past decisions in state courts have, however, extended the public-official designation deep into the ranks of public employees. Among those who have been held to be public officials are grand jurors, city inspectors, city street superintendents, prison wardens, assistant wardens, policemen, mental institution and welfare agency superintendents, agency secretaries, state oil inspectors, branch post office supervisors, and community center managers. Even a nursing "home" licensed by the state, a garbage collection "agency" employed by a city, an architect on a public building, and an engineer for a public water district have been declared public officials. These precedents, of course, are not uniform from state to state. Holdings have varied. Nevertheless, it is probable that state courts will continue to treat a number of miscellaneous public employees as public officials.

The question remains, however, as to where to draw the line between public employees with and without what the public believes to be substantial responsibility. Until this is resolved, one court may hold a public employee to be a public official while another court holds a public employee with similar duties to be a private citizen.[6] The "public official" employee would have to prove that defamatory falsehoods were published with knowledge of or reckless disregard of falsity. But the "private citizen" employee would simply have to prove that a publication was a defamatory falsehood. In the latter case, the publisher could seek an appeal on a claim that due process of law as guaranteed by the Constitution had been denied. Similar appeals seeking due process could continue indefinitely.

To prevent disparity, the United States Supreme Court must eventually make a more definitive announcement as to the meaning of the term "public official." And since the Court is committed to the principle that people have a right to discuss public affairs, it is hard to see how anyone on the public payroll could be excluded from such a definition. Furthermore, there can be no such exclusion without leaving questionable choices at the trial court level. The nation's courts cannot follow a uniform procedure in applying the public-official rule of libel until all agents of government are considered public officials.[7]

Procedural uniformity in the courts of the nation also hinges on the definition of official conduct. Here the Supreme Court has given wide latitude while simultaneously causing some confusion. In *Garrison v. Louisiana*, the Court held there was no libel even though criticism of judges' official conduct had an impact on their personal reputations. The Court said the public interest is paramount to an official's private reputation when criticism is about his conduct of public business. In another part of the decision, however, court dicta indicated rather strongly that criticism did not have to be aimed specifically at official conduct. It stated that "anything which might touch on an official's fitness for office" is relevant to the free flow of information.[8] Such personal attributes as dishonesty, malfeasance, or improper motivation, the Court said, are closely related to fitness for office.

The decision leaves questions unanswered. Would a public official, for instance, have to prove defamatory falsehoods were made with actual malice if his inner drives or dishonesty were discussed apart from his conduct in office? Conversely, does discussion have to center on official duties before a publisher can take advantage of the actual malice standard in exploring a public official's fitness for office? Again, it would appear that trial judges and juries would have to make a choice.[9] Interestingly, if a trial judge held that the actual malice standard did not apply to defamatory falsehoods about a public official's private character, even though it might affect his fitness for office, the appeal advantage would be with the publisher. The publisher could seek an appeal to the United States Supreme Court on the grounds that his constitutional right of discussion had been impaired without due process of law. In a proper case, the question of private character could be decided by the Supreme Court. Such a decision would appear to be necessary before the actual malice standard is applied uniformly in cases resulting from discussion of public officials' fitness for office.

Fitness for office certainly becomes a crucial issue during political campaigns, and the discussion generated affects both public officials and those opposing them for office. Both candidates and officials generally are required in lower courts to make the same proofs in obtaining libel judgments. The Supreme Court itself, however, has never stated that the actual malice standard applies to candidates for office. Nevertheless, it can be assumed that a candidate, as a public figure if not as an aspiring official, would have to prove actual malice. There appeared to be no question that Barry Goldwater, a presidential candidate, had to prove actual malice in his 1968 libel action. And the judgment he received was not overturned by the Supreme Court, perhaps implying that the actual malice standard was correctly applied in the case. Furthermore, Supreme Court dicta twice have included quotes from *Coleman* v. *MacLennon* to the effect that private character of a candidate is subject to scrutiny in so far as it affects his fitness for office. If candidates and public officials are to be equated by the Supreme Court, and it seems they must be,[10] the actual malice rule will have to be revised to permit discussion of much of their private lives as well as their official duties. Perhaps this indirectly has been done, but eventually it will have to be clarified.

The Supreme Court's task of clarification is not restricted to the conditions under which the public-official rule should be applied or to the types of people subject to it. If the confines of discussion on official duties are determined and the outer limits of the term public official are secured, however, lower courts can administer the federal public-official rule of libel with much greater uniformity. And it is possible that the Supreme Court under such circumstances would not disturb a great number of state judgments if the courts followed the proper procedures in applying the federal rule of law and if jury verdicts have reasonable bases in fact.[11]

Such a development would stress the role of juries in determining whether facts justify libel judgments for officials. And since jurors have human differences and emotional prejudices apart from the law, chances for public officials to obtain libel judgments possibly would increase. It is hard to see how the Supreme Court could overturn a jury verdict finding actual malice if evidence indicated a possible knowing or reckless falsehood. Still, erroneous or hostile decisions would be subject to review.[12] In formulating the constitutional standard for libel, the Supreme Court has set itself up as censor of both judge and jury.

The Supreme Court's position as censor of public-official libel judgments will of necessity not be changed as long as the people's constitutional freedom to discuss public officials is conditional. But there is a possibility, depending on the views of justices appointed, that the Court eventually will declare that the Constitution requires an unconditional freedom of discussion. Such a move appears highly improbable in the immediate future, however, as only two of the nine justices currently on the Supreme Court have publicly promoted unrestrained discussion.[13] Additionally, it is hard to conceive of an unrestrained liberty of discussion which would prohibit a public official from seeking legal redress from those who deliberately lie about him.

Still, future thinking may conceivably eliminate the condition of discussion, liberal as it is. Admittedly the condition, actual malice, provides the widest freedom to discuss public officials this nation has ever known. At this time, then, it could not be considered an impairment of liberties. But it rests on somewhat tricky ground. In granting a conditional privilege, the Supreme Court has in effect promulgated a federal rule which has the same force and effect as if it had been adopted by Congress. Yet it is questionable whether Congress itself, in the face of the First Amendment, could have passed such a law, even though it could be forcefully argued that liberty of speech and press would not be impaired but rather enhanced by the actual malice condition. The Supreme Court, then, has done something that Congress likely could not have done or likely would not have attempted to do. And future jurists may conclude that the Supreme Court has misinterpreted the Constitution in declaring a common-law rule that provides less than unrestrained freedom to discuss public affairs.

Meanwhile, the conditional privilege that now exists, limited only by actual malice, provides a balance between the people's right to free expression and the public officials' right to a good name as long as they have done nothing to warrant obloquy. Unfortunately, the fulcrum of balance, actual malice, still is open to interpretation. Although actual malice exists where the defendant has knowledge his statement was false or where he was reckless in publishing a falsehood, the standard is extremely fluid. The substantive limits of the actual malice standard, the element of balance itself, still must be formulated. These limits no doubt will be affected by decisions in state appellate courts, but the ultimate confines of the standard will be determined by the Supreme Court on a case-by-case basis.

The course that will be followed by the Supreme Court is subject to intangible variables, not the least of which is the inclination of the majority of the justices at any given time. Currently, the majority of the Court has pledged itself to the view that a public official cannot collect damages even for a false charge of crime unless it can be proved the publisher had serious doubts as to the truthfulness of the charge. Hence, the immediate outlook appears to be a wide freedom of discussion within the confines of the actual malice standard. However, even now there is no unanimity on the Court. The justices have never been in complete agreement as to the application or meaning of actual malice—of a knowing or reckless falsehood.[14] Moreover, this disagreement could be widened by either shifting viewpoints of current judges or by recent and future changes in the membership of the Court.[15] Decisions could continue to allow considerable latitude for discussing public officials, or they could take a more restrictive turn.

SUMMARY

With the possible exception of a dozen or so years immediately after the War of Independence, the freedom to discuss public officials is as broad today as it has ever been in the history of the United States. The freedom exists because the power of government has been severely limited in holding people responsible for what they can say about those who serve them in government. Because of this limitation, especially upon the courts, it is extremely difficult today for a public official to obtain damages for libel from anyone who discusses, criticizes, or comments on his conduct or fitness for office. Even falsehoods are tolerated. People have a constitutional right, in the absence of actual malice, to falsely expose public officials to hatred, ridicule, and contempt, and to falsely impeach their honesty, integrity, and virtue.

Such a right can be easily abused, especially by those who are in the business of communicating information about public officials. Moreover, extensive abuses could lead to a change in the federal rule of libel, to a loss in the freedom of discussion that has been gained. This has happened before. Newspapers after the War of Independence had an unrestrained freedom, but before fifteen years had elapsed, there were cries of press animosity, virulence, lies, and malicious slanders. One judge of the time said that "libeling has become a kind of national crime." [16] The result was suppression. States revived the English common law of criminal libel, and Congress passed the Sedition Law of 1798.

The Sedition Law, according to the United States Supreme Court, has been ruled unconstitutional by the court of history. And the concept of free speech and press today likely would prevent Congress from passing any laws to curtail expression. Even today, however, a deluge of vitriolic falsehoods about public officials in publications across the nation could draw sharp rebuttal, not only from the Supreme Court but from Congress as well.

Members of Congress, if they felt they, as public officials, were being mistreated by a rampant press, could initiate a constitutional amendment containing a more restrictive rule for libel.[17] Such a move would take a two-thirds vote of each house. Before the Constitution could be amended, however, it would have to be approved by three-fourths of the state legislatures.[18] These too are made up of public officials who might feel a need for a more stringent libel law. Although such a move at present is highly improbable, it is not beyond the realm of possibility. One needs look only to the highly critical remarks made of the media by Vice-President Spiro Agnew on several occasions in 1970. The support he drew from officials and even the public was indicative, perhaps, of a general mistrust of the press. Furthermore, the lesson of history clearly shows that real or imagined abuses of liberty can result in restrictive measures.

With the exception of the Sedition Law period, however, history also shows that freedom of speech and press has been progressively broadened. The ever-increasing latitude for discussing government and government officials has evolved because of the nation's needs—the needs in a particular period or the needs in specific geographic areas within particular periods. The current needs have been met by a liberal standard of libel that uniformly guarantees a wide freedom of discussion for everyone in the United States. The future needs, perhaps, will rest on how that freedom is exercised.

Abuse of the right to discuss public officials could lead to curtailment of our present level of liberty. Conversely, moderation could lead to even greater liberty. Since an extensive freedom for discussing public officials in the future could very well depend on moderation today, those who are in the business of communicating information about public officials have a somewhat frightening responsibility. It would appear that the responsibility is twofold. The first is to inform the people as to what their government and their government officials are doing.[19] The second is an ethical responsibility to deal fairly with all, including public officials, in reporting the news truthfully, accurately, and sincerely.[20] The total weight of these standards, regardless of legal freedom, requires that sincere efforts be made by all newsmen to provide the public with truthful and accurate reports about their public officials.

NOTES

SELECTED BIBLIOGRAPHY

TABLE OF CASES

INDEX

Notes

1. Colonial Heritage from England: *Religious, Seditious Libel*

[1] Nathaniel B. Shurtleff, ed. *Records of the Governor and Company of the Massachusetts Bay in New England*, 1 (Boston: William White Co., 1835), 160–61. The banishment was ordered September 2, 1635, by the General Court sitting at Newe Town. Earlier accounts of letters from the Salem church critical of the General Court are on pages 156–58.

[2] Clyde Augustus Duniway, *The Development of Freedom of the Press in Massachusetts* (New York: Longmans, Green, and Co., 1906), p. 19. Here it is stated that Williams instigated the circular letters because the General Court, which was upset over Williams's view and the fact he had been elected teacher in Salem, would not approve a grant of land to Salem.

[3] Great Britain, *Statutes of the Realm*, vol. 1, 3 Edw. 1, Stat.

[4] Ibid., vol. 2, 2 Ric. 2, c. 5 (1378); 2 Ric. 2. c. 10 (1388). The 1378 law names the great men as "prelattes, dukes, earls, barons, and other Nobles and Great Men of the Realm, and also of the chancellor, treasurer, clerk of the Privy Seal, steward of the King's House, justices of the one bench or of the other, and of other great officers of the realm." The three laws are defined as the Law *De Scandalis Magnatum*, among other places, in *Charles Earl of Macclesfield v. John Starkey* (1685), in *A Complete Collection of State Trials to 1783*, edited by Thomas Bayly Howell (London: T. Hansard, 1816–28), 10: 1329. This source will be cited as Howell's State Trials in the pages which follow.

5   Rex v. Sir Richard Knightly and Others (1588), 1 Howell's State Trials 1263 at 1264.
6   Ibid., p. 1267.
7   Ibid., p. 1269.
8   Rex v. John Udall (1590), 1 Howell's State Trial 1271 at 1277.
9   Ibid., p. 1279.
10   Ibid., pp. 1283, 1289. The assembly of judges meant the twelve highest judges in the land, drawn equally from the King's Bench, the Common Pleas, and the Exchequer. These judges met periodically to advise the Crown, to decide questions from trial courts, and to act as a court of appeals. See Irving Brant, *The Bill of Rights: Its Origin and Meaning* (New York: The New American Library, 1965), p. 506.
11   Van Vechten Veeder, "The History and Theory of the Law of Defamation," *Columbia Law Review*, 3 (1903), 553; R. C. Donnelly, "History of Defamation," *Wisconsin Law Review* (January 1949), p. 108.
12   Case de Libellis Famosis, 5 Coke Reports 125A (1606).
13   Ibid.
14   Ibid., p. 125B. Thomas Cooper in his *Treatise on the Law of Libel and the Liberty of the Press* (New York: G. F. Hopkins, 1830), p. 82, defies lawyers to show him any earlier precedent for this doctrine.
15   Case de Libellis Famosis, 5 Coke Reports 125A at 125B (1606).
16   That differing religious views were suppressed is shown by the fact that four Quakers and some twenty so-called witches were hanged by the Puritans in Massachusetts. The score was much, much higher in England and Europe. Rod W. Horton and Herbert W. Edwards, *Backgrounds of American Literary Thought* (New York: Appleton-Century-Crofts, 1952), p. 44.
17   Shurtleff, *Records of the Governor*, 1: 211.
18   Ibid., p. 213.
19   Rex v. Dr. John Bastwick, Henry Burton and William Prynn, Esq. (1637), 3 Howell's State Trials 711 at 730.
20   Ibid., p. 747.
21   Ibid., p. 766.
22   Frederick Seaton Siebert, *Freedom of the Press in England 1476–1776* (Urbana: University of Illinois Press, 1965), p. 212.
23   *Boston Gazette or Country Journal*, May 26, June 2, 1755, as cited in Duniway, *The Development of Freedom*, p. 119.
24   Lord Protector v. Sir Henry Vane (1656), 5 Howell's State Trials 791 at 795.
25   Shurtleff, *Records of the Governor*, vol. 4, pt. 2, p. 5.
26   Rex v. John Twyn (1663), 6 Howell's State Trials 513 at 535.
27   Ibid., p. 515.
28   Rex v. Benjamin Keach (1665), 6 Howell's State Trials 701 at 709.
29   Ibid.
30   Rex v. Edward Bushell (1670), 6 Howell's State Trials 999 at 1002.
31   Ibid., p. 1026.
32   Attorney General v. John Peter Zenger (1735), 17 Howell's State Trials 675 at 716–17.
33   Rex v. Benjamin Harris (1680), 7 Howell's State Trials 926.
34   Ibid., p. 927.
35   The Printing Act of 1662, *Statutes of the Realm*, vol. 5 (14 Charles 2 c. 33), was not in operation between 1679 and 1685, the end of Charles II's reign.

[36] Rex v. Harris (1680), 7 Howell's State Trials 926 at 929.

[37] It is stated in Siebert, *Freedom of the Press*, p. 220, that journalism, "controlled or uncontrolled, had become a permanent social and political phenomenon" during the period of the Commonwealth just prior to this time.

[38] Rex v. Harris, 7 Howell's State Trials 926 at 931.

[39] Rex v. Henry Carr or Care (1680), 7 Howell's State Trials 1111 at 1113.

[40] Ibid., p. 1112.

[41] Ibid., p. 1126. Chief Justice Scrogg's statements here and in the Harris trial were described by Cooper, *Treatise on the Law*, p. 62, as indicative of the Star Chamber.

[42] Proceedings Against Lord Chief Justice Scroggs (1680), 8 Howell's State Trials 163 at 198.

[43] Ibid., p. 199.

[44] Ibid., p. 216.

[45] It appears, however, that publication of news in the colonies could be illegal per se. Some ten years after Parliament had censured English judges for usurping legislative functions in declaring unlicensed news publications illegal, one of the men who played a prominent role in the affair, Benjamin Harris, attempted unsuccessfully to start the first newspaper in the American colonies. He published the first and only issue of *Publick Occurrences Both Foreign and Domestick* on September 25, 1690, in Boston. The governor and council of Massachusetts, in a summary proceeding four days later, found the newspaper "entertained reflections of a very high nature" and ordered it suppressed. This order is reprinted in *Proceedings of the Massachusetts Historical Society*, 2 d ser., 8 (Boston: For the Society, December 1892), 54. Harris was neither tried nor punished, nor was any official charge of libel lodged against him as it had been in England. Nevertheless, the council ordered that no one print anything without a license.

[46] Duke of York v. Titus Oates (1684), 10 Howell's State Trials 125.

[47] Rex v. Seven Bishops (1688), 12 Howell's State Trials 183 at 239.

[48] A petition circulated in the Province of New York in 1702 by Colonel Nicholas Bayard was cited in Bayard's trial for high treason as containing libelous statements also. In fact, it appears that he was tried for treason as a result of the overt act of getting soldiers to sign the "scandalous libels." Though found guilty by a colonial court, the verdict was overturned later by Lord Cornbury, the governor. Attorney General v. Nicholas Bayard (1702), 14 Howell's State Trials 471

[49] Rex v. Seven Bishops (1688), 12 Howell's State Trials 183 at 429.

[50] Ibid.   [51] Ibid.   [52] Ibid., p. 426.

2. Clash in the Law of Libel:
Colonial Liberalism v. English Totalitarianism

[1] George Keith, *New-England's Spirit of Persecution Transmitted to Pennsylvania; and the Pretended Quaker found Persecuting the True Christian-Quaker, in the Tryal of Peter Boss, George Keith, Thomas Budd, and William Bradford* (New York, 1693), pp. 5–6.

[2] The Proprietor v. George Keith, William Bradford, Thomas Budd and Peter Boss, Samuel W. Pennypacker, *Pennsylvania Colonial Cases* (Phila-

delphia: Rees Welsch & Co.: Law Book Publishers, 1892), p. 133. This source will be cited as *Pennypacker* in the pages which follow.
3   Ibid., p. 138, statement of Pennypacker.
4   Keith, *New-England's Spirit*, p. 33.
5   Ibid., p. 34.
6   Leonard W. Levy, *Freedom of Speech and Press in Early American History: Legacy of Suppression* (New York: Harper & Row, 1963), p. 28.
7   Keith, *New-England's Spirit*, p. 34; *Pennypacker* 117 at 135.
8   Keith, *New-England's Spirit*, p. 2.
9   *Pennypacker* 117 at 125. Deviation from English proceedings apparently was not unusual in Pennsylvania. Edmond Randolph in a letter to the Council of Trade and Plantations in England complained about this in 1697, stating Pennsylvania was an "arbitrary Quaker government" that was thoroughly independent of the Crown. He asked the King to take the governments of independent plantations into his own hands. J. W. Fortescue, ed. *Calendar of State Papers, Colonial Series, America and West Indies, October 1697–December 1698, Preserved in the Public Record Office*, 16 (London: Her Majesty's Stationers Offices, 1905; Reprinted at Vadiz: Kraus Reprint Lt., 1964), 182–83
10   Keith, *New England's Spirit*, p. 37. Both Isaiah Thomas in *The History of Printing in America, with a Biography of Printers, and an Account of Newspapers* (Albany, N.Y.: Joel Mansell, printer for American Antiquarian Society, 1874), 1: 222, and Frank Luther Mott in *American Journalism A History: 1690–1960* (New York: The Macmillan Co., 1962), p. 24, tell a story that jurors dropped Bradford's type form and had no evidence then that he printed the pamphlet, other than pied type. This story is not born out by Keith's original account of the trial. Further, the report in *Pennypacker*, p. 140, states the story of pied type is "utterly without foundation in fact."
11   The presiding judge in this case, Samuel Jennings, later wrote that he intended to let Peter Boss "read all that he had and make the most of it, for proof of any or all his charges." *Pennypacker* 117 at 125.
12   Clyde Augustus Duniway, *The Development of Freedom of the Press in Massachusetts* (New York: Longmans, Green, and Co., 1906), p. 73; Levy, *Freedom of Speech*, p. 34.
13   Theo Philanthes, *New-England Persecutors Mauled with Their Own Weapons* (New York, 1697), p. 58.
14   Ibid., p. 61.   15   Ibid., p. 62.   16   Ibid., pp. 60–61.
17   Ibid., p. 62; John D. Lawson, ed. *American State Trials* (St. Louis: H. H. Thomas Law Book Co., 1918), 5: 89.
18   Andrew Hamilton in arguing the John Peter Zenger case, 17 Howell's State Trials 675 at 717–18, refers to still another prosecution begun by Nicholson, then governor of Virginia, against a parson. Hamilton claimed that it was the only information that he knew of prior to the Zenger case for libeling a governor. He said that Nicholson had abused a parson, making the clergyman stand bareheaded in the hot sun while taking a tongue lashing. The parson, Hamilton said, wrote a doctor and said Nicholson was mad. Nicholson then prosecuted, but it was stopped by Queen Anne, according to Hamilton. Colonial state papers do disclose a severe political dispute in Virginia in 1703–5 in which Commissary Blair, founder of William and Mary College, and Nicholson were leaders of opposite factions. Blair, a member of the council and a parson, went to England to file official charges against Nicholson, one of which mentions abuse to parsons by making them

Notes to Pages 17–20   289
stand bareheaded in the hot sun. Correspondence of Nicholson to the Board of Trade further indicates that Nicholson wished to bring suit in England against Blair for a letter which Blair sent to a New York doctor. The letter apparently contained a printed ballad highly critical of Nicholson. Perhaps this is the case Hamilton referred to, as Queen Anne did remove Nicholson from the governorship at that time, leaving Blair and his faction in control of Virginia. See J. W. Fortescue, *Calendar of State Papers*, 22: 111, 417, 432, 437, and 480.

19   Ibid., 16: 503. Other entries on this incident, pp. 161, 154, 166, 169, 205, 392, 420, 407, 525, 526, and 529; also secs. 362, 371, 435, 619, 654, 780, 925.
20   Ibid., p. 399.
21   Ibid., p. 329.
22   Ibid., p. 413. See also secs. 762, 790, 812, 422, and 654.
23   Ibid., p. 525, sec. 975.
24   Ibid., pp. 526, 152.
25   Rex v. William Fuller (1702), 14 Howell's State Trials 517 at 530–31.
26   Ibid., pp. 534–35.
27   Ibid., p. 535.
28   Rex v. Dr. Henry Sacheverell (1710), 15 Howell's State Trials 360. Note to case prints "Proclamation of Queen Anne Against the Publication of Irreligious or Seditious Libels."
29   View of Chief Justice Morgan Lewis in People v. Croswell, 3 Johns. Cas. 336 at 389–90 (N.Y. 1804).
30   View of Justice James Kent in People v. Croswell, 3 Johns. Cas. at 386.
31   Rex v. John Tutchin (1704), 14 Howell's State Trials 1095 at 1097.
32   Ibid., p. 1128.   33   Ibid.   34   Ibid., p. 1129.
35   In the trial of People v. Croswell, Chief Justice Lewis and Justice Kent also disagreed on Lord Holt's instructions to the jury in Tutchin's case. Lewis said jurors considered only publication, while Kent said the entire case was left to them. The Howell's State Trials Index, p. 206, stated the case showed that Lord Holt "distinctly leaves the question of libel or no libel to the jury." This view also was adopted by Thomas Cooper, *Treatise on the Law of Libel and Liberty of the Press* (New York: G. F. Hopkins, 1830), p. 72. Cooper wrote the treatise after being prosecuted under the Alien and Sedition Act and after becoming president of Columbia College.
36   Rex v. John Tutchin, 14 Howell's State Trials, 1129.
37   Duniway, *The Development of Freedom*, pp. 101–2.
38   Thomas, *The History of Printing*, 1: 111. The article involved concerned pirates and the lack of government action against them.
39   *Boston Gazette*, January 29, 1722.
40   Livingston Rowe Schuyler, *The Liberty of the Press in the American Colonies Before the Revolutionary War* (New York: Thomas Wittaker, 1905), p. 13.
41   *Philadelphia Mercury*, no. 167, Tuesday, February 19 to February 26, 1722/23; "A Narrative of the Newspapers Printed in New England," *Collections of the Massachusetts Historical Society*, 1st ser., 6 (Boston: Samuel Hall, 1799), 64–65.
42   *Philadelphia Mercury*, no. 167, Feb. 19–26, 1722/23.
43   Thomas, *The History of Printing*, 2: 220.
44   Ibid.   45   Ibid., p. 221.
46   Duniway, *The Development of Freedom*, p. 108.

47 Rex v. Richard Francklin (1730), 17 Howell's State Trials 626 at 665.
48 Ibid., p. 658.   **49** Ibid., pp. 652, 659.   **50** Ibid., p. 672.
51 Ibid., p. 674.   **52** Ibid., p. 676.
53 This is especially true in the light of wide publicity given only four years before, in 1730, when editor S. Emlyn had written in the Preface to State Trials that he believed it would be difficult to maintain a libel indictment without the allegation that the publication was false, and that if falsity was alleged, persons proving truth shoul dbe found not guilty. Emlyn's 1730 Preface, 1 Howell's State Trials xxxi.
54 People v. Croswell, 3 Johns. Cas. at 388.
55 In 1720, prosecution of John Colman was ordered in Massachusetts for the publication of an alleged libelous book critical of trade policies, but the trial was never held. In the same year, a grand jury refused to indict Benjamin Gray for the publication of a pamphlet entitled *A Letter to an Eminent Clergyman in the Massachusetts Bay*, which argued for bills of credit. Duniway, *The Development of Freedom*, pp. 93–93; Thomas, *The History of Printing*, 2: 218.

3. Truth as a Defense: The Colonies Stand Alone

1 The case was reprinted in colonial and English newspapers and was reported in 17 Howell's State Trials at 675–747, because it had, the editor said, "made a general noise in the world." However, the editor also stated that "the decision is not allowed by the courts to be the law here (in England)." The State Trials report was followed by two legal opinions, signed by Anglo-Americanus and Indus Britanicus, which refuted Hamilton's arguments as not being consistent with the law in England. Further, James Alexander, Zenger's first attorney, wrote *A Brief Narrative of the Case and Trial of John Peter Zenger, Printer of the New-York Weekly Journal*, which was printed on the Zenger press. Articles pro and con were carried in newspapers of the day. For instance, Andrew Bradford in his *Philadelphia Mercury* printed the critical opinions of Anglo-Americanus and Indus Britanicus, which first appeared in the *Barbadoes Gazette*. Leonard W. Levy, *Freedom of Speech and Press in Early American History: Legacy of Suppression* (New York: Harper & Row, 1963), p. 134. In the same city, Benjamin Franklin in the *Pennsylvania Gazette* carried articles written by Alexander to belittle those in Bradford's newspaper. *Pennsylvania Gazette*, Nov. 17 to Dec. 8, 1737, issues 466–69. The case was termed by none other than William O. Douglas, U.S. Supreme Court justice, as marking a "milestone in the fight for the right to criticize the government." William O. Douglas, *The Right of the People* (Garden City, N.Y.: Doubleday & Co., Inc., 1958), p. 38.
2 Alexander's account of the trial was reprinted in 1756 for sale in New York by W. Dunlap. At the time libel charges were filed against Alexander McDougall in 1770, the account again was reprinted by newspaperman John Holt. In the same year, newspaperman Hugh Gaine reprinted the Anglo-Americanus and Indus Britanicus arguments.
3 Attorney General v. John Peter Zenger (1735), 17 Howell's State Trials 675 at 679.
4 Ibid., p. 690.   **5** Ibid., p. 691.   **6** Ibid., p. 692.

7   Ibid., p. 686.   8   Ibid., p. 689.   9   Ibid., p. 693.
10   Ibid., pp. 698, 699.   11   Ibid., p. 694.   12   Ibid., p. 696.
13   Ibid., p. 697.   14   Ibid., p. 703.   15   Ibid.
16   Ibid., p. 710.   17   Ibid., p. 719.   18   Ibid., p. 721.
19   Ibid., p. 707.   20   Ibid.

21   Ibid., p. 716. Hamilton also cited, on p. 717 of this account, Bushell's Case in England to show that jurors could determine the law without fear of reprisal from judges.

22   Ibid., p. 722.

23   Ibid., p. 723.

24   Leonard W. Levy, *Freedom of the Press from Zenger to Jefferson* (New York: Bobbs-Merrill Co., Inc., 1966), p. 43.

25   Attorney General v. John Peter Zenger, 17 Howell's State Trials at 710.

26   At this time only the second edition of State Trials, which had been published in 1730, was available in the colonies. It did not contain Francklin's case. In fact, the trials of Francklin and Zenger were printed one behind the other for the first time in the ninth and tenth editions of 1766. It is evident from the citations that both attorneys in the Zenger case relied on cases reported in State Trials. In fact, Hamilton's argument that the allegation of falsity was essential to a libel information appears, suspiciously, to parrot the words of the 1730 State Trials editor, S. Emlyn, who wrote in the preface that he believed it would be difficult to maintain an indictment without the allegation that the publication was false, and that if falsity was alleged, a person proving truth should not be found guilty. 1 Howell's State Trials xxxi. Also see Irving Brant, *The Bill of Rights* (New York: Mentor, 1965), p. 181, in which the author states that Lord Raymond's decision in Francklin's case was undocumented at the time of the Zenger trial.

27   Attorney General v. John Peter Zenger, 17 Howell's State Trials at 722.

28   Ibid., p. 697.

29   James Alexander, *A Brief Narrative of the Case and Trial of John Peter Zenger, Printer of the New-York Weekly Journal* (New York: W. Dunlap, 1756), pp. 37–39.

30   Harold L. Nelson, "Seditious Libel in Colonial America," *The American Journal of Legal History*, 3 (1959), 164, states that "court trials for seditious libel ended as a serious threat to printers in the American colonies with the decision in the Zenger case." Furthermore, the report of the case, 17 Howell's State Trials 675, while specifying that the Zenger principles were not allowed by the courts in England to be law there, did not question the fact that such was the law in the American colonies.

31   Isaiah Thomas, *The History of Printing in America, with a Biography of Printers and an Account of Newspapers* (Albany, N.Y.: Joel Mansell, printer for American Antiquarian Society, 1874), 2:48.

32   Ibid., 1:333–34.

33   Ibid., p. 334.

34   Massachusetts Bay Province, *Extract from the Journal of the House of Representatives* (Boston: Fowle & Tyler, 1756), p. 4.

35   Daniel Fowle, *A Total Eclipse of Liberty* (Boston, 1755), pp. 26, 27, 28. Also discussed in Thomas, *The History of Printing*, 2: 69–72.

36   Clyde Augustus Duniway, *The Development of Freedom of the Press in Massachusetts* (New York: Longmans, Green and Co., 1906), p. 118.

37   Among those called to account before assemblies were Andrew Brad-

ford, Hugh Gaine, and James Parker. Competent discussions of suppression through legislative action can be found in Levy, *From Zenger to Jefferson*, and Livingston Rowe Schuyler, *The Liberty of the Press in the American Colonies Before the Revolutionary War* (New York: Thomas Whittaker, 1905).

38 This was the case of Provost William Smith of the University of Pennsylvania, who was ordered imprisoned along with Judge William Moore. Smith took his case to England on appeal. See William Renwick Riddell, "Libel on the Assembly: A Prerevolutionary Episode," *Pennsylvania Magazine of History*, 52 (1928), 342; Levy, *From Zenger to Jefferson*, Libel for breach of privileges of a legislature, however, does not come within the scope of this work, which is concerned with court trials.

39 State v. William Owen (1752), 18 Howell's State Trials 1206 at 1223.
40 Ibid., p. 1228.
41 Ibid., p. 1230.
42 Ibid., p. 1206. Other cases cited were those of Bushell and the Seven Bishops.
43 *An Authentick Account of the Proceedings Against John Wilkes, Esq.* (London printed; Philadelphia reprinted: W. Dunlap, 1763), p. 11. Though arrested for the publication, he was released following a habeas corpus hearing on the grounds that Parliamentary privilege prevented imprisonment. See King v. John Wilkes (1763), 19 Howell's State Trials 982 at 990; 2 Wilson 159 (Eng. 1763). Following release, however, he was tried for libel.
44 King v. John Wilkes (1763-70), 19 Howell's Trials 1075 at 1123, 1136.
45 King v. John Almond (1770), 20 Howell's State Trials 803 at 819.
46 Considering that Owen was charged with falsity in his prosecution in 1752, this statement must be questioned. A note to the case report states that the word false was left out of the information against Wilkes because "all the crown lawyers knew very well that every word of the *North Briton* was true." Then the note summarized the then English law that "any writing, true of false, against a minister, is a libel." 20 Howell's State Trials 803 at 837. Mansfield himself as attorney general in 1754 had alleged in an information against Richard Nut, publisher of the *London Evening Post*, that the libel was false as well as scandalous and seditious.
47 Ibid., p. 839.
48 King v. Henry Simpson Woodfall (1770), 20 Howell's State Trials 895 at 903.
49 One attempt at an indictment was against the *Boston Gazette* for a Feb. 29, 1768, article written by Dr. Joseph Warren. It called Governor Francis Bernard cruel, obstinate, and insolent. Further, it described him as having a "diabolical thirst for Mischife" and as being "totally abandoned to Wickedness." Not only did the grand jury refuse an indictment, but the House refused to take notice of the governor's complaint about the newspaper, stating that the press was the "bulwark of the liberty of the people" and that if the proper bounds of press freedom were transgressed, punishment should be in the courts. After the indictment was refused, Samuel Adams had called newspapers the "bulwark of the People's liberties" in an article also printed in the *Boston Gazette*. The newspaper ran still another article in which toasts to the "worthy and independent grand jurors" were described, as well as a toast to the "worthy members of the House who vindicated

freedom of the press." Josiah Quincy, Jr., *Reports of Cases Argued and Adjudged in the Superior Court of Judicature of the Province of Massachusetts Bay Between 1761 and 1772* (Boston:Little, Brown and Co., 1865), pp. 260–70, 305.

50 Ibid., p. 309.

51 C. B. O'Callaghan, *Documentary History of the State of New York*, 3 (Albany: Week, Parson & Co., 1850), 528–36. Michael Cummings, hoping to get a reward from the governor, turned his boss, Parker, in as the printer. Parker was threatened with being removed from his post-office clerkship if he did not disclose the name of the author.

52 Arthur M. Schesinger, *Prelude to Independence* (New York: Alfred A. Knopf, 1958), pp. 115, 116. Schesinger cites the *Gazette* of June 2, 1770, and *New-York Journal* of April 19, 1770.

53 *A Brief Narrative of the Case and Trial of John Peter Zenger* (New York: John Holt, 1770).

54 Frank Luther Mott, *American Journalism A History:1690–1960* (New York: The Macmillan Co., 1962), p. 83. William Nelson in "The American Newspapers of the Eighteenth Century as Sources of History," *American Report of the American Historical Association For The Year 1908*, 1 (Washington: Government Printing Office, 1909), 219, states that Gaine served both English and American sides in the Revolutionary War. He published a newspaper in New York promoting the Tory view and one in East Newark promoting the colonial view, for a time.

55 Jonathan Blenman, *Remarks on Zenger's Trial* (New York: Gaine, 1770).

56 Alexander McDougall, *To The Freeholders and Freemen of the City and Colony of New York And To All The Friends of Liberty in The British Empire* (New York Broadside, Jan. 26, 1771).

57 O'Callaghan, *Documentary History*, p. 536.

58 Ibid.

59 *Massachusetts Spy*, No. 37, Nov. 15, 1771, p. 145 Also see *Boston Evening Post*, Nov. 18, 1771, where Thomas's article is cited with this description: "It is said that the piece referred to above (from its Nature, and Tendency) is the most production ever Published in America."

60 *Massachusetts Spy*, Nov. 29, 1771, p. 154.

61 Thomas, *The History of Printing*, 1: 168.

62 Schlesinger, *Prelude*, p. 147.

63 Thomas, *The History of Printing*, 2: 258.

64 This principle was continued even after the Revolutionary War had begun. English judges imprisoned John Horne in 1777 for publishing a libelous article in his *Morning Chronicle* and *London Advertiser*. The article stated that British troops had murdered loyal American subjects at Lexington and Concord. Jurors were allowed to determine only if Horne published the articles. 20 Howell's State Trials 788. It was not until 1793 with the passage of Fox's Libel Act that jurors were given the right in England to determine both the fact and the law. This act, entitled "An Act To Remove Doubts Respecting the Functions of Juries in Cases of Libel," 31 Geo. 3 c. 60, is listed along with House of Lords proceedings in King v. John Stockdale (1789), 22 Howell's State Trials 306. Also see T. C. Hansard, *Parliamentary History of England*, 29 (London, 1817), 551, 602. Also *Parliamentary Register*, 31 (London: J. Debrett, 1792), 57.

4. A New Nation:
Criticism of Public Officials a Crime

1   Frank Luther Mott, American Journalism a History:1690–1960 (New York: The Macmillan Co., 1962), p. 143.
2   Charles Warren, A History of the American Bar (New York: Howard Fertig, Inc., 1966), p. 237.
3   Ibid., pp. 224–39. An example of state constitutions was that of Maryland, which adopted the English common law as it was at the time of emigration and as since used. See Francis Newton Thorpe, Federal and State Constitutions, Colonial Charters and Other Organic Laws, 3 (Washington: Government Printing Office, 1909), 1689.
4   Ibid., 2: 789, Georgia; 3: 1092, Massachusetts; 5: 3083, Pennsylvania; 5: 2456, New Hampshire; 5: 2788, North Carolina; 6: 3257, South Carolina; 6: 3341, Vermont; 7: 3817, Virginia. These were the early guarantees. Other developments will be listed later.
5   Respublica v. Oswald, 1 Dall. 318 at 320 (U.S. 1788).
6   Ibid., p. 321.
7   "Original Draft of Letter From William Cushing, Chief Justice, To Hon. John Adams," Massachusetts Law Quarterly, 27, no. 4 (October 1942), 13.
8   Ibid.
9   "Copy of Original Letter To 'The Honourable William Cushing Esqr., Chief Justice of the Massachusetts Boston,'" Massachusetts Law Quarterly, 27, no. 4 (October 1942), 16.
10   "Original Draft," Massachusetts Law Quarterly, p. 15.
11   Freeman wrote that Gardiner's cruelty had murdered his wife. Further, Freeman claimed that Gardiner was preoccupied with New England, even on the Lord's day. This was claimed in the indictment to mean that Gardiner was a drunkard, with an affinity for New England rum. Though Gardiner was not mentioned by name, he was described in such a way that there could be no doubt who was meant. Herald of Freedom, March 4, 1791, p. 2.
12   Herald of Feedom, March 18, 1791, p. 1.
13   Boston Independent Chronicle, March 24, 1791, p. 2; Herald of Freedom, March 25, 1791, p. 1.
14   Warren, American Bar, p. 237.
15   Herald of Freedom, March 25, 1791, p. 1, col. 4.
16   Herald of Freedom, March 11, 1791, p. 2.
17   The claim was made in the Boston Independent Chronicle, February 24, 1791, and the Herald of Freedom, February 29, 1791, p. 2; March 11, 1791, p. 2, and March 18, 1791, p. 1.
18   Thorpe, Federal and State Constitutions, 5: 3100.
19   Ibid. 469 (Delaware); 3: 1274 (Kentucky); 6: 3423 (Tennessee).
20   "The Trial of William Cobbett for Libel, Philadelphia, Penn., 1797," in John D. Lawson, American State Trials, 6 (St. Louis: H. H. Thomas Law Book Co., 1916), 675–86, henceforth cited as American State Trials. Copy of indictment, as proposed, can be found in William Cobbett, Porcupine's Works; Containing Various Writings and Selections, Exhibiting a Faithful Picture of the United States of America; of Their Government, Laws, Politics, and Resources; of the Characters of Their Governors, Legislators, Magistrates, and Military Men: and of the Customs, Manners, Morals, Religions,

Virtues, and Vices of the People: Comprising also a Complete Series of Historical Documents and Remarks, From the End of the War in 1783, to the
Election of the President in March, 1801, 7 (London: Cobbett and Morgan,
1801), 335–36. Henceforth cited as *Porcupine's Works*.

²¹ *Porcupine's Works*, pp. 355–56; 6 American State Trials 680.

²² *Porcupine's Works*, pp. 346–48; 6 American State Trials 675.

²³ 6 American State Trials 681.

²⁴ Mott, *American Journalism*, p. 143.

²⁵ Clyde A. Duniway, *The Development of Freedom of the Press in
Massachusetts* (New York: Longmans, Green, and Co., 1906), p. 143.

²⁶ *Annals of Congress* (House), 5th Cong., 2 (Washington: Gales and
Seaton, 1851), 2139–71.

²⁷ United States v. Worrall, 2 Dall. 374 at 393–94 (U.S. 1798).

²⁸. Chase's decision was credited by John Quincy Adams some thirty-two
years later as ending the United States' common law jurisdiction in criminal
cases. Allan Nevins, ed. *The Dairy of J. Q. Adams*, 5 (New York: Longmans,
Green & Co., 1929), 247. Also "Review of DuPonceau's Dissertation on the
Nature and Extent of the Courts of the United States, April 22, 1824,"
North American Review, 21 (1825), 129, said Chase's decision 'gave rise to
one of the unfortunate measures of legislation, the Sedition Act." See foot-
note intimating the same, Frank M. Anderson, "The Enforcement of the
Alien and Sedition Laws," *Annual Report of the American Historical Associa-
tion for the Year 1912* (Washington, 1912), p. 119.

²⁹ Irving Brant, *The Bill of Rights: Its Origin and Meaning* (New York:
The New American Library, 1965), p. 251; Anderson, *Annual Report*, pp.
118, 119. Bache apparently obtained the information from official state papers
to which he was not supposed to have access.

³⁰ *Annals* (Senate), 2: 590, lists the date of June 26 for the introduction
of the bill. Anderson, *Annal Report*, p. 119, lists the same date for Bache's
indictment.

³¹ Anderson, *Annal Report*, p. 119 (footnote).

³² H. A. Washington, ed. *The Writings of Thomas Jefferson*, (Philadel-
phia: J. B. Lippincott & Co., 1871), 273.

³³ Ibid.

³⁴ U.S., *Statutes at Large*, 1: 596. Henceforth cited at *Stat*.

³⁵ 1 *Stat*. 10–21.

³⁶ Blair and Rives, ed. *The Congressional Globe, 26th Cong., 1st sess.,
Dec. 2–July 21, 1839–40* (Washington: Globe Office, 1840), p. 411. The
United States Supreme Court in New York Times v. Sullivan, 376 U.S. 254
at 292, stated the Sedition Act of 1798 had by 1964 been shown by the "court
of history" to be unconstitutional.

³⁷ Thomas Cooper, *Treaties on the Law of Libel and Liberty of the Press*
(New York; G. F. Hopkins, 1930), p. 78.

³⁸ United States v. Matthew Lyon, 15 Fed. Cas. No. 8646, at 1183 (Octo-
ber 9, 1798).

³⁹ Ibid.

⁴⁰ Ibid., p. 1184. The speeches referred to were those to Congress follow-
ing the XYZ affair, when United States delegates were ignored and ap-
proached concerning a bribe as the price for negotiations.

⁴¹ Ibid., p. 1185.

⁴² Ibid.

⁴³ United States v. Haswell, 26 Fed. Cas. 218 (May 5, 1800).

44   Ibid.   45   Ibid.   46   Ibid., p. 219.
47   United States v. Cooper, 25 Fed. Cas. No. 14, 865, at 638 (April 30, 1800).
48   Ibid., p. 632.   49   Ibid., p. 638.   50   Ibid., pp. 634–36.
51   Cooper, Treatise, pp. 79, 82.
52   United States v. Cooper, 25 Fed. Cas. at 634.
53   Ibid., p. 641.   54   Ibid., p. 642.   55   Ibid., p. 639.
56   Ibid., p. 635.
57   Rex v. James Thomson Callender, Walter Berry and James Robertson, 23 Howell's State Trials (1793), 79–83.
58   United States v. Callender, 25 Fed. Cas. No. 14, 709, at 240 (1800). Thomas Jefferson was accused of paying Callender for writing and publishing this tract, but he denied the charge. See his letter to Mrs. John Adams, Albert Ellen Beyh, ed. The Writings of Thomas Jefferson, 9 (The Jefferson Memorial Association: Washington, D.C., 1907), pp. 42–44.
59   United States v. Callender, 25 Fed. Cas. at 239.
60   Ibid., p. 253.   61   Ibid., p. 256.   62   Ibid., p. 257.
63   Ibid., p. 242.   64   Ibid., p. 243.   65   Ibid., p. 251.
66   United States v. Callender, 10 American State Trials 818.
67   United States v. Callender, 25 Fed. Cas. 239, Appendix on Chase's Impeachment Trial, p. 258.
68   Anderson, Annual Report, p. 120.
69   Ibid., p. 120; count also used by Mott, American Journalism, p .149.
70   Mott, American Journalism, p. 152.
71   Edward Chaning, History of the United States, 4 (New York: Macmillan Co., 1917), 232. There were claims the Sedition Law was the major factor defeating Adams. See Cooper, Treatise, p. 78.
72   Blair and Rives, The Congressional Globe, p. 412. Also see Jefferson's letter to Mrs. John Adams, Beyh, Thomas Jefferson, pp. 43–44.
73   Blair and Rives, The Congressional Globe, p. 412.
74   In the congressional debates on the Sedition Law, South Carolina Representative Robert Goodloe Harper said there had been four or five libel prosecutions in his state. Annals (House), 2: 2136.
75   Independent Chronicle, p. 2, April 8, 1799.
76   Ibid.
77   Ibid., April 29–May 2, 1799, p. 1, col. 4.
78   Ibid., March 4–7, March 7–11, 1799.
79   From April 8 through May 2 issues.
80   Henry Cabot Lodge, ed. The Works of Alexander Hamilton, 10 (New York: G. P. Putnam's Son, 1904), p. 354.
81   The Centinel of Freedom, Newark, N.J., Nov. 22, 1799, p. 3, col. 3.
82   Lodge, Alexander Hamilton, pp. 355–56.
83   Francis Wharton, State Trials of the United States During the Administrations of Washington and Adams (Philadelphia: Carey and Hart, 1849), p. 650. Also see People v. Croswell, 3 Johns. Cas. 352 (N.Y. 1804).
84   Broadus Mitchell, Alexander Hamilton, The National Adventure 1788–1804 (New York: The Macmillan Co., 1962), p. 431.
85   Centinel of Freedom, Nov. 22, 1799, p. 3, col. 3. The fine was reported in the edition of Nov. 26, an extra.
86   Warren, American Bar, p. 237; Duniway, The Development of Freedom, p. 145, quoting the records of the Supreme Judicial Court, 1800–1802.
87   Duniway, The Development of Freedom, p. 146.

88 Warren, *American Bar*, pp. 223, 224–36.
89 Mott, *American Journalism*, p. 143.
90 This was particularly evident from arguments by various state representatives in the debates on the Sedition Law. *Annals* (House), 2, pp. 2139–71.
91 This statement is made with knowledge of the provisions of the Espionage Act of 1917 and the 1918 amendment, sometimes referred to as the Sedition Act of 1918. The Espionage Act of 1917, however, was not a libel law in the sense that punishment was provided for defamatory criticism of those who ran the government. The act undoubtedly curtailed expression; it was a measure of suppression and, in the opinion of this writer, an unconstitutional infringment of free speech and press. But its avowed purpose was to punish expression that tended to incite insubordination and disloyalty during World War I, expression that tended to obstruct recruiting or that tended to curtail essential wartime production, expression that reflected on the *form* of government as opposed to the government itself, and expression that held the flag, military forces, or Constitution in contempt or scorn. The words of the Espionage Act had only slight resemblance to those in the Sedition Law of 1798. See Zechariah Chaffee, Jr., *Freedom of Speech* (New York: Harcourt, Brace and Howe, 1920), p. 56. The Sedition Law of 1798 was entitled a "Libel Law" in the federal statute books, and it not only provided punishment for statements that excited sedition but also provided penalities for statements that defamed the government or governors, that brought them into disrepute, or that provoked the hatred of the people against them. See 1 *Stat.* 596.
92 "Constitutionality of the Law of Criminal Libel," *Columbia Law Review*, 52 no. 4 (April 1952), 529.

5. Truthful Accounts: Defense to Criminal Libel

1 John E. Hallen, "Fair Comment," *Texas Law Review*, 8, no. 1 (December 1929), p. 53, points out that merit in the defendant's position began to be recognized.
2 Allan Nevins and Henry Steel Commanger, *The Pocket History of the United States* (New York: Pocket Books, Inc., 1951), p. 175, describes the spread of democracy to the masses, through a liberalized ballot and universal manhood suffrage during and after the Jacksonian administration.
3 *People* v. *Croswell* (1804), *Reports of Cases Adjudged in the Supreme Court of Judicature of the State of New York*, 3, ed. William Johnson (Philadelphia: E. F. Backus, 1834–36), 337 at 339–40.
4 Ibid., pp. 341–42.   5 Ibid., p. 355.   6 Ibid., pp. 360–61.
7 See chapter 4.
8 *People* v. *Croswell*, *Reports*, pp. 364, 377.
9 Ibid., p. 377.   10 Ibid.   11 Ibid.
12 Ibid., p. 401. Livingston, incidentally, defended Frothingham against Hamilton's libel prosecution in 1799. Frothingham did not plead truth as a defense.
13 Ibid., p. 402.
14 Ibid., p. 410. Both Justices Kent and Lewis reviewed the English common law of libel from early days until the time of the trial. They cited many of the same cases but came to different conclusions concerning them. Perhaps

their understanding of the law was based, to some extent, on their political
views. Kent was a Federalist as was Hamilton, and Lewis was a Democrat as
was Jefferson. However, the court's split opinion apparently was not based on
political ideologies. All the justices but Kent were Democrats. Kent was
joined in his opinion by Justice Thompson, a Democrat, and Lewis was joined
in his by Justice Livingston, a Democrat who in 1806 was to be named to the
United States Supreme Court by President Jefferson.

15   Ibid., p. 412, quoting the Act of April 6, 1805, Sess. 28, c. 90.
16   New York Constitution, Article 7, sec. 8 (1821).
17   *People v. Croswell, Reports*, p. 413.
18   "Constitutionality of the Law of Criminal Libel," *Columbia Law Review*, 52, no. 4 (April 1952), 531.
19   Respublica v. Dennie, 2 Am. Dec. 402 at 403 (Pa. 1803).
20   Ibid.   21   Ibid., p. 405.   22   Ibid.
23   Ibid.   24   Ibid., p. 407.
25   The 1790 Pennsylvania Constitution provided that citizens were free
to investigate public officials in their public capacities and that publications
proper for public information could be justified by truth in all prosecutions
for criminal libel.
26   Commonwealth v. Clapp, 4 Mass. 163 (1808).
27   Clyde A. Duniway, *The Development of Freedom of the Press in Massachusetts* (New York: Longmans, Green and Co., 1906), p. 152.
28   Commonwealth v. Clapp, 3 Am. Dec. 212 at 214. The importance of
the decision is underscored by showing other cases that cited the decision.
This decision was cited as a precedent in both criminal and civil suits for
years afterwards.
29   Commonwealth v. Clapp, 4 Mass. at 164.
30   Ibid., pp. 169-70.
31   Commonwealth v. Morris, 5 Am. Dec. 515 (Va. 1811).
32   Ibid., p. 516. This case, again, did not involve a newspaper; but it is
cited because of its importance in the evolving picture of the criminal law of
libel. The publication in this case was a petition to the legislature, claiming
a sheriff promised to ease tax collections for those supporting the construction of a court building on his land.
33   Francis Newton Thorpe, *Federal and State Constitutions, Colonial
Charters and Other Organic Laws*, vols. 1-7 (Washington: Government
Printing Office, 1909). States following the New York doctrine prior to the
Civil War included California, 1849, 1: 392; Florida, 1838, 2: 665; Iowa,
1846, 2: 1121; Michigan, 1835, 4: 1831; New Jersey, 1844, 4: 2599; Wisconsin, 1848, 7: 4077. After the Civil War other states placing the provision
in their constitutions were Nebraska, 1866, 4: 2349; Nevada, 1864, 4: 2403;
North Dakota, 1889, 4: 2855; Ohio (change in 1861), 4: 2941; South
Dakota, 1889, 6: 3370; Utah, 1895, 6: 3703; West Virginia, 1861-63, 6:
4015; Wyoming, 1889, 7: 4119.
34   Ibid., States following the "proper for public information" doctrine as
initiated in Pennsylvania were as follows: Arkansas, 1836, 1: 269; Connecticut, 1818, 1: 537; Illinois, 1818, 2: 983; Indiana, 1816, 2: 1037; Maine,
1819, 3: 1647; Mississippi, 1817, 4: 2033; Missouri, 1820, 4: 2164; Ohio,
1802, 4: 2910; Texas, 1836, 6: 3542, 3548. Similar provisions were made
after the Civil War in the following states: Colorado, 1876, 1: 476, 1: 476;
Alabama, 1865, 1: 117; Georgia, 1868, 2: 823; Montana, 4: 2302; South
Carolina, 1868, 6: 3257.

[35] United States v. Hudson and Goodwin, 7 Cranch 32 (U.S. 1812).

[36] Ibid.   [37] Ibid., p. 33.   [38] Ibid., p. 34.

[39] Federal officials, like state officials, took their grievances to state courts. An example was the civil suit filed in 1831 by United States District Attorney Beardsley of New York after he was charged in a newspaper article with misconduct in office. Maynard v. Beardsley, 7 Wend. 560 (N.Y. 1831).

[40] The State of Pennsylvania passed a law on March 16, 1809, preventing indictments for proper examinations of proceedings of the legislature or other governmental agencies, "or for investigating the official conduct of officers or men in public capacity." The law stopped a prosecution for libel against William Duane of the *Philadelphia Aurora*. See Commonwealth v. Duane, 2 Am. Dec. 497 (Pa. 1809). It states in this case that the civil remedy remained unimpaired.

[41] Commonwealth v. Child, 30 Mass. 198 (1832); Commonwealth v. Snelling, 32 Mass. 321 (1834); State v. Burnham, 31 Am. Dec. 217 (N.H. 1838).

[42] See chapter 6.

[43] The first civil libel suit involving an official and a newspaperman, that could be found by this writer, was Riggs v. Denniston, 3 Johns. Cas. 198 (N.Y. 1802). The suit involved an article about a commissioner of bankruptcy.

[44] Commonwealth v. Child, 30 Mass. at 198.

[45] Ibid., p. 199.

[46] Ibid., pp. 204, 206.

[47] Commonwealth v. Snelling, 32 Mass. at 321.

[48] Ibid., pp. 335, 336.

[49] State v. Burnham, 31 Am. Dec. at 217.

[50] Ibid., p. 221.   [51] Ibid.   [52] Ibid., p. 223.

[53] Ibid., p. 222.   [54] Ibid., p. 224.

[55] Thorpe, *Federal and State Constitutions*, 2, 1243. This was the constitution adopted by Kansas upon statehood.

[56] Banner Publishing Co. v. State, 57 Am. Rep. 214 at 222 (Tenn. 1885).

6. The Transition:
Public Officials Turn to Civil Libel Suits

[1] Frank Luther Mott, *American Journalism a History: 1690–1960* (New York: The Macmillan Co., 1962), pp. 111–326. He designates the early party press from 1783 to 1800, the middle party press period from 1801 to 1833 and the later party press period from 1833 to 1860.

[2] "The New Constitutional Definition of Libel and Its Future," *Northwestern University Law Review*, 60 no. 1 (March–April, 1965), 97.

[3] Plaintiffs in civil suits make claims, and defendants refute those claims. In a claim of libel, there is a presumption of falsity. To refute falsity, proof of truth is required.

[4] Tillotson v. Cheetham. 2 Johns. Cas. 62 at 74 (N.Y. 1806).

[5] Tillotson v. Cheetham, 3 Am. Dec. 459 at 563 (N.Y. 1808).

[6] Brewer v. Weakley, 5 Am. Dec. 656 at 658 (Tenn. 1807).

[7] Morris v. Duane, 1 Binn. 90 (Pa. 1808). It is reported by Mott, *American Journalism*, p. 187, that Duane had sixty to seventy libel suits pending against him in Pennsylvania. This is the only one recorded by the appellate courts.

8 Morris v. Duane, Binn. at 92.
9 Lewis v. Few, 5 Johns. R. 1 at 3–4 (N.Y. 1809). The article was printed March 12, 1807.
10 Ibid., p. 36.
11 Thomas v. Croswell, 7 Johns. R. 264 at 265 (N.Y. 1810).
12 Ibid., p. 273.
13 Powers v. Skinner, 1 Wend. 451 at 456 (N.Y. 1828).
14 Root v. King and Verplanck, 7 Cow. 613 (N.Y. 1827).
15 King and Verplanck v. Root, 4 Wend. 113 at 138 (N.Y. 1829).
16 Ibid., pp. 136–37.
17 A similar holding came in Powers v. Dubois, 17 Wend. 63 (N.Y. 1837). The suit resulted from an article claiming a candidate for state senator had agreed with the Albany Regency to defeat a public railway system in return for a bank charter. It was held the article implied corruption and was thus libelous.
18 Van Vechten Veeder, "Freedom of Public Discussion," *Harvard Law Review*, 23, no. 6 (April 1910), 436.
19 Act of the Legislature of the State of Massachusetts, 1826, ch. 107. Quoted in Alderman v. French, 1 Pick. 1 (1826).
20 Webster v. Lyman (1828), 12 American State Trials 327.
21 Ibid., p. 418.   22 Ibid., pp. 420–21.   23 Ibid., p. 422.
24 Ibid.   25 Ibid., p. 424.   26 Ibid., p. 424.
27 Usher v. Severance, 37 Am. Dec. 33 at 34 (Me. 1834).
28 Ibid., p. 35.
29 Robbins v. Treadway, 19 Am. Dec. 152 at 153 (Ky. 1829).
30 Ibid., pp. 154, 157.
31 Ibid., p. 152.
32 Sealey v. Blair, Wright (Ohio) Rep., 358 at 359 (1833).
33 Tappan v. Wilson, 7 Ohio 191 at 192 (1835).
34 Ibid., p. 193.
35 Cramer v. Riggs, 17 Wend. 209 at 210 (N.Y. 1837).
36 Mix v. Woodward, 12 Conn. 262 at 265 (1837).
37 Ibid., p. 267.   38 Ibid., p. 288.   39 Ibid., p. 293.
40 Henderson v. Hale, 19 Ala. App. 154 at 162 (1851).
41 Johnson v. Stebbins, 5 Ind. App. 364 at 366 (1854).
42 Ibid., pp. 366–67.
43 Lansing v. Carpenter, 76 Am. Dec. 281 (Wisc. 1859).
44 Ibid., p. 282.
45 Barrows v. Bell, 66 Am. Dec. 479 (Mass. 1859). This decision was cited by the Delaware Supreme Court in 1904 as having "established practically the American rule" on the privilege of reporting official and quasi-official hearings. See Star Publishing Co. v. Donahoe, 58 Atl. 513 at 522 (Del. 1904).
46 Barrows v. Bell, 66 Am. Dec. at 484.
47 Ibid., p. 485.
48 Ibid., p. 479.
49 It was held in Simpson v. Wiley, 4 Porter (Ala.) 251, in 1836 that the presentation of a newspaper in court, though similar to one with an alleged libel, could not prove publication if the witness who read the libel originally could not prove that it was issued from the newspaper office.
50 Dolloway v. Turrill, 26 Wend. 383 at 397–98 (N.Y. 1841).
51 Hunt v. Bennett, 19 N.Y. (5 Smith) 173 at 176 (1859).

[52]   Ibid., p. 177.
[53]   Ibid., p. 176.
[54]   The New York Code of Practice, passed in 1849, did, however, allow truth and any mitigating circumstances to be given in evidence in such libel cases, Bush v. Proser, 11 N.Y. 347 at 350.
[55]   Brewer v. Weakley, 5 Am. Dec. 656 at 658 (Tenn. 1807).
[56]   Charles Warren, *A History of the American Bar* (New York: Howard Fertig, Inc., 1966), pp. 446–74. The author claims that legal development between 1830 and 1860 in both state and federal law was "greater than any period in the legal history of the country."

7. Greater Privilege of Discussion:
Belief in Truth

[1]   John E. Hallen, "Fair Comment," *Texas Law Review*, 8, no. 1, (December 1929), 41–100; Jeremiah Smith, "Are Charges against the Moral Character of a Candidate for Elective Office Conditionally Privileged?" *Michigan Law Review*, 18, no. 1 (November 1919), 104–26; James J. Bierbower, "Fair Comment on a Political Candidate," *Georgetown Law Journal*, 37, no. 3 (March 1949), 404–17; Van Vechten Veeder, "Freedom of Public Discussion," *Harvard Law Review*, 23, no. 6 (April 1910), 413–40.
[2]   Chief Justice William Tilghman of Pennsylvania allowed a plea of good faith publication, with belief in truth, to mitigate damages in Morris v. Duane, 1 Binn. 90 (Pa. 1808). See chapter 6.
[3]   See State v. Burnham, 31 Am. Dec. 217 (N.H. 1838). Discussed in chapter 5.
[4]   See discussion on the Kansas Constitution, chapter 5.
[5]   White v. Nichols, 3 How. 266 (U.S. 1845).
[6]   Ibid., pp. 267, 291.   [7]   Ibid., p. 291.   [8]   Ibid., pp. 286–87.
[9]   This did not come until 1931 in Near v. Minnesota, 283 U.S. 697. More specifically, civil suits were not brought under the provision, though the Fourteenth Amendment due process clause, until the case New York Times v. Sullivan, 376 U.S. 254 (1964).
[10]   Hotchkiss v. Porter, 30 Conn. Supp. 414 at 415 (1862).
[11]   Ibid., p. 417.
[12]   Ibid., p. 420.
[13]   It was held by the Connecticut Supreme Court of Errors toward the end of the century that malicious attacks through reckless disregard of the truth, even though the occasion was privileged, destroyed any privilege of comment. Atwater v. Morning News Co., 34 Atl. 865 at 866, 868 (Conn. 1896).
[14]   Palmer v. Concord, 97 Am. Dec. 605 at 607 (N.H. 1868). Articles and poems were printed by Palmer on Aug. 3, 1861.
[15]   Ibid., pp. 612–13. Italics mine. The court recognized that this decision differed from State v. Burnham by ruling that true articles could be libelous if motives were bad and there was no good faith publication.
[16]   Arthur M. Schlesinger Sr., *The Rise of the City 1887–1898* (New York: Macmillan, 1932).
[17]   Edwin Emery and Henry Ladd Smith, *The Press and America* (New York: Prentice-Hall, Inc., 1954), p. 345
[18]   Aldrich v. Press Printing Co., 86 Am. Dec. 84 at 86 (Minn. 1864).
[19]   Ibid., p. 87.

20   Marks v. Baker, 9 N.W. 678 at 679 (Minn. 1881). The article was printed April 2, 1880.

21   Ibid., p. 679.

22   Larrabee v. Minnesota Tribune Co., 30 N.W. 462 (Minn. 1886).

23   State v. Balch, 2 Pac. 609 (Kan. 1884).

24   Express Printing Co. v. Copeland, 64 Tex. 354 at 359 (1885).

25   Ibid., p. 358.

26   Cotulla v. Kerr, 11 S.W. 1058 at 1060 (Tex. 1889). This decision often is quoted as embodying the "public officers rule" in libel, to be discussed later.

27   Commonwealth v. Odell, 3 Pitts. Rep. 449 (Pa. 1867).

28   Constitution of 1874, Article 1, par. 7. Cited in Barr v. Moore, 30 Am. Rep. 367 (Pa. 1878).

29   Barr v. Moore, 30 Am. Rep. at 370.

30   Briggs v. Garrett, 2 Atl. 513 (Pa. 1886); Neeb v. Hope, 2 Atl. 568 (1886). In the latter case no probable cause was found for claiming a coroner had not given the county goods taken from the dead, when he had.

31   Jackson v. Pittsburgh Times, 25 Atl. 613 at 616 (Pa. 1893).

32   Ibid., pp. 614, 616.   33   Ibid., p. 616.   34   Ibid., pp. 616, 617.

35   Commonwealth v. Rudy (Quart. Sess.), 5 Pa. Dist. 270 (1896); Commonwealth v. Disbrow (Quart. Sess.), 5 Pa. Dist. 276 (1896).

36   Augusta Evening News v. Radford, 17 S.E. 612 (Ga. 1893).

37   Cox v. Strickland, 28 S.E. 655 at 661 (Ga. 1897).

38   Ibid.

39   This privilege was limited in different ways by different states, as will be seen on later pages. In some states there were no definite rulings. Such was Rhode Island, but it was indicated that privilege was recognized in Tiepke v. Times Publishing Co., 37 Atl. 1031 (R.I. 1897). It was held in this Rhode Island suit that a plea of privilege could not be considered on a question of demurrer because the official had alleged malice as well as falsity. Indications were that the plea would be considered under other circumstances.

40   Boucher v. Clark Pub. Co., 84 N.W. 237 at 241 (S.D. 1900); O'Rourke v. Leiston Daily Sun Pub. Co., 36 Atl. 398 (Me. 1900).

41   Ibid.

42   Sweeney v. Baker, 31 Am. Rep. 757 at 759 (W.Va. 1878).

43   Ibid.

44   Ibid. The dictum also stressed that facts upon which criticism rested had to be proved unless admitted.

45   Ibid., p. 766.

46   See King and Verplanck v. Root in chapter 6. Also Hunt v. Bennett in chapter 6.

47   Hamilton v. Eno, 81 N.Y. 116 at 127 (1880).

48   Ibid., p. 123.

49   Ibid., p. 127.

50   In Mattice v. Wilcox, 42 N.E. 270 (N.Y. 1895) privilege was denied for charges of corruption, dishonesty and malpractice. In McIntyre v. Journal Co., 75 N.Y. 389 (1896), a charge of maladministration was not privileged. Also in Ulrich v. New York Press Co., 50 N.Y. 788 (1898) it was held that criticism was not libelous and did not need a plea of privilege to shield it. See section on criticism being privileged, found later in this chapter.

51   Rearick v. Wilcox, 81 Ill. 77 (1876).

52 Fitzpatrick v. Daily States Pub. Co., 20 So. 173 (La. 1896). Editorial printed July 23, 1894.

53 Upton v. Hume, 33 Pac. 810 (Ore. 1893).

54 Rearick v. Wilcox, 81 Ill. at 79–80; Fitzpatrick v. Daily States Pub. Co. 20 So. at 181; Upton v. Hume, 33 Pac. at 814.

55 Upton v. Hume, 33 Pac. at 813; Fitzpatrick v. Daily States Pub. Co., 20 So. at 174.

56 Upton v. Hume, 33 Pac. at 812.

57 Jones v. Townsend's Administrativix, 58 Am. Rep. 676 at 679 (Fla. 1885).

58 Ibid., p. 679.

59 Bronson v. Bruce, 26 N.W. 671 (Mich. 1886).

60 Ibid., p. 674.

61 Wheaton v. Beecher, 33 N.W. 503 at 505 (Mich. 1887).

62 Post Publishing Co. v. Maloney, 33 N.E. 921 at 926 (Ohio 1893).

63 Ibid., p. 926.

64 Wahle v. Cincinnati Gazette Co., 6 Ohio Dec. 709 (1878).

65 Negley v. Farrow, 45 Am. Rep. 715 (Md. 1883).

66 Ibid., p. 717.

67 Veeder, "Freedom," p. 434.

68 Neeb v. Hope, 2 Atl. 568 (Pa. 1886).

69 Bourreseau v. Detroit Evening Journal Co., 30 N.W. 376 (Mich. 1886).

70 Arthur T. Turnbull and Russell N. Baird, *The Graphics of Communication* (New York: Holt, Rinehart and Winston, 1964), p. 18. Zincographs for line illustrations came into vogue in the Uinted States in the 1870s, and halftone engravings were in use after 1886.

71 Randall v. Evening News Association, 44 N.W. 783 at 786 (Mich. 1890).

72 Eviston v. Cramer, 3 N.W. 392 at 393 (Wisc. 1879).

73 Ibid.

74 Buckstaff v. Viall, 54 N.W. 111 at 113 (Wisc. 1893).

75 Ibid.

76 Crane v. Waters, 10 Fed. 619 at 620–21 (1882). The case involved the *Boston Daily Advertiser* and an article about the manager of a railway. The court said he was a public man. The cited quotation specifically was applied to officials, however.

77 Vance v. Louisville Courier Journal Co., 23 S.W. 591 at 592 (Ky. 1893).

78 Ibid.

79 Veeder, "Freedom," pp. 432–33.

80 Cincinnati Gazette Co. v. Bishop, 6 Ohio Dec. 1113 (1882).

81 Belknap v. Ball, 47 N.W. 674 (Mich. 1890).

82 Michigan previously had held that in certain cases, falsehoods about officials made in honest belief of the truth and published in good faith were privileged, McAllister v. Detroit Free Press, 43 N.W. 431 at 437 (Mich. 1889).

83 Michigan courts were consistent in allowing juries to consider good faith belief in truth to mitigate damages. This was true in 1891 when it was held that the concluding sentence of an article—stating a marshall had been thoroughly corrupt—was not a summing up or opinion, but rather factual allegation and libelous. Hay v. Reid, 48 N.W. 507 (Mich. 1891). A similar

holding on mitigation was voiced in Orht v. Featherly, 49 N.W. 640 (Mich. 1891).

84   Burt v. Advertiser Newspaper Co., 28 N.E. 1 (Mass. 1891).

85   Printed Jan. 29, 1891. Three articles were involved. The newspaper was feuding with the *New York Evening Post.*

86   Burt v. Advertiser Newspaper Co., 28 N.E. at 5.

87   Ibid.   88   Ibid., p. 1.   89   Ibid., p. 4.

90   Ibid., p. 6.

91   Bailey v. Kalamazoo Publishing Co., 40 Mich. 251 at 257 (1879).

92   Scripps v. Foster, 3 N.W. 216 at 218 (Mich. 1879).

93   Dunneback v. Tribune Printing Co., 65 N.W. 583 at 585 (Mich. 1895).

94   See the Michigan cases of Bronson v. Bruce, 26 N.W. 671 (1886); Bourreseau v. Detroit Evening Journal, 30 N.W. 376 (1886); Wheaton v. Beecher, 33 N.W. 503 (1887); Belknap v. Ball, 47 N.W. 674 (1890); Hay v. Reid, 48 N.W. 507 (1891); Orth v. Featherly, 49 N.W. 640 (1891).

95   Account can be found earlier in chapter 6.

96   Account can be found earlier in chapter 6.

97   Thomson v. Powning, 15 Nev. 195 at 209 (1880).

98   Ibid., p. 210.

99   Ibid., p. 207.

100   Edwards v. San Jose Printing and Publishing Co., 34 Pac. 128 at 129 (Cal. 1893).

101   Ibid., p. 130.

102   Accounts given earlier in chapter.

103   Accounts given earlier in chapter.

104   Accounts given earlier in chapter.

105   Banner Publishing Co. v. State 57 Am. Rep. 214 (Tenn. 1885).

106   Ibid., p. 216.   107   Ibid., p. 222.   108   Ibid.

109   Price v. Whitely, 50 Mo. 439 at 442 (1872).

110   Ibid.

111   Ibid.

112   Prosser v. Callis, 19 N.E. 735 at 737 (Ind. 1889).

113   State v. Bush, 23 N.E. 677 at 678 (Ind. 1890).

114   Wintrode v. Renbarger, 50 N.E. 570 at 572 (Ind. 1898).

115   Sol Tax, *Evolution after Darwin,* 3 (Chicago: University of Chicago Press, 1960), 1–40; Rod W. Horton and Herbert W. Edwards, *Backgrounds of American Literary Thought* (New York: Appleton-Century-Crofts, 1952), pp. 153–58.

116   Horton and Edwards, *Backgrounds,* pp. 209, 227.

117   Woodbridge Riley, *American Thought From Puritanism to Pragmatism and Beyond* (Peter Smith: Gloucester, Mass., 1959), pp. 279–331. James's philosophy specifically outlined on pages 310–12; Horton and Edwards, *Backgrounds,* pp. 163–68.

118   Oliver Wendell Holmes, Jr., *The Common Law* (Boston: Little Brown and Co., 1949; 43rd Printing), p. 139.

119   Holmes, *The Common Law,* pp. 1–2, 35–36. Also see Oliver Wendell Holmes, *Collected Legal Papers* (New York: Peter Smith, 1952), p. 129.

8. Crystallization and Conflict: *The Jurisprudence of Libel Emerges*

1   The Tenth Amendment reserved to the individual states, or to the people, all powers not delegated to the United States government in the Constitution itself. There was nothing in the Constitution about United States courts reviewing state court decisions on libel. There were guarantees of basic liberties, including freedom of the press. But it had been held by Mr. Chief Justice John Marshall in the 1883 case of Barron v. Baltimore, 7 Pet. 243, that the guarantees of individual liberty in the first ten amendments restrained only the national government in these areas, not the state governments. Following this reasoning, there could not be a review of state libel judgments on the grounds that the state had infringed upon the liberty of the press.

2   Near v. Minnesota, 283 U.S. 697 (1931). The Supreme Court did not interfere with state libel judgments until 1964 in the case of New York Times v. Sullivan, 376 U.S. 254.

3   Gandia v. Pettingill, 222 U.S. 452 at 458–59 (1912).

4   Ibid., p. 457.

5   One can only speculate, if false facts had been involved, whether Mr. Justice Oliver Wendell Holmes, who rendered this Supreme Court decision, would have repeated his ruling in *Burt v. Advertiser Publishing Co.* to the effect that comment and not factual statements were privileged.

6   Patterson v. Colorado, 205 U.S. 454 at 462 (1907).

7   Prudential Insurance Co. v. Cheek, 259 U.S. 530 at 542–43 (1920). This case contested a Missouri law requiring employers to give employees leaving them for any reason a letter showing true causes for leaving. The insurance company claimed its right of privacy was being invaded.

8   Gitlow v. New York, 268 U.S. 652 at 666 (1925).

9   Ibid., p. 666.

10   Ibid., p. 672.

11   Near v. Minnesota, 283 U.S. 697 (1931).

12   The Court did list exceptions, such as the legality of prior restraints to protect violent overthrow of the government, to protect interference with recruiting, and to keep sailing dates secret in war times.

13   Near v. Minnesota, 283 U.S. at 708, 714.

14   Ibid., p. 704.

15   J. Edward Gerald, *The Press and the Constitution, 1931–47* (Minneapolis: University of Minnesota Press, 1948), p. 127.

16   Near v. Minnesota, 283 U.S. at 713.

17   Ibid., p. 723.   18   Ibid., p. 718.   19   Ibid., p. 721.

20   Ibid., p. 720.   21   Ibid., p. 715.

22   Beauharnais v. Illinois, 343 U.S. 250 at 256 n. 5 (1951).

23   Ibid.

24   Ibid., p. 257 n.5.

25   Baker v. Warner, 231 U.S. 588 at 594 (1913).

26   Arnold v. Ingram, 139 N.W. 111 at 117 (Wisc. 1912).

27   Kutcher v. Post Printing Co., 147 Pac. 517 at 519 (Wy. 1915).

28   People v. Strauch, 93 N.E. 126 at 131 (Ill. 1910). Also see People v. Fuller, 87 N.E. 336 (Ill. 1909).

29   Ziebell v. Lumbermen's Printing Co., 127 Pac. 677 at 680 (Wash.

1942); Herringer v. Ingberg, 97 N.W. 460 at 462 (Minn. 1903); Oliveros v. Henderson, 106 S.E. 855 at 857 (S.C. 1921).
30   Oklahoma Publishing Co. v. Kendall, 221 Pac. 762 (Okla. 1923).
31   Walsh v. Miami Herald Publishing Co., 80 So. 2d 669 (Fla. 1955); McClellan v. L'Engle, 77 So. 270 at 272 (Fla. 1917).
32   Kilgour v. Evening Star Newspaper Co., 53 Atl. 716 at 718 (Md. 1902); Commercial Tribune Publishing Co. v. Haines, 15 S.W.2d 306 at 307 (Ky. 1929); Kilgore v. Koen, 288 Pac. 192 at 196 (Ore. 1930).
33   Gaffney v. Scott Publishing Co., 212 P.2d 817 at 820 (Wash. 1949).
34   Ingalls v. Hastings & Sons Publishing Co., 22 N.E.2d 657 at 659 (Mass. 1939).
35   See Jackson v. Record Publishing Co., 178 S.E. 833 at 835 (S.C. 1935).
36   See Rowan v. Gazette Printing Co., 239 Pac. 1035 at 1037 (Mont. 1925); Oliveros v. Henderson, 106 S.E. 855 at 857 (S.C. 1921); Chase v. New Mexico Pub. Co., 203 P.2d 594 at 595 (N.M. 1949).
37   Bowie v. Evening News, 129 Atl. 797 at 799 (Md. 1925).
38   See Kilgore v. Koen, 288 Pac. 192 at 196 (Ore. 1930).
39   Ziebell v. Lumbermen's Printing Co., 127 Pac. 677 at 680 (Wash. 1942).
40   Kutcher v. Post Printing Co., 147 Pac. 517 (Wy. 1915).
41   Oklahoma Publishing Co. v. Tucker, 254 Pac. 975 at 977 (Okla. 1927).
42   Downer v. Tubbs, 139 N.W. 820 at 824 (Wisc. 1913).
43   Sheibley v. Fales, 116 N.W. 1035 (Neb. 1908).
44   Bennet v. Commercial Advertiser Association, 129 N.E 343 at 344 (NY. 1921).
45   McCormick v. Hawkins, 135 N.W. 1066 at 1067 (Mich. 1912), the superintendent; Aronson v. Baldwin, 146 N.W. 206 at 208 (Mich. 1914), the sheriff; People v. Talbot, 162 N.W. 1017 (Mich. 1917), the county clerk; Smith v. Hubbell, 106 N.W. 547 (Mich. 1906), the village attorney; MacWeston v. Grand Rapids Publishing Co., 87 N.W. 258 at 259 (Mich. 1901), the slot machines.
46   MacInnis v. National Herald Printing Co., 167 N.W. 550 at 551 (Minn. 1918).
47   Shaw v. Crandon Printing Co., 143 N.W. 698 (Wisc. 1918).
48   Kutcher v. Post Printing Co., 147 Pac. 517 (Wy. 1915).
49   Wooley v. Plaindealer Publishing Co., 84 Pac. 473 at 475 (Ore. 1906).
50   Gaffney v. Scott Publishing Co., 212 P.2d 817 (Wash. 1949), the prosecuting attorney; Hanson v. Parks, 246 Pac. 589 (Wash. 1926).
51   Aldrich v. Boyle, 101 N.E.2d 295 at 296 (Mass. 1951).
52   Davis v. Ferguson, 246 Ill. App. 318 (1928).
53   Watkins v. Augusta Chronicle Pub. Co., 174 S.E. 199 at 201 (Ga. 1934).
54   State v. Landy, 153 N.W. 258 (Minn. 1915).
55   Lydiard v. Wingate, 155 N.W. 212 at 214 (Minn. 1915).
56   Sweeney v. Newspaper Printing Corp. 147 S.W.2d 406 (Tenn. 1941).
57   Dawson v. Baxter, 42 S.E. 456 at 457 (N.C. 1902).
58   Hendriz v. Mobile Register, 81 So. 558 at 559 (Ala. 1919).
59   Wofford v. Meeks, 20 So. 625 at 628 (Ala. 1901).
60   Brown v. Journal Newspaper Co., 107 N.W. 358 at 359 (Mass. 1914).
61   Welch v. Tribune Publishing Co., 47 N.W. 562 (Mich. 1890); McIntyre v. Bransford, 17 S.W. 359 (Ky. 1891); Byers v. Martin, 25 Am.

Dec. 755 at 756 (Colo. 1875); Carter v. King, 94 S.E. 4 at 6 (N.C. 1917).
[62] Swearingen v. Parkesburg Sentinel Co., 26 S.E.2d 209 at 214 (W.Va. 1943).
[63] Fullerton v. Thompson, 143 N.W. 260 at 263 (Minn. 1913).
[64] Ewell v. Boutwell, 121 S.E. 912 at 916 (Va. 1924).
[65] Hartford v. State, 49 Am. Rep. 186 at 187 (Ind. 1884).
[66] Lent v. Underhill, 66 N.Y. Supp. 1086 (1900).
[67] Byrne v. Funk, 80 Pac. 772 (Wash. 1905).
[68] Smith v. Lyons, 77 So. 896 at 904 (La. 1918).
[69] Houston Press Co. v. Smith, 3 S.W.2d 900 at 907 (Tex. 1928).
[70] Josephson v. New York World-Telegram Corp., 38 N.Y.S.2d 986 (1943).
[71] Clark v. McBaine, 252 S.W. 428 at 432 (Mo. 1923). The court said the affairs of all departments at the University of Missouri were subject to comment by the press.
[72] Ibid. Also see Collins v. Press Publishing Co., 246 N.W. 363 (Wisc. 1933), for privilege being extended to invited criticism.
[73] Charles A. and Mary R. Beard, *The Making of American Civilization* (New York: The Macmillan Co., 1948), p. 720. The authors stated that the questioning spirit of these years became violent, with the critical mood and spirit of reform being reflected in magazines, essays, pamphlets, editorials, news stories, and novels. Charges in this age of the muckrakers, they write, were in many instances false and exaggerated. Still, they led to wholesale remedies of abuses. See pp. 720–23.
[74] See Post Publishing Co. v. Hallam, 59 Fed. 530 at 541 (1893). This case quotes the English decision Davis v. Shepstone, 11 App. Cas. 187, as did the decision of Holmes in the Burt case.
[75] Burt v. Advertiser Newspaper Co., 28 N.E. 1 at 4 (Mass. 1891).
[76] Post Publishing Co. v. Hallam, 59 Fed. at 531.
[77] Ibid., p. 541.   [78] Ibid., p. 535.   [79] Ibid., p. 536.
[80] Ibid., pp. 540–41. Italics added.
[81] Ibid., p. 539.
[82] See chapter 9. They include Alabama, Arkansas, Florida, Illinois, Kentucky, Louisiana, Maine, Maryland, Massachusetts, Mississippi, New Jersey, New York, North Dakota, Oregon, Vermont, Virginia, Washington, Wisconsin, Ohio, Tennessee, South Carolina, and the territory of Hawaii.
[83] Coleman v. MacLennan, 98 Pac. 281 (Kan. 1908).
[84] Ibid., p. 288.
[85] See State v. Balch, 2 Pac. 609 (Kan. 1884). Reported in chapter 7.
[86] Coleman v. MacLennan, 98 Pac. at 289.
[87] Ibid., pp. 281–82.
[88] Ibid., p. 292. That the plaintiff must show express malice when false articles were published was again sanctioned in 1919 in Carver v. Greason, 177 Pac. 539. The article in this case claimed a country attorney had not fulfilled his duty to investigate a record of a man tried on a criminal indictmen. In 1901 the Kansas Supreme Court also held accusations of bribery, drunkeness, gambling, etc., within the bounds of privilege. State v. Grinstead, 64 Pac. 49 (Kan. 1901).
[89] Coleman v. MacLennan, 98 Pac. at 286.
[90] Ibid., p. 291
[91] Ibid.

92 See chapter 9. They include Arizona, California, Colorado, Connecticut, Iowa, Kansas, Michigan, Minnesota, Montana, Nebraska, New Hampshire, North Carolina, Pennsylvania, South Dakota, Utah, and West Virginia.
93 Post Publishing Co. v. Hallan, 59 Fed. 530 (1893).
94 Coleman v. MacLennan, 98 Pac. 281.
95 A more complete discussion of these two rules, along with variations made upon them, will be found in chapter 9.

9. The Evolving Law: Majority v. Minority View

1 E. B. Morris, "Annotation to "Washington Times Co. v. Bonner," *American Law Reports*, 10 (1946), 412–40. Here he discusses the division of states as to the majority rule and minority rule of privilege, as of the time of the case in 1936.
2 Wofford v. Meeks, 30 So. 625 at 627 (Ala. 1901)
3 Advertiser Co. v. Jones, 53 So. 759 at 761–62 (Ala. 1910).
4 Parsons v. Age-Herald Pub. Co., 61 So. 345 at 350 (Ala. 1913).
5 The Alabama Supreme Court reiterated the rule a year later in Starks v. Comer, 67 So. 440 (1914), a suit brought by a candidate for president of the Railroad Commission of Alabama.
6 Murray v. Galbraith, 128 S.W. 1047 at 1049 (Ark. 1910).
7 Ibid., p. 1049.
8 Ibid., p. 1050.
9 Ibid., p. 1051. The Arkansas Supreme Court also said in West Memphis News v. Bond, 206 S.W.2d 449 (1947), that truth was the only defense to libel when officials, in this case a county judge, were charged with violating the law, p. 454.
10 McClellan v. L'Engle, 77 So. 270 at 272 (Fla. 1917).
11 State ex rel Tom Arnold v. Henry R. Chase, 114 So. 856 at 858 (Fla. 1928).
12 Metropolis Co. v. Croasdell, 199 So. 568 at 569 (Fla. 1941).
13 Rearick v. Wilcox, 81 Ill. 77 (1876). Discussed in chapter 7.
14 People v. Fuller, 87 N.E. 336 at 338 (Ill. 1909). The official had used money to pay help that had not been allocated by the budget, but it was approved by the proper officials.
15 Cooper v. Lawrence, 204 Ill. App. 261 (1917). This case resulted from articles claiming a judge was sympathetic to criminal elements and unfit for office. Also see Cooper v. Illinois Publishing and Printing Co., 218 Ill. App. 95 (1917).
16 Ogren v. Rockford Star Printing Co., 123 N.E. 587 at 592 (1919).
17 Ibid., p. 591. Also see Ogren v. Rockford Star Printing Co., 237 Ill. App. 349 (1926).
18 People v. Doss, 48 N.E.2d 213 (Ill. 1943), certiorari denied, 321 U.S. 789.
19 Ibid., p. 520.
20 Hotz v. Alton Telegraph Printing Co., 57 N.E.2d 137 at 139 (Ill. 1944).
21 Evening Post Co. v. Richardson, 68 S.W. 665 at 666 (Ky. 1902).
22 Ibid.
23 Ibid., p. 669.
24 Democrat Pub. Co. v. Harvey, 205 S.W. 908 at 910 (Ky. 1918).

25 Cole v. Commonwealth, 300 S.W. 907 at 908–9 (Ky. 1928).
26 Commercial Tribune Publishing Co. v. Haines, 15 S.W.2d 306 at 308 (Ky. 1929).
27 Levert v. Daily States Publishing Co., 49 So. 206 at 211 (La. 1909).
28 Addington v. Times Publishing Co., 70 So. 784 at 786 (La. 1916).
29 Egan v. Signal Pub. Co., 70 So. 556 at 557 (La. 1917).
30 Ibid., p. 559.
31 Cadro v. Plaquemines Gazette, 11 So. 2d 10 at 11 (La. 1943).
32 Martin v. Markley, 11 So. 2d 593 at 599 (La. 1943).
33 Ibid., p. 596–98.
34 O'Rourke v. Leiston Daily Sun Publishing Co., 36 Atl. 398 (Me. 1900).
35 Pattangall v. Mooers, 94 Atl. 561 at 563 (Me. 1915).
36 Ibid., p. 564.
37 The Maine Supreme Judicial Court did hold in 1918 in Sweeney v. Higgins, 104 Atl. 791 at 792, that honest belief in truth of false statements refuted malice for statements in a petition to a mayor. This, however, was not a general publication. There were no additional newspaper cases prior to the end of World War II from which to gauge privilege. It would appear that privilege extended only to fair comment and criticism for general publications.
38 Negley v. Farrow, 60 Md. 158 at 175 (1883). This case is reported in chapter 7.
39 Ibid., p. 177.
40 Kilgour v. Evening Star Newspaper Co., 53 Atl. 716 at 719 (Md. 1902).
41 Bowie v. Evening News, 129 Atl. 797 at 800 (Md. 1925).
42 Ibid., p. 799.
43 Dow v. Long, 76 N.E. 667 at 669 (Mass. 1906). Burt v. Advertiser Newspaper Co. is discussed in the previous two chapters.
44 Commonwealth v. Pratt, 95 N.E. 105 at 106 (Mass. 1911).
45 Oakes v. State, 50 So. 79 at 84 (Miss 1910).
46 Though privilege was denied, the case was reversed to give the publisher, J. C. Oakes, an opportunity to show good motives. Since the law made this a material part of the defense, along with truth, the court ruled that he had a right to show it.
47 Benton v. State, 36 Atl. 1041 at 1045 (N.J. 1897).
48 Merrey v. Guardian Printing and Publishing Co., 74 Atl. 464 at 467 (N.J. 1911), affirmed, 80 Atl. 331.
49 State v. Fish, 102 Atl. 378 at 379 (N.J. 1917).
50 State v. Dedge, 127 Atl. 539 at 544 (N.J. 1925).
51 Lindsey v. Evening Journal Ass'n, 163 Atl. 245 at 248 (N.J. 1933).
52 Bingham v. Gaynor, 96 N.E. 84 at 85 (N.Y. 1911).
53 Ibid., p. 85.
54 Ibid.
55 Also see Hills v. Press Co., 202 N.Y. Supp. 678 (1924), where criticism of favoritism by a county fuel administrator was ruled criticism on acts, not criticism of private character.
56 Hoeppner v. Dunkirk Printing Co., 172 N.E. 139 at 142 (N.Y. 1930).
57 Ibid.
58 Ibid., p. 143.
59 Cohalan v. New York Tribune, 15 N.Y.S.2d 58 (1939). Also see Cohalan v. New York World-Telegram, a companion case, 16 N.Y.S.2d 706 (1940).

[60]   Hall v. Binghamton Press Co., 70 N.E.2d 537 (N.Y. 1941), affirming, 29 N.Y.S.2d 760.
[61]   Englund v. Townley, 174 N.W. 755 (N.D. 1919); McCue v. Equity Co-Op Pub. Co., 176 N.W. 225 (N.D. 1918); Langer v. The Courier-News, 179 N.W. 909 (N.D. 1920).
[62]   Langer v. The Courier-News, 179 N.W. at 915.
[63]   Roethke v. North Dakota Taxpayers Association, 10 N.W.2d 738 at 741 (N.D. 1943). This decision did state that privilege existed when communications were made without malice by one interested person to other interested persons. But the issue was not so much comment and criticism as it was fair and accurate report of official records.
[64]   Todd v. East Liverpool Pub. Co., 29 Ohio C.C.R. 155 (1906). Original holding was in Cincinnati Gazette Co. v. Bishop, 6 Ohio Dec. 1113 (1882), discussed in chapter 7.
[65]   Banner Pub. Co. v. State, 57 Am. ep. 214 (1885). Discussed in chapter 7.
[66]   Territory v. Ota, 36 Hawaii 80 (1945).
[67]   Peck v. Coos Bay Times Pub. Co., 259 Pac. 307 at 312 (Ore. 1927).
[68]   Ibid., p. 312.
[69]   Ibid.
[70]   Jackson v. Record Publishing Co., 178 S.E. 833 at 836 (S.C. 1935).
[71]   Ibid.   [72]   Ibid., p. 837.
[73]   Ibid., p. 835.
[74]   State v. Colby, 162 Atl. 510 at 512 (Vt. 1924).
[75]   Williams Printing Co. v. Saunders, 17 S.E. 472 at 477 (Va. 1912).
[76]   Ibid., p. 488.
[77]   Ibid., p. 477.
[78]   Carpenter v. Meredith, 98 S.E. 635 at 637 (Va. 1918).
[79]   Quinn v. Review Pub. Co., 104 Pac. 181 (Wash. 1909).
[80]   State v. Sefrit, 144 Pac. 725 (Wash. 1914).
[81]   McKillip v. Grays Harbor Pub. Co., 171 Pac 1026 at 1028 (Wash 1918).
[82]   Ibid., p. 1029
[83]   Graham v. Star Pub. Co., 233 Pac. 625 at 626 (Wash. 1925).
[84]   Arnold v. Ingram, 138 N.W. 111 at 119 (Wisc. 1912). In this case it was proved a district attorney had prosecuted only half the pending cases, and the charge that he disapproved of the laws and hence would not prosecute the others was ruled as justified.
[85]   Putnam v. Browne, 155 N.W. 910 at 913 (Wisc. 1916).
[86]   Ibid., p. 914.
[87]   Walters v. Sentinel Co., 169 N.W. 564 (Wisc. 1918), and Hanson v. Temple, 185 N.W. 225 (Wisc. 1921).
[88]   Lukaszewicz v. Dziadulewicz, 225 N.W. 172 at 173 (Wisc. 1929).
[89]   Grell v. Hoard, 239 N.W. 428 at 429 (Wisc. 1932).
[90]   Ibid., p. 430.
[91]   Hoan v. Journal Co., 298 N.W. 228 (Wisc. 1941).
[92]   A discussion of this rule is given in David Riesman's "Democracy and Defamation: Fair Game and Fair Comment II," Columbia Law Review, 42, no. 8 (November 1942), 1294.
[93]   Donahoe v. Star Pub. Co., 58 Atl. 513 at 517 (Del. 1904).
[94]   Ibid., pp. 515, 522.
[95]   Ibid., p. 522.

[96] Washington Times Co. v. Bonner, 86 F.2d 836 at 848 (D.C. Cir. 1936).

[97] Ibid., pp. 840–41.

[98] Ibid., p. 848.

[99] Sweeney v. Patterson, 128 F.2d 457 at 458 (D.C. Cir. 1942).

[100] Ibid., p. 458.

[101] See chapter 7. Augusta Evening News v. Radford, 17 N.E. 612 (Ga. 1893); Cox v. Strickland, 28 S.E. 655 (Ga. 1897).

[102] Lowe v. News Publishing Co., 70 S.E. 607 (Ga. 1911).

[103] McIntosh v. Williams, 128 S.E. 672 at 673 (Ga. 1925).

[104] Kirkland v. Constitution Publishing Co., 144 S.E. 821 at 822 (Ga. 1928).

[105] Constitution Publishing Co. v. Kirkland, 149 S.E. 869 (Ga. 1929).

[106] See chapter 7: Prosser v. Callis, 19 N.S. 735 (Ind. 1889); State v. Bush, 23 N.E. 677 (Ind. 1890), and Wentrose v. Renbarger, 50 N.E. 570 (Ind. 1898).

[107] Cummings v. State, 166 N.E. 155 at 157 (Ind. 1929).

[108] Ibid.

[109] Cook v. Pulitzer Pub. Co., 145 S.W. 480 at 488 (Mo. 1912).

[110] Branch v. Publishers: George Knapp & Co., 121 S.W. 93 at 100 (Mo. 1909).

[111] Cooke v. Globe Printing Co., 127 S.W. 332 at 350 (Mo. 1910).

[112] Walsh v. Pulitzer Pub. Co., 157 S.W. 326 at 330 (Mo. 1913).

[113] Ibid., p. 329.

[114] McClung v. Pulitzer Pub. Co., 241 S.W. 193 at 200 (Mo. 1919).

[115] Ibid., p. 202.

[116] Ibid., p. 201. Also see McClung v. Star-Chronicle Pub. Co., 202 S.W. 571 (Mo. 1918), a companion case.

[117] Kleinschmidt v. Johnson, 183 S.W.2d 82 at 86 (Mo. 1944).

[118] Ibid., pp. 84, 86. State ex rel Zorn v. Cox, 298 S.W. 837 (1927), involved a truthful charge that a sheriff had ignored a request to investigate a source of liquor in a community.

[119] Oklahoma Pub. Co. v. Kendall, 221 Pac. 762 at 764 (Okla. 1923).

[120] Ibid., pp. 767–68.

[121] Oklahoma Pub. Co. v. Tucker, 254 Pac. 975 at 979 (Okla. 1927).

[122] Holway v. World Pub. Co., 44 P2d 881 at 882, 886 (Okla. 1935). See "Fair Comment," *Harvard Review*, 62 (Spring 1962), 1210.

[123] Holway v. World Pub. Co., 44 P.2d at 888–89, quoting Oklahoma Statutes 1931, sec. 726.

[124] The Texas Commission of Appeals judgments were, in effect, the same as those of the Texas Supreme Court. The commission was set up in Texas to help the supreme court clear its docket of a tremendous overland of cases, and commission decisions were adopted by the supreme court as its own.

[125] A. H. Belo & Co. v. Looney, 246 S.W. 777 at 778 (Tex. 1923).

[126] Ibid., p. 784. The case Express Printing Co. v. Copeland, 64 Tex. 354 (1885) is discussed in chapter 7.

[127] Webster v. Nunn, 769 S.W. 157 at 158 (Tex. 1924).

[128] Enterprise Co. v. Wheat, 290 S.W. 212 at 218 (Tex. Cir. App. 1927) and Houston Press Co. v. Smith, 3 S.W.2d 900 (Tex. Cir. App. 1928).

[129] Ferguson v. Houston Press Co., 12 S.W.2d 125 (Tex. 1929)

[130] Moore v. Leverett, 52 S.W.2d 252 at 255 (Tex. 1932). The determination was left to a jury.

131 Enterprise Co. v. Wheat, 290 S.W. at 219.
132 Fort Worth Press Co. v. Davis, 96 S.W.2d 414 at 419 (Tex. Cir. App. 1936).
133 Yecker v. State, 152 S.W.2d 355 at 357 (Tex. 1941).
134 Sweeney v. Caller-Times Pub. Co., 41 F. Supp. 163 at 168 (1941).
135 Ibid., pp. 166–67.
136 Ibid., p. 169.
137 Kutcher v. Post Printing Co., 147 Pac. 517 at 519 (Wy. 1915).
138 Ibid., on rehearing denied, 149 Pac. 552 at 553 (Wy. 1915).
139 Nicholson .v State, 157 Pac. 1013 (Wy. 1913). A county attorney was charged with misconduct.
140 Coleman v. MacLennan, 98 Pac. 291 (Kan. 1908).
141 Arizona Pub. Co. v. Harris, 181 Pac. 373 at 374 (Ariz. 1919).
142 Ibid., p. 377
143 Ibid.
144 Conner v. Timothy, 33 P.2d 293 at 295 (Ariz. 1934).
145 Snively v. Record Pub. Co., 198 Pac. 1 at 7 (Cal. 1921).
146 Ibid., p. 3.
147 Ibid., p. 3.
148 See Eva v. Smith, 264 Pac. 803 (Cal. 1928) for restriction on private lives and Morcom v. San Francisco Shopping News Co., 40 P.2d 940 (Cal. 1935) for holding that newspapers and citizens have some privilege.
149 Harris v. Curtis Pub. Co., 121 P.2d 761 at 768 (Cal. 1942).
150 Ibid., p. 767.
151 Knapp v. Post Printing & Publishing Co., 144 P.2d 981 at 985 (Colo. 1944).
152 Ibid., p. 985.
153 Moynahan v. Waterbury Republican. 102 Atl. 653 at 654 (Conn. 1918).
154 Ibid.
155 Ibid., p. 654.
156 Ott v. Murphy, 141 N.W. 463 at 467 (Iowa 1913).
157 Ibid.
158 Children v. Shinn, 150 N.W. 864 at 869 (Iowa 1915).
159 Salinger v. Cowles, 191 N.W. 167 at 174 (Iowa 1922). Another case involving Justice Salinger was heard by the Supreme Court in 1928. Here it was ruled that Salinger's advocacy of an additional judgeship to lighten the work load was not libelous. However, the court said that an accompanying charge that court decisions were one-man judgments was susceptible of meaning that the advocated a new judgeship to violate his duty of considering every case. This, the court said, was a question for the jury. Salinger v. Des Moines Capital, 217 N.W. 555 at 557 (Iowa 1928).
160 Taylor v. Hungerford, 217 N.W. 83 at 84 (Iowa 1928).
161 Coleman v. MacLennan, 98 Pac. 291 (Kan. 1908).
162 Carver v. Greason, 177 Pac. 539 (Kan. 1919).
163 Steenson v. Wallace, 62 P.2d 144 (Kan. 1937).
164 Lawrence v. Herald Pub. Co., 122 N.W. 1081 at 1086 (Mich. 1909).
165 Madill v. Currie, 134 N.W. 1004 at 1011 (Mich. 1912).
166 Moore v. Booth Pub. Co., 185 N.W. 780 at 781 (1921).
167 Poleski v. Polish American Pub. Co., 235 N.W. 841 at 843 (Mich. 1931).
168 State v. Ford, 85 N.W. 217 at 218 (Minn. 1901).

169 Friedell v. Blakely Printing Co., 203 N.W. 974 at 976 (Minn. 1925).
170 Ibid., p. 975.
171 Ibid., p. 976.
172 Clancy v. Daily News Corp. 277 N.W. 264 at 269 (Minn. 1938).
173 Cooper v. Romney, 141 289 at 292 (Mont. 1914).
174 Griffin v. Opinion Pub. Co., 138 P.2d 580 at 583 (Mont. 1943).
175 Ibid., p. 585.
176 Ibid., p. 586.
177 Bee Pub. Co. v. Shields, 94 N.W. 1029 at 1031 (Neb. 1903).
178 Mertens v. Bee Pub. Co., 99 N.W. 847 at 850 (Neb. 1904).
179 Farley v. McBride, 103 N.W. 1036 (Neb. 1903)
180 Estelle v. Daily News Pub. Co., 156 N.W. 645 at 648 (Neb. 1916).
181 Ibid., p. 650.
182 Lafferty v. Houlihan, 121 Atl. 92 at 96 (N.H. 1923).
183 Ibid., p. 98.
184 See Palmer v. Concord, 97 Am. Dec. 605 (N.H. 1868), discussed in chapter 7.
185 Lewis v. Carr, 101 S.E. 97 at 98 (N.C. 1919).
186 Ibid.
187 State v. Greenville Pub. Co., 102 S.E. 318 at 319 (N.C. 1920).
188 The same rule of privilege was abided by in Alexander v. Vann. 104 S.E. 360 (N.C. 1920), though this involved a letter from one sheriff to another stating that a deputy was no better than a Negro ex-convict.
189 See Jackson v. Pittsburgh Times, 25 Atl. 613 (Pa. 1893), discussed in chapter 7.
190 Weglein v. Golder, 177 Atl. 47 at 49 (Pa. 1935).
191 Bausewine v. Norristown Herald, 41 A.2d 736 at 741 (Penn. 1945).
192 Ibid., p. 742.
193 Boucher v. Clark Pub. Co., 84 N.W. 237 (S.D. 1900), sheriff; Schull v. Hopkins, 127 N.W. 550 (S.D. 1910), state's attorney; Myers v Longstaff, 84 N.W. 223 (S.D. 1900), candidate for mayor; Howe v. Thompson, 150 N.W. 301 (S.D. 1914), county auditor; Niblo v. Ede, 152 N.W. 284 (S.D. 1915), candidate for the legislature
194 Egan v. Dotson, 155 N.W. 783 at 787 (S.D. 1915).
195 Ibid., p. 788. The same rule was upheld in relation to an article about a campaign manager against the women's suffrage amendment in 1920. See McLean v. Merriman, 175 N.W. 878 (S.D. 1920).
196 Williams v. Standard-Examiner Pub. Co., 27 P.2r 1 at 14–16 (Utah. 1933).
197 Ibid., p. 14.   198 Ibid., p. 18.   199 Ibid., p. 17.
200 Ibid., p. 16.
201 Swearingen v. Parkersburg Sentinel Co., 26 S.E.2d 209 at 213 (W.Va. 1943).
202 Ibid., p. 215.
203 Ibid., pp. 210, 215–16.
204 Sweeney v. Baker, 31 Am. Rep. 757 (W.Va. 1878). Discussed in chapter 7.
205 Bailey v. Charleston Mail Association, 27 S.E.2d 837 at 844 (WVa 1944).
206 Ibid, p. 841.   207 Ibid., p. 844.   208 Ibid.
209 Tiepke v. Times Pub. Co., 37 Atl. 1031 (R.I. 1897).
210 Dwyer v. Libert, 167 Pac. 651 (Idaho, 1917).

211 United States Constitution, Article 2, sec. 2. Private citizens, of course, have the same right.
212 It had been ruled by the United States Supreme Court in the 1842 case of Swift v. Tyson, 16 Pet. 1, that federal courts had to follow the statutory laws of the states but that common law principles of the states did not have to be followed.
213 This case is discussed in chapter 8. See 59 Fed. 530 (1893).
214 Nevada State Journal Co. v. Henderson, 294 Fed. 60 at 62–63 (9th Cir. 1924).
215 Ibid., p. 63. The Post Publishing Co. v. Hallam decision also was cited in Washington Times Co. v. Bonner, 86 F.2d 836 at 848 (D.C. Cir. 1936).
216 Erie Railroad Co. v. Thompkins, 403 U.S. 64 (1938).
217 James J. Bierbower, "Fair Comment on a Political Candidate," Georgetown Law Journal, 37, no. 3 (March 1949), 413. Also see Dix W. Noee, "Defamation of Public Officers and Candidates," Columbia Law Review, 49 no. 7 (November 1949), 882.
218 Sweeney v. Philadelphia Record Co., 126 F.2d 53 (1942), held not libelous under Pennsylvania law of libel and privilege; Sweeney v. Patterson, 128 F.2d 457 at 458 (1942), discounted errors in fact and partially adopted liberal rule for District of Columbia; Sweeney v. Caller-Times Pub. Co., 41 F. Supp. 163 at 168 (1941) held statements not libelous under Texas law granting privilege except when falsehoods are grounds for removal from office. In Schenectady Union Publishing Co. v. Sweeney, 122 F.2d 288 (C.C.A.N. Y. 1941), the disposition of other cases is listed, p. 28, and it states Sweeney won his case in two unreported Illinois decisions.
219 Schenectady Union Publishing Co. v. Sweeney, 122 F.2d 288.
220 Ibid., pp. 291–92.
221 Schenectady Union Publishing Co. v. Sweeney, 314 U.S. 605 (1942).
222 Schenectady Union Publishing Co. v. Sweeney, 316 U.S. 642 (1942).
223 See opinion in New York Times v. Sullivan, 376 U.S. 254 at 268 (1964), where the court states that the Schenectady Union case was the only previous case considered by the court in which constitutional limitations were a direct issue.
224 The Minnesota Supreme Court in Friedell v. Blakely Printing Co., 203 N.W. 974 (1925), stated it was the jury's job to consider good and bad faith. The New Hampshire court in Lafferty v. Houlihan, 121 Atl. 92 (1923), stated the court ruled if the occasion was privileged, and the jury determined abuse. Also see Weglein v. Golder, 177 Atl. 47 (Pa. 1935), in which the right of the jury to determine malice was upheld.
225 The South Carolina Supreme Court also adhered to the policy that substantial truth was all that was required for privilege, as did the courts in Kentucky and Louisiana. See Clark v. Bullock, 28 S.W.2d 991 (Ky. 1930); Otero v. Ewing, 115 So. 633 at 636 (La. 1928).
226 This case turned on a charge of assault. See Peck v. Coos Bay Times Pub. Co. discussion earlier in this chapter.
227 See Charles A. and Mary R. Beard, The Making of American Civilization (New York: The Macmillan Co., 1948), pp. 611–920.
228 See Zachariah Chaffee Jr., Free Speech in the United States (Cambridge: Harvard University Press, 1964), chapter 2.
229 See Samuel Hopkins Adams, Incredible Era (Boston: Houghton Mifflin Co., 1939), pp. 312–32, 341–65.
230 Education and communications had undergone an explosive expansion,

and radio allowed individuals to learn more quickly of developments in the world. The number of newspapers served by national wire services grew from one hundred to fourteen hundred between 1914 and 1940, and prominence began to be given to political columnists who interpreted the news. See Frank L. Mott, *American Journalism a History* (New York: The Macmillan Co., 1962), pp. 691–92, 710. President Franklin D. Roosevelt was one of those in government who saw the advantage of informing the people through the media. See Elmer E. Cornwell Jr., *Presidential Leadership of Public Opinion* (Bloomington: University of Indiana Press, 1965), pp. 143–73, and p. 339 where it discusses the tremendous growth of accredited members of the press attending presidential press conferences. The figure is placed at 475 in 1935 an dat 829 in 1961.

231 See Gitlow v. New York, 268 U.S. 625 (1925) and Near v. Minnesota, 238 U.S. 697 (1931), discussed in chapter 8. Also Fiske v. Kansas, 274 U.S. 380 at 387 (1927), held a state criminal syndicalism law as applied to a prosecution of a workers' group was an unconsitutional impairment of free speech guarantees.

232 They were convicted under the Espionage Act of 1917 and the amendment of 1918, sometimes referred to as the Sedition Act of 1918. See 40 *Stat.* 217 at 219 and 40 *Stat.* 553. Also see Chaffee, *Free Speech*, chapter 2, where he says there were more than two thousand prosecutions. Also Robert E. and Robert F. Cushman, *Cases in Constitutional Law* (New York: Appleton-Century-Crofts, 1963), pp. 631–32.

233 Hartzel v. United States, 322 U.S. 680 (1944).

234 Alabama, Arkansas, Illinois, Kentucky, Louisiana, Massachusetts, New Jersey, New York, Ohio, Tennessee, Washington, Wisconsin, Maine, Maryland, and Mississippi. Of these, Kentucky and New Jersey shifted to a more liberal rule after World War I but returned to the original doctrine.

235 South Dakota, Utah, West Virginia, Arizona, California, Colorado, Connecticut, North Carolina. Also partially the District of Columbia and Oklahoma.

236 The Morris report in "Annotation," 412–40, showed that in 1936 the states following the majority view numbered twenty-eight. With them the District of Columbia and several federal jurisdictions. The list then showed eleven states in the liberal rule camp. The findings for this work differ in some respects from the findings of Morris, who did not cover the same period of time and who did not attempt to place cases in historical perspective.

237 This case, Hoeppner v. Dunkirk Printing Co., 172 N.E. 139 (N.Y. 1930), clearly indicated, however, that privilege did not extend to attacks upon the professional capacity of a teacher. The Arizona case of Conner v. Timothy, 33 P.2d 293 (Ariz. 1934), said privilege did not apply to a teacher who was a noncandidate and not in a job depending on votes of the people.

238 Snively v. Record Publishing Co., 198 Pac. 1 at 3 (Cal. 1921).

239 Sweeney v. Patterson, 128 F.2d 457 at 458 (1942). It was in this case that the court switched from the narrow to liberal rule of privilege.

10. Public Proceedings: *Privilege to Publish Fair and Accurate Reports*

1 Thomas v. Croswell, 7 Johns. R. 264 (N.Y. 1818); Powers v. Skinner, 1 Wend. 451 at 456 (N.Y. 1828).

2 White v. Nichols, 3 How. 266 (U.S. 1845). This case concerned a letter

to the President of the United States which allegedly libeled a collector of customs. It is reported in chapter 7.

3   Barrows v. Bell, 66 Am. Dec. 479 (Mass. 1859). See Star Publishing Co. v. Donahoe, 48 Atl. 512 at 522 (Del. 1904), where it is stated the Barrows case established the American rule on the subject of public meeting privilege.

4   A detailed account will follow in chapter.

5   Cowley v. Pulsifer, 50 Am. Rep. 318 (Mass. 1884). Holmes at this time was sitting on the Supreme Judicial Court of Massachusetts.

6   Fairbanks Pub. Co. v. Francisco, 390 P.2d 784 at 793 (Alaska 1964); Abram v. Odham, 89 So. 2d 334 at 335 (Fla. 1956); Pulverman v. A. S. Abel, 288 F.2d 797 at 802 (1955); Coleman v. Newark Morning Ledger, 149 A.2d 193 at 203 (N.J. 1959).

7   Wallis v. Bazet, 34 La. Ann. 131 (La. 1882).

8   Ibid., p. 133.   9   Ibid., p. 135.   10   Ibid.

11   Buckstaff v. Hicks, 68 N.W. 403 (Wisc. 1896).

12   Shields v. Commonwealth, 55 S.W. 881 (Ky. 1900).

13   Sarasohn v. Workingmen's Publishing Association, 60 N.Y. Supp. 640 (N.Y. 1890).

14   As examples see Williams Printing Co. v. Saunders, 73 S.E. 472 at 477 (Va. 1912); Kilgore v. Koen, 288 Pac. 192 at 194 (Ore. 1930); State v. Sheridan, 93 Pac. 656 at 660 (Idaho 1908).

15   Ingalls v. Morrissey, 143 N.W. 681 at 687 (Wisc. 1913).

16   Light Pub. Co. v. Huntress, 199 S.W. 1168 at 1173 (Tex. 1918).

17   Brown v. Providence Telegram Pub. Co., 54 Atl. 1061 at 1062 (R.I. 1903).

18   Henderson v. Dreyfus, 191 Pac. 442 (N.M. 1919).

19   Lyon v. Fairweather, 218 Pac. 477 (Cal. 1823).

20   Oliveros v. Henderson, 106 S.E. 855 at 857 (S.C. 1921).

21   Grossman v. Globe-Democrat Pub. Co., 149 S.W.2d 362 (Mo. 1941).

22   Alexandria Gazette Corp. v. West, 93 S.E.2d 274 at 279 (Va. 1956).

23   Rockafellow v. New Mexico State Tribune Co., 397 P.2d 303 at 306 (N.M. 1963).

24   Henderson v. Evansville Press, Inc., 142 N.E.2d 920 at 924 (Ind. 1957).

25   Ibid., p. 925.

26   Savannah News-Press, Inc. v. Hartridge, 138 S.E.2d 172 at 177 (Ga. 1964).

27   See Oliveros v. Henderson, 106 S.E. at 860; Rockafellow v. New Mexico State Tribune Co., 397 P.2d at 306; Lyon v. Fairweather, 218 Pac. at 477.

28   Lubore v. Pittsburgh Courier Pub. Co., 200 F.2d 355 at 356 (1952).

29   Kilgore v. Koen, 288 Pac. at 196.

30   Anne McCoy Campbell v. New York Evening Post, 157 N.E. 153 at 156 (N.Y. 1927).

31   Rhodes v. Star Herald Printing Co., 113 N.W.2d 658 at 661 (Neb. 1962).

32   Little v. Allen, 87 P.2d 510 (Kan. 1960).

33   Bennett v. Stockwell, 163 N.W. 482 (Mich. 1917).

34   Parsons v. Age-Herald Pub. Co., 61 So. 345 at 349 (Ala. 1913).

35   Houston Press Co. v. Ferguson, 12 S.W.2d 125 at 126 (Tex. 1928).

36   Merriam v. Star-Chronicle Publishing Co., 74 S.W.2d 592 at 595 (Mo. 1934).

37 Williams v. Journal Co., 247 N.W. 435 at 438 (Wisc. 1933).
38 See Matthews v. Oklahoma Pub. Co., 219 Pac. 947 at 949 (Okla. 1923); Schomberg v. Walker, 64 Pac. 290 at 291 (Cal. 1901); Rhodes v. Star Herald Printing Co., 113 N.W.2d 656 at 661 (Neb. 1962).
39 Westbrook v. Houston Chronicle Publishing Co., 102 S.W.2d 197 at 199 (Tex. 1934).
40 Swede v. Passaic Daily News, 153 A.2d 36 at 43–44 (N.J. 1959).
41 Leninger v. New Orleans Item Publishing Co., 101 So. 411 at 412 (La. 1924).
42 Bush-Moore Newspaper Inc., v. Pollitt, 151 Atl. 530 at 533 (Md. 1959).
43 Ibid., p. 534.
44 Ibid., p. 532.
45 Cafferty v. Southern Tier Pub. Co., 173 N.Y. Supp. 774 (N.Y. 1919), for school board; Gattis v. Kilgo, 38 S. E. 931 at 932 (N. C. 1901), for college board.
46 Nehrling v. Herald Co., 88 N. W. 614 at 617 (Wisc. 1902), for museum board; Holway v. World Pub. Co., 44 P.2d 881 at 888 (Okla. 1935), for water board.
47 Madill v. Currie, 134 N. W. 1,004 (Mich. 1912).
48 Reardon v. News-Journal Co., 164 A.2d 263 (Del. 1960).
49 Fairbanks Pub. Co. v. Francisco, 390 P.2d 784 (Alaska 1960).
50 Nickson v. Avalanche Journal Pub. Co., 334 S. W.2d 749 at 750 (Tex. 1959).
51 Davis v. Missourian Pub. Ass'n, 19 S. W.2d 650 at 653 (Mo. 1929).
52 Ryan v. Wilson, 300 N. W. 707 at 716 (Iowa 1941).
53 Begley v. Louisville Times Co., 115 S. W.2d 345 at 348–49 (Ky. 1938).
54 Schneph v. New York Times Co., 233 N. Y. S.2d 90 at 94 (N.Y. 1961).
55 Jackson v. Record Pub. Co., 187 S. E. 833 at 837 (S. C. 1935).
56 Abram v. Odham, 89 So. 2d 334 at 335 (Fla. 1956).
57 Phoenix Newspapers Inc. v. Choisser, 312 Pac. 150 at 154 (Ariz. 1957).
58 Pulvermann v. A. S. Abell Co., 288 F.2d 797 at 802 (1955).
59 Borg v. Boas, 231 F.2d 788 at 794 (1956).
60 Ibid., p. 795.
61 Ibid., p. 794.
62 Cresson v. North American Co., 124 Atl. 495 at 496 (Pa. 1924); Cresson v. Wortham-Carter Pub. Co., 248 S. W. 1,077 (Tex. 1923); Cresson v. Dispatch Printing Co., 291 Fed. 632 (U. S. D. C. Minn. 1923); Cresson v. Louisville Courier-Journal, 299 Fed. 487 (U. S. C. C. A. Ky. 1924).
63 Coleman v. Newark Morning Ledger Co., 149 A.2d 193 at 203 (N. J. 1959).
64 Ibid.
65 Ibid., p. 206.
66 McGovern v. Martz, 182 F. Supp. 343 at 346 (D. D. C. 1960).
67 Ibid., p. 347.
68 Ibid., p. 348. The United States Supreme Court in Barr v. Matteo, 360 U.S. 564 (1959), also held that public officers in federal posts have a complete privilege to speak out on matters involving their legal duties. Also see Glass v. Ickes, 177 F.2d 273 (D. C. Cir. 1940), *certiorari denied by Supreme Court*, 311 U.S. 718 (1940).
69 Curtis Pub. Co. v. Vaughan, 278 F.2d 23 at 29 (D. C. Cir. 1960).
70 Ibid., p. 31.

11. Shift to Liberalism:
Greater Tolerance of Discussion

[1]   As was seen in chapter 10, courts began to talk about the duty of news-papers to inform the people, Phoenix Newspapers Inc. v. Choisser, 312 Pac. 150 at 154 (Ariz. 1957), and the right of the people to know about matters relating to national problems such as national security and defense, Coleman v. Newark Morning Ledger Co., 149 A.2d 193 at 203 N. J. 1959). Further-more, personal liberties, including civil and political rights, became a major concern of the nation's courts of all levels. See John R. Schmidhauser, *The Supreme Court As Final Arbiter in Federal-State Relations, 1789–1957* (Chapel Hill: The University of North Carolina Press, 1958), pp. 193–202. In increasing numbers after World War II, state cases involving liberties were reviewed by the United States Supreme Court to determine whether the de-cisions rendered were in accordance with the provisions of the Bill of Rights in the United States Constitution. This concern with basic liberties rep-resented a shift of emphasis for the Court, though it had its beginnings in the period shortly after World War I. By 1941, with the decision in Olsen v. Nebraska *ex rel* Western Reference & Bond Association, 313 U.S. 236, the Supreme Court had largely abandoned substantive due process review of state economic legislation and had become increasingly occupied with the protection of civil and political rights. See William B. Lockhart, Yale Kam-isar, and Jesse H. Choper, *Constitutional Rights and Liberties* (St. Paul: West Publishing Co., 1964), specifically p. 47. The new emphasis of the Supreme Court was felt in the state courts as the constitutional decisions forced modifications in public policies. State judges had to render decisions based on these modifications.

[2]   Home Building and Loan Association v. Blaisdell, 290 U.S. 398 at 422 (1934).

[3]   Pennecamp v. Florida, 328 U.S. 331 at 347 (1946). Also in Craig v. Harney, 331 U.S. 367 at 376 (1947) the Court said the law of contempt was "not made for the protection of judges who may be sensitive to the winds of public opinion."

[4]   Farmers Educational & Cooperative Union of America, North Dakota Division v. WDAY Inc., 360 U.S. 525 (1959). This case is discussed later in this chapter.

[5]   Their right to do so was upheld by the United States Supreme Court in the 1952 case of *Beauharnais v. People of the State of Illinois*. In this case it again was ruled that individual state libel laws did not violate constitutional guarantees of free speech and press. The case did not involve an official. See 343 U.S. 250 at 256–57 (1952).

[6]   Babcock v. McClatchy Newspapers, 186 P.2d 737 at 740 (Cal. 1947); Brown v. Barnes, 296 P.2d 739 at 741 (Colo. 1956).

[7]   Gogerty v. Covins, 124 N. E.2d 605 (Ill. App. 1955).

[8]   Piacenti v. Williams Press, 107 N. E.2d 45 (Ill. App. 1952).

[9]   Caufield v. El Paso Times Inc., 280 S. W.2d 766 (Tex. Civ. App. 1955).

[10]   Puhr v. Press Pub. Co., 25 N. W.2d 62 at 64 (Wisc. 1946).

[11]   Garland v. State, 84 S. E.2d 9 at 12 (Ga. 1954).

[12]   Sanders v. Evening News Association, 21 N. W.2d 152 at 155 (Mich. 1946).

13 Aldrich v. Boyle, 101 N. E.2d 495 (Mass. 1951).

14 Thompson v. Newspaper Printing Corp., 325 P.2d 945 at 948 (Okla. 1958).

15 Reasonable susceptibility still was regarded by most jurisdictions as the rule for trials. See Thompson v. Newspaper Printing Corp., 325 P.2d 945 at 948 (Okla. 1958). Still, more judges were beginning not to find such reasonable susceptibility.

16 People v. Quill, 177 N. Y. S.2d 380 at 383–84 (1958).

17 Ibid., p. 382.

18 John D. Stevens, Robert L. Bailey, Judith F. Krueger, and John M. Mollwitz, "Criminal Libel as Seditious Libel, 1916–1965," *Journalism Quarterly*, 43 No. 1 (Spring 1966), 112. Criminal libel prosecutions in the last half of the nineteenth century were listed at approximately 235 as compared to 148 in the fifty years ending in 1965.

19 Krasner v. State, 26 So. 2d 519 (Ala. App. 1946).

20 Krasner v. State, 26 So. 2d 526 at 529 (Ala. 1946).

21 Ibid., pp. 527–28.

22 See comment in Garrison v. Louisiana, 379 U.S. 64 at 70 (1964), where the Proposed Official Draft of the Model Penal Code of the American Law Institute is quoted to the effect that penal control of personal defamation is inappropriate and "this probably accounts for the paucity of prosecutions and the near desuetude of private criminal libel legislation in this country."

23 Ross v. Gore, 48 So. 2d 412 at 415 (Fla. 1950).

24 Miami Herald Pub. Co. v. Brautigam, 127 So. 2d 718 at 723 (Fla. 1961).

25 Ibid., p. 724.

26 McCormick v. Miami Herald Pub. Co., 139 So. 2d 197 at 201 (Fla. 1962).

27 Ibid., p. 200.

28 Ross v. Gore, 48 So. 2d at 412. The Law required retractions within ten days.

29 Brogan v. Passaic Daily News, 123 A.2d 473 at 477 (N. J. 1956).

30 Ibid., p. 478.

31 Ibid., pp. 477, 482.

32 Leers v. Green, 131 A.2d 781 at 790 (N. J. 1957).

33 Ibid., p. 792.

34 Coleman v. Newark Morning Ledger Co., 149 A.2d 193 at 206 (N. J. 1959).

35 Krebs v. McNeal, 76 So. 2d 693 at 701 (Miss. 1955).

36 Edmonds v. Delta Democrat Pub. Co., 93 So. 2d 171 (Miss. 1957).

37 Henry v. Collins, 150 So. 2d 28 at 38 (Miss. 1963).

38 Harold J. Spaeth, *The Warren Court* (San Francisco: Chandler Publishing Co., 1966). p. 181.

39 Henry v. Collins, 380 U.S. 356 (1965). See detailed account in chapter 12.

40 See McKillip v. Grays Harbor Publishing Co., 171 Pac. 1026 at 1028 (Wash. 1918).

41 Owens v. Scott Publishing Co., 284 P.2d 296 at 306–11 (Wash. 1955). The court still was split in its views of privilege through 1964. See Jolly v. Valley Publishing Co., 388 P.2d 129 (Wash. 1964).

42 Owens v. Scott Publishing Co., 284 P.2d at 302. Privilege later was ruled

not to excuse charges of misconduct in office, Lamanna v. Scott Publishing Co., 296 P.2d 321 (Wash. 1956), with improper counting of votes being the specific issue.

43   Farrar v. Tribune Pub. Co., 358 P.2d 792 at 794 (Wash. 1961). If jurors found lack of malice, even compensatory damages could be reduced.

44   Brewster v. Boston Herald-Traveler Corp., 188 F. Supp. 565 at 578 (1960). The decision was based on state law.

45   Mencher v. Chesley, 75 N. E.2d 257 at 260 (N.Y. 1947); Toomey v. Farley, 138 N. E.2d 221 at 225 (N.Y. 1956).

46   Fischer v. Brockway Co., 218 N. Y. S.2d 309 at 311 (1961).

47   Ibid., p. 310.

48   Crosby v. Rockland County Citizen Pub. Co., 232 N. Y. S.2d 819 at 822 (1962).

49   Ibid., p. 821.

50   Cook v. East Shore Newspapers, 64 N. E.2d 751 at 760 (Ill. 1946).

51   Ibid., p. 766.

52   Cadwell v. Crowell-Collier Pub. Co., 161 F.2d 333 at 336 (2d Cin. 1947).

53   Ibid., p. 335.

54   Ibid., p. 336.

55   Murphy v. Farmers Educational and Co-Op Union of America, North Dakota Division, 72 N. W.2d 636 at 647 (N. D. 1955).

56   Cross v. Guy Gannett Pub. Co., 121 A.2d 355 at 358–59 (Me. 1956).

57   Westropp v. E. W. Scripps Co., 74 N. E.2d 340 at 346 (Ohio. 1947).

58   Madison v. Bolton, 102 So. 2d 433 (La. 1955).

59   DeShotel v. Thistlethwaite. 121 So. 2d 222 at 225 (La. 1960).

60   A. S. Abell Co. v. Kirby, 176 A.2d 340 (Md. 1961).

61   Ibid., p. 351.

62   Panhandle Pub. Co. v. Fitzgarald, 215 S. W.2d 659 (Tex. App. 1950).

63   Fitzgarald v. Panhandle Pub. Co., 228 S. W.2d 499 at 505 (Tex. 1950).

64   See Herald-Post Pub. Co. v. Hervey, 282 S. W.2d 410 at 413 (Tex. App. 1955).

65   Rawlins v. McKee, 327 S. W.2d 633 at 636 (Tex. App. 1959).

66   See Constitution Pub. Co. v. Kirkland, 144 S. E. 821 (Ga. 1928) and at 149 S. E. 869 Ga. 1929).

67   See McIntosh v. Williams, 128 S. E. 672 (Ga. 1925), and quoted in Camp v. Maddox, 92 S. E.2d 581 at 585 (Ga. 1956).

68   Gough v. Tribune Journal Co., 275 P.2d 663 at 667 (Idaho 1954).

69   Reynolds et al v. Arentz, 119 F. Supp. 82 at 90–91 (1954).

70   Nevada State Journal v. Henderson, 294 Fed. 60 at 62 (1929), decided by a federal court prior to the decision of the United States Supreme Court in Erie Railroad Co. v. Tompkins, 403 U.S. 64 (1938), which required that federal courts follow state common law in arriving at decisions.

71   Story v. Norfolk-Portsmouth Newspapers Inc., 118 S. E.2d 688 at 670 (Va. 1956).

72   Ibid., p. 671.

73   McAndrew v. Scranton Pepublican Publishing Co., 72 A.2d 780 at 785 (Pa. 1950).

74   Ibid., p. 783.

75   Ponder v. Cobb, 126 S. E.2d 67 at 76 (N. C. 1962).

76   Ibid., p. 81.

77   Yancey v. Gillespie, 87 S. E. 2d 210 at 212 (N. C. 1955).

78 Hammersten v. Reiling, 115 N. W.2d 259 at 264 (Minn. 1962).
79 Catalfo v. Shenton, 149 A.2d 871 at 874 (N. H. 1959)
80 Stice v. Beacon Newspaper Corp. 340 P.2d 396 at 400 (Kan. 1959).
81 England v. Daily Gazette Co., 104 S. E.2d 306 at 314, 316 (W. Va. 1958); Bower v. Daily Gazette Co., 104 S. E.2d 317 at 319 (W. Va. 1958).
82 Howser v. Pearson, 95 F. Supp. 936 at 938 (1951).
83 Ibid.
84 Privilege for misstatement of fact was not allowed in Oregon and Washington and, at this time, in Nevada.
85 Gearheart v. WSAZ. 150 F. Supp. 98 at 112 (1953).
86 Ibid., p. 109.
87 Ibid., p. 107.
88 Charles Parker Co. v. Silver City Crystal Co., 116 A.2d 440 at 445 (Conn. 1955).
89 Ibid., p. 446.
90 Farmers Educational & Cooperative Union of America, North Dakota Division v. WDAY, Inc., 360 U.S. 525 at 531–35 (1959).
91 Ibid., pp. 526–27.
92 Beauharnais v. People of the State of Illinois, 343 U.S. 250 at 256–57 (1952).
93 See Associated Press v. United States, 326 U.S. 1 at 20 (1945), in which it is stated that the First Amendment freedom "rest on the assumption that the widest possible dissemination of information from diverse and antagonistic sources is essential to the welfare of the public." Also see Bryce W. Rucker, *The First Freedom* (Carbondale: Southern Illinois University Press, 1968), particularly p. 222.
94 Barr v. Matteo, 360 U.S. 564 at 571, 575 (1959).
95 Ibid., p. 571.
96 Howard v. Lyons, 360 U.S. 593 at 597 (1959).
97 Hogan v. New York Times Co., 211 F. Supp. 99 at 106–7 (1962).
98 Hogan v. New York Times Co., 313 F.2d 354 at 356–57 (1963).
99 New York Times v. Sullivan, 376 U.S. 254 (1964), to be discussed fully in the next chapter.
100 Spaeth, *The Warren Court*, pp. 13–17, points out that starting with the Vinson direction of the Supreme Court and going through the Warren direction, individual states were required "to measure up to the standards of the Bill of Rights."
101 William E. Leuchtenburg, *The Great Age of Change*, vol. 12, *The Life History of the United States*, ed. Henry T. Graff (New York: Times, Inc., 1964), pp. 148–58.
102 Internal Security Act of 1950, 64 Stat. 987.
103 *Public Papers of the Presidents of the United States, Harry S. Truman, 1950* (Washington, D.C.: United States Government Printing Office, 1965), p. 650.
104 See John F. Kennedy's Inaugural Address, January 20, 1961, *Public Papers of the Presidents of the United States, John F. Kennedy, 1961* (Washington, D.C.: United States Government Printing Office, 1962), pp. 1–3.
105 Irving Brant, *The Bill of Rights: Its Origin and Meaning* (New York: The New American Library, 1965), p. 490.
106 L. Brent Bozall, *The Warren Revolution* (New Rochelle, N.Y.: Arlington House, 1966), pp. 34–35, stated that the Supreme Court had instituted

a new system of Constitution making. By reviewing state judgments, the Supreme Court became lawmakers, not expounders.

[107] Those states in which courts allowed misstatements of fact are Arizona, California, Connecticut, Georgia, Idaho, Iowa, Kansas, Michigan, Minnesota, Montana, Nebraska, Nevada, New Hampshire, North Carolina, Pennsylvania, South Dakota, Utah, Virginia, and West Virginia. Also see chapter 9.

[108] Those states following the majority view of fair comment also are listed in chapter 9. They are Alabama, Arkansas, Florida, Hawaii, Illinois, Kentucky, Louisiana, Maine, Maryland, Massachusetts, Mississippi, New Jersey, New York, North Dakota, Ohio, Oregon, South Carolina, Tennessee, Vermont, Washington, and Wisconsin. Other states either followed independent views or had established no precedent in court decisions.

12. A Nationwide Libel Standards:
The United States Supreme Court Speaks

[1]   New York Times v. Sullivan, 376 U.S. 254 at 279–80 (1964). This case also included the decision to Abernathy et al. v. Sullivan, which had been combined with the New York Times case by the Supreme Court.

[2]   Ibid., p. 264.

[3]   Garrison v. Louisiana, 379 U.S. 64 at 75 (1964).

[4]   Rosenblatt v. Baer, 383 U.S. 75 at 85 (1966).

[5]   Curtis Publishing Co. v. Butts, 383 U.S. 130 at 145 (1967). This case also included Associated Press v. Walker, on certiorari from a Texas Court of Civil Appeals.

[6]   New York Times v. Sullivan, 376 U.S. at 257.

[7]   Ibid., pp. 257–58.

[8]   Ibid., pp. 258–59.

[9]   "The New Constitutional Definition of Libel and Its Future,"Northwestern University Law Review, 66 No. 1 March-April 1965), 110. This study lists the largest libel judgment prior to this time at $67,000; it was reduced to $45,000.

[10]   See Shelly v. Kraemer, 334 U.S. 1 at 4 (1948), where the opinion reads: "That the action of state courts and judicial officers in their official capacities is to be regarded as action of the State within the meaning of the Fourteenth Amendment, is a proposition which has long been established by decisions of this court."

[11]   New York Times v. Sullivan, 376 U.S. at 265.

[12]   Ibid., p. 266.   [13]   Ibid., p. 273.   [14]   Ibid., p. 279.

[15]   Ibid., p. 264.   [16]   Ibid., p. 283.   [17]   Ibid., pp. 279–80.

[18]   Ibid., 201–2, Mr. Justice Goldberg's concurring opinion, stresses that private defamation is not protected by the Constitution.

[19]   The decision extensively quotes from the pace-setting liberal decision of Coleman v. MacLennan, 98 Pac. 281 (Kan. 1908).

[20]   New York Times v. Sullivan, 376 U.S. at 298.

[21]   Ibid., p. 295.

[22]   Ibid., pp. 295, 304.

[23]   Ibid., p. 285. Also see Samuel Gray McNamara, "Recent Developments Concerning Constitutional Limitations on State Defamation Laws," Vanderbilt Law Review, 18 (June 1965), 1455.

[24]   New York Times v. Sullivan, 376 U.S. at 285–86.

[25]   Ibid., p. 287.   [26]   Ibid., p. 288.   [27]   Ibid., p. 292.

[28] Ibid., p. 282.   [29] Ibid., p. 276.

[30] Discussions of this can be found in Harold J. Spaeth, *The Warren Court* (San Francisco: Chandler Publishing Co., 1966), p. 151; McNamara, "State Defamation Laws," p. 1453; and "Libel and Its Future," p. 102.

[31] The *New York Times* decision also determined the *Abernathy et al* case.

[32] Spaeth, *The Warren Court*, p. 151.

[33] New York Times v. Sullivan, 376 U.S. at 264–95.

[34] Ibid., p. 270.

[35] Oliver Wendell Holmes, Jr., *The Common Law* (Boston: Little Brown and Company, 1949; 43rd Printing), p. 2.

[36] Garrison v. Louisiana, 379 U.S. at 67.

[37] Ibid., p. 78.   [38] Ibid., p. 66.   [39] Ibid., p. 77.

[40] Ibid., p. 73.   [41] Ibid., p. 74.   [42] Ibid., p. 75.

[43] Ibid.   [44] Ibid., p. 79.   [45] Ibid.

[46] Ibid., p. 74. Even this standard, however, was deemed too strict by Mr. Justices Black and Douglas, who again wrote concurring opinions stating there should be absolutely no restrictions on public discussion. "If malice is all that is needed, inferences from facts as found by the jury will easily oblige," Mr. Justice Douglas wrote, pp. 79–83.

[47] See Barr v. Matteo, 360 U.S. 564 (1959), discussed in chapter 11.

[48] New York Times v. Sullivan, 376 U.S. at 282–83; Garrison v. Louisiana, 379 U.S. at 74.

[49] Henry v. Collins joined with Henry v. Persons, 380 U.S. 356 at 357 (1965).

[50] Garrison v. Louisiana, 379 U.S. at 69.

[51] Ashton v. Kentucky, 384 U.S. 195 at 198 (1966).

[52] Ibid., p. 200. Perhaps a criminal libel statute could be drawn for publications that cause a clear and present danger of disturbing the peace. This test has been adopted in other free speech cases. See Dennis v. United States, 341 U.S. 494 (1951). But even then, there would have to be proof of "actual malice."

[53] Ashton v. Kentucky, 384 U.S. at 198.

[54] Rosenblatt v. Baer, 383 U.S. at 79–82.

[55] Ibid., p. 82.   [56] Ibid.   [57] Ibid., p. 84.

[58] Ibid., p. 85.   [59] Ibid., p. 87.

[60] The New Hampshire Supreme Court since has ruled that Baer on retrial is entitled to have a jury determination as to whether he is a public official and whether a privileged occasion existed. See Baer v. Rosenblatt, 237 A.2d 130 (N.H. 1967).

[61] Rosenblatt v. Baer, 383 U.S. at 87.

[62] Ibid., p. 94.   [63] Ibid., p. 89.   [64] Ibid., p. 93.

[65] Ibid., p. 100.   [66] Ibid., p. 100.

[67] Of course, Mr. Justices Douglas and Black preferred absolute immunity from libel rather than the conditional rule.

[68] Rosenblatt v. Baer, 383 U.S. at 85.

[69] Butts v. Curtis Publishing Co., 242 F. Supp. 390 (1964).

[70] Associated Press v. Walker, 393 S.W.2d 671 (Tex. 1965).

[71] New York Times, June 12, 1967, p. 1, cols. 2–3. Also see Walker v. Louisville Courier-Journal & Louisville Times Co., 246 F. Supp. 231 (1965), and Walker v. Associated Press, 191 So. 2d 727 (La. 1966). In Walker v. Pulitzer Publishing Co., 394 F.2d 800 (1969), a list of the suits is included on p. 807. Walker sued the Associated Press in Florida, Texas, and Arkansas.

He also brought suits against the *St. Louis Post-Dispatch*, the *New Orleans Times-Picayune*, the *Denver Post*, the *Kansas City Star*, the *Louisville Courier-Journal*, the *Atlanta Journal*, the *Little Rock Gazette*, and the *Arkansas Democrat* for printing the same article. He lost them all, with the exception of a reduced judgment in a Louisiana suit against the Associated Press.

[72]   Curtis Publishing Co. v. Butts, 388 U.S. 130 at 154 (1967).

[73]   Ibid., pp. 158–59.   [74]   Ibid., p. 155.   [75]   Ibid., p. 165.

[76]   Ibid., pp. 165, 170, and 172. Mr. Justices Brennan and White, incidentally, felt the publication was made with reckless disregard for the truth but also felt a new trial should be held at the state level.

[77]   Ibid., p. 165.

[78]   Ibid., pp. 165, 173.

[79]   Further, the Supreme Court in 1967 also applied what it then termed the "calculated falsehood" rule to a right of privacy case originating in New York. The suit was brought by a family named Hill who had been held hostages by hoodlums in 1952. Later, a fictitious play was written about hostages who were subjected to treatment similar to that experienced by the Hills, as well as to other degrading abuses. The suit was not against the author but rather against *Life* magazine, which published an article with pictures, stating the play was a reenactment of the Hill experiences. The Hills won an invasion of privacy judgment in New York. But on appeal, the Supreme Court in *Time* v. *Hill* held that the Hills would have to prove that a "calculated falsehood" had been published. The rationale again was that a public issue was involved. Time v. Hill, 385 U.S. 374 (1967).

[80]   New York Times v. Sullivan, 376 U.S. at 270.

[81]   See Farmers Educational & Cooperative Union of America, North Dakota Division v. WDAY, Inc., 360 U.S. 525 (1959). Discussion can be found in chapter 11.

13. State Conformity:
Unity Under A Developing Law

[1]   See Harmon Zeigler, *Interest Groups in American Society* (Englewood Cliffs, N.J.: Prentice-Hall Inc., 1965), pp. 328–29, where he discussed possible ways to erode Supreme Court decisions—by legal questions, hostile interpretation, and noncompliance.

[2]   Pauling v. News Syndicate Co., 335 F.2d 659 (1964).

[3]   Pauling v. Globe Democrat, 362 F.2d 188 at 196 (1966).

[4]   Pauling v. National Review, 269 (N.Y.S.2d 11 (N.Y. 1966).

[5]   Curtis Publishing Co. v. Butts, 388 U.S. 130 at 154 (1967).

[6]   Short v. News-Journal Co., 212 A.2d 716 at 720–22 (Del. 1965). Barr v. Matteo is discussed in chapter 11.

[7]   Sheridan v. Crisona, 198 N.E.2d 359 at 361–62 (N.Y. 1964).

[8]   Williams v. Daily Review, Inc., 46 Cal. 135 at 144 (1965).

[9]   Lulay v. Peoria Journal-Star, Inc., 214 N.E.2d 746 at 748–49 (Ill. 1966).

[10]   Gilbert v. Goffi, 251 N.Y.S.2d 823 at 831 (N.Y. 1964).

[11]   Pearson v. Fairbanks Publishing Co., 413 P.2d 711 at 715 (Alaska 1966).

[12]   Curtis Publishing Co. v. Butts, 388 U.S. 130 (1967).

[13]   Krutech v. Schimmel & Independent Pub. Co., 278 N.Y.S.2d 25 (App. Div. 1967).

14 News-Journal Co. v. Gallagher, 233 A.2d 166 at 170 (Del. 1967).
15 Rose v. Koch, 154 N.W.2d 409 at 421, 426 (Minn. 1967).
16 Ibid., p. 426. The Alaska Supreme Court also sidestepped the issue as to whether a public school teacher is a public official. See Fairbanks Pub. Co. v. Pitka, 445 P.2d 685 at 690 (1968). Like Wallace Butts, however, Washington University basketball coach John Grayson was declared a public figure. It was ruled in Grayson v. Curtis Publishing Co., 436 P.2d 756 (1968) that he had to prove actual malice before he could collect libel damages for a magazine article accusing him of precipitating a riot at a basketball game.
17 El Paso Times, Inc. v. Trexler, 447 S.W.2d 403 at 405 (Tex. 1969).
18 Tilton v. Cowles Pub. Co. 459 P.2d 8 (Cal. 1969).
19 Cerrito v. Time Inc., 302 F. Supp. 1071 at 1973 (1969). Also a $12.5 million libel suit brought by Mayor Joseph Alioto of San Francisco against Look magazine was pending at the time this book went to press. Alioto sued the magazine over an article published Sept. 23, 1969, which alleged Alioto was "enmeshed in a web of alliances with at least six members of the Mafia." The suit went to trial in May 1970, but a mistrial resulted when an eight-woman, four-man jury could not reach a verdict. Fort Worth Star-Telegram, Saturday morning, May 16, 1970, p. 20-A.
20 Tait v. King Broadcasting Co., 460 P.2d 307 at 310 (Wash. 1969).
21 Time, Inc. v. McLaney, 406 F.2d 565 (Fla. 1969).
22 Aber v. Stahlin, 159 N.W.2d at 156, 157 (Mich. 1968). The news story did not mention individual names but instead listed organizations. In addition to the public figure ruling, the court said that since individuals were not named, there was no libel of individuals.
23 Thompson v. Evening Star, 394 F.2d 774 at 775, 776 (1968).
24 Clark v. Allen, 204 A.2d 42 at 44 (Pa. 1964).
25 Ibid., p. 47.
26 Robbins v. Evening News Association, 130 N.W.2d 404 at 405 (Mich. 1964).
27 Pears v. Palladium Publishing Co., 142 N.W.2d 502 at 504 (Mich. 1966).
28 Wade v. Sterling Gazette Co., 205 N.E.2d 44 at 48 (Ill. 1965).
29 Noonan v. Rousselot, 49 Cal. 817, 819–21 (1966).
30 Matassa v. Bel, 164 So. 2d 332 at 335 (La. 1964).
31 Tucker v. Kilgore, 338 S.W.2d 112 at 116 (Ky. 1964).
32 Ibid.
33 Cabin v. Community Newspapers, Inc., 275 N.Y.S.2d 396 at 398 (App. Div. 1966).
34 Fegley v. Morthimer, 202 A.2d 125 at 126 (Pa. Super. Ct. 1964).
35 Kennedy v. Mid-Continent Telecasting, Inc., 394 P.2d 400 at 407 (Kan. 1965).
36 Driscoll v. Block, 210 N.E.2d 899 at 911 (Okla. 1965).
37 Bell v. Courier-Journal and Louisville Times Co., 402 S.W.2d 84 at 88 (Ky. 1966).
38 State v. Browne, 206 A.2d 591 at 596 (N.J. 1965).
39 Ibid., p. 600.
40 McGuire v. Roth, 219 N.E.2d 319 at 322 (Ohio 1965).
41 Powell v. Monitor Publishing Co., 217 A.2d 193 at 196 (N.H. 1966).
42 Klahr v. Winterble, 418 P.2d 404 at 451 (Ariz. 1966).
43 Lathan v. Journal Company, 140 N.W.2d 417 at 420 (Wisc. 1966).

44   New York Times Co. v. Connor, 365 F.2d 567 at 576 (5th Cir. 1966). This decision was rendered by Justice Homer Thornberry, who two years later received an appointment but not confirmation to the United States Supreme Court. He was appointed to a seat that was not vacated as expected by Mr. Justice Abe Fortas. Both Thornberry and Fortas were caught in the midst of political maneuvering that prevented Fortas from becoming chief justice and denied Thornberry a seat on the Court.

45   Ibid., p. 576.

46   Oswalt v. State-Record Co., 158 S.E.2d 204 at 207 (S.C. 1967).

47   Beckley Newspapers Corp. v. C. Harold Hanks, 389 U.S. 81; 19 L. Ed. 2d 248 at 250 (1967).

48   19 L. Ed. 2d 250.

49   Ibid., p. 251.

50   Theckston v. Triangle Publications Ind., 242 A.2d 629 at 630–31 (N.J. 1968).

51   Phoenix Newspapers Inc. v. Church, 447 P.2d 840 at 849, 853 (Ariz. 1969).

52   Grabovoy v. Wilson dba The Spectator, 230 N.E.2d 581 at 585 (Ill. 1967).

53   Suchomel v. Suburban Life Newspapers Inc., 228 N.E.2d 172 (Ill. 1967).

54   Coursey v. Greater Niles Township Pub. Co., 239 N.E.2d 837, overruling 227 N.E.2d 164 (Ill. 1968).

55   Turley v. WTAX Inc., 236 N.E.2d 778 at 780 (Ill. 1968).

56   Doctors Convalescent Center Inc. v. East Shore Newspapers Inc. 244 N.E.2d 373 at 377 (Ill. 1968).

57   Bienvenue v. Angell, 211 So. 2d 395 at 396 (La. 1968).

58   Silbowitz v. Lepper, 285 N.Y.S.2d 456 at 459 (N.Y. 1967).

59   Arizona Biochemical Co. v. Hearst Corp., 302 F. Supp. 412 (1969).

60   Brown v. Kitterman, 443 S.W.2d 146 (Mo. 1969).

61   Rowden v. Amick, 446 S.W.2d (Mo. 1969).

62   Dodd v. Pearson, 277 F. Supp. 469 at 471 (1967).

63   Dodd v. Pearson, 279 F. Supp. 101 at 102–5 (1967).

64   Joseph J. Baldine v. Sharon Herald Co., 280 F. Supp. 440 and 391 F.2d 703 at 706–7 (1968).

65   Pape v. Time Inc., 354 F.2d 558 at 559 (7th Cir. 1965).

66   Ibid., p. 560.

67   Ibid., p. 562. Time filed for appeal with the United States Supreme Court in 1966 but met a denial, Time Inc. v. Pape, 384 U.S. 909 (1966) and the jury trial order went into effect. Pape in his suit was asking for $350,000. The United States Court of Appeals for the 7th Circuit again reconsidered the case on Dec. 15, 1969, and again ordered a jury trial. At this time, one judge said he believed the magazine writer did act with reckless disregard.

68   Time Inc. v. Pape, No. 1309, 38 L.W. 3413, April 21, 1970.

69   Time Inc. v. Pape, No. 1309, 38 L.W. 3419, April 28, 1970.

70   Keogh v. Pearson, 244 F. Supp. 482 at 485 (1965).

71   Washington Post Co. v. Keogh, 367 F.2d 965 at 972–73 (D.C. Cir. 1966).

72   Keogh v. Washington Post Co., 385 U.S. 1011 (1967).

73   Hackworth v. Larson, 165 N.W.2d 705 (S.D. 1969).

74   New York Times, April 26, 1968, p. 18, cols. 4–5. Gilligan v. Farmer,

289 N.Y.S.2d 846 (N.Y. 1968). This decision also has been hailed as extending the public official rule to civil rights organizations, though it is Gilligan, an officer, who is suing, p. 847.

75 Also see Gilligan v. King, 265 N.Y.S.2d 309 at 315 (N.Y. 1965).

76 *Editor & Publisher*, June 1, 1968, p. 69, col. 3. The judgment included $75,000 in punitive damages and $1 in compensatory damages.

77 Goldwater v. Ginzburg, 261 F. Supp. 784 (1966).

78 *Editor & Publisher*, June 1, 1968, p. 60, col. 3; *New York Times*, May 25, p. 1, col. 2 (1968).

79 Goldwater v. Ginzburg, 261 F. Supp. at 787.

80 *New York Times*, May 17, p. 20, col. 4.

81 Ginzburg never did dispute that the article was false but did say it was fair opinion and that it was vital to free debate to discuss fitness for the presidency. He testified that he was not interested in truth or falsity, that he just wanted to show what the psychiatrists said. *New York Times*, May 25, p. 22 (1969).

82 Goldwater v. Ginzburg, 414 F.2d 324 at 340, 342 (1969); Ginzburg v. Goldwater, 38 L.W. 3280 (1–27–70).

83 38 L.W. 3288.

84 Mahnke v. Northwest Publications Inc., 160 N.W.2d 1 at 10, 11 (Minn. 1968).

85 Sas Jaworsky v. Padfield, 211 So. 2d 122 at 125, 126 (La. 1968).

86 St. Amant v. Thomspon, Supreme Court Bulletin No. 517, October 1967 Term, April 29, 1968, p. 3.

87 Ibid., p. 5.

88 Thompson v. St. Amant, 184 So. 2d 314 at 321–23 (La. 1966).

89 Thompson v. St. Amant, 196 So. 2d 255 at 262 (La. 1967).

90 St. Amant v. Thompson, Supreme Court Bulletin No. 517. Mr. Justice Abe Fortas dissented, stating that if a public official is "needlessly, heedlessly, falsely accused of crime," he should have a remedy in law. St. Amant, he said, had not even checked the accuracy of his charges. This to Mr. Justice Fortas was reckless disregard of falsity, p. 1 of dissent.

91 Ibid., p. 4. 92 Ibid. 93 Ibid.

94 Ibid., quote of Curtis Publishing Co. v. Butts, 388 U.S. 130 at 153.

95 St. Amant v. Thompson, Supreme Court Bulletin No. 517, p. 5.

96 Ibid.

97 Goldwater v. Ginzburg, 38 L.W. 3280.

98 Tunnell v. Edwardsville Intelligencer Inc., 241 N.E.2d 28 at 39 (Ill. 1969).

99 Tunnell v. the Edwardsville Intelligencer Inc., 252 N.E.2d 538 at 542 (Ill. 1969).

100 Tunnell v. Edwardsville Intelligencer, Inc., 38 L.W. 3388 (4–7–70).

101 Thomas T. Tagawa v. Maui Publishing Co., Ltd., 38 L.W. 3122 (1969).

102 Rosenbloom v. Metromedia Inc., 38 L.W. 3290, 3309 (1970).

103 "Supreme Court Curbs Libel Suits on Reports of Exaggerated Charges," *New York Times*, Tuesday, May 19, 1970, p. 25-C. "Supreme Court Shields Papers In Reporting of Public Debate," *For Worth Star-Telegram*, evening edition, May 18, 1970, p. 14-A. See also Greenbelt Cooperative Pub. Assn. Inc. v. Bresler, 252 A.2d 755 at 760 (Md. 1969); also 8 L.W. 3139 (10–21–69).

104 Pape v. Time, 38 L.W. 3421 (May 5, 1970).

105   Monitor Patriot Co. v. Roy, 254 A.2d 832 at 833 (N.H. 1970).
106   Monitor Patriot Co. v. Roy, 38 L.W. 3309 (1970).
107   Ocala Star-Banner Co. v. Leonard Damron, 38 L.W. 3425, 3430 (1970).
108   Ocala Star-Banner Co. v. Leonard Damron, 221 So. 2d 459 at 461 (Fla. 1969).
109   Cepeda v. Cowles Magazine and Broadcasting Inc., 292 F.2d 417 at 419 (1968).
110   *Editor & Publisher*, June 15, 1968, p. 84, col. 3. This case apparently was never appealed but involved an article stating city property was missing from city hall after a defeated city councilman cleared out his office.

14. Public Officials and Libel: *An Overview*
1   Brewer v. Weakley, 5 Am. Dec. 656 at 658 (Tenn. 1807).

15. The Future: *Alternatives and Consequences*
1   As an example, the United States Supreme Court in Toledo Newspaper Co. v. United States, 247 U.S. 402 (1918), established the rule that newspapers could be held in contempt of court for criticism "tending to obstruct and prevent" justice. The rule was revised by the time the Court delivered its opinion in Bridges v. California, 314 U.S. 252 (1941), to require a "clear and present danger of subverting justice" before newspapers could be held in contempt of court. The prevailing views concerning fair trial and free press had shifted, as the views concerning defamation of public officials also could shift.
2   The Court in Prudential Insurance Co. v. Cheek, 259 U.S. 530 (1920), interpreted the Constitution to mean that there were no restrictions on the states concerning freedom of speech. Yet, five years later, in Gitlow v. New York, 268 U.S. 652 (1925), it was held that freedom of speech and press were among the fundamental personal rights protected against state impairment. The interpretation of the Constitution had changed.
3   Though free press was recognized as being protected by the Constitution, the Court rule as of 1931, announced in Near v. Minnesota *ex rel* Olson, 283 U.S. 697 (1931), was that only previous restraints on the press impaired freedom and that postrestraints on the press in the form of libel laws were not in violation of constitutional rights. The variation came thirty-three years later in New York Times v. Sullivan, 376 U.S. 254 (1964), when the Court held that prior restraints in the form of libel did violate liberty when judgments concerned public officials. Thus, the Court has the prerogative of changing its mind.
4   One jury in New Hampshire was given a choice of determining where "public" or "private" libel was involved. Monitor Patriot Co. v. Roy, 254 A.2d 832 at 833 (N.H. 1970). The case is pending for review by the United States Supreme Court at this printing. See 38 L.W. 3309 (1970).
5   Rosenblatt v. Baer, 383 U.S. 75 at 83 (1966).
6   This has happened. In Missouri, for instance, a college professor was placed in the position of a public official because the University of Missouri was established by law and supported by taxpayers. See Clark v. McBaine, 252 S.W. 428 at 432 (1923). The issue was avoided in Minnesota in Rose v.

Koch, 154 N.W.2d 409 at 426 (1967) and no decision was made on the public official designation for a college professor. A school football coach was ruled a "semi-official" in Hoeppner v. Dunkirk Printing Co., 172 N.E. 139 at 142 (1930) in New York but such a designation was not applied to Wallace Butts in Butts v. Curtis Publishing Co., 242 F. Supp. 390 (1964), though Butts was a public university athletic director later to be declared a public figure by the Supreme Court.

7   See opinions of Justices Black and Douglas in Rosenblatt v. Baer, 383 U.S. 75 at 89, 94.

8   Garrison v. Louisiana, 379 U.S. 64 at 77 (1964).

9   This too has been done. For instance, in Kentucky, criticism of a personal nature about a policeman who was performing an official duty was declared not to be subject to the federal rule, Tucker v. Kilgore, 338 S.W.2d 112 at 116 (Ky. 1964). But in New York, criticism of a personal nature about a school board member who was not acting officially was declared subject to the federal rule, Cabin v. Community Newspapers, Inc., 275 N.Y.S.2d 396 at 398 (App. Div. 1966).

10   The public-official rule of libel was applied in the trial of presidential candidate Barry Goldwater for a personality analysis purportedly published to assess his fitness for office. Here, then, a candidate's personality is subject to the constitutional protections of discussion, and candidates surely are subject to no deeper scrutiny than officials.

11   There of course could be procedural due process reviews by the Court to determine if fair trials had been given. See "The New Constitutional Definition of Libel and Its Future," *Northwestern University Law Review*, 66, no. 1 (March–April 1965) 104–6. There also is precedent for the Supreme Court's backing out of substantive due process reviews when governmental regulation was bound by reasonableness. See Nebbia v. New York, 291 U.S. 502 (1934).

12   An independent examination of a libel suit record was made by the Supreme Court in Beckley Newspapers Corp. v. C. Harold Hanks, 389 U.S. 81; 19 L. Ed. 2d 248 (1967). Also see statement in New York Times v. Sullivan, 376 U.S. 254 at 285.

13   Mr. Justices Douglas and Black in opinions to New York Times v. Sullivan, 376 U.S. at 293, 298; Garrison v. Louisiana, 379 U.S. at 79, 80. Also see Goldwater v. Ginzburg, 38 L.W. 3280 (1970).

14   Curtis Publishing Co. v. Butts, 388 U.S. 130 (1967), disclosed several viewpoints. Four judges felt *Saturday Evening Post* departed from responsible standards; Justices Warren, Brennan, and White felt the magazine was reckless in regard to falsity, and Justices Black and Douglas felt there was no libel.

15   Since precedent-setting cases on the actual malice rule, Warren Berger has replaced Earl Warren as chief justice, and Harry A. Blackmun has replaced Abe Fortas as an associate justice. Specific views of these men had not been published at the time this book was written.

16   The Trial of William Cobbett for Libel, 6 Am. State Trials 675 at 681 (1797).

17   See Coleman v. Miller, 307 U.S. 433 (1939). Here the Supreme Court held in effect that Congress was the sole and complete authority in the amending process, subject to no judicial review.

18   Approval could be by three-fourths of the states in convention, but Congress in such a case likely would bypass a convention of the people. This it has

the authority to do. See Hawke v. Smith, 253 U.S. 221 (1920), in which the
Supreme Court held that Congress and not the state determines how amendments will be ratified.

[19] This has even been called a duty of the press. See Pulverman v.
A. S. Abell Co. 288 F.2d 797 at 802 (1955). Also see New York Times v.
Sullivan, 376 U.S. at 282, where the Court points to a duty to criticize gov-
ernment.

[20] See Code of Ethics for the American Society of Newspaper Editors,
Secs. 4, 6, Curtis D. MacDougall, Newsroom Problems and Policies, (New
York: The Macmillan Co., 1941), p. 827

Selected Bibliography

Articles and Periodicals

"A Narrative of the Newspapers Printed in New England," in *Collections of the Massachusetts Historical Society*, 1st ser. 6 (Boston: Samuel Hall, 1799), 64–77.

Anderson, Frank M. "The Enforcement of the Alien and Sedition Laws," in *Annual Report of the American Historical Association for the Year 1912*. (Washington, 1912), pp. 109–22.

Bierbower, James J. "Fair Comment on a Political Candidate," *Georgetown Law Journal*, 37,3 (March 1949), 404–17.

Boston Evening Post, Nov. 18, 1771.

Boston Gazette, Jan. 29, 1722.

Centinel of Freedom, Newark, N.J., Nov. 22, 26, 1799.

"Constitutionality of the Law of Criminal Libel," *Columbia Law Review*, 52,4 (April 1952), 521–34.

Donnelly, Richard C. "History of Defamation," *Wisconsin Law Review*, 49,1 (January 1949), 99–126.

Editor & Publisher, 1968.

Hallen, John E. "Fair Comment," *Texas Law Review*, 8,1 (December 1929), 41–100.

Herald of Freedom, Boston, Mass., Feb. 29 and Mar. 4, 11, 18, 25, 1791.

Independent Chronicle, Boston, Mass., Feb. 24 and Mar. 24, 1791; Apr. 8, 29 and May 2, 1799; Mar. 4, 11, 1799.

McNamara, Samuel Gray. "Recent Developments Concerning Constitutional Limitations on State Defamation Laws," *Vanderbilt Law Review*, 18,3 (June 1965), 1429–55.

Massachusetts Spy, Nov. 15 and Nov. 29, 1771.

Morris, E. B. "Annotation to Washington Times v. Bonner," *American Law Reports*, 10 (1946), 412–41.

Nelson, Harold L. "Seditious Libel in Colonial America," *The American Journal of Legal History*, 3,2 (1959), 160–72.

Nelson, William. "The American Newspapers of the Eighteenth Century as Sources of History," *Annual Report of the American Historical Association for the Year 1908*, 1 (1909), 200–223.

New York Times, June 12, 1967 and Apr. 26, 1968; May 8–25, 1968.

Noel, Dix W. "Defamation of Public Officers and Candidates," *Columbia Law Review*, 49,7 (November 1949), 875–903.

Pennsylvania Gazette, Nov. 17 to Dec. 8, 1737.

Philadelphia Mercury, Feb. 19–26, 1722/23.

"Review of Peter S. Du Ponceau's Dissertation on the Nature and Extent of the Courts of the United States, April 22, 1824," *North American Review*, 21,48 (July 1825), 104–41.

Riddell, William Renwick. "Libel on the Assembly: A Pre-Revolutionary

Episode," *Pennsylvania Magazine of History*, 52,2, 3, 4 (April, July, October 1928), 176–92, 249–79, 342–66.

Riesman, David. "Democracy and Defamation: Fair Game and Fair Comment II," *Columbia Law Review*, 42,8 (November 1942), 1282–1318.

St. Louis Globe Democrat, June 27, 1968.

Smith, Jeremiah. "Are Charges Against the Moral Character of a Candidate for Elective Office Conditionally Privileged?" *Michigan Law Review*, 18, 1, 2 (November and December 1919), 1–15, 104–26.

Southern Illinoisan, Carbondale, Illinois, May 26 and July 1, 1968.

Stevens, John D., Robert L. Bailey, Judith F. Krueger, and John M. Mollwitz. "Criminal Libel as Seditious Libel, 1916–1965." *Journalism Quarterly*, 43,1 (Spring 1966), 110–13.

"The Early Law of Criminal Libel in Massachusetts," *Massachusetts Law Quarterly*, 27,4 (October 1942), 9–16.

"The New Constitutional Definition of Libel and Its Future," *Northwestern University Law Review*, 60,1 (March–April 1965), 95–113.

Veeder, Van Vechten. "Freedom of Public Discussion," *Harvard Law Review*, 23,6 (April 1910), 413–40.

———. "The History and Theory of the Law of Defamation," *Columbia Law Review*, 3,8 (December 1903), 546–73.

Books

Adams, Samuel Hopkins. *Incredible Era*. Boston: Houghton Mifflin Co., 1939.

Beard, Charles A. and Mary R. *The Making of American Civilization*. New York: The Macmillan Co., 1948.

Biesanz, John and Mavis. *Modern Society*. Englewood Cliffs, N.J.: Prentice Hall, Inc., 1964.

Beyh, Albert Ellen, ed. *The Writings of Thomas Jefferson*. Vol. 11. Washington, D.C.: The Jefferson Memorial Association, 1907.

Blaisdell, Donald C., ed. *Unofficial Government: Pressure Groups and Lobbies*. Vol. 319 of *The Annals of the American Academy of Political and Social Science*, edited by Thorsten Sellin. Philadelphia, 1958.

Bozall, L. Brant. *The Warren Revolution*. New Rochelle, N.Y.: Arlington House, 1966.

Brant, Irving. *The Bill of Rights: Its Origin and Meaning*. New York: The New American Library, 1965.

Chaffee, Zechariah, Jr. *Free Speech in the United States*. Cambridge: Harvard University Press, 1964.

———. *Freedom of Speech*. New York: Harcourt, Brace and Howe, 1920.

Chaning, Edward. *History of the United States*. Vol. 4. New York: Macmillan Co., 1917.

Cooper, Thomas. *Treatise on the Law of Libel and Liberty of the Press*. New York: G. F. Hopkins, 1830.

Cornwell, Elmer E., Jr. *Presidential Leadership of Public Opinion*. Bloomington, Ind.: Indiana University Press, 1965.

Cushman, Robert E. and Robert F. *Cases in Constitutional Law*. New York: Appleton-Century-Crofts, 1963.

Douglas, William O. *The Right of the People*. Garden City, N.Y.: Doubleday & Co., Inc., 1958.

Duniway, Clyde Augustus. *The Development of Freedom of the Press in Massachusetts.* New York: Longmans, Green, and Co., 1906.

Emery, Edwin and Henry Ladd Smith. *The Press and America.* New York: Prentice-Hall, Inc., 1954.

Gerald, J. Edward. *The Press and the Constitution, 1931–1947.* Minneapolis: University of Minnesota Press, 1948.

Horton, Rod W. and Herbert W. Edwards. *Backgrounds of American Literary Thought.* New York: Appleton-Century-Crofts, 1952.

Holmes, Oliver Wendell, Jr. *The Common Law.* 43rd printing. Boston: Little Brown and Company, 1949.

Howell, Thomas Bayly, ed. *A Complete Collection of State Trials to 1783.* London: T. Hansard, 1816–28.

Johnson, William, ed. *Reports of Cases Adjudged in the Supreme Court of Judicature of the State of New York.* Vol. 3. Philadelphia: E. F. Backus, 1834.

Klapper, Joseph T. *The Effects of Mass Communications.* Glencoe, Ill.: The Free Press, 1960.

Lawson, John D., ed. *American State Trials.* 16 vols. St. Louis: H. H. Thomas Law Book Co., 1914–28.

Leuchtenburg, William E. *The Great Age of Change.* The Life History of the United States, edited by Henry T. Graff, vol. 12. New York: Time, Inc., 1964.

Levy, Leonard W. *Freedom of Speech and Press in Early American History: Legacy of Suppression.* New York: Harper & Row, 1963.

———. *Freedom of the Press from Zenger to Jefferson.* New York: Bobbs-Merrill Co., Inc., 1966.

Lockhart, William B., Yale Kamisar, and Jesse H. Choper. *Constitutional Rights and Liberties.* St. Paul: West Publishing Co., 1964.

Lodge, Henry Cabot, ed. *The Works of Alexander Hamilton.* Vol. 10. New York: G. P. Putnam's Son, 1904.

MacDougall, Curtis D. *Newsroom Problems and Policies.* New York: The Macmillan Co., 1941.

Massachusetts Historical Society. *Proceedings of the Massachusetts Historical Society.* Series 2, vol. 8. Boston: For the Society, December, 1892.

Mitchell, Broadus. *Alexander Hamilton, The National Adventure 1788–1804.* New York: The Macmillan Co., 1962.

Mott, Frank Luthur. *American Journalism A History: 1690–1960.* New York: The Macmillan Co., 1962.

Nevins, Allan, ed. *The Diary of J. Q. Adams.* Vol. 5. New York: Longmans, Green & Co., 1929.

Nevins, Allan and Henry Steele Commanger. *The Pocket History of the United States.* New York: Pocket Books, Inc., 1951.

O'Callagham, C. B. *Documentary History of the State of New York.* Vol. 3. Albany, N.Y.: Week, Parson & Co., 1850.

Pennypacker, Samuel W. *Pennsylvania Colonial Cases.* Phailadelphia: Rees Welsch & Co., Law Book Publishers, 1892.

Quincy, Josiah, Jr. *Reports of Cases Argued and Adjudged in the Superior Court of Judicature of the Province of Massachusetts Bay Between 1761 and 1772.* Boston: Little, Brown and Co., 1865.

Riley, Woodbridge. *American Thought From Puritanism To Pragmatism and Beyond.* Gloucester, Mass.: Peter Smith, 1959.

Rucker, Bryce W. *The First Freedom*. Carbondale, Ill.: Southern Illinois University Press, 1968.

Schlesinger, Arthur M. *Prelude to Independence*. New York: Alfred A. Knopf, 1958.

Schlesinger, Arthur M., Sr. *The Rise of the City 1887–1898*. New York: Macmillan, 1932.

Schmidhouser, John R. *The Supreme Court as Final Arbiter in Federal-State Relations, 1789–1957*. Chapel Hill: The University of North Carolina Press, 1958.

Schuyler, Livingston Rowe. *The Libery of the Press in the American Colonies before the Revolutionary War*. New York: Thomas Whittaker, 1905.

Shurtleff, Nathaniel B., ed. *Records of the Governor and Company of the Massachusetts Bay in New England*. Vol. 1. Boston: William White Co., 1853.

Siebert, Frederick Seaton. *Freedom of the Press in England 1476–1776*. Urbana: University of Illinois Press, 1965.

Spaeth, Harold J. *The Warren Court*. San Francisco: Chandler Publishing Co., 1966.

Tax, Sol. *Evolution After Darwin*. Vol. 3. Chicago: University of Chicago Press, 1960.

Thomas, Isaiah. *The History of Printing in America, with a Biography of Printers, and an Account of Newspapers*. 2 vols. Albany, N.Y.: Joel Mansell, printer for American Antiquarian Society, 1874.

Thorpe, Francis Newton. *Federal and State Constitutions, Colonial Charters and Other Organic Laws*. 7 vols. Washington: Government Printing Office, 1909.

Turnbull, Arthur T. and Russell N. Baird. *The Graphics of Communication*. New York: Holt, Rinehart and Winston, 1964.

Warren, Charles. *A History of the American Bar*. New York: Howard Fertig, Inc., 1966.

Washington, H. A., ed. *The Writings of Thomas Jefferson*. Vol. 4. Philadelphia: J. B. Lippincott & Co., 1871.

Wharton, Francis. *State Trials of the United States during the Administrations of Washington and Adams*. Philadelphia: Casey and Hart, 1849.

Zeigler, Harmon. *Interest Groups in American Society*. Englewood Cliffs, N.J.: Prentice-Hall, Inc., 1965.

Legal Digests

American Digest System, Century Edition of the American Digest, 1658 to 1896. 50 vols. St. Paul: West Publishing Co., 1904.

————. *First Decennial Digest, 1897–1906*. 20 vols. St. Paul: West Publishing Co., 1910.

————. *Second Decennial Digests, 1906–1916*. 23 vols. St. Paul: West Publishing Co., 1922.

————. *Third Decennial Digest, 1916–1926*. 28 vols. St. Paul: West Publishing Co., 1929.

————. *Fourth Decennial Digest, 1926–1936*. 33 vols. St. Paul: West Publishing Co., 1938.

————. *Fifth Decennial Digest, 1936–1946*. 47 vols. St. Paul: West Publishing Co., 1949.

————. *Sixth Decennial Digest, 1946–1956.* 32 vols. St. Paul: West Publishing Co., 1957.

————. *Seventh Decennial Digest, 1956–1966.* 34 vols. St. Paul: West Publishing Co., 1968.

General Digest, American Digest System, 1966–1968. 6 vols. St. Paul: West Publishing Co., 1967–68.

United States Supreme Court Digest. Lawyer's Edition. 18 vols. Rochester, N.Y.: The Lawyer's Cooperative Publishing Co., 1948–68.

Public Documents

Great Britain, Fortesque, J. W., ed. *Calendar of State Papers, Colonial Series, America and West Indies, 1704–1705, Preserved in the Public Record Office.* Vol. 22. London: Her Majesty's Stationers Offices, 1905; Reprinted at Vadez: Kraus Reprint Lt., 1964.

Great Britain, Fortescue, J. W., ed. *Calendar of State Papers, Colonial Series 16, October 1697, to December 1698.* London: Her Majesty's Stationers Offices, 1905.

Great Britain, Hansard, T. C., ed. *Parliamentary History of England.* Vol. 29. London, 1817.

Great Britain, *Parliamentary Register.* Vol. 31. London: J. Debrett, 1792.

Great Britain, *Statutes of the Realm.* Vols. 1, 2, 5.

U.S., *Annals of Congress* (House). 5th Cong., vol. 2. Washington: Seaton, 1851.

U.S., Blair and Rives, eds. *The Congressional Globe, 26th Congress, 1st Session, Dec. 2–July 21, 1839–40.* Washington: Globe Office, 1840.

U.S., *Constitution.*

U.S., *Public Papers of the Presidents of the United States, Harry S. Truman, 1950.* Washington, D.C.: United States Government Printing Office, 1965.

U.S., *Public Papers of the Presidents of the United States, John F. Kennedy, 1961.* Washington, D.C.: United States Government Printing Office, 1962.

U.S., *Statutes at Large.* Vols. 1, 40.

Reports and Pamphlets

Alexander, James. *A Brief Narrative of the Case and Trial of John Peter Zenger, Printer of the New-York Weekly-Journal.* New York: W. Dunlap, 1756.

An Authentick Account of the Proceedings against John Wilkes, Esq. London printed; Philadelphia, reprinted: W. Dunlap, 1763.

Blenman, Jonathan. *Remarks on Zenger's Trial.* New York: Gaine, 1770.

Fowle, Daniel. *A Total Eclipse of Liberty.* Boston: 1755.

Holt, John. *A Brief Narrative of the Case and Trial of John Peter Zenger.* New York: John Holt, 1770.

Keith, George. *New-England's Spirit of Persecution Transmitted to Pennsylvania; And the Pretended Quaker Found Persecuting the True Christian-Quaker, in the Tryal of Peter Boss, George Keith, Thomas Budd, and William Bradford.* New York: 1693.

McDougall, Alexander. *To The Freeholders and Freemen of the City and*

Colony of New York And To All The Friends of Liberty in The British Empire. New York Broadside, Jan. 26, 1771.

Massachusetts Bay Province. Extract From The Journal of the House of Representatives. Boston: Fowle & Tyler, 1756.

Philanthes, Theo. New-England Persecutors Mauled With Their Own Weapons. New York: 1697.

Table of Cases

Index

Circulation: extent affects privilege, 169, 177, 182; is improper basis for damage award, 197; problems caused by broadcast media, 203

City Council reports: privileged, 177–82

Civil libel suits: grow as criminal libel prosecutions dwindle, 65, 193, 269, 299n43. See also Criminal libel; Defense to libel against officials; Libel

Civil Rights, 219, 318n1

Clarke, Philip, 17, 23

Cobbett, William: called champion libeler, 42, 43

Colonial court trials: of Roger Williams, 2, 5, 13; of Mrs. Ann Hutchinson, 5; of John Wheelright, 5; of John Eliot, 6, 7; of William Bradford, 14–16; of George Keith, Thomas Budd, and Peter Boss, 15, 23; of Thomas Maule, 16, 23; of James Franklin, 19, 24; of John Peter Zenger, 25–30; of Thomas Fleet, 30; of William Parks, 30–31; of Daniel Fowle, 31; of Alexander McDougall, 34–35; of John Colman, 290n55. See also Religious libel; Seditious libel

Colorado cases, 152, 154, 191, 298n34

Common law libel prosecutions: heritage from England, 1–13; modified in colonies, 14–37 passim; reinstituted in new United States, 39, 40, 41, 52, 54, 266, 267–68, 283; not within power of U.S. government, 44, 64–65, 68, 295; left to states, 58–60; 65, 111, 115; are harder to sustain because of people's right to know, 61–64, 67; begin to dwindle as civil suits increase, 65, 68, 70. See also Criminal libel

Communicators: responsibility, 188, 206, 318n1, 330n19; duty of, 284

Communists: libel suits based on charges of being, 185–86, 197, 202, 237, 239–40, 246, 252–53, 260

Congress: privilege to report about, 185–86; determines constitutional amendment process, 284, 329n17. See also Fair and accurate reports; Privilege

Connecticut cases, 78, 83, 84, 89–90, 92, 105, 152, 155, 168, 204–5, 206–7, 298n34

Constitution: procedures to amend, 284, 329n17, 329n18, 330; interpretational changes in, 328n2, 328n3

Constitutional guarantees of press freedom: in the states, 33–34, 60, 64, 294n3, 294n4, 298n33, 298n34; as interpreted by U.S. Supreme Court, 45, 89, 114–15, 172, 190, 205, 209–

10, 213–16, 217, 221, 223, 229, 242–43, 259, 272, 274, 277, 283, 301n9, 305n1, 318n5, 321n93, 322n10. See also Press freedom; United States Supreme Court

Constitutional Law: new status of public-official libel law, 213–32. See also Constitutional privilege of discussion; Public-official libel rule

Constitutional privilege of discussion: originated to limit libel judgments to public officials, 213–21, 239–64; established by U.S. Supreme Court, 213–32, 274, 283; replaces old state privileges, 213, 232, 233, 259, 274, 283; conditioned upon lack of actual malice, 217, 221, 228, 245–46, 250–52, 253–54, 260–63, 282; based upon right to discuss public issues, 220, 231, 234–35, 236, 237, 239; does apply to criminal libel, 221, 223, 229, 275; extended to publications on government employees, 224–24, 237, 275; does not apply to private libels, 225–26; protects commentary on public figures, 228–29, 233–34, 275; an all-inclusive, nationwide privilege, 232, 274–75, 283; interpretated by state courts, 233–64 passim; can be abused, 248–52, 283; limits libel judgments on reports of government proceedings, 257, 275; is subject to change, 277, 278, 282, 284. See also Actual malice standard; Public-official libel rule

Contempt of court, 190, 318n3

Convincing clarity: an actual malice standard, 245–46, 263

Cooper, Thomas: tried under Sedition Act, 46–49; denied rights, 55

County commissioner court reports: carry privilege, 182

Court trials: privileged, 176–80

Cresson, Charles, 185

Criminal accusations against officials: were libelous per se in early days, 73–74, 98–99, 119; privileged in some states if made in good faith, 142–43, 170; basis of many libel judgments in recent years, 196, 197–200, 209; now privileged if not made with actual malice, 254, 327n90

Criminal libel: common in early days of nation, 39–56 passim; prosecutions become difficult, 57–66 passim; prosecutions by federal government end, 64–65, 68; gives way to civil libel, 65, 70–85 passim; prosecutions few in modern times, 193, 223, 242, 269, 319n19,

Index

355

Retraction: rules outlined, 195; mentioned, 76, 169
Revere, Paul, 42
Rhode Island cases, 165–66, 171, 178, 302n39
Right to know: belongs to public, 60–61, 63, 64, 68, 298n33, 298n34; is basis of truth becoming a defense for libel, 61–63, 68, 70–86 passim, 268; gives press privilege to print nonmalicious falsehoods, 153, 155, 164, 270; basis for privilege to make fair and accurate report, 176, 177, 186, 188; basis for fair comment and criticism privilege, 194, 204, 318n1, 321n93; coupled with right to discuss is basis for constitutional privilege in libel, 221, 226, 228; is basis for libel defense of probable cause for believing truth, 270–71, 91–92, 125, 127. See also Constitutional privilege of discussion
Robbins, Jonathan, 48, 50
Roosevelt, Franklin D., 171

St. Amant, Phil A.: is involved in television libel suit, 253–55; has suit which establishes guidelines for juries, 255, 263, 276
School board meetings: privileged, 183
Scroggs, William, Sir, 8, 9, 10, 12
Sedition Law: reasons for, 44; quoted, 44–45; combined U.S. and English libel heritage, 45–46, 55; sanctioned idea that criticism of officials is criminal, 46; prosecution of Matthew Lyon, 46–47; prosecution of Anthony Haswell, 47; prosecution of Dr. Thomas Cooper, 48–49; prosecution of James Callender, 50–51; had widespread effect, 51–52; died with John Adams's term, 52, 56; was last libel act ever passed by Congress, 56, 297n91; declared unconstitutional by the court of history, 219, 220
Seditious libel: English prosecutions, 1–3; heritage from England, 1–3; colonial prosecutions, 2, 5, 6–7, 13, 14–18, 25–30; defined, 4–5, 18; reinstituted in the United States on independence, 40; prosecuted under Sedition Law, 45–52; today unconstitutional, 219, 224, 231, 243. See also Colonial court trials; Common law libel prosecutions; English prosecutions
Self-protection right: in libel suits, 122
Seven Bishops Case: shows confusion in English common law of libel, 10–11, 12, 27

Sly, Gerald, 17, 23
South Carolina cases, 117, 129, 139–40, 179, 183, 245, 298n34
South Dakota cases: 96, 152, 163, 169, 250, 298n33
Star Chamber Court: trial of Richard Knightly, 3, 11; trial of Lewis Pickering (Case de Libellis Famosis), 4, 12; renders judgment in Libellis Famosis, 5; mentioned, 266
State courts: issued final judgments in libel suits, 112; determined own laws on libel, 114; are subjected to U.S. Supreme Court review on libel judgments, 213–20, 232, 254; conform to constitutional standard of libel, 233–64 passim; limited from interfering with discussion on public issues, 277
Statute de Scandalus Magnatum: declaratory law, 2; restriction concerning false statements discarded, 11; quoted 285n4
Stewart, Potter, 226
Substantive due process, 329n11
Sullivan, L. B.: brings libel suit that changes law in United States, 214–15, 216
Sweeney, Martin L., 151, 167
Syndicated columns: privileged unless high degree of awareness of probable falsity, 249

Taft, William Howard: renders decision in leading narrow-rule-of-privilege case, 123, 124, 129, 166, 271
Television. See Broadcasting
Tennessee cases, 42, 71–72, 106, 109, 120, 129, 139
Texas cases, 94, 106, 122, 143, 149–51, 168, 170, 178, 181, 185, 191, 199–200, 209, 227–28, 237
Thomas, Isaiah, 35
Thornberry, Homer, 326n44
Truman, Harry S, 187, 208
Truth: not material in English libel defenses, 4–5, 22; accepted as libel defense in John Peter Zenger trial, 25–30, 267; not always a defense after independence, 40–41, 42, 52, 53, 54; defense under Sedition Law, 45, 55, 56, 58, 269; often used to defeat malice, 57, 58; becomes defense when coupled with good motives, 58–60, 65; becomes full defense in considering a good motive as informing people, 61–63, 68, 70–86; remains general defense through nineteenth century, 82, 107; belief in truth often sufficient when discussing officials, 87–110 passim, 123–27, 152–